# THE PENTECOSTAL GENDER PARADOX

**T&T Clark Systematic Pentecostal and Charismatic Theology**

*Series editors*

Wolfgang Vondey
Daniela C. Augustine

# THE PENTECOSTAL GENDER PARADOX

## Eschatology and the Search for Equality

Joseph Lee Dutko

LONDON • NEW YORK • OXFORD • NEW DELHI • SYDNEY

T&T CLARK

Bloomsbury Publishing Plc, 50 Bedford Square, London, WC1B 3DP, UK
Bloomsbury Publishing Inc, 1385 Broadway, New York, NY 10018, USA
Bloomsbury Publishing Ireland, 29 Earlsfort Terrace, Dublin 2, D02 AY28, Ireland

BLOOMSBURY, T&T CLARK and the T&T Clark logo are trademarks of
Bloomsbury Publishing Plc

First published in Great Britain 2024
Paperback edition published 2025

Copyright © Joseph Lee Dutko, 2024

Joseph Lee Dutko has asserted his right under the Copyright, Designs and Patents Act, 1988, to be identified as Author of this work.

For legal purposes the Acknowledgments on p. xi constitute an extension of this copyright page.

Cover design by Anna Berzovan
Cover image © naqiewei / GettyImages

All rights reserved. No part of this publication may be: i) reproduced or transmitted in any form, electronic or mechanical, including photocopying, recording or by means of any information storage or retrieval system without prior permission in writing from the publishers; or ii) used or reproduced in any way for the training, development or operation of artificial intelligence (AI) technologies, including generative AI technologies. The rights holders expressly reserve this publication from the text and data mining exception as per Article 4(3) of the Digital Single Market Directive (EU) 2019/790.

Bloomsbury Publishing Plc does not have any control over, or responsibility for, any third-party websites referred to or in this book. All internet addresses given in this book were correct at the time of going to press. The author and publisher regret any inconvenience caused if addresses have changed or sites have ceased to exist, but can accept no responsibility for any such changes.

A catalogue record for this book is available from the British Library.

Library of Congress Cataloging-in-Publication Data
Names: Dutko, Joseph Lee, author.
Title: The Pentecostal gender paradox: eschatology and the search for equality / Joseph Lee Dutko.
Description: New York: T&T Clark, 2023. | Series: T&T Clark systematic Pentecostal and charistmatic theology | Includes bibliographical references and index.
Identifiers: LCCN 2023023088 (print) | LCCN 2023023089 (ebook) |
ISBN 9780567713681 (hardback) | ISBN 9780567713650 (paperback) |
ISBN 9780567713674 (pdf) | ISBN 9780567713698 (epub)
Subjects: LCSH: Pentecostalism. | Pentecostal women. | Eschatology. | Sex discrimination against women. | Women and religion. | Feminism–Religious aspects.
Classification: LCC BR1644 .D88 2023 (print) | LCC BR1644 (ebook) |
DDC 269/.4082–dc23/eng/20230731
LC record available at https://lccn.loc.gov/2023023088
LC ebook record available at https://lccn.loc.gov/2023023089

ISBN: HB: 978-0-5677-1368-1
PB: 978-0-5677-1365-0
ePDF: 978-0-5677-1367-4
ePUB: 978-0-5677-1369-8

Series: T&T Clark Systematic Pentecostal and Charismatic Theology

Typeset by Deanta Global Publishing Services, Chennai, India

For product safety related questions contact productsafety@bloomsbury.com.

To find out more about our authors and books visit www.bloomsbury.com and sign up for our newsletters.

*For my daughters*
*Anya & Junia*

# CONTENTS

Acknowledgments    xi
List of Abbreviations    xiii

Introduction
GENDER EQUALITY: BEGINNING WITH THE END    1
    The Decline of Women in Leadership and the Rise of the Gender Paradox    5
    Why Eschatology?    12
        The Revival of Eschatology: The End Is the New Beginning    13
        A Transformational Method: The Dialectic of Imagination and Participation    18
    Why the Problem (and a Solution) Matter    22
    Outline of Procedure    27

Chapter 1
ESCHATOLOGY: ENEMY OF EQUALITY?    31
    1.1 Eschatology and Equality: Three Existing Views    34
        1.1.1 The Antagonistic View: Eschatology Is Incompatible    34
        1.1.2 The Agnostic View: Eschatology Is Irrelevant    39
        1.1.3 The Augmented View: Eschatology Is Insufficient    43
    1.2 The Pentecostal Potential: Toward a Positive Eschatology for Women    48
    1.3 Conclusion and Contribution    52

Chapter 2
WOMEN AND ESCHATOLOGY IN THE EARLY PENTECOSTAL MOVEMENT: IN SEARCH OF AN AUTHORIZING HERMENEUTIC    55
    2.1 Methodology and Parameters    56
    2.2 Eschatology as Authorizing Hermeneutic for Women    59
        2.2.1 Background: Nineteenth-Century Foundations    59
        2.2.2 Early Writings and Periodicals    61
        2.2.3 Three Case Studies    67
        2.2.4 Outcomes of Historical Investigation    76

|  |  |  |
|---|---|---|
| 2.3 | The Early-Years Argument | 77 |
|  | 2.3.1 The Egalitarian Heart of the Movement | 79 |
|  | 2.3.2 The Eschatological Heart of the Movement | 83 |
| 2.4 | The Function(s) of Eschatology | 86 |
| 2.5 | Conclusion | 88 |

Chapter 3
THE LOSS OF ESCHATOLOGY AS AUTHORIZING HERMENEUTIC   91

|  |  |  |
|---|---|---|
| 3.1 | Historical Developments: The Shifting of Eschatology and Hermeneutics | 92 |
|  | 3.1.1 Hermeneutics: From Eschatological to Restorationist | 93 |
|  | 3.1.2 Eschatology: From Latter Rain to Dispensational | 99 |
| 3.2 | The Impact: The Loss of Eschatology as Authorizing Hermeneutic | 103 |
| 3.3 | Modern Developments: The Re-Visioning of Eschatology and Hermeneutics | 112 |
|  | 3.3.1 Eschatology: From Dispensational to Transformational | 113 |
|  | 3.3.2 Hermeneutics: From Scripture-Centered to Spirit-Centered | 117 |
| 3.4 | The Need for an Eschatological Authorizing Hermeneutic | 120 |
|  | 3.4.1 The Eschatological Hermeneutic | 121 |
|  | 3.4.2 The Eschatological Spirit | 123 |
|  | 3.4.3 The Eschatological Word: Imagination | 125 |
|  | 3.4.4 Eschatological Experience (in Community): Participation | 127 |
| 3.5 | Conclusion | 129 |

Chapter 4
IMAGINING THE *ESCHATON*: (RE)CONSTRUCTING THE
ESCHATOLOGICAL AUTHORIZING HERMENEUTIC   131

|  |  |  |
|---|---|---|
| 4.1 | The Hermeneutical Priority of Eschatological Texts on Gender | 134 |
|  | 4.1.1 The Premise of Hermeneutical Priority | 135 |
|  | 4.1.2 The Promise of an Eschatological–Egalitarian Hermeneutical Priority | 137 |
|  | 4.1.3 The Procedure for Constructing the Hermeneutic | 141 |
| 4.2 | In the Beginning Is the End: Genesis 1–3 and Creation | 142 |
|  | 4.2.1 Importance | 142 |
|  | 4.2.2 Relevant Background | 144 |
|  | 4.2.3 Eschatological Significance | 145 |
|  | 4.2.4 Hermeneutical Priority | 147 |
|  | 4.2.5 Imagination and Participation | 148 |
| 4.3 | In the End Is the Beginning: Galatians 3:28 and the Ministry of Jesus | 149 |
|  | 4.3.1 Importance | 149 |

|   |     | 4.3.2 | Relevant Background | 150 |
|---|---|---|---|---|
|   |     | 4.3.3 | Eschatological Significance | 152 |
|   |     | 4.3.4 | Hermeneutical Priority | 158 |
|   |     | 4.3.5 | Imagination and Participation (the Ministry of Jesus) | 159 |
|   | 4.4 | The Beginning of the End: Acts 2:17-18 and Pentecost | | 162 |
|   |     | 4.4.1 | Importance | 162 |
|   |     | 4.4.2 | Relevant Background | 163 |
|   |     | 4.4.3 | Eschatological Significance | 165 |
|   |     | 4.4.4 | Hermeneutical Priority | 166 |
|   |     | 4.4.5 | Imagination and Participation | 168 |
|   | 4.5 | The Eschatological–Egalitarian Narrative as Hermeneutical Guide | | 169 |
|   | 4.6 | Conclusion | | 172 |

Chapter 5
PRE-ENACTING THE PROMISE: SOLVING THE GENDER PRAXIS PROBLEM  175
- 5.1 The Pentecostal Gender Praxis Problem  176
- 5.2 Pre-Enactment and Re-Enactment Praxis Models  179
- 5.3 Pentecostal Eschatology and Praxis: Potentiality and Problem  181
  - 5.3.1 Eschatology as Praxis-Driven Discipline  182
  - 5.3.2 Pentecostal Theology as Praxis Centered  183
  - 5.3.3 Pentecostal Eschatology as (a) Praxis  185
  - 5.3.4 The Eschatological Praxis Problem  187
- 5.4 Solving the Praxis Problem(s): Eschatological–Egalitarian Praxis as Pre-Enactment  190
  - 5.4.1 Pre-Enactment: Dialectical, Experiential, Experimental  191
  - 5.4.2 Pre-Enactment and Biblical Authority: The (Ongoing) Eschatological Drama  195
  - 5.4.3 Potential Concerns  197
- 5.5 Conclusion  200

Chapter 6
PARTICIPATING IN THE *ESCHATON*: TOWARD A PENTECOSTAL ESCHATOLOGICAL–EGALITARIAN PRAXIS  203
- 6.1 Organizational Leadership: Reifying Eschatological Equality  206
  - 6.1.1 In Denominational Structures  206
  - 6.1.2 In the Local Church  209
- 6.2 Theological Education: Forming an Eschatological Consciousness  214
  - 6.2.1 Eschatological Pedagogy: Incorporating Women's Voices  215
  - 6.2.2 Eschatological Anthropology: Ontological Outcomes  220
  - 6.2.3 Eschatological Trinitarianism: Gender Implications  223

    6.3  Corporate Worship: Participating in Eschatological–Egalitarian Realities    227
        6.3.1  Imagination: Eschatological Language    229
        6.3.2  Story: Eschatological Inclusivity    236
        6.3.3  Embodiment: Eschatological Sacramentality    242
    6.4  Conclusion    249

CONCLUSION    251
    Review of Major Contributions and Invitation to Further Research    251
    Impact: Global and Ecclesiastical Implications    254
    Concluding Word    259

Bibliography    261
Index    292

## ACKNOWLEDGMENTS

The original idea for this project was birthed ten years ago in a seminar course entitled "Women's Voices: Issues in Women's Faith and Development." Through the eleven women in that class, and under the pastoral and academic guidance of Dr. Barbara Mutch, I decided that when (or if) I wrote my first book, I would use the opportunity to contribute to women's equality. Ten years later, here it is! Therefore, I would first like to thank Barbara Mutch for her support and the women in that class for sharing their stories. This project is in honor of them and the endless number of women's voices in the church, both past and present, that they represent.

Since then, several people have helped me tremendously to complete this book's journey. I want to thank John G. Stackhouse Jr. for his early encouragement toward both the idea of this work and my pursuit of the academic qualifications necessary to publish it. From there, Michael Wilkinson provided the initial belief in this project and helped me in the early process of developing a research proposal and connecting me with the right people at the University of Birmingham and the Centre for Pentecostal and Charismatic Studies. Without him, the bridge between wanting to do this and actually doing it might never have been built. Thank you, Allan Anderson, for getting me started in the program at Birmingham and for proactively pursuing me even after I fell silent for months at a time while considering acceptance!

To my doctoral program supervisor, Wolfgang Vondey, I am so thankful that we came to Birmingham at the same time. It was truly a privilege to work with you over these years. You have provided generous amounts of advice and resources to bring this project to where it is. Your rigorous standards, eye for detail, and constant challenges to strive for clear and convincing scholarship (among many other things) have made me a better scholar for life. I am incredibly grateful for the writer and critical thinker you have helped me become (although I, of course, accept all shortcomings in this project as my own!). Along the way, you also extended kindness and pastoral guidance regarding the challenges of writing a doctoral thesis amid raising a family and pastoring a church full time. I am forever proud to name you as my *Doktorvater*.

I would like to thank my previous schools, departments, and professors that helped form me both as a person and academic. I am grateful for the overwhelmingly positive experience of my undergraduate years at Evangel University and with my professors in the Theology Department. I am especially grateful for the mentorship and friendship of Martin W. Mittelstadt. Thank you for your encouragement that now spans two decades and for being the first to introduce me to Pentecostal scholarship. Many of our conversations along this journey are forever etched in my memory, including our long walk along the Fraser River in one of your trips "up north" to your homeland. Thank you to Missouri State University and the Department of Religious Studies for their generous funding of my master's program and research there. The professors, including my thesis supervisor John Schmalzbauer, installed a love and passion in me for academic research and teaching. My (unexpected) second master's program at Regent College shaped me as a person more than any other season in my life and cultivated in me a desire for "intelligent, vigorous, and joyful commitment to Jesus Christ, His church, and His world." Thanks to all these institutions (and for access to their libraries!).

I would like to gratefully acknowledge the love and support of my church family. Thank you, Oceanside Community Church (Parksville, BC), for supporting my studies and writing over these last eight years with time off, some funding, and your prayers. One of the great privileges of my life was to author this book in the context of leading and pastoring a beautiful group of people as we write our God-story together. Thank you also to my fellow pastors and staff members for your support, including covering for me on my writing breaks and trips overseas and regularly asking about my project (and at least pretending to show interest!). And thanks to the greater family of the BC & Yukon Network of the Pentecostal Assemblies of Canada. Hannah and I have never felt so "at home" in a fellowship of churches and leaders as we do here.

Lastly, to my wife and fellow minister, scholar, and co-lead pastor, I cannot say thank you enough. There is no one with whom I would rather lead a church. Thank you for your help in reading and offering suggestions for each chapter. I am aware of the irony that my time and dedication to this work on women's leadership has at times unintentionally caused me to fail at properly supporting your extraordinary leadership—both in the church and in the home—in the ways you needed. There is truly no pastor or spiritual leader I have more respect for or learn more from than you. To my son Amos and especially to my two daughters, Anya and Junia, this work is dedicated to you and your God-given freedom to pursue whatever God calls you to do, without limitation.

# ABBREVIATIONS

| | |
|---|---|
| *AF* | *The Apostolic Faith* |
| *JPT* | *Journal of Pentecostal Theology* |
| *NIDPCM* | *The New International Dictionary of Pentecostal and Charismatic Movements* |
| *Pneuma* | *Pneuma: The Journal of the Society for Pentecostal Studies* |

# Introduction

## GENDER EQUALITY

### BEGINNING WITH THE END

The distinct subjects of eschatology and gender equality[1] have seen an explosion of interest in recent decades, particularly within the Pentecostal movement.[2] Pentecostalism is widely considered to be a thoroughly eschatological movement reflecting the idea that the "last days" had been initiated with the day of Pentecost (Acts 2:17). Recent attention to and debate on eschatology by Pentecostals reflects a renewed interest in the subject and the search for an eschatology that is authentically Pentecostal.[3] Pentecostalism is also regarded ideally as an egalitarian

---

1. Due to their concomitant relationship within Pentecostalism (as argued throughout this work, see especially Chapter 3), the terms "eschatology" and "gender equality" vary in the order in which they appear (often intentionally). However, this is primarily a work on gender that uses the heuristic tool of eschatology (see Chapter 1, note 1). As is often the case, the term "gender equality" is used in the context of and refers to women's equality. They are used interchangeably throughout this work. See discussion of the term "gender" in this section.

2. On defining Pentecostalism, particularly as a "movement," see Wolfgang Vondey, *Pentecostal Theology: Living the Full Gospel* (London: Bloomsbury T&T Clark, 2017), 4; Wolfgang Vondey, *Pentecostalism: A Guide for the Perplexed* (London: Bloomsbury, 2013), 2, 155; Wolfgang Vondey, *Beyond Pentecostalism: The Crisis of Global Christianity and the Renewal of the Theological Agenda* (Grand Rapids: Eerdmans, 2010), 8–13. Some prefer to not capitalize the term, or some use the plural "Pentecostalisms" to describe the diversity of the movement. However, Vondey prefers to keep the term Pentecostalism as a transitional term reflecting its emerging theology. The focus of this project is mostly North American classical Pentecostalism, although the global nature of Pentecostalism necessitates considering the wider impact of this study (see the end of this chapter and my Conclusion chapter).

3. See Daniel D. Isgrigg, *Imagining the Future: The Origins, Development, and Future of Assemblies of God Eschatology* (Tulsa, OK: Oral Roberts University Press, 2021); Larry R. McQueen, *Toward a Pentecostal Eschatology: Discerning the Way Forward* (Blandford Forum, UK: Deo, 2012); Matthew K. Thompson, *Kingdom Come: Revisioning Pentecostal Eschatology* (Blandford Forum, UK: Deo, 2010); Peter Althouse and Robby Waddell, eds., *Perspectives in Pentecostal Eschatologies: World Without End* (Eugene, OR: Pickwick, 2010); Peter Althouse, *Spirit of the Last Days: Pentecostal Eschatology in Conversation with Jürgen*

community, embodying the Pentecost story of the Spirit poured out on "all flesh ... sons and daughters ... both men and women" (Acts 2:16-18; cf. Joel 2:28-32).⁴ However, many Pentecostals have lamented the inconsistency between this core egalitarian impulse and the often-restrictive practices within the movement.⁵ This situation is described by sociologist Bernice Martin as the so-called Pentecostal "gender paradox," a helpful phrase adopted in this work to refer to the conflicting freedoms and limitations experienced by women in the Pentecostal movement. This paradox has plagued the movement for a century and resulted in constant tension and uncertainty concerning women's roles in Pentecostal churches and organizations.⁶

Both women's equality and eschatology share a rich history within the Christian and Pentecostal tradition, and their declining prominence has attracted the attention of Pentecostal and other scholars. However, little research has been done to put these two areas into conversation with each other: eschatological convictions are often absent in the debate on gender roles in the church. In the rare occasions they are discussed together, eschatology is often dismissed as incompatible with,

---

*Moltmann* (London: T&T Clark, 2003); D. William Faupel, *The Everlasting Gospel: The Significance of Eschatology in the Development of Pentecostal Thought* (1996; repr., Blandford Forum, UK: Deo, 2009).

4. All Scripture quotations throughout this work are from the New Revised Standard Version Updated Edition (NRSVue).

5. See the next section for a more detailed articulation of this problem. Some Pentecostal works and resources that touch on this tension and inconsistency: Cheryl Bridges Johns and Lisa P. Stephenson, eds., *Grieving, Brooding, and Transforming: The Spirit, The Bible, and Gender* (Leiden: Brill, 2021); Joy E. A. Qualls, *God Forgive Us for Being Women: Rhetoric, Theology, and the Pentecostal Tradition* (Eugene, OR: Wipf & Stock, 2018); Margaret English de Alminana and Lois E. Olena, eds., *Women in Pentecostal and Charismatic Ministry: Informing a Dialogue on Gender, Church, and Ministry* (Leiden: Brill, 2017); Kimberly Ervin Alexander and James P. Bowers, *What Women Want: Pentecostal Women Ministers Speak for Themselves* (Lanham, MD: Seymour, 2013); Lisa P. Stephenson, *Dismantling the Dualisms for American Pentecostal Women in Ministry: A Feminist-Pneumatological Approach* (Leiden: Brill, 2012); Estrelda Y. Alexander and Amos Yong, eds., *Philip's Daughters: Women in Pentecostal-Charismatic Leadership* (Eugene, OR: Pickwick, 2009); Shane Clifton and Jacqueline Grey, eds., *Raising Women Leaders: Perspectives on Liberating Women in Pentecostal and Charismatic Contexts* (Sydney: Australian Pentecostal Studies, 2009); Kimberly Ervin Alexander and R. Hollis Gause, *Women in Leadership: A Pentecostal Perspective* (Cleveland, TN: Center for Pentecostal Leadership and Care, 2006). For a website with articles from a Pentecostal perspective, see the "Gender Equality" page of Pentecostals and Charismatics for Peace and Justice (PCPJ), updated June 7, 2021, https://pcpj.org/category/gender-equality/.

6. Bernice Martin, "The Pentecostal Gender Paradox: A Cautionary Tale for the Sociology of Religion," in *The Blackwell Companion to Sociology of Religion*, ed. Richard K. Fenn (Oxford: Blackwell, 2001), 52–66. See note 31 of this chapter.

irrelevant to, or insufficient for advancing women's equality in the church.[7] For Pentecostals, eschatology has often been about urgency in "saving souls" rather than attending to social issues.[8] Therefore, partnering Pentecostal eschatology with gender equality sounds like an uneasy marriage. The question might be asked: can Pentecostal eschatology make a positive contribution for those seeking greater equality for women in the church?

The purpose of this project is to critically assess the relationship between gender and eschatology in the early Pentecostal movement, key biblical texts, theology, and praxis, in order to develop a thoroughly eschatological basis for the full flourishing and unrestricted inclusion of women in all parts and at all levels of church life, ministry, and society.[9] By examining gender through an eschatological lens in Pentecostal history, hermeneutics, theology, and ecclesiology,[10] I argue that eschatology provides a valid and valuable critical approach in the Pentecostal gender debate for furthering women's equality because it provides a consistent

---

7. These three positions are discussed in the next chapter, but most notable is Rosemary Radford Ruether, *Sexism and God-Talk: Toward a Feminist Theology*, 10th anniversary ed. (Boston: Beacon, 1993), see 99–102 and her Chapter 10, "Eschatology and Feminism." Eschatology is mostly left out of full-scale theological works on women's equality, even ones claiming to be comprehensive or systematic in their approach (see 1.1.2).

8. However, cf. Murray W. Dempster, "Christian Social Concern in Pentecostal Perspective: Reformulating Pentecostal Eschatology," *JPT* 1, no. 2 (1993): 51–64. See also Veli-Matti Kärkkäinen, "Are Pentecostals Oblivious to Social Justice? Theological and Ecumenical Perspectives," *Missiology: An International Review* 29, no. 4 (2001): 417–31. In addition to or alongside social justice issues, Pentecostals are increasingly writing about the work of the Spirit in public life. See Mark J. Cartledge, *The Holy Spirit and Public Life: Empowering Ecclesial Praxis* (Lanham, MD: Lexington Books/Fortress Academic, 2022); Daniela C. Augustine and Chris E. W. Green, eds., *The Politics of the Spirit: Pentecostal Reflections on Public Responsibility and the Common Good* (Lanham, MD: Seymour, 2022).

9. This is essentially my (eschatologically inspired) definition for gender equality, influenced by similar definitions (minus the eschatological element) in Rebecca S. Chopp, *The Power to Speak: Feminism, Language, God* (New York: Crossroad, 1989), 2, 37, 68; Bettina Tate Pedersen, "Christian Feminist or Feminist Christian: What's Feminism Got to Do with Evangelical Christians," in *Being Feminist, Being Christian: Essays from Academia*, ed. Allyson Jule and Bettina Tate Pedersen (New York: Palgrave Macmillan, 2006), 9; Lisa Sowle Cahill, *Sex, Gender, and Christian Ethics* (Cambridge: Cambridge University Press, 1996), 110; and Andrea Hollingsworth, "Spirit and Voice: Toward a Feminist Pentecostal Pneumatology," *Pneuma* 29, no. 2 (2007): 189–213.

10. Unlike history, hermeneutics, and ecclesiology (praxis), there is no dedicated chapter to theology (but do see the theological history in Chapter 3 as well as the theological discussion in 6.2). However, this entire work put together creates a theological contribution to the gender debate. Overall, developing a Pentecostal eschatology of gender is a theological task that relies on history, hermeneutics, and praxis.

authorizing hermeneutic capable of resolving the Pentecostal gender paradox.[11] This previously overlooked heuristic tool of eschatology has the capacity to awaken the Pentecostal eschatological imagination by offering a clear biblical and theological authorization for gender equality which leads to the complete and unhindered participation of women in ecclesial leadership.

Although the term "gender" is a "highly theorized" and often "unstable" term or category,[12] in the Pentecostal gender debate we are talking about perceived differences between men and women with regard to their authority and leadership roles in the church.[13] The terms "gender roles" and the "role of women" are used in this work in the context of ecclesiastical practices, positions, or places where women's participation is denied, limited, or questioned. Pentecostal historian Leah Payne calls these ecclesiastical differences "gender binaries," which establish practices and realms that are considered normative for each sex in a way that limits the freedoms of women in church leadership.[14] Most scholars who argue for gender equality do not argue that there are no differences between men and women, but rather that the differences are of equal value and importance and should not be used to grant men any advantages in authority or to discriminate against women in any way.[15] Discovering the reasons these gender binaries

---

11. There is an unavoidable overlap of "hermeneutics" as it applies to biblical interpretation, and a "hermeneutic," meaning a way of approaching a theological issue. This project is the latter—applying an eschatological hermeneutic to gender—but necessarily involves the former, which is the focus of much of my work and especially Chapters 3 and 4. The line is always a bit blurred, for to articulate a biblical hermeneutic is to articulate a theology. See J'annine Jobling, *Feminist Biblical Interpretation in Theological Context: Restless Readings* (Hampshire: Ashgate, 2002), 100.

12. Leah Payne, *Gender and Pentecostal Revivalism: Making a Female Ministry in the Early Twentieth Century* (New York: Palgrave Macmillan, 2015), 15; Marcella Althaus-Reid, "Class, Sex and the Theologian: Reflections on the Liberationist Movement in Latin America," in *Another Possible World: Reclaiming Liberation Theology*, ed. Marcella Maria Althaus-Reid, Ivan Petrella, and Luiz Carlos Susin (London: SCM, 2007), 34. For gender in evangelical history, see Part 1 of Michelle Lee-Barnewall, *Neither Complementarian nor Egalitarian: A Kingdom Corrective to the Evangelical Gender Debate* (Grand Rapids: Baker Academic, 2016), 17–67.

13. Men and women are sometimes used interchangeably with male and female, including sometimes in this work and most of the works cited in this discussion. However, some helpfully distinguish them by understanding male and female more as a referent to biological sex and men and women referring to gender as a sociological construct. See Rom Harré, *Physical Being: A Theory for a Corporeal Psychology* (Oxford: Blackwell, 1991), 42–60.

14. Payne, *Gender*, 15–16.

15. See John G. Stackhouse Jr., *Finally Feminist: A Pragmatic Christian Understanding of Gender* (Grand Rapids: Baker Academic, 2005), 17–18; Cahill, *Sex, Gender*, 1–2; Bradley C. Hanson, *Introduction to Christian Theology* (Minneapolis: Fortress, 1997), 37. Other terms for this position include "egalitarianism," "biblical equality," or "evangelical feminism." See

currently exist and how (or if) they might be resolved through eschatology is part of the aim of this work.

Some may contest that a critical-theological approach is actually needed in the gender debate, particularly within Pentecostalism. The following section therefore briefly outlines the historical decline and current plateauing of women in Pentecostal leadership and the rise of the gender paradox, all of which are fueled by the lack (or weakening) of a consistent theological authorizing hermeneutic. I then suggest that the recent revival of eschatological thinking in Christianity and Pentecostalism creates a (re)new(ed) opportunity for an eschatological solution to this century-old problem. Eschatology has the methodological potential to resolve the Pentecostal gender paradox because it acts as a transformational method ideal for motivating social action. I then discuss why this Pentecostal problem (and a potential critical solution) has global impact beyond just the Pentecostal movement. The chapter closes with an overview of the argument and outline of the procedure.

## The Decline of Women in Leadership and the Rise of the Gender Paradox

The narrative of women in Pentecostalism begins with a significant rise in women's participation in both official and unofficial church leadership during the early twentieth century.[16] The historical evidence reveals a surprising consensus on how the Scriptures authorized the full equality of women, particularly in ecclesial situations.[17] However, as the movement grew and formalized, this initial egalitarian impulse began to fade and was never fully recovered as hermeneutical uncertainty and the gender paradox replaced earlier hermeneutical and egalitarian convictions. This story of the rise, decline, and continued waning or plateauing of women's leadership in Pentecostalism is a well-known narrative.[18] Scholars and historians of Pentecostalism have consistently documented this gradual decline

---

Cherith Nordling, "Gender," in *The Oxford Handbook of Evangelical Theology*, ed. Gerald R. McDermott (Oxford: Oxford University Press, 2010), 503–4. The opposite perspective is usually labeled the "complementarian" position which does distinguish roles based on sex and believes the Bible does place restrictions on women. For further explanation, as well as an argument to move beyond this debate and reframe the issue, see Lee-Barnewall, *Neither Complementarian nor Egalitarian*, esp. 1–7, 167–74; Stackhouse, *Finally Feminist*, 19.

16. See Section 2.3.1 for more.

17. See my Chapter 2 for this evidence. This is not to say it was a "golden age" to be duplicated (see 2.2.4).

18. See 3.2 for more. For summaries and statistics, see Margaret English de Alminana, "Introduction," in English de Alminana and Olena, *Women*, 1–2; Edith L. Blumhofer, "Women in Evangelicalism and Pentecostalism," in *Women and Church: The Challenge of Ecumenical Solidarity in an Age of Alienation*, ed. Malanie A. May (Grand Rapids: Eerdmans, 1991), 4; Frank D. Macchia, *Baptized in the Spirit: A Global Pentecostal Theology* (Grand

of women's involvement and influence as well as the increased limitations placed upon women.[19] They point to the "alarming diminishing number of women under the age of 30 holding ministerial credentials"[20] and have concluded there is "little indication that women's position within pentecostalism has improved over 100 years."[21] This modern gender imbalance in Pentecostal leadership is true not only of churches but also of parachurch and missions organizations as well.[22] Recent research confirms that many Pentecostal women feel compelled to leave Pentecostal churches and organizations due to the lack of freedom to fully exercise their callings,[23] often pointing out the irony that women now have less freedom in Pentecostal circles than they do in some denominations that once rejected the Pentecostal empowerment of women.[24] This overall decline and its reasons are briefly discussed below and in Chapters 2 and 3, but the result is that despite Pentecostal women historically being treated equally on paper—such as being given full ordination—current practice and experience tell a different

---

Rapids: Zondervan, 2006), 219; Janet Everts Powers, "Pentecostalism 101: Your Daughters Shall Prophesy," in Alexander and Yong, *Philip's Daughters*, 149.

19. See Estrelda Y. Alexander, "Introduction," in Alexander and Yong, *Philip's Daughters*, 6; Payne, *Gender*, 132–3. For the Canadian story, see Michael Wilkinson and Linda M. Ambrose, *After the Revival: Pentecostalism and the Making of a Canadian Church* (Montreal & Kingston: McGill-Queen's University Press, 2020), 86–94.

20. Alexander and Bowers, *What Women Want*, 128. See Appendix 2, "Female Ministers in the USA: Demographic Profile," in Alexander and Bowers, *What Women Want*, 162.

21. R. Marie Griffith and David G. Roebuck, "Women, Role of," in *NIDPCM*, rev. ed., ed. Stanley M. Burgess and Eduard M. van der Maas (Grand Rapids: Zondervan, 2002), 1208. See also Deidre Helen Crumbley, "Sanctified Saints—Impure Prophetess: A Cross-Cultural Study of Gender and Power in Two Afro-Christian Spirit-Privileging Churches," in *The Spirit in the World: Emerging Pentecostal Theologies in Global Contexts*, ed. Veli-Matti Kärkkäinen (Grand Rapids: Eerdmans, 2009), 117–18.

22. Julie C. Ma and Wonsuk Ma, *Mission in the Spirit: Towards a Pentecostal/Charismatic Missiology* (Eugene, OR: Wipf & Stock, 2010), 206.

23. See particularly the chapter "Hearing Their Voices," in Alexander and Bowers, *What Women Want*, 14, 17–20. See also Alexander, "Introduction," 7; Loralie Robinson Crabtree and Joy E. A. Qualls, "Women as Assemblies of God Church Planters: Cultural Analysis and Strategy Formation," in English de Alminana and Olena, *Women*, 305. Mary Daly was one of the first to encourage women to leave the church or form their own churches in *The Church and the Second Sex* (Boston: Beacon, 1968). For misogyny as one of the main reasons evangelicals are leaving the church, see Bradley Onishi, "The Rise of #Exvangelical," *Religion and Politics*, April 9, 2019, John C. Danforth Center on Religion & Politics at Washington University (St. Louis), https:// religionandpolitics.org/2019/04/09/the-rise-of-exvangelical/.

24. See James P. Bowers, "Foreword," in Alexander and Gause, *Women*, vii.

story. Women are losing their once prominent place in the Pentecostal story, and Pentecostalism is losing its once promising egalitarian trajectory.[25]

The early rise and later decline of women in leadership reveals a tension within Pentecostalism: the capacity to encourage and to discourage egalitarian practices, or what Martin termed the Pentecostal gender paradox. Pentecostal scholars have alternatively articulated Martin's argument as the competing impulses of liberation and limitation,[26] freedom and formalization,[27] affirmation and denial,[28] opportunity and constraint,[29] and exclusion and embrace[30] concerning women in leadership.[31] The conclusion among these authors is that these competing impulses lead to tremendous uncertainty, hesitancy, or ambiguity about the place of women

---

25. Janet Everts Powers, "'Your Daughters Shall Prophesy': Pentecostal Hermeneutics and the Empowerment of Women," in *The Globalization of Pentecostalism: A Religion Made to Travel*, ed. Murray W. Dempster, Byron D. Klaus, and Douglas Petersen (Oxford: Regnum Books, 1999), 313–14, 332. See also Deborah M. Gill, "The Contemporary State of Women in Ministry in the Assemblies of God," *Pneuma* 17 (Spring 1995): 34–6.

26. Estrelda Y. Alexander, *Limited Liberty: The Legacy of Four Pentecostal Women Pioneers* (Cleveland, OH: Pilgrim, 2008); Andrea Hollingsworth and Melissa D. Browning, "Your Daughters Shall Prophesy (As Long as They Submit): Pentecostalism and Gender in Global Perspective," in *A Liberating Spirit: Pentecostals and Social Action in North America*, ed. Michael Wilkinson and Steven M. Studebaker (Eugene, OR: Pickwick, 2010), 176–8.

27. Charles H. Barfoot and Gerald T. Sheppard, "Prophetic vs. Priestly Religion: The Changing Role of Women Clergy in Classical Pentecostal Churches," *Review of Religious Research* 22, no. 1 (September 1980): 2–17. This article obviously precedes Martin's and has been equally influential. Its context is more the early Pentecostal movement; therefore, it will be discussed in Chapter 2. Similarly, Frederick L. Ware discusses "spiritual egalitarianism" versus "ecclesial pragmatism" in "Spiritual Egalitarianism, Ecclesial Pragmatism, and the Status of Women in Ordained Ministry," in Alexander and Yong, *Philip's Daughters*, 215. See also Powers, "Pentecostal Hermeneutics," 314.

28. Pamela Holmes, "The Spirit, Nature, and Canadian Pentecostal Women: A Conversation with Critical Theory," in Alexander and Yong, *Philip's Daughters*, 187.

29. Qualls, *Forgive Us*, 153. See also the observation of Diedre Helen Crumbley concerning "Pentecostal paradoxes that liberate the body in worship while constraining its sexuality" in "Dressed as becometh Holiness: Gender, Race and the Body in a Storefront Sanctified Church," in *Spirit on the Move: Black Women and Pentecostalism in Africa and the Diaspora*, ed. Judith Casselberry and Elizabeth A. Pritchard (Durham, NC: Duke University Press, 2019), 91.

30. Cheryl Bridges Johns, "Spirited Vestments: Or, Why the Anointing Is Not Enough," in Alexander and Yong, *Philip's Daughters*, 170–1.

31. It should be noted the starting premise for these Pentecostal scholars is the opposite of Martin. Whereas Martin sees Pentecostalism as a mostly patriarchal movement that sometimes surprisingly brings new freedoms for women, most Pentecostal scholars view Pentecostalism ideally as an egalitarian movement that often surprisingly restricts the ministry of women. Nevertheless, the important conclusion and consensus is that there are

in Pentecostal circles, what they also refer to as the gender problem, gender question, gender issue, or gender debate within Pentecostalism.[32]

If the problem (or solution) were merely official policy concerning the full ordination of women, then there would not be much of an issue. Most Pentecostal denominations now ordain women and endorse women's leadership in official statements, although some only after a painful and lengthy process.[33] However, as Cheryl Catford comments, "Just as it would be ridiculous to suggest that the legal end to segregation achieved by the Civil Rights Movement in the 1960s ended all discrimination against African-Americans, so the acceptance of the ordination of women ministers in Pentecostal denominations is not a one-dimensional, 'solve-all' action."[34] Many Pentecostal leaders (particularly men) tend to think women's equality is "no longer an issue" due to the appearance of a few women and official documents and policy that affirm women's leadership and ordination.[35] But both Catford and Joy Qualls separately conclude from their research that even when official statements and full ordination for women exist or when Pentecostal denominations see a rise in female clergy, a serious gap and disconnect still remains between the formal policy of an organization and actual practices in local churches.[36] The research of others has also shown that there is little correlation between access to ordination and women being given authority and influence

---

two competing impulses which create a paradox in Pentecostalism regarding gender and the role of women.

32. These terms will be used interchangeably throughout my work to refer to the issue of women's (in)equality in Pentecostalism.

33. However, some Pentecostal denominations such as the Church of God (Cleveland, TN) have repeatedly voted to restrict leadership positions and full ordination for women (including most recently at the 2016, 2010, and 2008 General Assembly) as well as voting rights in their general assembly. See the painful stories relayed by Alexander and Bowers, *What Women Want*, 17–20; Stephenson, *Dismantling*, 1–2; Qualls, *Forgive Us*, 218. See also Joel Daniels, "Gender and Pentecostalism: Men Voting on Whether Women Should Get to Vote," Engaged Pentecostalism (website), October 26, 2017, http://engagedpentecostalism.com/gender-and-pentecostalism-men-voting-on-whether-women-should-get-to-vote/. For the story of women's ordination in other contexts, denominations, and countries, see Ian Jones, Janet Wootton, and Kirsty Thorpe, *Women and Ordination in the Christian Churches: International Perspectives* (New York: T&T Clark, 2008).

34. Cheryl Catford, "Women's Experiences: Challenges for Female Leaders in Pentecostal Contexts," in Clifton and Grey, *Raising Women*, 40. This is why some works which argue solely for ordination or just "women in ministry" as the end goal, while helpful, fall short. For example, see Stanley J. Grenz and Denise Muir Kjesbo, *Women in the Church: A Biblical Theology of Women in Ministry* (Downers Grove, IL: IVP Academic, 1995).

35. Catford, "Women's Experiences," 41.

36. Qualls, *Forgive Us*, 217; Catford, "Women's Experiences," 26–7. See also Shane Clifton, "Sexism and the Demonic in Church Life and Mission," in Clifton and Grey, *Raising Women*, 51–70.

in churches: ordination does not eliminate discriminatory practices.[37] Leading Assembly of God historian Edith Blumhofer summarizes: "For women, ordination does not translate into equal access to positions of leadership traditionally available to clergy." In fact, she argues, it can make it harder because organizations feel they are no longer on the hook for discrimination.[38] Women's leadership and influence has declined even as official policies have often changed for the better. If the main problem (or solution) is not official policy concerning women's leadership, what is fueling the decline of women in Pentecostal leadership and keeping them on the margins of institutional influence and decision-making?

At the root of the perpetual decline of women's leadership in Pentecostalism and the rise of the gender paradox is the lack of a consistent authorizing hermeneutic for the ministry of women. The Pentecostal gender paradox is primarily fueled by hermeneutical hesitancy and inconsistency,[39] leading to what scholars have described as a strong "theological ambiguity"[40] or "rhetorical dichotomy"[41] within the movement. This constant ambiguity or consistent "dissonance"[42] describes the tension of competing beliefs about women in leadership that leads to theological uncertainty and to paradoxical messages and practices, all of which burden and limit women in their God-given callings. The gender paradox is partly due to Pentecostal leaders' desire to stay faithful to the Bible and its seeming position that women must play a subordinate role in leadership (a problem addressed in

---

37. Payne, *Gender*, 9; Stephenson, *Dismantling*, 7–8, 57, 139. For more on authority see Payne, *Gender*, 13–15.

38. Edith L. Blumhofer, *Restoring the Faith: The Assemblies of God, Pentecostalism, and American Culture* (Urbana, IL: University of Illinois Press, 1993), 176.

39. This is the observation of several Pentecostal scholars, but see especially Powers who argues Pentecostals have been "hermeneutically inconsistent" ("Pentecostal Hermeneutics," 317).

40. Catford, "Women's Experiences," 30. Many, if not most, Pentecostal historians, theologians, and hermeneuts use the term "ambiguity" to describe or refer to the situation surrounding the gender problem. For example, Kimberly Ervin Alexander describes the last century as "fraught with ambiguity" and a "period of ambiguity" as well as the "ambiguous rhetoric" women face and "ambiguous space" in which they fulfill their call ("'With Blessings They Cover the Bitterness': Persisting and Worshipping through Brokenness – Pentecostal Women and the Pentecostal Tradition(s)," in Johns and Stephenson, *Grieving, Brooding, and Transforming*, 144, 149, 158). Linda Ambrose also uses the term "ambiguities" to describe the complicated results surrounding the promotion of women leaders in a theologically and socially conservative movement such as Pentecostalism. See Linda M. Ambrose, "Thinking through the Theological and Methodological Quandaries of Gender and Canadian Pentecostal History," *Canadian Journal of Pentecostal-Charismatic Christianity* 3 (2012): 72. I consider ambiguity more a symptom, consequence, or further description of the gender paradox rather than the underlying cause or problem.

41. Qualls, *Forgive Us*, 17.

42. A key word for Qualls's description of the situation (*Forgive Us*, 3, 8, 31, 203).

Chapter 4). Catford's research shows that even where men (or women) may biblically accept the right of women to minister, the majority (67 percent in her study) still maintain a theological conviction that women must be under the "covering" of another man.[43] This "need for submission," she says, creates the problem of a very small percentage of women in senior or denominational leadership.[44] For example, as of 2021, Assemblies of God women in the United States make up 27 percent of credential holders and 19 percent of ordained ministers. However, less than half a percent (0.49) of churches are led by a female pastor.[45] The research of Kimberly Alexander and James Bowers shows that many Pentecostal groups still oppose full ministerial equality for women, and that the majority of men have a problem with women in leadership because they believe it "violates God-ordained order."[46] There is a barrier of a cultural norm within Pentecostal churches that assumes leadership is male, driven by the lack of a consistent theological authorizing hermeneutic that is able to resolve the gender paradox.[47]

A lack of theological conviction concerning women's equal status in the church has created a century of "mixed experiences,"[48] "conflicting messages,"[49] and "confusion and ambivalence,"[50] as Pentecostal women have attempted to navigate the gender paradox. In his theological introduction to Pentecostalism, Wolfgang Vondey summarizes the conflict concerning gender.[51] He does see an "egalitarian impulse" in the Pentecostal movement but describes how this ideal of egalitarianism inevitably encounters resistance when attempting to put it into practice: the movement is both revolutionary and regressive. Therefore, Pentecostalism is full of "unresolved tensions" and is "torn" between its egalitarian intentions and the reality of gender discrimination which is alive and well.[52]

---

43. Cheryl Catford, "Explaining the Recent Increase in Numbers of CRC Women Pastors" (PhD diss., Deakin University, 2008), 161–2.

44. Catford, "Women's Experiences," 31–2, 35.

45. "Female Lead Pastors: A Discussion Worth Having," A Collaborative Resource by Assemblies of God District/Network Superintendents, curated by Gene Roncone, September 2021, https://penndel.org/wp-content/uploads/2021/09/Female-Lead-Pastors.pdf (page 1).

46. Alexander and Bowers, *What Women Want*, 44–6, 60.

47. Payne, *Gender*, 15–16.

48. Alexander, *Limited Liberty*, 26, 14.

49. Martin W. Mittelstadt, "Reimagining Luke-Acts: Amos Yong and the Biblical Foundation of Pentecostal Theology," in *The Theology of Amos Yong and the New Face of Pentecostal Scholarship: Passion for the Spirit*, ed. Wolfgang Vondey and Martin William Mittelstadt (Leiden: Brill, 2013), 34. See also Qualls, *Forgive Us*, 31–5.

50. Alexander, "Persisting and Worshipping through Brokenness," 144.

51. See Vondey, *Perplexed*, 111–31.

52. Vondey, *Perplexed*, 119–26, 128. Because of all this, Vondey prefers to refer to Pentecostalism as an "egalitarian movement-in-development" or "egalitarianism-in-the-making" (125, 131).

Part of the reason these tensions exist, suggests Vondey, is that the concerns of gender have yet to occupy a central place in Pentecostal theology. Like Pentecostal churches, Pentecostal scholars have often been silent in articulating a solid theological defense for the leadership of women.[53] There is a deficiency, a "significant shortage of research" so that "an intellectual basis for the realization of egalitarian practices" has yet to be established.[54] In their intriguing chapter discussing the limiting and liberating aspects of Pentecostalism for women, Andrea Hollingsworth and Melissa Browning claim that emancipatory theological resources exist for women "to both subvert gender oppression and find empowerment"; however, these resources have yet to be mined and appropriated in a way that leads to the flourishing of women in Pentecostalism.[55]

As Pentecostalism becomes a more mature movement, Pentecostal scholars are being encouraged to construct theologies that are authentically Pentecostal, shaped by Pentecostal concerns and resources.[56] This call to "think pentecostally"[57] extends especially to the gender paradox. In the postscript to his important work on Pentecostal theology, Keith Warrington identifies one of the chief challenges ahead for Pentecostals as the role of women in leadership, and he warns that the Pentecostal revival "will slow down and even implode" if this and other issues "are not seriously examined and conclusions carefully implemented."[58] Others have similarly warned that unless suggestions for change regarding the role of women come from within and are faithful to the Pentecostal tradition, then they will not create change at all.[59] Although there is some variation as to what an authentically Pentecostal approach involves, most agree it must: (1) reflect the earliest years of the movement; (2) be deeply biblical and interpret Scripture in light of Pentecost; (3) be pneumatological in its theological reflection while remaining orthodox and ecumenical; and (4) contain a strong emphasis on praxis and real-time participation with the Spirit.[60] No single work has comprehensively addressed and

---

53. For silence from Pentecostal churches on women's equality, see Powers, "Pentecostalism 101," 145–9, esp. 148. This is, of course, changing as evidenced by the increasing amount of books dedicated to the gender problem in Pentecostalism. However, these works still fall short in contributing a unified and methodologically connected theological defense that fully incorporates all the necessary areas of a Pentecostal approach.

54. Vondey, *Perplexed*, 128, 131.

55. Hollingsworth and Browning, "Daughters," 176–8.

56. Chris E. W. Green, *Toward a Pentecostal Theology of the Lord's Supper: Foretasting the Kingdom* (Cleveland, TN: CPT, 2012), 244.

57. Amos Yong, *The Spirit Poured Out on All Flesh: Pentecostalism and the Possibility of Global Theology* (Grand Rapids: Baker Academic, 2005), 9.

58. Keith Warrington, *Pentecostal Theology: A Theology of Encounter* (London: T&T Clark, 2008), 324.

59. Powers, "Pentecostal Hermeneutics," 315.

60. There are numerous sources that could be cited here, and the importance of each discipline is discussed in its corresponding chapter of this work, but a few Pentecostal

integrated each of these areas with a consistent theological method that authorizes the leadership and full participation of women at all levels of Pentecostal church life, despite calls to do so.[61] Thus, the Pentecostal gender paradox is and will remain alive and well until a convincing, unified, and authentically Pentecostal solution is applied across each of these fields of study in a way that can "clear away the dissonance."[62]

Women's leadership continues to wane or at least plateau in almost all Pentecostal denominations despite advancements on paper. The overall deficiency in research and lack of work directed at mining emancipatory resources for Pentecostal women means the gender paradox, fueled by hermeneutical inconsistency and theological uncertainty concerning women's roles in the church, is the current inheritance of the next generation of Pentecostal women and men. The following section suggests why eschatology might have the potential to become the needed foundational resource and theological basis for the full realization of unrestricted egalitarian practices in Pentecostal churches and organizations.

## Why Eschatology?

The purpose of this section is to present why eschatology carries promise for resolving the Pentecostal gender paradox. Numerous explanations have been given over the years for the decline of women's leadership in the movement. The most common include the theological and hermeneutical influence of fundamentalism and evangelical theology, fear of secular feminism and other liberal movements, institutionalization, and the professionalization of ministry.[63] No matter the reason for the decline, what is increasingly apparent is the need for a consistent and critical solution to the gender paradox across historical, biblical, and practical Pentecostal disciplines. Scholars have successfully identified the vast scope of the *problem* and

---

scholars that articulate the above in various ways are Green, *Lord's Supper*, 1–2; Steven M. Studebaker, *From Pentecost to the Triune God: A Pentecostal Trinitarian Theology* (Grand Rapids: Eerdmans, 2012), 1–3; Vondey, *Perplexed*, 33, 44–6.

61. Stephenson admits her work mostly focuses on the historical and theological elements of women in ministry but suggests we must also pay attention to hermeneutical issues: "one must be able to give an account from all three perspectives when dealing with the issue of women in ministry" (*Dismantling*, 195). My work answers that call while also adding the key and perhaps most crucial element of praxis.

62. For the importance of a unified voice (rhetoric) to "clear away the dissonance," see Qualls, *Forgive Us*, 186.

63. These and other reasons are mentioned or listed in Qualls, *Forgive Us*, 153; Powers, "Pentecostalism 101," 133–51; Powers, "Pentecostal Hermeneutics," 316, 332; Alexander, "Introduction," 6–7; Blumhofer, "Women," 4; Barbara L. Cavaness, "Leadership Attitudes and the Ministry of Single Women in Assemblies of God Mission," in Alexander and Yong, *Philip's Daughters*, 125–6, 128; Catford, "Women's Experiences," 39–40; Holmes, "Canadian."

some of its reasons; what is missing is a distinctively Pentecostal *solution* that takes into account Pentecostal history, hermeneutics, and theology, and leads to praxis on the ground.[64] I propose eschatology as the methodological starting point for women's equality and as an authorizing hermeneutic for the ministry of women that fits the ethos and essence of the Pentecostal movement. My work is not just about identifying and resisting the patriarchal exclusion of women but offering "proactive measures" to ensure a better future for women in Pentecostal churches, a strategy championed by other Pentecostals.[65]

In her work *Limited Liberty*, Estrelda Alexander divides existing strategies for dealing with the unjust treatment of women into three categories: accommodationist, reformist, or activist. While the first two try to make the best of a bad situation and do what is possible within certain limitations (in other words, they embrace the gender paradox), the activist response—which Alexander calls for—seeks to change the injustice by questioning the system(s) and theological premise(s) for actions and seeks to demonstrate a better way.[66] I am responding to the call of Alexander to question theological approaches that perpetuate the gender paradox as well as to suggest a solution that brings a promising theological lens to this societal and religious problem. Eschatology—despite being overlooked in the gender debate—has the potential to resolve the existing tensions and provide a unique and effective way forward in the quest for women's equality in Pentecostalism.

For eschatology to be considered an appropriate, even ideal, methodological lens to address the gender paradox, two hypotheses need to be tested. First, if Pentecostalism is a thoroughly eschatological movement, then eschatology can (and must) play a crucial role in engaging any ethical or social issue within Pentecostalism, including gender. Second, if eschatology is considered a transformational method, meaning it has major implications for present practice, then it must have potential to lead to social action and legitimate long-term change. In other words, if there is a strong relationship between eschatology and ethics, then eschatology would be positioned as an essential theological approach for developing a social critique. These two working hypotheses will continue throughout this work and its chapters, and a brief introduction to both will help lay the foundation for the possibility of an eschatological resolving of the Pentecostal gender paradox.

*The Revival of Eschatology: The End Is the New Beginning*

Eschatology has often been a speculative afterthought in Christian theology, hidden away at the end of books and reserved for the ultra-curious. But several

---

64. The overemphasis on the problems and the lack of a distinctively Pentecostal solution is the lament of Powers, "Pentecostal Hermeneutics," 332, and the assessment of Blumhofer, "Women," 3.
65. Clifton, "Sexism," 63.
66. Alexander, *Limited Liberty*, xi–xiv.

prominent theologians since the mid-twentieth century have begun to challenge this thinking and are increasingly reviving eschatology's importance in Christian life and theology.[67] With this revival, eschatology has been called "the definitive vantage point from which to contemplate the entirety of Christian revelation, theology, spirituality, ethics, and wisdom"[68] and the "ultimate perspective" for theological understanding and for allowing the Spirit to accomplish God's work through the church.[69] John Shields suggests "a new genre for eschatology," not as speculation but rather as exhortation that leads to action.[70] Some have gone as far to say that apart from an eschatological orientation "every Christian doctrine becomes distorted."[71] The argument of these and other theologians is that the "last things" are really the "first things" to contemplate when it comes to Christian theology, practice, and the mission of God in the world.[72] We must begin with the end, for we live for what we hope for.[73]

Trevor Hart, one of the most prominent voices on the revival of eschatology and the eschatological imagination, warns of the danger of placing eschatology last in our theological thinking and treating it as "a detachable appendix without any apparent purchase on most of what precedes it." "Christian faith and theology are, or should properly be," he says, "eschatological from first to last."[74] This renewed emphasis on eschatology has even led some Pentecostal theologians to reverse

---

67. See discussion and overview in John M. Shields, *An Eschatological Imagination: A Revisionist Christian Eschatology in the Light of David Tracy's Theological Project* (New York: Peter Lang, 2008), 1–7; Wolfhart Pannenberg, *Systematic Theology*, vol. 3, trans. Geoffrey W. Bromiley (Edinburgh: T&T Clark, 2004); Joseph Ratzinger, *Eschatology: Death and Eternal Life*, 2nd ed., trans. Michael Waldstein (Washington, DC: The Catholic University of America Press, 1988). An example of developing an ethical argument around an eschatological foundation is Stanley Grenz, *The Moral Quest: Foundations of Christian Ethics* (Downers Grove, IL: IVP Academic, 1997), see 203. See discussion of this work in 5.3.1.

68. Paul O'Callaghan, *Christ Our Hope: Introduction to Eschatology* (Washington, DC: The Catholic University of America Press, 2011), 329. See his chapter "The Central Role of Christian Eschatology in Theology," 329–37.

69. Stanley Grenz, *Renewing the Center: Evangelical Theology in a Post-Theological Era*, 2nd ed. (Grand Rapids: Baker Academic, 2006), 255.

70. Shields, *Eschatological Imagination*, 173.

71. Daniel Migliore, *Faith Seeking Understanding: An Introduction to Christian Theology* (Grand Rapids: Eerdmans, 1991), 231.

72. See Christian A. Smith's classic article "The Eschatological Drive of God's Mission," *Review and Expositor* 82 (Spring 1985): 209–16. See also Byron Klaus, "The Holy Spirit and Mission in Eschatological Perspective: A Pentecostal Viewpoint," *Pneuma* 27, no. 2 (2005): 322–42; Andrew M. Lord, "Mission Eschatology," *JPT* 11 (1997): 111–23.

73. See Amos Yong, *Renewing Christian Theology: Systematics for a Global Christianity* (Waco, TX: Baylor University Press, 2014), 55.

74. Trevor Hart, "Eschatology," in McDermott, *Handbook*, 262.

the classical order for systematic theology and to begin with eschatology.⁷⁵ Amos Yong argues in his *Renewing Christian Theology* that a systematic theology from a renewalist perspective must be thoroughly eschatological.⁷⁶ The entire volume has an eschatological orientation and *begins* with eschatology, which Yong believes constitutes a major paradigm shift for doing theology.⁷⁷ Yong suggests elsewhere that eschatology cannot be set apart as a separate topic removed from the rest of theology; rather, it "runs as a thread woven throughout the entirety" of all theology.⁷⁸

Yong's emphasis on eschatology reflects the critical role it has historically played in the Pentecostal movement⁷⁹ and among Pentecostal theologians. The eschatological fervor of early Pentecostalism was and still is key to its rapid growth, vitality, and way-of-being in the world.⁸⁰ Robert Mapes Anderson was one of the first to argue that eschatology is the unifying concept and central element of the Pentecostal worldview.⁸¹ Since then, Pentecostal historians and theologians such as William Faupel, Donald Dayton, Matthew Thompson, and others have written extensive works arguing, in different ways, that eschatology is the central theme and heartbeat of the movement.⁸² More recent Pentecostal theologians such as

---

75. Hence the subtitle of this section, which is the title of Chapter 6 in Thompson's *Kingdom Come*, 89–108.

76. Yong, *Renewing*, 15. "Renewalist" is an all-inclusive term used by Yong that refers to "the pentecostal and charismatic forms of Christianity around the world" (6).

77. Yong, *Renewing*, 18.

78. Yong, *Spirit Poured Out*, 97. Cf. also Yong's *In the Days of Caesar* where he comments in the last chapter entitled "Pentecostal Hope: A Political Theology of History and the Eschaton" that "the entire book points in the eschatological direction explicated here" and that the entire flow of the book "begs for" an eschatological theology of the political" (Amos Yong, *In the Days of Caesar: Pentecostalism and Political Theology* [Grand Rapids: Eerdmans, 2010], 316–17).

79. See 2.3.2 for more on the eschatological fervor of early Pentecostals.

80. See Grant Wacker, *Heaven Below: Early Pentecostalism and American Culture* (Cambridge, MA: Harvard University Press, 2001), 251–65. The historical and recent developments in Pentecostal eschatology and their significance will be more fully discussed in Chapter 3.

81. Robert Mapes Anderson, *Vision of the Disinherited: The Making of American Pentecostalism* (Oxford: Oxford University Press, 1979), 79–97. See Peter Althouse, "Pentecostal Eschatology in Context: The Eschatological Orientation of the Full Gospel," in Althouse and Waddell, *Eschatologies*, 207.

82. Faupel, *Everlasting Gospel*; Donald W. Dayton, *Theological Roots* (Peabody, MA: Hendrickson, 1987); Thompson, *Kingdom Come*. Dayton does distinguish himself from Faupel by saying "I am arguing here that eschatology is *a* crucial element, but not *the* central theme of Pentecostalism (33n44; Dayton speaks of Faupel's dissertation as in progress). See also Matthew K. Thompson, "Eschatology as Soteriology: The Cosmic Full Gospel," in Althouse and Waddell, *Eschatologies*, 189–204. For a sort of literature review of those who

Frank Macchia, Simon Chan, Vondey, and others have mentioned frequently in their works the crucial role eschatology plays in Pentecostal belief and practice.[83] A number of Pentecostals have also engaged with Jürgen Moltmann,[84] "the theologian par excellence of eschatology,"[85] who argues that "Christian ethics *are* eschatological ethics."[86] Following Moltmann, several Pentecostals have included eschatology in discussions on ethics and social issues, such as Robby Waddell's article on "Apocalyptic Sustainability" which encourages an eschatologically oriented ecology that cares for creation "in light of the end,"[87] or Monte Lee

have argued for an eschatological impulse as the best way for understanding Pentecostalism, see Althouse, "Pentecostal Eschatology," 205–31.

83. Macchia, *Baptized in the Spirit*, 27, 38–40, 46–9; Simon Chan, *Pentecostal Theology and the Christian Spiritual Tradition* (Sheffield: Sheffield Academic, 2000), 109 (see 108–16 for Chan's discussion of eschatology in Pentecostalism); Vondey, *Pentecostal Theology*, 131–51 (and every subsequent chapter has an eschatological section; for example, see 171–4). Vondey's assessment of both the recovery and reinterpretation of eschatological urgency in Pentecostalism is addressed in my Chapter 3. For some of the problems or difficulties of Pentecostal eschatological urgency in the twenty-first century, see Monte Lee Rice, "Practicing the Passion of Pentecost: Re-envisioning Pentecostal Eschatology through the Anatheistic Sacramentality of Richard Kearney," *Pneuma* 43, no. 1 (2021): 43–71.

84. Some examples are Althouse's work *Pentecostal Eschatology in Conversation with Jürgen Moltmann*, and Thompson's *Kingdom Come*, 89–102. Thompson's constructive chapter in *Kingdom Come* is heavily influenced by Moltmann. Moltmann has taken notice of Pentecostal eschatology, stating that "Pentecostal movements *are* eschatological movements" (Jürgen Moltmann, "Foreword," in Althouse, *Moltmann*, vii; italics mine). Dialogue between Pentecostals and Moltmann has been ongoing for decades. For some examples, see the several articles and responses, including by Moltmann, in vol. 2, no. 4–5 (1994) of *JPT* and again in vol. 13, no. 2 (2005). See also Jürgen Moltmann and Frank D. Macchia, "A Pentecostal Theology of Life," *JPT* 4, no. 9 (1996): 3–15; Andrew Lord, "The Pentecostal-Moltmann Dialogue: Implications for Mission," *JPT* 11, no. 2 (2003): 271–87; Néstor Medina, "Jürgen Moltmann and Pentecostalism(s): Toward a Cultural Theology of the Spirit," *Toronto Journal of Theology* 24, supplement 1 (January 2008): 101–14. Because of Moltmann's congeniality to Pentecostal eschatology (Althouse, *Moltmann*, 195), his influence is evident throughout the chapters of my work.

85. Margaret A. Farley and Serene Jones, "Introduction," in *Liberating Eschatology: Essays in Honor of Letty M. Russell*, ed. Margaret A. Farley and Serene Jones (Louisville, KY: Westminster John Knox, 1999), xiii. For a summary of Moltmann's eschatology and contributions, see Shields, *Eschatological Imagination*, 15–17, 25–35.

86. Jürgen Moltmann, "Liberating and Anticipating the Future," trans. Margaret Kohl, in Farley and Jones, *Liberating Eschatology*, 205; italics mine.

87. Robby Waddell, "Apocalyptic Sustainability: The Future of Pentecostal Ecology," in Althouse and Waddell, *Eschatologies*, 99. See also Murray W. Dempster, "Eschatology, Spirit Baptism, and Inclusiveness: An Exploration into the Hallmarks of a Pentecostal Social Ethic," in Althouse and Waddell, *Eschatologies*, 155–88.

Rice's eschatological-ethical response to global violence and world hunger.[88] But perhaps the most influential theological argument for the revival of eschatology in Pentecostalism comes from Steven Land's *Pentecostal Spirituality*.

In this important and oft-cited work, Land argues that Pentecostalism was and is primarily an eschatological movement and that "a passion for the kingdom" (his subtitle) is an eschatological passion.[89] He asserts that "the faith, worldview, experience, and practice of Pentecostals were thoroughly eschatological" so that one cannot understand Pentecostal spirituality apart from its eschatological context.[90] For Land, Pentecostalism is an apocalyptic movement of the Spirit and as such should "have the eschatological context and horizon prominently displayed" in an approach to any issue.[91] Any theological task within Pentecostalism, he says, should include reflection on eschatology and issues within Pentecostalism should receive fresh attention from an eschatological perspective.[92] A weakness of Land's work, by his own admission, is that he does not go into depth with any one single issue to propose how this might work eschatologically on the ground.[93] Land does suggest that "the reason for [the] overcoming of social and economic barriers was the eschatological perspective which accompanied the fall of the Latter Rain" and that it is this lack of eschatological imagination that has led Pentecostals to become ambivalent about the ministry of women.[94] However, gender (in)equality is not featured prominently in Land's work or any of the works cited above that encourage eschatological living.

What this current work attempts to do is to respond to Land's invitation to approach an issue within Pentecostalism solely from an eschatological perspective. If Pentecostalism is a thoroughly eschatological movement, one "fired by the eschatological imagination"[95] with an "eschatological impulse" at its core,[96] and if an eschatological conviction is "the driving belief of the fivefold gospel in Pentecostalism"[97] and the heartbeat of the movement, then eschatology must have

---

88. Rice, "Practicing the Passion of Pentecost," 49, 61–5, 69–71.

89. Steven Jack Land, *Pentecostal Spirituality: A Passion for the Kingdom* (1993; repr., Cleveland, TN: CPT, 2010), 3.

90. Land, *Pentecostal Spirituality*, 46–7.

91. Land, *Pentecostal Spirituality*, 196. Land interchanges the terms "apocalyptic" and "eschatology" when explaining the core of early Pentecostalism. For an overview and analysis of Land, see Christopher Stephenson, *Types of Pentecostal Theology: Method, System, Spirit* (Oxford: Oxford University Press, 2013), 29–56. Stephenson says Land never precisely states what he means by apocalyptic and combines the two terms into one to refer to Land's "apocalyptic eschatology" (34).

92. Land, *Pentecostal Spirituality*, 91, 196.

93. Land, *Pentecostal Spirituality*, 91.

94. Land, *Pentecostal Spirituality*, 209–10.

95. Thompson, "Eschatology," 189.

96. Thompson, *Kingdom Come*, 3.

97. Jon K. Newton, "The Full Gospel and the Apocalypse," *JPT* 26, no. 1 (2017): 103.

18   *The Pentecostal Gender Paradox*

*something* to say with regard to one of the most complex problems the movement faces: the gender paradox and resulting limitations on the ministry of women. The next challenge, then, is whether eschatology, particularly Pentecostal eschatology, has the potential to enact change and transformation in such a way that resolves the tension of the gender paradox and liberates women in their ecclesial praxis.

*A Transformational Method: The Dialectic of Imagination and Participation*

An eschatological method has the potential to succeed in resolving the gender paradox because it transforms both theological thinking and ecclesial praxis. Eschatology does this by accomplishing two things. First, as the doctrine about "the highest good"[98] and "the final reality,"[99] it engages our theological *imagination* to show us *what should be* with regard to gender equality.[100] Second, because of

---

98. Trutz Rendtorff, *Ethics*, trans. Keith Crim (Philadelphia: Fortress, 1986), 1:187. See also Grenz, *Moral Quest*, 125, 345–6.

99. Zachary Hayes, *Visions of a Future: A Study of Christian Eschatology* (Collegeville, MN: Liturgical, 1989), 11.

100. The meaning of the term "imagination" from a Pentecostal-eschatological perspective will be unpacked in the proceeding chapters and particularly 3.4.3. The main concern of this project is the eschatological imagination as a key for the transformational activity of the Holy Spirit. For the central role of the imagination in Christian eschatology and discussion of the "eschatological imagination," see Garrett Green, *Imagining Theology: Encounters with God in Scripture, Interpretation, and Aesthetics* (Grand Rapids: Baker Academic, 2020), particularly Part 3 which consists of four chapters on the role of eschatology in the Christian imagination; Thomas P. Rausch, *Eschatology, Liturgy, and Christology: Toward Recovering an Eschatological Imagination* (Collegeville, MN: Liturgical, 2012), esp. Chapter 1, "The Eschatological Imagination"; Shields, *Eschatological Imagination*; Richard Bauckham and Trevor Hart, *Hope Against Hope: Christian Eschatology at the Turn of the Millennium* (Grand Rapids: Eerdmans, 1999), esp. 84–108; Trevor Hart, "Imagination for the Kingdom of God? Hope, Promise, and the Transformative Power of an Imagined Future," in *God Will Be All in All: The Eschatology of Jürgen Moltmann*, ed. Richard Bauckham (Edinburgh: T&T Clark, 1999), 49–76. For a historic overview of imagination as well as the significance of the imagination for theology, see Amos Yong, *Spirit-Word-Community: Theological Hermeneutics in Trinitarian Perspective* (Eugene, OR: Wipf & Stock, 2002), 123–32, 141–9; Vondey, *Beyond Pentecostalism*, 17–25. For the centrality of the imagination in Christian thinking and definitions, see James K. A. Smith, *Imagining the Kingdom: How Worship Works* (Grand Rapids: Baker Academic, 2013), 6–18. For more on the Pentecostal imagination, see Vondey, *Perplexed*, 42–6; James K. A. Smith, *Thinking in Tongues: Pentecostal Contributions to Christian Philosophy* (Grand Rapids: Eerdmans, 2010), 84. Lastly, for the epistemic qualities of the imagination/imaginative see Smith, *Imagining*, 18; Hart, "Eschatology," 263–4.

the strong relationship between eschatology and ethical action,[101] eschatology demands *participation* now to the fullest extent possible in *what can be* regarding egalitarian practices in the church. As a "rhetoric of virtue" and rhetoric of hope, Christian eschatology inherently persuades and exhorts to action.[102] Eschatology is therefore a practical discipline that motivates action more than merely quenching curiosity.[103] The biblically inspired eschatological imagination activates a passion to work presently toward change in light of a future hope.[104] The result is a transformational method that provides both theological authority (imagination) and practical urgency (participation) to the gender problem by incorporating hope with ethics, the hereafter with the here and now. In short, the end is the beginning—where we start now—when it comes to the question of equality. And it is Pentecostal eschatology in particular, because of both its central place historically in the movement and its current development, that is primely positioned to utilize this eschatological dialectic of imagination and participation that frees women from exclusion and embraces their ecclesial callings.

Although eschatology is literally "thinking about the end," that does not exclude present-day implications. Land argues that "if Pentecostal theology is a discerning reflection upon living reality in the light of the end, then the shape of the eschatological expectation is crucially important."[105] Therefore, approaching gender eschatologically is not a fruitless theological exercise; rather, it either validates or invalidates the pursuit of equality in the here and now. For Pentecostals, their beliefs about the ultimate future determine their actions in the present: eschatological urgency fuels a passion for transformative social action.[106] My work uses what is often called "inaugurated," "proleptic,"

---

101. Rendtorff, *Ethics*, 1:187. See here also Vigen Guroian, "Liturgy and the Lost Eschatological Vision of Christian Ethics," *The Annual of the Society of Christian Ethics* 20 (2000): 227–38; Miroslav Volf, "On Loving with Hope: Eschatology and Social Responsibility," *Transformation* 7 (July/Sept 1990): 28–31.

102. Shields, *Eschatological Imagination*, 4, 160. See also Shields's longer discussion, 165–77. For more on eschatology and the genre of rhetoric, see Shields, *Eschatological Imagination*, 4–7, 173–5.

103. See Miroslav Volf, "After Moltmann: Reflections on the Future of Eschatology," in Bauckham, *Moltmann*, 252–3. For further discussion of eschatology as praxis-driven, see section 5.3.1.

104. Shields, *Eschatological Imagination*, 4.

105. Land, *Pentecostal Spirituality*, 223.

106. Dwight J. Wilson, "Eschatology, Pentecostal Perspectives On," in *NIDPCM*, 601. An example of this would be Elizabeth Rios's study of Pentecostal Puerto Rican women in New York City who blend their passion for justice with an eschatological urgency inspired by Joel 2:28. See Elizabeth D. Rios, "'The Ladies are Warriors': Latina Pentecostalism and Faith-Based Activism in New York City," in *Azusa Street and Beyond: 100 Years of Commentary on the Global Pentecostal/Charismatic Movement*, ed. Grant McClung (Gainesville, FL: Bridge-Logos, 2006), 217–18.

"holistic," or "practiced" eschatology,[107] for this kind of eschatology is most consistent with Pentecostal belief and practice.[108] This approach avoids the two poles or extremes of eschatological thought: the mostly otherworldly dispensational fundamentalism that is primarily concerned with the future, speculates on the second coming of Christ, and debates millennial theologies; and the mostly this-worldly liberal eschatology that is primarily concerned with the present, diminishes the role of Christ, and reduces eschatology to a way of speaking about social betterment and utopian visions divorced from theology.[109] The eschatological method used in this work embraces the theological tension between God's future kingdom and its present inauguration, the ultimate and the penultimate, living responsibly in the present while preaching fidelity to the future.[110] It is, as Moltmann consistently argues for, an eschatology of hope that is both heavenly and earthly, a union between the new heavens and the new earth.[111]

---

107. See Rice, "Practicing the Passion of Pentecost"; Benjamin L. Gladd and Matthew S. Harmon, *Making All Things New: Inaugurated Eschatology for the Life of the Church* (Grand Rapids: Baker Academic, 2016); J. Richard Middleton, *A New Heaven and a New Earth: Reclaiming Biblical Eschatology* (Grand Rapids: Baker Academic, 2014); Peter Althouse, "Ascension—Pentecost—Eschaton: A Theological Framework for Pentecostal Ecclesiology," in *Toward a Pentecostal Ecclesiology: The Church and the Fivefold Gospel*, ed. John Christopher Thomas (Cleveland, TN: CPT, 2010), 226-7; For a thorough "textbook" and systematic introduction and approach to the topic, see Markus Mühling, *T&T Clark Handbook of Christian Eschatology*, trans. Jennifer Adams-Maßmann and David Andrew Gilland (London: Bloomsbury T&T Clark, 2015).

108. As the proceeding chapters will argue, particularly Chapter 3 (see 3.3.1) and Chapter 5 (see 5.3.3).

109. For more on distinguishing these eschatologies, see Rausch, *Eschatology*, esp. xi; Althouse, "Ascension," 242. For the "contours" of contemporary eschatologies and the "complex" task of the meaning or meanings of eschatological reflection, see Shields, *Eschatological Imagination*, 9-38, esp. 36-8.

110. See Rausch, *Eschatology*, 160; Glenn Tinder, *The Fabric of Hope: An Essay* (Grand Rapids: Eerdmans, 1999), 40-1, 180.

111. See Jürgen Moltmann, *Theology of Hope: On the Ground and the Implications of a Christian Eschatology*, trans. James W. Leitch (Minneapolis: Augsburg Fortress, 1964), which reacts to other approaches in eschatology and argues for a transformational eschatology, and *The Coming of God: Christian Eschatology*, trans. Margaret Kohl (Minneapolis: Augsburg Fortress, 1996). Miroslav Volf calls these two works the foundation and capstone of Moltmann's eschatology of hope (Volf, "After Moltmann," 233). There is a strong movement to articulate the final destiny of human beings in a new heaven and new earth rather than an otherworldly existence in heaven. See, for example, Middleton, *New Heaven*; N. T. Wright, *Surprised by Hope: Rethinking Heaven, the Resurrection, and the Mission of the Church* (New York: HarperOne, 2008).

Understanding eschatology as transformational is critical not only for developing an eschatological basis for women's equality but also for contesting what is potentially one of the main critiques to developing an eschatological authorization for the ministry of women, namely, why one's eschatological convictions matter at all. If our hope is only for the future, if equality is consigned to the *eschaton*, why bother trying to change things now? Doesn't otherworldly hope lead to this-worldly indifference? Said another way regarding a different social concern, should we bother planting trees if our hope is only in the future?[112] But eschatology and its corresponding dialectic of imagination and participation does not take the focus off the present. That is a misunderstanding of eschatological hope. As Glenn Tinder argues, eschatological hope does not undermine responsibility; on the contrary, it heightens responsibility, resists injustice, and keeps one steadfast, for only those who are playing a part in moving toward the ultimate end will have a part in that end.[113]

The eschatological imagination leads to, inspires, and sustains participation in social action and public transformation.[114] The move toward a holistic, transformational, and participatory eschatology among Pentecostal theologians, and eschatology's overall revival in Christian theology, positions it as a viable lens for which to critically examine a practical problem such as the Pentecostal gender paradox. An eschatological approach to gender may not be free from concerns, and there is always a need for appropriate epistemic humility when working within an eschatological framework.[115] Nevertheless, I boldly propose eschatology as the most promising methodology for resolving the gender paradox.[116] A methodology is not about creating a set of rules to be followed blindly, a "methodolatry,"[117] but about developing "a framework for creativity" in approaching a problem in an

---

112. Bauckham and Hart, *Hope Against Hope*, 176. For an affirmative answer with some eschatological nuance, see A. J. Swoboda, *Tongues and Trees: Towards a Pentecostal Ecological Theology* (Blandford Forum, UK: Deo, 2013), esp. 227.

113. Tinder, *Hope*, 192–3.

114. Vondey, *Pentecostal Theology*, 132, 148; Smith, *Imagining*, 32.

115. See 5.4.3 for more. I occasionally use the phrase "fullest extent possible" throughout this work as a reminder of the need for humility regarding eschatological promises. However, one should not "underestimate the epistemic status of the imaginative as a respectable form of 'knowledge' in the broader sense" (Hart, "Eschatology," 263–4). Christian faith is not imaginary (fiction), but imaginative (Bauckham and Hart, *Hope Against Hope*, xii). For more on the eschatological imagination as a source of truth, see Isgrigg, *Imagining the Future*, 205–9; Shields, *Eschatological Imagination*, esp. 170–5. For more on methodology and humility, see Bernard J. F. Lonergan, *Method in Theology* (Toronto: University of Toronto Press, 1971), 332.

116. Yong advises that an eschatological approach must be simultaneously bold and humble, advice this project will seek to follow and hopefully embody (Yong, *Renewing*, 16).

117. Mary Daly, *Beyond God the Father: Toward a Philosophy of Women's Liberation* (Boston: Beacon, 1973), 11–12.

effective and convincing manner.[118] Eschatology has methodological potential for resolving the gender paradox and therefore deserves attention and testing across the areas of history, biblical hermeneutics, and ecclesial praxis. Before outlining the procedure for the argument, it is important to discuss why the gender paradox matters, why a Pentecostal solution is particularly important, and how that solution could have an impact beyond the Pentecostal world.

## Why the Problem (and a Solution) Matter

Gender inequality has been identified as the paramount human rights problem of this century.[119] Studies reveal that achieving greater equality for women improves public life, decreases war and violence, creates greater economic stability, and increases sustainable development.[120] Empirical research reports that women are excluded from leadership in various ways around the globe[121] and that religious beliefs greatly impact one's views on gender.[122] Therefore, those interested in furthering the equality of women on a global scale must show concern for the gender beliefs of arguably the fastest-growing and most influential Christian movement in the world: Pentecostalism.[123] There is a growing consensus that Pentecostalism will play a crucial role in the development of global Christianity

---

118. Lonergan, *Method*, xii.

119. See Nicholas D. Kristof and Sheryl WuDunn, *Half the Sky: Turning Oppression into Opportunity for Women Worldwide* (New York: Vintage Books, 2009), xiii, xvii. For a more academic resource, see Janet Mancini Billson and Carolyn Fluehr-Lobban, eds., *Female Well-Being: Toward a Global Theory of Social Change* (London and New York: Zed Books, 2005).

120. See "Guiding Documents," UN Women, https://www.unwomen.org/en/about-us/guiding-documents; "Ending Violence Against Women," UN Women, https://www.unwomen.org/en/what-we-do/ending-violence-against-women; "Tackling Violence Against Women and Girls in the Context of Climate Change," UN Women, https://www.unwomen.org/en/digital-library/publications/2022/03/tackling-violence-against-women-and-girls-in-the-context-of-climate-change. All sites accessed or updated April 21, 2022. Gender inequality is heavily connected to violence against women and girls.

121. See Vondey, *Perplexed*, 123–4. For resources, see the UN Women website, https://www.unwomen.org/.

122. See Timothy J. Steigenga's empirical research in *The Politics of the Spirit: The Political Implications of Pentecostalized Religion in Costa Rica and Guatemala* (Lanham, MD: Lexington, 2001), 131–5. For more, see Lisa P. Stephenson, "Toxic Spirituality: Reexamining the Ways in Which Spiritual Virtues can Reinforce Violence Against Women," in *Sisters, Mothers, Daughters: Pentecostal Perspectives on Violence against Women*, ed. Kimberly Ervin Alexander et al. (Leiden: Brill, 2022), 33–48.

123. Philip Jenkins, *The Next Christendom: The Coming of Global Christianity*, rev. ed. (Oxford: Oxford University Press, 2007), 8–9.

and social engagement through at least the middle of this century,[124] especially among women, the poor, and the oppressed.[125] In many developing countries, Pentecostalism is one of the primary contributors to gender attitudes in society.[126] In their widely read book *Half the Sky*, a nonreligious journalistic introduction to gender inequality around the world, Nicholas Kristof and Sheryl WuDunn make the startling assessment that it is "particularly crucial to incorporate Pentecostalism into a movement for women's rights around the globe, because it is gaining ground more quickly than any other faith," especially in poor countries.[127] They openly petition for Pentecostalism to be a part of the global solution to emancipate and empower women around the world.[128]

Similar to Kristof and WuDunn, Martin's sociological research shows that those who actually consider Pentecostalism's influence on women in developing countries continually find that it makes "deeper inroads into the everyday reality of gender equality than all the official policies of gender enacted by the government."[129] Part of Martin's work is to demonstrate how little attention scholars have paid to Pentecostalism's influence on gender equality due to intellectual bias and the misunderstanding of Pentecostalism as a regressive, "conservative throw-back."[130] Despite its patriarchal tendencies and some official restrictions on women, Martin maintains that Pentecostalism has still led to surprisingly new freedoms and influence for women. She cites about a dozen sociological studies that show that women in the developing world are advantaged in new and crucial ways by the Pentecostal movement.[131]

The story of Pentecostalism's influence on women in the emerging world, however, is complicated and one of conflicting narratives and trajectories,

---

124. See Yong, *Renewing*, 6, who cites demographers. See also Vondey, *Perplexed*, 91–6; Vondey, *Beyond Pentecostalism*, 1–2. Potentially more than 85 percent of the world's Pentecostals live in Africa, Asia, and Latin America. See Douglas Jacobsen, "Review Essay: Pentecostalism Today; A Review of Brill's Encyclopedia of Global Pentecostalism," *Pneuma* 44, no. 2 (2022): 255.

125. This is a common and well-researched observation. See Carol Ann Drogus, "Private Power or Public Power: Pentecostalism, Base Communities, and Gender," in *Power, Politics, and Pentecostals in Latin America*, ed. Edward L. Cleary and Hannah W. Stewart-Gambino (Oxford: Westview, 1998), 55, 61; Vondey, *Perplexed*, 91; Lene Sjorup, "Pentecostals: The Power of the Powerless," *Dialog: A Journey of Theology* 41, no. 1 (Spring 2002): 16–25; Yong, *Spirit Poured Out*, 192–3; Jenkins, *Next Christendom*, 88–90; Douglas Petersen, "A Moral Imagination: Pentecostals and Social Concern in Latin America," in Kärkkäinen, *Spirit in the World*, 53; Harvey Cox, *The Seduction of the Spirit* (New York: Simon and Schuster, 1974), 178.

126. See Drogus, "Private Power," 57, 60.

127. Kristof and WuDunn, *Half the Sky*, 143.

128. Kristof and WuDunn, *Half the Sky*, 244.

129. Martin, "Gender Paradox," 63.

130. Martin, "Gender Paradox," 58, 60–1.

131. Martin, "Gender Paradox," 54.

reflecting Martin's "paradox" thesis.[132] Some champion the egalitarian impulse of Pentecostalism which gives a voice to women and the marginalized as its explosive growth among the global poor brings the movement face-to-face with social injustices such as gender inequality.[133] Two decades ago, sociologist David Martin argued that the egalitarian structure of Pentecostalism works to the advantage of women around the world and therefore represents a worldwide "women's movement."[134] However, others have countered Martin's thesis, claiming Pentecostalism's patriarchal tendencies eventually overcome any initial egalitarian structures as churches quickly assume more traditional forms of authority that ultimately inhibit the participation of women.[135] Most scholars describe the global situation for Pentecostal women more in line with the gender paradox described in this work, a convoluted "egalitarian patriarchalism"[136] and complex "conundrum" that has yet to be solved.[137] In her research on Latin American Pentecostal women, Carol Ann Drogus shows that Pentecostalism contains a "mixture of opportunity and traditionalism."[138] Pentecostalism incorporates conservative gender attitudes and some patriarchal values. But, she says, it also acts a source of emancipation that has the potential to increase equality between the genders, a sentiment echoed by several scholars studying Pentecostalism in Latin America.[139]

---

132. For example, see the essays in Alexander et al., *Sisters, Mothers, Daughters*.

133. For this emphasis on the positive impact, see Petersen, "Moral Imagination," 56, 61; Dempster, "Eschatology," 158; Waddell, "Apocalyptic Sustainability," 110; Vondey, *Perplexed*, 119; Donald Miller and Tetsunao Yamamori, *Global Pentecostalism: The New Face of Christian Social Engagement* (Berkeley: University of California Press, 2007), 209–10; Jenkins, *Next Christendom*, 89; Hollingsworth, "Spirit and Voice," 197–201. Martin was one of the first to articulate these positive contributions (see "Gender Paradox," esp. 54–7, 60–3).

134. David Martin, *Forbidden Revolutions: Pentecostalism in Latin America and Catholicism in Eastern Europe* (London: SPCK, 1996), 52. See also his *Tongues of Fire: The Explosion of Protestantism in Latin America* (London: Basil Blackwell, 1990); and *Pentecostalism: The World Their Parish* (Oxford: Blackwell, 2002). Cf. Bernice Martin: "if there is a 'women's movement' among the poor of the developing world, Pentecostalism has a good claim to the title" ("Gender Paradox," 56). Cf. also Maria Frahm-Arp, *Professional Women in South African Pentecostal Charismatic Churches* (Leiden: Brill, 2010).

135. See Jane E. Soothill, *Gender, Social Change and Spiritual Power: Charismatic Christianity in Ghana* (Leiden: Brill, 2007), 138–9. Julie Ma outlines some of the challenges, limitations, and gender imbalance facing modern Pentecostal women in Asia (Ma and Ma, *Mission*, 194–207).

136. Yong, *Spirit Poured Out*, 41.

137. Vondey, *Perplexed*, 124, 108–9; See also Jenkins, *Next Christendom*, 232.

138. Drogus, "Private Power," 61.

139. Drogus, "Private Power," 55–6, 59, 63–4; Cecília Loreto Mariz and María Das Dores Campos Machado, "Pentecostalism and Women in Brazil," in Cleary and Stewart-Gambino, *Power*, 42, 47–52; Elizabeth E. Brusco, *The Reformation of Machismo: Evangelical*

Which direction Pentecostals end up taking on the gender question in their churches could impact women around the world.¹⁴⁰ In their work on global Pentecostalism, Donald Miller and Tetsunao Yamamori posit that the democratic, antiauthoritarian, egalitarian spirit of what they call "Progressive Pentecostalism" has the potential to help develop democracies, challenge totalitarian politicians and governments, and further the idea of the equality of all persons in such a way that improves the lives of women.¹⁴¹ But they also report that although Pentecostalism can at times be favorable toward women's empowerment, there are still relatively few females in positions of church leadership.¹⁴² In his similarly extensive research, Phillip Jenkins suggests the immense positive changes Pentecostalism and its churches can make in the lives of women and in gender relations across the globe.¹⁴³ However, he also points to the patriarchal tendencies of Pentecostalism in some places in Africa, where little gender balance exists and churches are "overwhelmingly male-dominated, and often unsympathetic to women's causes and interests."¹⁴⁴ For example, Pentecostal women in some African and Asian churches face intense limitations and restrictions such as being prohibited from sitting near men, attending church when menstruating, or being in "men only" areas such as the altar.¹⁴⁵ Jenkins laments that Pentecostal clergy unwilling to distance themselves from the subordination of women has often led to widespread sexual exploitation and rape, even by male clergy.¹⁴⁶ Other scholars also warn of Pentecostalism's potential influence in aiding oppression and stagnating women's equality, especially in the two-thirds world.¹⁴⁷ There is a link between social issues such as human trafficking or domestic abuse and theological beliefs that support

*Conversion and Gender in Columbia* (Austin: University of Texas Press, 1995); see discussion of Brusco in Yong, *Spirit Poured Out*, 39–42.

140. This is something frequently emphasized by Kristof and WuDunn in *Half the Sky* (see 159, 248).

141. Miller and Yamamori, *Global Pentecostalism*, 4, 33–4, 178, 210–12, 223.

142. Miller and Yamamori, *Global Pentecostalism*, 209.

143. Jenkins, *Next Christendom*, 89, 94–5.

144. Jenkins, *Next Christendom*, 233. Countries (and churches) in the global South tend to be more patriarchal and teach a more traditional role for women (see Jenkins, *Next Christendom*, 232).

145. See Crumbley's study of West African women in "Sanctified Saints," 121; Julie C. Ma, "Changing Images: Women in Asian Pentecostalism," in Alexander and Yong, *Philip's Daughters*, 203–14, esp. 211; Ma and Ma, *Mission*, 194–207. See also Jenkins, *Next Christendom*, 232–3. For some of the complexities of being a Christian woman in these contexts, see Maria Frahm-Arp, "Singleness, Sexuality and the Dream of Marriage," in her *Professional Women in South African Pentecostal Charismatic Churches*, 183–244.

146. Jenkins, *Next Christendom*, 233.

147. See discussions in Beth (A. Elizabeth) Grant, "Merchandised Women: Priceless, Called and Empowered," in English de Alminana and Olena, *Women*, 273–80; Martin, "Gender Paradox," 60–3; Hollingsworth, "Spirit and Voice," 198–201, 210. See also Lesley

patriarchal and misogynistic systems that directly or indirectly teach that women's lives are not equal to men's and potentially not worth saving.[148]

Thus, the stakes could hardly be higher for how Pentecostals approach the gender question; it is quite literally a matter of life or death for many women. Discrimination against women in Pentecostal churches "is only the tip of an iceberg of global proportions"[149] but a part of the iceberg nonetheless. Kristof and WuDunn document how the problems of sexism, misogyny, and indifference have led to forced prostitution, gender-based violence such as honor killings and rape, and unnecessary maternal mortality around the globe.[150] In addition, 70 percent of the world's refugees are women, many who are dehumanized, victimized by violence, and discriminated against.[151] Consequently, not resolving the gender paradox could potentially continue to prop up oppression and discrimination toward women around the globe, especially where Pentecostalism is growing.

In contrast, a clear and consistent theological vision for gender equality may liberate and free women from oppressive practices, such as the stories reported by Miller and Yamamori of women freed from selling their bodies with the help of Pentecostal social entrepreneurs and the Pentecostal experience of the Spirit.[152] Drogus shares her cautious optimism by stating "the opening that Pentecostalism provides for the empowerment of women is narrow, but it is an opening."[153] What I hope to achieve is to widen that opening by showing how the (revived) Pentecostal eschatological–egalitarian imagination leads to the full flourishing of women in church and society. A specifically eschatological approach to the gender problem would be especially crucial and beneficial in developing countries where eschatological expectancy and fervency is more vibrant.[154] Given the current

---

Gill, "'Like a Veil to Cover Them': Women and the Pentecostal Movement in La Pas," *American Ethnologist* 17, no. 4 (1990): 708–21.

148. See Sarah Bessey, *Jesus Feminist: An Invitation to Revisit the Bible's View of Women* (New York: Howard Books, 2013), 169–74; Estrelda Yvonne Alexander, "When Liberation Becomes Survival," in English de Alminana and Olena, *Women*, 333, 342; Kristof and WuDunn, *Half the Sky*, 116.

149. Alexander, "When Liberation Becomes Survival," 331.

150. This is not just a problem in the developing world. For example, young aboriginal women in Canada are five times more likely to die from physical violence than others. See some of this Canadian perspective in Sally Armstrong, *Ascent of Women* (Toronto: Random House Canada, 2013), esp. 219–24.

151. Ma and Ma, *Mission*, 196–200. See also here Elaine Storkey, *Scars Across Humanity: Understanding and Overcoming Violence Against Women* (Westmont, IL: IVP Academic, 2018).

152. Miller and Yamamori, *Global Pentecostalism*, 223.

153. Drogus, "Private Power," 64.

154. Land, *Pentecostal Spirituality*, 63. This may be partly due to an increased desire for liberation and overcoming unjust social structures. See Gustavo Gutiérrez's discussion of eschatology in Latin America in *A Theology of Liberation*, rev. ed. (Maryknoll, NY: Orbis

global crisis of women's inequality, this work hopefully contains an appropriate degree of (eschatological) urgency and intensity.[155] As Nimi Wariboko appeals, "Anywhere we see potentials for expanding possibilities for human flourishing we will make it a subject of radical [theological] inquiry."[156] This work proposes that eschatology is one of these "potentials" due to its theological centrality and transformational nature. The following section outlines how the proposed eschatological method—"beginning with the end"—will be applied in each chapter to address the problem of the Pentecostal gender paradox in the key areas of history, hermeneutics, and praxis.

## Outline of Procedure

The nature of the eschatological framework proposed in this work and its corresponding dialectic of imagination and participation require the procedure be viewed more as a spiral than a linear argument.[157] Nonetheless, the arrangement is intentional and not arbitrary. Chapter 1 begins by analyzing and categorizing the three dominant views concerning the relationship between women's equality and eschatology. The first view, and most influential, is the antagonistic attitude made popular by Rosemary Radford Ruether. This view treats eschatology as incompatible with the concerns of women, claiming eschatology must be exposed for what it is: a male-centered and oppressive theological system that takes the focus off present injustices toward women. Less antagonistic but equally dismissive is the agnostic view. This view is less concerned with proactively dismantling eschatology; rather, these authors purposely ignore eschatology or treat it as completely irrelevant to the concerns of women. The third view is the augmented position which considers eschatology a potential friend to the cause of women's equality; however, it is insufficient as a comprehensive methodological approach and therefore must be supplemented with more versatile approaches that can be utilized across several areas such as history, hermeneutics, and praxis. Chapter 1 closes with identifying

---

Books, 1988), 91–7, 121–2. See also the chapter "The Christian Hope: Eschatology in Global Perspective," 137–55 in William A. Dyrness and Oscar García-Johnson's book *Theology without Borders: An Introduction to Global Conversations* (Grand Rapids: Baker Academic, 2015). For ethnically and geographically contextualized eschatologies and the challenges eschatology faces in various places, see section 4 of Althouse and Waddell, *Eschatologies*, 315–400.

155. Tinder calls hope "a virtue for crises" (*Hope*, 148).

156. Nimi Wariboko, *The Pentecostal Principle: Ethical Methodology in New Spirit* (Grand Rapids: Eerdmans, 2012), 213. See also Wolfgang Vondey and Martin W. Mittelstadt, who say that Pentecostal scholarship that engages the Spirit's work of renewal is "a means to engage in the struggle against the structures that hinder human flourishing" ("Introduction," in Vondey and Mittelstadt, *Amos Yong*, 11, 17–18).

157. Cf. Yong, *Spirit-Word-Community*, 23.

the problems caused by these views and articulates why my methodology represents an original and effective contribution to the problem.

Chapter 2 examines the impact eschatology made on gender practices in the early Pentecostal movement and hypothesizes that the eschatological imagination fueled the initial freedoms experienced by women. Historical investigation reveals that eschatology functioned as an authorizing hermeneutic that legitimized the ministry of women in the first few decades of Pentecostalism because it rescinded previous perceived limitations concerning the role of women. This eschatological authorization of the ministry of women cut through any previous hesitancy concerning women's roles and led to newfound openness to women leaders because they were now seen as the fulfillment of biblically based eschatological promises. Using a feminist-functional interpretive approach to primary sources and three biographical case studies, the chapter investigates how eschatology, and its critical and constructive functions, encouraged egalitarian participation and worked as a newfound liberating agent for Pentecostal women. However, these newfound freedoms for women slowly waned, along with the eschatological mindset that caused early Pentecostals to celebrate women leaders.

Eschatological and hermeneutical shifts in the post-organizational era of classical Pentecostalism removed eschatology as the dominant framework for determining and authorizing gender praxis. As the eschatological urgency of early Pentecostalism faded, egalitarian practices faded with it; the rise and fall of women in leadership was potentially concomitant with the rise and fall of the centrality of eschatology for Pentecostal praxis. Chapter 3 investigates this hypothesis and the possible reasons for the decline of Pentecostal women leaders. I argue that historical shifts and changes in both Pentecostal eschatology and hermeneutics slowly led to the loss of eschatology as authorizing hermeneutic for women and increased restrictions on women in the church, ultimately birthing the gender paradox. Therefore, a re-visioning of Pentecostal eschatology and hermeneutics, faithful to the heart of the movement, is needed to (re)develop the eschatological hermeneutic used by early Pentecostals. For eschatology to once again be a cornerstone for the legitimization of the unrestricted ministry of women, the original eschatological authorization of women in Pentecostal leadership must be (re)discovered and methodologically applied to the key areas of biblical hermeneutics and ecclesiology.

The eschatological–egalitarian heart of early Pentecostalism was fueled by eschatological texts from the Scriptures that promoted women's equality. Chapter 4 attempts to recover and (re)construct this early eschatological authorizing hermeneutic and reappropriate its previously unarticulated function. I seek to establish a unified eschatological–egalitarian narrative thread in Scripture through three key biblical narratives: creation (Gen. 1–3), the ministry of Jesus (Gal. 3:28), and Pentecost (Acts 2:17-18). By proposing and defending the hermeneutical priority of these eschatological texts on gender and interpreting non-eschatological gender texts through this lens, a hermeneutical guide emerges that can resolve the hermeneutical inconsistency that led to and has sustained the gender paradox. The importance, relevant background, eschatological significance, hermeneutical priority, and call to imagine and participate in eschatological realities are examined for each of these three interconnected biblical narratives. Reading the Bible with an eschatological hermeneutical lens overcomes the crippling ambiguity and gender binary created by other supposedly limiting passages and authorizes the full and unhindered participation of women in Pentecostal church leadership.

The final two chapters take the historical and hermeneutical arguments of the previous chapters and attempt to apply them to Pentecostal praxis with the goal of constructing an authorizing eschatological–egalitarian praxis. Chapter 5 seeks to create and justify a conceptual eschatological framework or "model" for a liberating egalitarian praxis. I suggest a pre-enactment praxis model that is dialectical, experiential, and experimental over against a re-enactment praxis model. The articulation of a preferred (and eschatological) praxis model ensures my work does not fall short where so many theoretical and theological works on eschatology or egalitarianism do, namely, developing a methodologically connected praxis that leads to actual changes on the ground. This "praxis problem" is examined for both Pentecostal works on gender and eschatological works in general, and I demonstrate how my eschatological pre-enactment model solves these problems by closing the praxis gap.

The closing chapter lays out some practical suggestions for leaders and churches by applying the proposed eschatological–egalitarian hermeneutic and its pre-enactment praxis model to the areas of Pentecostal leadership, education, and worship. An eschatological praxis corrects male-dominated practices that push women to the margins and also constructs egalitarian practices congruent with the eschatological vision of the biblical story. Leadership in Pentecostal organizations and churches can reify eschatological truths by creating egalitarian structures that reflect the coming kingdom. Furthermore, theological education in Pentecostal places of learning can help form an eschatological consciousness that informs pedagogy, ontological assumptions, and the gender praxis implications of trinitarian doctrines. The chapter culminates by suggesting how corporate worship and worshippers can participate in eschatological–egalitarian realities by eschatologically reimagining the language that is used, the stories that are told, and the way equality is embodied in sacramental activity. When gender practices are fully supported by an imaginative and authoritative hermeneutic, the gender paradox can be resolved, and the unrestricted participation and ministry of women can become the norm in Pentecostal churches.

The work closes with a review of its major contributions as well as considerations on the global and ecclesiastical impact of an eschatological resolving of the Pentecostal gender paradox. Overall, a comprehensive picture will materialize of how eschatology resolves the hermeneutical inconsistency and theological ambiguity that defines the gender paradox. Adopting an eschatological authorization for women in Pentecostal leadership creates a unified, transdisciplinary, methodologically connected argument for the full flourishing and unhindered inclusion of women in all parts and at all levels of church life and ministry. An eschatological method causes one to review historically, reinterpret hermeneutically, redefine theologically, and reimagine practically the role of women in and beyond Pentecostal churches.

# Chapter 1

## ESCHATOLOGY

## ENEMY OF EQUALITY?

The previous chapter explained the nature of the so-called Pentecostal gender paradox and suggested the promise and potential impact of an eschatological solution. Given the revival of eschatology in Christian and Pentecostal theology and eschatology's link with transformative social action, it may appear puzzling that eschatological hope has not received much attention in the gender debate. If Christianity in general and Pentecostalism in particular are thoroughly eschatological movements, and if eschatology has much to say about Christian practices, injustices, and social responsibility, why has so little been written on the relationship between women's equality and eschatology?

The task of this chapter is to analyze and categorize the existing views in recent literature on the relationship between eschatology and gender equality in order to distinguish the different approaches and the challenges they present to my argument. The goal is to show the need for—and hint at the viability of—a thoroughly eschatological resolving of the Pentecostal gender paradox. Each section examines the major figures and key works behind each view and analyzes their attitude toward and influence on the use of eschatology in the gender debate. I end by pivoting toward Pentecostal works that appeal to an eschatological perspective for an alternative way of imagining present roles for women and men in the church. The chapter concludes with a summary of what is missing in these discussions and why my eschatological proposal provides an important and original contribution for resolving the gender paradox. But before analyzing the existing views on the relationship between gender and eschatology, a brief word is needed on some of the literature discussed in this and following chapters and why engaging this literature is necessary for a work such as mine.

Examining the literature on the relationship between gender and eschatology necessarily involves engaging works in feminist theology, for that is one of the few places that bring together the feminist concern for the equality of women with a theological concern such as eschatology.[1] In addition, almost every major

---

1. This book is a work on gender that uses eschatology as the methodological starting point. Therefore, this section reviews primarily works on gender that mention eschatology,

Pentecostal work on gender that mentions eschatology engages with feminist theologians and is influenced by them to some extent.[2] This current project is a Pentecostal work on gender, and for some bringing Pentecostalism into constructive conversation with feminism may seem at best like a difficult "tightrope walk"[3] and at worst "may seem impossibly oxymoronic."[4] But most feminist literature in general is a commonsense fit for a work such as this one, for the basic definition of a feminist is one who advocates for the complete equality and full personhood of women and men[5] such that gender in no way determines restrictions on roles or

---

not works on eschatology that consider implications for gender. However, it is interesting to note how often gender is ignored in full-scale works on eschatology (see 5.3.4 for Pentecostal examples). For example, Bauckham and Hart's book *Hope Against Hope* is an apology for the importance of Christian eschatology for Christian hope and praxis, but gender is never mentioned in their lengthy discussion of images of hope (see 109–73) or in their section on "eschatology and the liberation of the oppressed" about the "progress" we should strive for (193–8).

2. See the third "augmented view" in 1.1.3, but a few examples: Stephenson, *Dismantling*; English de Alminana and Olena, *Women*.

3. English de Alminana, "Introduction," 6–7.

4. Hollingsworth, "Spirit and Voice," 189. For more on the dilemma of being Pentecostal and feminist, see Catford, "Women's Experiences," 47; English de Alminana, "Introduction," 6; Yong, *Spirit Poured Out*, 192–3; Vondey, *Perplexed*, 123. See also Shane Clifton, "Pentecostal Hermeneutics and First-Wave Feminism: Mina Ross Brawner, MD," *Journal of the Pentecostal Charismatic Bible Colleges*, no. 2 (2006): Article 01, no longer available online, but previously accessed on August 8, 2019, at: http://webjournals.ac.edu.au/ojs/index .php/PCBC/article/view/8854/8851. Christians in general, particularly evangelical ones, may experience the same tensions and struggles. See Mary Stewart Van Leeuwen, *Gender and Grace* (Downers Grove, IL: InterVarsity, 1990), 9; Allyson Jule and Bettina Tate Pedersen, "Introduction: Being Feminist, Being Christian," in Jule and Pedersen, *Being Feminist*; Pedersen, "Christian Feminist." Sarah C. Williams cites several others in the argument that the roots of the modern feminist movement are in evangelical Christianity ("Evangelicals and Gender," in *Global Evangelicalism: Theology, History and Culture in Regional Perspective*, ed. Donald M. Lewis and Richard V. Pierard [Downers Grove, IL: IVP Academic, 2014], 292).

5. The consensus definitions of both Letty Russell and Elizabeth Schüssler Fiorenza. See Letty M. Russell, *Household of Freedom: Authority in Feminist Theology* (Philadelphia: Westminster, 1987), 18; Elisabeth Schüssler Fiorenza, "A Critical Feminist Emancipative Reading. Invitation to 'Dance' in the Open House of Wisdom: Feminist Study of the Bible," in *Engaging the Bible: Critical Readings from Contemporary Women*, ed. Choi Hee An and Katheryn Pfisterer Darr (Minneapolis: Fortress, 2006), 82. There are, of course, a myriad of definitions of feminism as well as descriptions of feminism's different phases, waves, and streams of thought, which all approach the commitment to equality in diverse ways. See Janice Rees, "Sarah Coakley: Systematic Theology and the Future of Feminism," *Pacifica: Australasian Theological Studies* 24, no. 3 (October 2011): 300; Linda Woodhead,

results in any form of hierarchy.⁶ Feminist *theology* in its most rudimentary sense takes the egalitarian impulse of feminism and applies it to argue *on a theological basis* for the full equality of women in the church and other spheres of society.⁷ In feminist theology, gender roles are not divinely preordained by God, and therefore women and men are free to live out their callings and giftings to the fullest extent without limitations.⁸

To move the gender conversation forward in Pentecostalism, we must look for the "shared values" and "rich meeting ground" between feminist theology and Pentecostal spirituality so that they become mutual dialogue partners.⁹ However, one major hurdle in partnering an eschatologically oriented movement like Pentecostalism with the egalitarian pursuits of feminist theology is that many

---

"Feminism and the Sociology of Religion: From Gender-blindness to Gendered Difference," in Fenn, *Blackwell Companion*, 67–84; Denise L. Carmody, *Christian Feminist Theology: A Constructive Interpretation* (Cambridge, MA: Blackwell, 1995), x–xi; Peter C. Phan, "Woman and the Last Things: A Feminist Eschatology," in *In the Embrace of God: Feminist Approaches to Theological Anthropology*, ed. Ann O'Hara Graff (Maryknoll, NY: Orbis Books, 1995), 209, 225–26n15; Margaret Koch and Mary Stewart Van Leeuwen, *After Eden: Facing the Challenge of Gender Reconciliation* (Grand Rapids: Eerdmans, 1993), 21–5; Sandra M. Schneiders, *Beyond Patching: Faith and Feminism in the Catholic Church* (New York: Paulist, 1991), 15–25. One must be careful not to argue that woman is equal *to* man which sets men as the standard to which women must be "pulled up" (Alexander and Gause, *Women*, 25).

6. See Stackhouse, *Finally Feminist*, 17–19, 35–6; Nordling, "Gender," 498–500.

7. Chopp, *Power to Speak*, 3. For more definitions of Christian feminism, see Lisa Bernal Corley and Carol Blessing, "Speaking Out: Feminist Theology and Women's Proclamation in the Wesleyan Tradition," in Jule and Pedersen, *Being Feminist*, 145; Van Leeuwen, *Gender*, 36; Carmody, *Feminist Theology*, 10. For more on the shape and major themes of feminist theology, see Susan Frank Parsons, "Preface," in *The Cambridge Companion to Feminist Theology*, ed. Susan Frank Parsons (Cambridge: Cambridge University Press, 2002); Carmody, *Feminist Theology*, 67. There is immense diversity within feminist theology so that it may be more accurate to refer to feminist theologies in the plural. See Marjorie Procter-Smith, "Feminist Ritual Strategies: The *Ekklēsia Gynaikōn* at Work," in *Toward a New Heaven and a New Earth: Essays in Honor of Elisabeth Schüssler Fiorenza*, ed. Fernando F. Segovia (Maryknoll, NY: Orbis Books, 2003), 503. I deal mostly with feminist theology from a North American perspective. For other perspectives, see Ursula King, ed., *Feminist Theology from the Third World: A Reader* (London: SPCK, 1994). For a work specific to the Canadian context, see Mary Ann Beavis with Elaine Guillemin and Barbara Pell, eds., *Feminist Theology with a Canadian Accent: Canadian Perspectives on Contextual Feminist Theology* (Ottawa: Novalis, 2008).

8. See Alexander, "When Liberation Becomes Survival," 325.

9. Hollingsworth, "Spirit and Voice," 190. For an example of this, see *JPT* 26, no. 1 (2017), which dedicates three full-length articles to Sarah Coakley's *God, Sexuality, and the Self: An Essay "On the Trinity"* (Cambridge: Cambridge University Press, 2013), the inaugural volume of her revision of the task of systematic theology. The journal also contains a response article by Coakley.

feminist theologians and works have denounced eschatology and eschatological movements as a threat to women's equality, claiming it adds to rather than clarifies the theological ambiguity surrounding the issue. Instead of the revival of the eschatological imagination leading to the full flourishing of women (as this project argues), most feminist theologians argue the exact opposite and dismiss eschatology as incompatible with, irrelevant to, or insufficient for the cause of women's equality. It is to these works and to this challenge we now turn.

## 1.1 Eschatology and Equality: Three Existing Views

In order to categorize the existing views in recent literature on the relationship between eschatology and women's (in)equality, major works in feminist theology over the last forty years were searched and read for their discussions on eschatology and related topics such as future hope, eternal life, heaven, last things, and more. The works were analyzed for how they approached and defined eschatology, how they used (or did not use) it, where it appeared in their works and arguments, and how it impacted their work and the work of others. Two primary figures emerged as the most prolific in their discussions and most influential in their attitudes concerning eschatology's place in the gender debate: Rosemary Radford Ruether and Letty Russell. Ruether and Russell represent the perimeters of the topography of literature relating to attitudes toward eschatology in feminist theology, categorized respectively as the antagonistic and augmented view. These two influential scholars are at times joined by other feminist theologians, while others fall somewhere in between the views of Ruether and Russell, what I term the agnostic view.

### 1.1.1 The Antagonistic View: Eschatology Is Incompatible

The topography of literature begins with the antagonistic view because it presents the most significant challenge facing an eschatological argument for women's equality. It also is likely the most dominant view within feminist theology due to the pioneering work of Rosemary Radford Ruether in feminist systematic theology. The antagonistic view treats any traditional eschatology that looks to a future existence as incompatible with and dialectically opposed to present egalitarian ideals, arguing that eschatology suppresses the message of equality. The antagonistic view proactively seeks to expose and denounce eschatology as a threat and distraction to egalitarian goals and therefore attempts to remove it from any theology that promotes the equality of women.

The history of eschatology being employed to support the oppression of women dates back to at least the second century and the *Gospel of Thomas*, which advises that "every woman who will make herself male will enter the kingdom of heaven."[10]

---

10. Thomas O. Lambdin, trans., *The Gospel of Thomas*, in *The Nag Hammadi Library in English*, 3rd ed., ed. James M. Robinson (San Francisco: HarperSanFrancisco, 1988), 138 (saying 114).

This eschatological understanding that women must transcend or overcome their femaleness to become spiritually fit for the afterlife is popular in early mystic writings and among some eschatologically driven modern mystical groups.[11] Several orthodox church fathers also utilized eschatology as a way to dismiss the equal status of women. Fourth-century church fathers Augustine of Hippo and Gregory of Nyssa were some of the first to propose an eschatologically oriented understanding of gender, proposing equality for women in heaven only through accepting their subordination on earth.[12] This history of eschatology's relationship to gender, albeit brief here, has caused many modern feminist theologians, most notably Ruether, to hold an antagonistic view toward eschatology's relationship with women's equality.

In her widely cited book *Sexism and God-Talk: Toward a Feminist Theology*, first published in 1983, Ruether makes the first full-scale attempt at a feminist systematic theology. This work became the foundation that all future feminist theologies built on and a standard work that any Christian feminist argument must still engage. It is also the first feminist work to write explicitly on Christian eschatology.[13] Because of that, what she says about eschatology—and the antagonistic position her work takes—matters greatly and has been influential in how feminist theologians have approached eschatology, hindering its use as a viable approach to the gender question.

In the first chapter of *Sexism and God-Talk*, Ruether claims that one of the main problems Christianity has faced when it comes to the equality of men and women is its interpretation of equality "in a spiritual and eschatological way that suppressed its relevance for the sociology of the church."[14] Ruether later argues that throughout history there have been three main egalitarian anthropologies, the first being eschatological feminism.[15] Eschatological feminism spiritually affirmed the restored equality of men and women by referring to an original transcendent

---

11. See Ruether, *Sexism*, 128 for examples. The argument of these groups centers on two main points: (1) Adam as the original and unified spiritual being and eschatological body, a condition lost when woman was "taken out of the man" (Gen. 2:22-23); and (2) the resurrected Jesus as representative of the superior maleness being eschatologically restored. See Ruether, *Sexism*, 128. For further discussion and rebuttal of these conclusions, see my Chapter 4 (esp. 4.2) and section 6.2.

12. See Rosemary Radford Ruether, "Eschatology in Christian Feminist Theologies," in *The Oxford Handbook of Eschatology*, ed. Jerry L. Walls (Oxford: Oxford University Press, 2008), 331–2. The works of Gregory and Augustine are discussed more in 6.2.2.

13. This is confirmed by Phan in his summary of Ruether's *Sexism and God-talk* in his "Feminist Eschatology," 210–14. See also Ruether's later work "Eschatology and Feminism" where she does not change her position much (in *Lift Every Voice: Constructing Christian Theologies from the Underside*, rev. & exp. ed., ed. Susan Brooks Thistlethwaite and Mary Potter Engel [Maryknoll, NY: Orbis Books, 1998], 129–42).

14. Ruether, *Sexism*, 35.

15. See Ruether, *Sexism*, 99–102, for full discussion, which is summarized in this paragraph. The other two are liberal feminism and romantic feminism.

anthropology. This united androgynous humanity represented by Adam was eventually split into male and female by the Fall and only restored by Christ, the new androgynous Adam.

The problem for Ruether with this Gnostic-inspired eschatological feminism, which she traces as influential to all eschatologically oriented movements that followed, is that it "has no message of equality of women *in the world*."[16] The transcendent and escapist message of this eschatology becomes subject to historical conditions such as patriarchy brought about by the Fall, and therefore hope for equality is reserved only for the *eschaton*. Even if or when equality was affirmed in the church, says Ruether, it belonged to the transcendent sphere. Therefore, the male is still to rule in the present world. Ruether labels this interpretation a dualism where patriarchy is regarded as appropriate for the order of society, and equality of the genders is only an eschatological idea anticipated by the church. Eschatological groups past and present affirm this dualism by separating the eschatological realm from the material world so that the eschatological world cannot be put in conversation with the current order of creation.[17] Therefore, Ruether dismisses eschatological feminism as unhelpful because, although it affirms equality as the ideal, it does so in a transcendent fashion that inevitably upholds male domination and present injustice against women. She suggests the church can only bring real change to gender inequality in church leadership by dismissing eschatological feminism. The church is to be set apart "not as a representative of an eschatological humanity outside of and beyond history," but rather as a this-worldly example of redeemed humanity and social reform.[18]

At the end of the book, Ruether dedicates an entire chapter to "Eschatology and Feminism," where she takes a primarily negative approach to eschatology. Citing others, she first argues that women think of immortality different than men and that traditional eschatology is a male-centered, individualized way of thinking mostly concerned about self-perpetuation in the future and is "severed from historical hope."[19] Ruether proposes that the idea of an eschatological "spiritual body" (1 Cor. 15:42-44) that is potentially genderless traces its roots to male thinkers such as Gregory of Nyssa, Thomas Aquinas, and others. This idea juxtaposes the more spiritual male body with the more carnal female body so that the church fathers questioned whether women will exist in the resurrection or if the female body might be transformed into male.[20] Ruether argues that an eschatological orientation to gender has crippled the quest for equality for centuries and must be

---

16. Ruether, *Sexism*, 101; italics mine.

17. Ruether, *Sexism*, 196.

18. Ruether, *Sexism*, 104. I embrace Ruether's idea of the church as bearer of redeemed humanity, but I argue that eschatology helps and is even essential in this endeavor rather than a threat to it.

19. Ruether, *Sexism*, 245.

20. Ruether, *Sexism*, 247-8. Some, such as Augustine and Jerome, argued for the resurrection of male and female bodies for various reasons, but often with the female body

rejected because it devalues life in this world by transferring egalitarian ideals to an unrealized future beyond history.[21]

As an alternative to a transcendent or apocalyptic eschatology, Ruether then proposes a more cyclical and less linear eschatology that does not rely on an eschatological hope based in eternity or the new creation. She downplays more traditional eschatology in favor of our responsibility "to use our temporal life span to create a just and good community for our generation and for our children."[22] She concludes that we can be at best agnostic about what eschatology means for gender equality in the present and in the future, and therefore it need not play a major role in any discussions on equality.[23] Although many have followed Ruether's advice of an agnostic approach by simply dismissing eschatology as irrelevant (as examined below), others have followed her more antagonistic view of eschatology. This view actively refutes traditional eschatology as incompatible with and even damaging to the cause of women, a position Ruether continued to affirm fifteen and twenty-five years later.[24]

In his survey of central themes in feminist theology, Manfred Hauke traces the devaluing of eschatology within feminist thought back to the works of Ruether. In his chapter on "Feminist Eschatology, or the Lost Hope of Eternal Life,"[25] he references how eschatology is often viewed as a piece of patriarchal ideology and the recent "phasing out" of individual immortality, life after death, bodily resurrection, and the new creation as a future hope. What is notable is that he proposes this development is due to the influence of Ruether who treated the subject most extensively and who concluded that traditional eschatology is a distraction from the current problems facing women. He suggests Ruether is potentially influenced by the Marxist position that eschatological hope "is a deceptive consolation that only diverts attention from the political struggle."[26] According to Hauke's summary on the feminist view, traditional eschatology represents a linear masculine way of

---

being transformed since sex and childbearing would no longer be necessary (see Ruether, *Sexism*, 249).

21. Ruether, *Sexism*, 250, 254, 256.

22. Ruether, *Sexism*, 258.

23. Ruether, *Sexism*, 258.

24. See Ruether, "Eschatology and Feminism" (1998), and "Eschatology in Christian Feminist Theologies" (2008) where she reviews her own literature on eschatology (338–9).

25. Manfred Hauke, *God or Goddess? Feminist Theology: What Is It? Where Does It Lead?* trans. David Kipp (San Francisco: Ignatius, 1995), 239–44. The chapter on eschatology is the shortest of the fourteen chapters in the book, a pattern that is repeated frequently in works on feminist theology. Hauke's survey is especially interested in feminist theology in German-speaking countries. Hauke himself is not a feminist and at times is critical of feminist theology, but he does believe the questions raised by feminists are worthy of attention, and his main goal is to lay out the positions and let the reader decide (13–15).

26. Hauke, *God or Goddess*, 239–41. For a discussion on feminism's relationship to Marxism as well as its influence in Ruether's works, see Hauke, *God or Goddess*, 50–2.

thinking that is not useful for women's equality. To be of use, eschatological hope must be reinterpreted to apply *only* to the this-worldly sphere, and any speculation on future hope for equality is incompatible with the feminist cause.[27] He makes no reference to any potential positive treatments of eschatology in feminist theology nor offers any alternative ideas himself. And there is ample evidence, as analyzed in the following paragraph and proceeding section, that Hauke's assessment of the topic is correct.

A review of all works arguing for women's equality that mention eschatology since Ruether's initial systematic contribution would be beyond the current task. Although, as seen in the next section, it is surprising how many feminist works that claim to be a comprehensive overview of traditional Christian theology completely ignore eschatology altogether. However, a few examples confirm Ruether's influence on the treatment of eschatology. In her book on women's experiences with Christian spirituality and theology, the only concern Catholic Latin American theologian Ivone Gebara places on eschatology is to expose how it suppresses equality and distracts from the real concerns of women. Gebara is critical of any sort of "trans-historic beyond" type of eschatology that moves beyond the mortal, claiming that immortal ways of thinking rob us of the importance of daily acts of salvation and resurrection.[28] The yearning for the "eschatological salvation of the beyond" only fuels our desire for power, stability, and constancy and thereby only hurts women.[29] Because eschatological religions keep injustices alive, Gebara argues that we must establish another explanation. In her critique of traditional eschatology, she notably singles out only one faith group, Pentecostal churches, for spreading "a simplistic and dangerous message" that causes people to become "dangerously alienated" from this world and damn them from participating in concrete history.[30] She prefers a this-world-only eschatology that has no need for imagination beyond this earth or this body.[31] Similarly, in an edited collection of feminist essays, Amy Plantinga Pauw writes in her chapter "Some Last Words about Eschatology" (by far the shortest chapter in the book) that from a feminist perspective, "eschatology presents special doctrinal dangers" due in part to being individualistic, disembodied, justifying the status quo, and other reasons. Eschatology has "often functioned destructively, serving

---

27. Hauke, *God or Goddess*, 244.

28. Ivone Gebara, *Out of the Depths: Women's Experience of Evil and Salvation*, trans. Ann Patrick Ware (Minneapolis: Fortress, 2002), 129–30. Gebara is a Brazilian Sister of Notre Dame. See review of Gebara's work on eschatology in Ruether, "Eschatology in Christian Feminist Theologies," 337–8.

29. Gebara, *Depths*, 130.

30. Gebara, *Depths*, 131. Critiques like this on Pentecostal eschatology are discussed in my Chapter 3. See also Vondey, *Perplexed*, 111; Vondey, *Pentecostal Theology*, 179.

31. Gebara, *Depths*, 131.

the interest of oppression and denial" and therefore feminists are "wary of grand eschatological pronouncements."[32]

In summary, authors such as Pauw, Gebara, and Ruether denounce traditional eschatology—and particularly imaginative eschatology as found in Pentecostalism—as incompatible with the cause of women because it emphasizes future hope but deemphasizes present problems and injustices. Therefore, eschatology as a system of theological thought is devalued because it props up systems of domination such as patriarchy and gender hierarchy and distracts attention from the struggle of women. The hesitancy by Pauw, Gebara, Ruether, and others is understandable;[33] the type of eschatology they are critiquing does have the potential to create indifference to current issues surrounding injustices toward women.[34] Dualist conceptions of the afterlife can be dangerous and critiques such as theirs are helpful. But dismissing eschatology and future hope as completely incompatible with egalitarian pursuits due to a very narrow view of eschatology is to miss the transformative character of eschatology and its dialectic of imagination and participation. Making sweeping generalizations about groups (including Pentecostals) and focusing on disembodied existence and general conceptions of the afterlife as the main or only tenets of Christian eschatology does not align with the history and current state of eschatological thought. Ruether and others determine that completely rejecting eschatology is the necessary conclusion for anyone seriously interested in women's equality in the church. So, is eschatology forever an enemy of gender equality? Is the future *for* feminist theology to have no future *in* feminist theology at all?[35] That has been the conclusion of the many who hold the agnostic view, treating eschatology as completely irrelevant in the quest for women's equality.

*1.1.2 The Agnostic View: Eschatology Is Irrelevant*

The second most significant challenge facing an eschatological methodology for solving the gender paradox is the agnostic view. Whereas the antagonistic view seeks to expose traditional eschatology as incompatible with an egalitarian position by proactively arguing that it suppresses equality, the agnostic view takes the next

---

32. Amy Plantinga Pauw, "Some Last Words about Eschatology," in *Feminist and Womanist Essays in Reformed Dogmatics*, ed. Amy Plantinga Pauw and Serene Jones (Louisville, KY: Westminster John Knox, 2006), 221–4. The chapter is only four pages in a book comprising chapters that are almost all fifteen pages or longer.

33. This hesitancy is most prominently displayed by the lack of engagement with eschatology by other feminist theologians after Ruether as discussed in the following section on the agnostic view, but see Jobling, *Feminist Biblical Interpretation*, esp. 99–163.

34. Pauw does hint at a better way when she rightly states, "the last things cannot be divorced from present things" ("Last Words," 224).

35. Playing off the title *Is There a Future for Feminist Theology?*, ed. Deborah F. Sawyer and Diane M. Collier (Sheffield: Sheffield Academic, 1999).

logical step and treats eschatology as irrelevant to theological arguments for gender equality. Therefore, the agnostic view is represented by feminist theologians who surprisingly pay little or no attention to eschatology *in works and places where one would normally expect it.* Instead of dedicating time to denouncing eschatology as a threat or distraction to equality, these theologians often let absence speak louder than words: what they leave out of their works on gender is often as important as what they put in. Because eschatology is irrelevant to the concerns of women, it is not worth engaging in theological works. Although not necessarily antagonistic toward eschatology (although there are traces of that), this view is influenced by and the result of the position of Ruether, who devalued eschatological inquiry into feminist issues. The result of the agnostic perspective is that eschatology is treated at best with skepticism or minimal attention, or, more often, it is ignored altogether.

Since the agnostic view identifies the *absence* of eschatology in feminist works, there is no dominant voice for this position; instead, there is a consistent pattern of neglect found in key works in the field. Several scholars have highlighted this curious absence: for example, J'annine Jobling questions the complete lack of eschatological hope found in well-known works by feminist theologians.[36] This lack is even more surprising when considering the renewed emphasis on systematic theology among feminist theologians[37] combined with the renewed interest in eschatology within systematics.[38] Why the disinterest in eschatology among feminist theologians? Following the lead of Ruether, they tend to take the position that speculation about eternal life or immortality is unnecessary and unfruitful because it cannot address the present concerns of women.

Perhaps the strongest example of the agnostic position is Denise Carmody's well-received *Christian Feminist Theology: A Constructive Interpretation.* Her book claims to be an "overview of traditional Christian theology" in light of feminist sensibilities.[39] Carmody ascribes to "moderate feminism" and asserts that she is not radical or separatist but seeks to contribute a feminist theology that takes seriously the good news of the advent and victory of Jesus.[40] In order to remove traditional patriarchy and accommodate the insights of women, Carmody rightly argues that Christian theology needs a reform and "overhaul."[41] The work of feminist theology, she states, is to champion the full equality of women with men and weed out any sexism in theology that denies this full equality.[42] However, what is conspicuous for a book claiming to encapsulate all the key tenets of traditional Christian theology

---

36. Jobling, *Feminist Biblical Interpretation.* She looks specifically at the works of Elizabeth Schüssler Fiorenza and Phyllis Trible.
37. See Rees, "Sarah Coakley," 300–14.
38. See Shields, *Eschatological Imagination*, 1–2, 9–38.
39. Carmody, *Feminist Theology*, ix.
40. Carmody, *Feminist Theology*, x–xi, 242.
41. Carmody, *Feminist Theology*, 66, xii.
42. Carmody, *Feminist Theology*, 6.

and make them "applicable to the needs and hopes of women" is that there is no distinct section on and very little mention of eschatology.[43]

Unlike Ruether, who spends a chapter on eschatology in her systematic contribution to show its incompatibility, Carmody chooses not to engage eschatology at all. The tacit implication is that in order to reform and overhaul Christian theology in light of feminist concerns (the purpose of her work), one must dismiss eschatology. Carmody has constructive chapters on creation, ecclesiology, anthropology, and theology, also covering topics such as suffering, the Trinity, and others while discussing what Christian feminism can add. In her effort to ponder some "neglected" stimuli to reflect on the religious experience and praxis of Christian women, eschatology would seem like a prime candidate but instead remains ignored.[44] In the rare mention of an eschatological topic, Carmody is dismissive and skeptical: "All imagination of heaven is speculative, to say the least, and not overly profitable. Sufficient for earthly days are the evils thereof."[45] Carmody sees no potential connection between eschatological hope and present praxis with regard to gender equality.

If Carmody were only an isolated example, then the case for the agnostic view would be tentative. But Carmody's pattern of dismissal is continually repeated. In the edited collection *Freeing Theology: The Essentials of Theology in Feminist Perspective*, the editor and authors consider where theology can liberate both men and women from the harmful effects of patriarchy. They look for liberating elements for equality within the "essentials" of the Christian tradition.[46] Among chapters on the Bible, Trinity, Christology, anthropology, ecclesiology, the sacraments, and others, there is no mention of eschatology in the entire book, implying that eschatology is neither "essential" nor contains any liberating elements for Christian women. A chapter or section on eschatology is normally necessary for any work on the "essentials" of Christian theology; therefore, its absence speaks volumes about the supposed irrelevance of eschatology to feminist concerns.

Most feminist works that claim to be comprehensive and do mention eschatology do so only in cursory and often dismissive fashion. In *Theology and Feminism,* influential feminist thinker Daphne Hampson dismisses eschatology as an individualistic male doctrine. She argues that the only effective approach for achieving equality is to focus solely on the present without any mention of a new

---

43. Carmody, *Feminist Theology*, x. There is a section on hope (30–8), a brief mention of church as eschatological community in context of church as sacramental (127), a mention of the future in a non-eschatological sense (243), and a quick mention of the hope of heaven (249), but there are no connections made to any usefulness for gender equality and no constructive contribution.

44. Carmody, *Feminist Theology*, 10.

45. Carmody, *Feminist Theology*, 256.

46. Catherine Mowry LaCugna, ed., *Freeing Theology: The Essentials of Theology in Feminist Perspective* (New York: HarperOne, 1993). See the "Introduction" by LaCugna, 1–4. The book is primarily concerned with or contains contributions from Catholic theology.

creation or eschatological hope.[47] In *An A to Z of Feminist Theology*, editor Lisa Isherwood writes the entry for "Eschatology." It is worth consideration here both for its brevity (one of the shortest entries in the book) and because Isherwood does a quick overview of biblical eschatology and tersely concludes that the eschatological perspective that "all will be well in some other realm at the end of time" has nothing in common with feminist theology and nothing to do with the causes it champions.[48] She affirms the common thought in feminist theology that there is no personal continuation after death and that eschatological thinking offers no present benefit for women. In her overview of feminist theology, Natalie Watson takes a similar stance. In her two pages dedicated to eschatology (which almost entirely focus on ecofeminist theology), she notes that "feminist theologians have so far not taken much interest in the study of a possibility of a future world,"[49] and she has no interest in doing so either. She observes that traditional Christian eschatology is usually dismissed by feminist theologies and affirms that this is the correct approach because eschatology promotes the destruction of the earth, which corresponds to the oppression of women by men.[50]

All these works are supposedly "comprehensive" works on gender that view eschatology in an agnostic manner, treating it as irrelevant to women's equality.[51] The brief but dismissive mentions of eschatology by Carmody, Hampson, and Isherwood serve as examples of authors who deliberately choose to ignore eschatology. They either discard it as a sexist doctrine or deem it unprofitable to engage with due to its lack of concern for the present. There is no hint of the liberative components of a more holistic eschatology, which demonstrates how future hope changes present practice. Carol Christ sums up the agnostic position of feminist theologians by saying that one does not have to rule out the possibility of life after death, but "we ought not live our lives in the light of such a possibility."[52] So must eschatology be dismissed from any theology that is serious about women's equality? Despite the popularity and influence of the antagonistic and agnostic views, some concerned with gender equality have attempted to go against the grain and treat eschatology more positively. However, their contributions still leave the

---

47. Daphne Hampson, *Theology and Feminism* (Oxford: Basis Blackwell, 1990), 137–45. Hampson is a self-defined post-Christian who believes Christianity and feminism to be incompatible. However, in a book that discusses theology's relationship to feminism, it is still telling that she mostly ignores eschatology.

48. Lisa Isherwood, "Eschatology," in *An A to Z of Feminist Theology*, ed. Lisa Isherwood and Dorothea McEwan (Sheffield: Sheffield Academic, 1996), 53–5.

49. Natalie K. Watson, *Feminist Theology* (Grand Rapids: Eerdmans, 2003), 49.

50. Watson, *Feminist Theology*, 49–51.

51. However, all these authors make positive contributions to the cause for equality, and some are considered helpful in other parts of my work.

52. Carol P. Christ, *Laughter of Aphrodite: Reflections on a Journey to the Goddess* (San Francisco: Harper & Row, 1987), 215. This quote is from her chapter on "Finitude, Death, and Reverence for Life."

door wide open for the possibility of a thoroughly eschatological contribution to the gender problem.

### 1.1.3 The Augmented View: Eschatology Is Insufficient

The third challenge facing a comprehensive eschatological approach to gender across several disciplines is the augmented view. This view takes eschatology seriously and even engages it as helpful but ultimately treats it as insufficient as a definitive method for resolving gender issues, and it therefore augments eschatology with other approaches. Like the antagonistic view (and unlike the agnostic view), these feminist authors do engage eschatology but do so in a mostly positive manner. These theologians see traditional eschatology and beliefs about the future as potentially valuable resources for liberative gender practices. However, whether explicitly or implicitly, they view eschatology as an insufficient distinctive methodological starting point from which to approach the gender problem. This section first reviews the most prolific voice in promoting an eschatological framework for egalitarianism, Letty Russell, and then discusses other key authors and works that have followed in her footsteps.

Letty Russell is considered a pioneer in feminist theology and her work has inspired and influenced a generation of Christian feminist thinkers.[53] Important for this study is that Russell is primarily known and remembered for her eschatological orientation to the subject of gender equality in the church.[54] Several of Russell's early works lay out the eschatological framework she would become known for. In *The Future of Partnership*, Russell searches for eschatological "clues" in the new creation that might inspire the present practice of equal partnership for women and men in the work of Christ.[55] She lays out several approaches to eschatology and argues for what she calls an adventological eschatology "in which God's New Creation is coming into our lives now, bringing the dimension of the holy into everyday dynamics of human interaction and expectancy."[56] The church,

---

53. As a pastor, scholar, and Christian educator, Russell wrote nearly a dozen books over a twenty-year period beginning in 1974.

54. See M. Shawn Copeland, "Journeying to the Household of God: The Eschatological Implications of Method in the Theology of Letty Mandeville Russell," in Farley and Jones, *Liberating Eschatology*, 26–44.

55. Letty M. Russell, *The Future of Partnership* (Philadelphia: Westminster, 1979), 16, 95.

56. Russell, *Future*, 82. Russell says the four approaches to eschatology are apocalyptic (future is imminent), teleological (focus on the end of life), axiological (future is taking place now), and adventological (the new that is coming into history). Russell's adventological approach is influenced by Moltmann and it is fitting that he contributes to the volume of essays in honor of her (Moltmann, "Liberating"). For Moltmann's influence on Russell, see Rosemary Radford Ruether, "The Theological Vision of Letty Russell," in Farley and Jones, *Liberating Eschatology*, 16–25, 20–1.

asserts Russell, lives in "advent shock" where "we seek to anticipate the future in what we do, opening ourselves to the working of God's Spirit and expecting the impossible" in spite of the world in which the church dwells.[57] She encourages the church to focus its theological reflection, such as questions on the image of God,[58] from an eschatological point of view so that we look toward God's ultimate goal for humanity as the basis for contradicting any present practices that dehumanize women (or men) in any way.[59] She then spends the final pages of the book briefly summarizing what an eschatological hermeneutic would look like for approaching biblical texts.[60]

*Future of Partnership* and other earlier works[61] are eventually summarized and incorporated into Russell's main attempt to approach gender equality from an eschatological orientation, *Household of Freedom: Authority in Feminist Theology*. In this work, Russell attempts a theological reflection on the problem of authority from an eschatological perspective. Russell uses what she labels an eschatological metaphor or image—God's future "household of freedom"[62]—which she states elsewhere is an alternative translation for "kingdom of God" or the new creation.[63] Instead of looking to present (patriarchal) authority, Russell proposes the church appeal to "the authority of God's future" in order to disable gender hierarchy in the present.[64] Advocacy for women "requires a utopian faith that understands God's

---

57. Russell, *Future*, 102. Russell first used the phrase "advent shock" in *Ferment of Freedom: A Guide to Help Women Relate the Christian Faith and Participation in Social Change* (New York: National Board of the Young Women's Christian Association of the USA, 1972), 188. She is engaging with the popular term and title of the widely read book by Alvin Toffler, *Future Shock* (New York: Bantam Books, 1970). Whereas Toffler's "future shock" is a mostly negative experience describing people's maladjustment to the present due to being overwhelmed by the rapidity of change (and therefore holding on to the traditions of the past and the status quo), Russell's "advent shock" is used more positively as a way of expressing one's freedom in Christ in the present based on the future (Russell, *Future*, 102).

58. See her Chapter 2, "God Utopia," esp. 45–6.

59. Russell, *Future*, 167.

60. Russell, *Future*, 171–6. See her previous work as editor in *The Liberating Word: A Guide to Nonsexist Interpretation of the Bible* (Philadelphia: Westminster John Knox, 1977).

61. Such as Letty M. Russell, *Growth in Partnership* (Philadelphia: Westminster John Knox, 1981).

62. Russell, *Household*, 13–14, 67. Russell defines a metaphor as "an imaginative way of describing what is still unknown by using an example from present concrete reality" (*Household*, 37).

63. Russell, *Household*, 26. See also *Household*, 84 where she uses Mark 3:24-25 as an example of this interchangeability of terms.

64. Russell, *Household*, 18–20. For her other work on issues of authority and power and another metaphor, see *Church in the Round* which proposes the "round table" metaphor for developing a new paradigm of authority and power (Philadelphia: Westminster John Knox, 1993).

future as an impulse for change in the present."[65] In addition to "household of freedom," Russell introduces two key eschatological concepts or phrases in this work. The first one, "memories of the future," describes biblical events that already happened and that give glimpses of God's promised and future household of freedom.[66] These "glimpses" happen in the present and act as a "sign," "foretaste," and "first taste" of the future household of God.[67] The second concept is Russell's idea of working or beginning "from the other end."[68] In doing this, the church imaginatively looks to the egalitarian authority of the future so that it can envision and participate in that egalitarian freedom in the present.[69] Russell then attempts to spend most of the rest of the book giving examples of "memories of the future" or "working from the other end" in the biblical text and in church life. However, part of the problem with Russell's work is how ineffectively she does this and how frequently she completely abandons her appeal to eschatology as well as these key metaphors and phrases.

While Russell should be applauded for being the first to attempt a full-scale eschatological argument for women's equality in the church, her work falls short. Instead of consistently following her eschatological paradigm and metaphors throughout, Russell somewhat inexplicably leaves her eschatological framework behind and springboards into other discussions without making any eschatological connection. For example, Chapter 3 on language and images for God ("Power of Naming") makes almost no mention of her eschatological metaphor or phrases introduced in the first two chapters and is mostly a generic chapter about God-talk in feminist theology. Other chapters lose their eschatological orientation for long stretches, and some completely abandon it.[70] A similar critique could be made of *The Future of Partnership*, in which Russell incorporates eschatology when convenient but leaves it out for full chapters at a time.

Russell's approach is also narrow, which is likely why she has difficulty following her eschatological method all the way through her works. Instead of engaging the broader theological field of traditional eschatology and what it can contribute, she proposes only one eschatological metaphor and attempts to support her arguments throughout with that single image, which results in a work that is not persuasively or thoroughly theological. Similarly, she focuses on the problem of authority as the main issue but only vaguely defines that problem and leaves it out of several

---

65. Russell, *Household*, 18.

66. Russell, *Household*, 18–21, 26–8; see also 71–2. Some of these memories include the Exodus and the life of Jesus.

67. Russell, *Household*, 26, 37, 92. There is quite a bit of trajectory language in Russell's works. For example, see *Household*, 61.

68. Russell, *Household*, 60, 67. Working from the other end is also an important theme in her earlier work *The Future of Partnership* (see 15–16).

69. Russell, *Household*, 67–8.

70. For example, see her Chapter 5, "Household, Power, and Glory."

chapters.[71] Although Russell sees great potential in an eschatological approach to present-day gender problems in the church, the evidence of her works is that it is ultimately insufficient in its ability to be consistently applied across various disciplines. As evidence, it is not surprising that in the collection of essays in her honor that are supposedly dedicated to her theme of liberating eschatology, only a few essays explicitly approach the theme of eschatology.[72]

However, what does set Russell firmly apart from the antagonistic and agnostic views is her important insight that eschatology—an appeal to the authority of the future—is not an otherworldly escapist tool for circumnavigating present gender problems; rather, it contributes to the actualization of hope and changes in practice in the here and now.[73] Russell seems aware of her unique contribution and this void of eschatology within feminist theology. In her conspicuously short attempt to give an overview of some other feminist views of eschatology, she concludes that not much exists and that "none of these feminist writers would necessarily say that authority of the future is a key element in their feminist theory" and in fact they were more in search of a "usable past."[74] That Russell is grasping for other examples of positive uses of eschatology for women in the church is evidence of how little there is and the opportunity for more work to be done. Some other feminist writers have eschewed the antagonistic or agnostic view and have at least hinted at the potential for eschatology to make a positive contribution to the gender problem. Most mention or use eschatology for a brief section, approach a specific topic with it, or occasionally indicate its possible usefulness throughout their discussion while using other approaches.[75] These authors are engaged and cited throughout my work but do not make enough of a contribution to review here. However, two articles are worth mentioning now.

71. Russell, *Household*, 20-1.

72. Interestingly and similarly, the collection edited by Segovia, *Toward a New Heaven and a New Earth*, is also not nearly as eschatological as the title suggests. Not a single essay out of the thirty included is dedicated to eschatology.

73. See Russell, *Household*, 20, 68.

74. Russell, *Household*, 71. The whole section is only 68-71. She reviews the work of Ruether, Elizabeth Schüssler Fiorenza, and (for reasons that are unclear) Alice Walker. She cannot find much from Schüssler Fiorenza, but see *In Memory of Her: A Feminist Theological Reconstruction of Christian Origins*, 10th anniversary ed. (New York: Crossroad, 1994); Elisabeth Schüssler Fiorenza, *Bread Not Stone: The Challenge of Biblical Interpretation* (1984; repr., Boston: Beacon, 1995), xiv-xvii. Schüssler Fiorenza's works are discussed in my Chapter 4, esp. 4.1.

75. Examples: Stackhouse, *Finally Feminist*, 41-5, 84; see also Stackhouse's revision of this work, *Partners in Christ: A Conservative Case for Egalitarianism* (Downers Grove, IL: InterVarsity, 2015), which has an "Eschatology" chapter (55-9), but is actually the same exact material as *Finally Feminist*; Cherith Nordling, "Gender," 506-9; Grenz and Kjesbo, *Women in the Church*, chapters 5 and 6; Van Leeuwen, *Gender*, last chapter "All Things Made New," 231-50, although she never calls it an eschatological argument.

In "Woman and the Last Things: A Feminist Eschatology," Peter Phan accurately observes that despite the renewed interest in eschatology and the growth in feminist theology, the two have rarely been put together in conversation.[76] He finds it odd that although feminist theology has made contributions in nearly every fundamental Christian doctrine, there is a puzzling silence when it comes to eschatology. Eschatology is "still in its infancy"[77] when compared with other themes in feminist theology. Phan's intention is merely to "explore" what a feminist eschatology might look like in conversation with traditional eschatology.[78] His essay, which focuses on the works of Ruether and Sallie McFague, is by his own admission more of an ecofeminist eschatology.[79] As Phan notices, and as demonstrated in the agnostic view, several books that claim to be comprehensive studies of feminist theology completely ignore eschatology.[80] His focus is on developments within the Catholic Church regarding eschatology, and he speculates what issues in eschatology may need to be reformulated based on women's experiences.[81]

Much of the article is a literature review on the critiques made by Ruether and McFague regarding eschatology, pointing out their intense suspicion of traditional eschatology and their accusation that it does little to solve the current inequality that women face.[82] However, in his closing section Phan offers seven contributions that (eco)feminist eschatology can make toward traditional eschatology, four doctrines of traditional eschatology that feminist theologians have dismissed without adequate justification, and three lines of development ecofeminist eschatology might consider moving forward.[83] While Phan's contribution is helpful as one of the few attempts to lay out the problem clearly—particularly in arguing that a feminist eschatology does not need to focus only on the present—he does not move the conversation forward or spend time offering a solution of how eschatology might act as a potential friend to the feminist cause. His short essay, which is mostly a literature review, acts more as an invitation for further work to be done than a substantial contribution to the problems articulated.

Like Phan, Valerie Karras begins her article on eschatology in feminist theology by showing that most feminist theological literature gives the impression of being

---

76. Phan, "Feminist Eschatology," 206.

77. Phan, "Feminist Eschatology," 218.

78. Phan, "Feminist Eschatology," 223n1.

79. Phan, "Feminist Eschatology," 207, 223n1. This emphasis is not surprising since McFague is his focus. See Sallie McFague's chapter, "Eschatology: A New Shape for Humanity," in her *The Body of God: An Ecological Theology* (Minneapolis: Augsburg, 1993), 197–212.

80. He cites as examples Anne E. Carr, *Transforming Grace: Women's Experience and Christian Tradition* (San Francisco: Harper & Row, 1988) and LaCugna, *Freeing Theology*.

81. Phan, "Feminist Eschatology," 209–10.

82. Phan, "Feminist Eschatology," 210–18.

83. Phan, "Feminist Eschatology," 219–23. Some of these are referenced later in this work.

anti-eschatological. Feminist theologians seek to distance themselves from any talk of immortality, resurrection, new creation, or an ultimate "end" by instead concerning their "eschatology" with ecological sustainability.[84] She traces the familiar argument among feminists that traditional eschatology is a patriarchal concept that suffers from an anthropocentric bias which unhelpfully focuses on unrealized events that are "not yet."[85] She raises the question, "Is 'feminist eschatology,' then, an oxymoronic expression?"[86] Karras, a self-described believing and practicing Eastern Orthodox Christian,[87] presents Eastern Orthodox thinking as a way to reject the "unbalanced eschatologies" of both feminist eschatology (this-worldly) and patriarchal eschatology (otherworldly) and instead to see eschatology as both realized and unrealized, simultaneously "now" and "not yet" in a way that is helpful to the cause of women.[88] Although Karras's approach to eschatology is nothing new, her attempt to bring it into conversation with feminist theology represents an important step forward and aligns closely with the approach of this work. Karras's contribution is brief, but her call for a balanced eschatology that makes a positive contribution for women is important. What Karras neglects is to flesh out what this contribution could look like and how it might be applied to the gender problem. She gives no practical suggestions, focuses solely on Genesis 1–2 for her eschatology, and gives no evidence for how this approach has played out for women in history.

The works of Russell and articles by Phan and Karras do not make a convincing case for the sufficiency of a solely eschatological solution to women's inequality, but they do make important contributions as some of the only feminist attempts to treat eschatology positively. Karras sees Eastern Orthodox theology and eschatology as a potential solution or way forward. Can the same be said for Pentecostal eschatology? Might it provide a way to resolve the Pentecostal gender paradox? My work seeks to critique the antagonistic, agnostic, and augmented view of eschatology in the gender debate by constructing a thoroughly eschatological approach to gender in the areas of Pentecostal history, hermeneutics, theology, and praxis. I now turn to the few Pentecostal works that have laid a foundation—albeit incomplete—to accomplish that task.

### 1.2 The Pentecostal Potential: Toward a Positive Eschatology for Women

Since Pentecostalism is an eschatological movement, it is not surprising that most Pentecostals have not subscribed to the antagonistic or agnostic view when

---

84. Valerie A. Karras, "Eschatology," in Parsons, *Feminist Theology*, 243–4. She also mentions Ruether and McFague.
85. Karras, "Eschatology," 247.
86. Karras, "Eschatology," 244.
87. Karras, "Eschatology," 245.
88. Karras, "Eschatology," 245–7.

it comes to eschatology and gender.[89] However, what is surprising, considering the centrality of eschatology in the movement is how infrequently eschatology is mentioned in what is arguably one of Pentecostalism's most pressing issues, the gender paradox.[90] Eschatology occasionally receives positive mentions as a potential tool of liberation in theological discussions on women's equality, but it is rarely developed and is treated more as an addition to or support for other approaches.[91] No comprehensive Pentecostal study exists that addresses the gender paradox entirely through the lens of eschatology, but some helpful works do exist. This section looks at the contributions of three Pentecostal authors who illustrate a positive eschatology for women, but still reflect the augmented view that eschatology is insufficient as a methodological starting point for gender equality.[92]

Cheryl Bridges Johns is one of the most prolific and consistent voices on women's equality in Pentecostalism. One of her most influential articles marks the first Pentecostal attempt to make eschatology central in the quest for the full liberation and participation of women in church life. In "Pentecostal Spirituality and the Conscientization of Women," Johns, heavily influenced by Moltmann as well as Walter Brueggemann's prophetic imagination, argues that our understanding of the reality of the future is the template we should use to live now through the power of the Holy Spirit. As this happens, we are "actualizing" God's future in the historical present which leads to the conscientization of women and the ability to live out their eschatological-ontological vocations now.[93] Johns

---

89. For Pentecostalism as an eschatological movement see my Introduction. I am not aware of any Pentecostal work which actively refutes eschatology as incompatible with gender equality (the antagonistic view) or purposely dismisses it as irrelevant (the agnostic view).

90. Arguments have been made about racial integration in Pentecostalism and the importance of eschatology. See especially Iain MacRobert, *The Black Roots and White Racism of Early Pentecostalism in the USA* (New York: St. Martin's, 1988), 80, and other places. On the relationship between ecological concern and Pentecostal eschatology, see Waddell, "Apocalyptic Sustainability," 95–110.

91. For example, see Alexander and Gause, who say Pentecostalism must articulate the role of women in the church based on a Pentecostal eschatology (among other things) but barely mention eschatology throughout the entire work (*Women*, 22).

92. As with the previous section, there are other works that briefly mention the role of eschatology in relation to the gender paradox and these works are cited in later chapters. Works on feminism and women's issues in general by Pentecostal scholars are covered in the Introduction and in later chapters.

93. Cheryl Bridges Johns, "Pentecostal Spirituality and the Conscientization of Women," in *All Together in One Place: Theological Papers from the Brighton Conference on World Evangelization*, ed. Harold D. Hunter and Peter D. Hocken (Sheffield: Sheffield Academic, 1993), 155–6. As her title suggests, the concept of conscientization is key for Johns. She is picking up the term from Brazilian scholar Paulo Freire, describing how women and men become aware of their sociocultural reality and act as subjects of a (divine) historical

seeks to offer eschatologically based "tangible signs" and "symbols of hope" for this conscientization, "which announce, in the present, God's future for women and men."[94] In order to do this, she looks at biblical precedents and historical antecedents for "liberating memories" of our "unattained future."[95]

Some of Johns's approach to these eschatological symbols is discussed more fully in later chapters of my work, but important here is Johns's solution for the realization of conscientization among women, namely, to read the Bible eschatologically and recapture the eschatological urgency of early Pentecostalism.[96] She draws a connection—one that is usually overlooked—between the waning of women in ministry with the waning of the eschatological edge of early Pentecostalism. She closes by claiming "it is the task of pentecostals to interpret our present in light of God's future" and that Pentecostal spirituality "marked by an eschatological vision" is what will lead to the present experience of women's equality through what Johns calls conscientization.[97] Although this article is by her own admission brief, it has opened the door for a more in-depth look at an eschatological perspective on gender in Pentecostalism, a door nudged open further twenty years later by Lisa P. Stephenson.

In *Dismantling the Dualisms for American Pentecostal Women in Ministry*, Stephenson seeks a methodological approach that leads to a fully liberating praxis for Pentecostal women.[98] She turns to pneumatology and feminist theology, which she claims are two missing perspectives in other works on Pentecostal women. Stephenson's work is important and nearest to my own project for three reasons. First, it is a full-length, authentically Pentecostal, constructive approach to the gender problem as opposed to the predominantly descriptive works that explain the problem, examine the history, but do not propose a way forward.[99] Like my work, Stephenson sees the problem and solution as theological.[100] Second, it is not

---

future (156, 161). See also her work, *Pentecostal Formation: Pedagogy among the Oppressed*, particularly Chapter 4, "Pentecostalism as a Movement of Conscientization" (Eugene, OR: Wipf & Stock, 1998), 62–110. Despite being a later and more developed work, I find it no more (and perhaps even less) eschatological than the article discussed here (but do see 69–70 in *Pentecostal Formation*). For more on the background of conscientization, see Stephenson, *Dismantling*, 77n39.

94. Johns, "Conscientization," 156.
95. Johns, "Conscientization," 157.
96. Johns, "Conscientization," 157, 162. For more on reading eschatologically see Johns's article, "Grieving, Brooding, and Transformation: The Spirit, the Bible, and Gender," *JPT* 23, no. 2 (2014): 141–53, which is discussed more in 4.3 and 5.4.1. See also Schüssler Fiorenza, "Emancipative Reading," who mentions the goal of conscientization for biblical interpreters.
97. Johns, "Conscientization," 165.
98. Stephenson, *Dismantling*, 2.
99. Stephenson, *Dismantling*, 59–60.
100. Stephenson, *Dismantling*, 19.

afraid to engage feminist theology, treating it as a friend of Pentecostal theology and integral to moving forward in the gender debate.[101] Third, and most important, Stephenson's pneumatological methodology is unavoidably an eschatological approach.

The above third and final point is made because, as is fully supported in my later chapters and as Stephenson herself suggests, to take a pneumatological approach is by necessity to incorporate an eschatological approach.[102] The starting point for Stephenson's thesis is the Acts 2 outpouring of the Spirit at Pentecost, an event she and others interpret as an eschatological event.[103] Using her "Isaianic New Exodus paradigm," Stephenson argues that the restored people of God and eschatological Spirit prophesied in Isaiah are fulfilled at Pentecost, which signals the fulfillment of the eschatological promise and arrival of the eschatological age.[104] One of her conclusions is that Pentecostal churches should model full equality for they are "representative of the new creation of God."[105] *Dismantling the Dualisms* does not use an eschatological lens throughout to argue for the full inclusion of women in ministry; but it is eschatological in its approach because it is pneumatological, whereas my own work aims to be pneumatological because it is eschatological.

The single Pentecostal work that most clearly makes an eschatological argument for women's equality and hints that it may be the best or most comprehensive approach to the gender paradox is an article by Zachary Tackett.[106] Tackett offers three interpretive grids for understanding the theological dynamics in the historical developments of the decline of women in ministry in Pentecostalism, the third being the nature of Pentecostal eschatology as it relates to egalitarianism.[107] Before discussing his three grids, Tackett introduces the topic by arguing that the theological foundation for the full inclusion of women in leadership is "the eschatological Pentecost Proclamation" of Joel 2/Acts 2, and the implications of this are a radical, egalitarian gospel.[108] The early endorsement of women in ministry among Pentecostals was built on their radical eschatological message of

---

101. Stephenson claims her work is the first monograph by a Pentecostal explicitly to engage feminist theology (3). She specifically engages Schüssler Fiorenza, Ruether, and Letty Russell. She says that by ignoring feminist theology, Pentecostals will continue to fuse "an ideology of Spirit empowerment with a hierarchical anthropology" (86). Incorporating feminist ecclesial models and insights is especially important for her work (189–90).

102. Stephenson, *Dismantling*, 6; see my 3.4.2.

103. Stephenson, *Dismantling*, 74, 81, 109.

104. Stephenson, *Dismantling*, 109. See Isa. 32:14-17; 42:1; 44:1-4.

105. Stephenson, *Dismantling*, 190.

106. Zachary Michael Tackett, "Callings, Giftings, and Empowerment: Preaching Women and American Pentecostalism in Historical and Theological Perspective," in English de Alminana and Olena, *Women*, 73–98.

107. The other two are institutionalization and radicalization followed by embourgeoisement.

108. Tackett, "Callings," 73.

inclusion and participation in the eschatological work of the Spirit which fueled egalitarian praxis.[109] However, Tackett shows that Pentecostals quickly struggled with the implications of this eschatological inclusion in light of cultural pressures and expectations.[110] He also intimates the potential connection between the increase in limitations on women with the decrease in eschatological fervor.[111] Tackett's eschatological emphasis is unsatisfyingly short—just a few pages at the beginning and end of his argument. But it is important in that it makes a tacit claim that an eschatological framework for equality is the best approach because, unlike other methods, it leads to more than just spiritual or ecclesial freedom and does more than just give women a voice. An eschatological egalitarianism leads to an ontological wholeness, full inclusion, and authority in all aspects of life.[112]

All three of these Pentecostal scholars make valuable contributions in that they see potential for an eschatological method to solve the Pentecostal gender paradox, even if concluding that it must be augmented by other approaches. However, none offer a thoroughly eschatological approach nor indicate what it might look like to consider each of the key areas of Pentecostal history, hermeneutics, theology, or ecclesiology through the lens of eschatology. Johns focuses on an eschatological reading of the Scriptures and early Pentecostal eschatology. Stephenson's study, by her own admission, is mostly historical and theological; she acknowledges the critical importance of hermeneutical issues, but she does not contribute an actual hermeneutic out of her methodology.[113] Both are significantly lacking in praxis. Johns offers almost no practical suggestions for what her eschatologically based conscientization might look like for Pentecostal churches, and Stephenson gives only three pages to praxis in her conclusion. Tackett's sections on Pentecostal eschatology and egalitarianism are too brief to develop his argument thoroughly for any specific area of study. Therefore, all three only represent partial eschatological approaches to gender and end up being augmented with other approaches; they experiment with eschatology but in the end consider it insufficient as a primary theological-orienting argument for the full liberation of Pentecostal women.

### 1.3 Conclusion and Contribution

The purpose of this chapter was to analyze and categorize recent literature on the relationship between eschatology and gender by examining how feminist theologians approach and use (or do not use) eschatology in their arguments for women's equality. The result reveals three dominant views concerning the

---

109. Tackett, "Callings," 74, 86.
110. Tackett, "Callings," 75–6.
111. Tackett, "Callings," 78.
112. Tackett, "Callings," 93–5.
113. Stephenson, *Dismantling*, 195, see also 72. She does imply that her theological paradigm is able to offer a "hermeneutical framework" for reading Luke-Acts (99).

relationship between gender and eschatology: (1) the antagonistic view, which exposes eschatology as incompatible with the quest for gender equality; (2) the agnostic view, which dismisses eschatology as irrelevant to the concerns of women; (3) the augmented view, which sees potential in eschatology for women's liberation but ultimately deems it as insufficient by itself. Each of these perspectives present potential challenges to the eschatological approach proposed in this work, while also opening the door to develop a new view, one that adopts eschatology as a liberative tool for the full flourishing of Christian women.

We can conclude there is no work, Pentecostal or otherwise, that is entirely dedicated to the relationship of gender to eschatology (or vice versa) and that follows an eschatological framework consistently in a way that resolves the complexities of the gender question. The consequence of the current feminist antagonism or ambivalence toward eschatology is it implies a choice: one must choose between participation in the this-worldly feminist quest for equality or the otherworldly male-driven eschatological imagination, for they cannot work together.[114] Some antagonist perspectives even go out of their way to criticize specifically Pentecostal eschatology as part of the problem.[115] All these works determine that a robust eschatological hope cannot adequately address the varied present-day concerns of women in the church nor act as an authoritative method for solving a problem such as the Pentecostal gender paradox. What the remaining chapters argue is that Pentecostal eschatology surprisingly emerges out of this mostly antagonistic history as a valuable dialogue partner in the quest to implement egalitarian ideals in the church. An eschatological resolving of the Pentecostal gender problem may be the authoritative and authentically Pentecostal method needed to finally end the gender debate.

To make a meaningful and lasting contribution to the gender issue in Pentecostalism and to avoid perpetuating the gender paradox, an argument must engage and be faithful to Pentecostal history, hermeneutics, theology, and praxis. Although general Pentecostal works that have done this are surprisingly few, including these four areas is not the unique contribution of my work. What is unique is applying an eschatological lens in all four areas to develop a thoroughly eschatological argument for the full flourishing and liberation of women in Pentecostal life. The eschatological dialectic of imagination and participation offers a clear biblical and theological mandate to both think and act eschatologically when it comes to gender, which, as the next chapter shows, is exactly what the early Pentecostals did.

---

114. See Charlotte Perkins: one must choose between a "posthumous egotism" and an "immediate altruism" (*His Religion and Hers: A Study of the Faith of Our Fathers and the Work of our Mothers* [Westport, CT: Hyperion, 1976], 46–7). But see Farley and Jones, "Introduction," xiv.

115. See 1.1.1 as well as Farley and Jones who say that an eschatology that includes the liberation of all persons is a vision different from the consumerist eschatology dominant within much of Pentecostalism and evangelicalism ("Introduction," viii).

## Chapter 2

## WOMEN AND ESCHATOLOGY IN THE
## EARLY PENTECOSTAL MOVEMENT

### IN SEARCH OF AN AUTHORIZING HERMENEUTIC

The previous chapters articulated why eschatology may have the potential to solve the Pentecostal gender paradox, the notion that the beliefs and practices of Pentecostalism are in a constant tension of competing impulses that simultaneously liberate and limit women in church leadership. To provide a valuable critical contribution to resolving the problem, a Pentecostal approach must consider the historical, biblical-theological, and ecclesiological questions surrounding the gender issue. The argument of this chapter is that eschatology functioned as an authorizing hermeneutic that legitimized the ministry of women in the first few decades of Pentecostalism because it rescinded previous perceived limitations concerning the role of women. This eschatological authorization of women in church leadership led to newfound freedoms for women as well as acceptance of their ministry by peers and parishioners. This new affirmation of women was primarily due to the belief that their present ministry was helping to bring about the future *eschaton* by fulfilling prophetic and eschatological Scriptures such as the promise that in the "last days . . . sons and daughters will prophesy" and God will pour out his Spirit on "both men and women" (Acts 2:17-18). The eschatological urgency of early Pentecostals created an egalitarian impulse that led to the unprecedented promotion and practice of gender equality in the first few decades of the movement.

Beginning with a historical approach is important because many Pentecostal scholars argue the first few decades represent the "heart" of the Pentecostal movement and are foundational for Pentecostalism's ongoing beliefs and practices.[1] The beginnings of the Pentecostal movement are often considered the height of women in leadership and in prominent positions. Therefore, potentially locating the early eschatological motivations that contributed to the increased participation of women is key for building an eschatological basis for the full flourishing and unhindered inclusion of women in all parts of contemporary Pentecostal life and

---

1. See 2.3.

ministry. A (re)discovery of how early Pentecostals used eschatological texts and beliefs to legitimize and authorize women in leadership will also validate how the approaches in the subsequent chapters on hermeneutics and ecclesiology are in step with the historical heart of the movement.

The primary interest of this work and this chapter is first in Pentecostal women leaders and how applying the methodological lens of eschatology addresses the gender paradox. However, an undeniable interdependence emerges between eschatology and egalitarianism in a way that reflects this work's dialectic of imagination and participation. That is, just as the ministry of women was buttressed by the eschatological fervor of early Pentecostals, so also the eschatological convictions of early Pentecostals were intensified by their experience of a Spirit-inspired egalitarianism. The historical evidence presented in this chapter demonstrates how the egalitarian impulse and eschatological fervor of early Pentecostals are intimately and mutually related, a pattern that runs throughout the rest of this book.

This chapter begins by presenting the methodology used in reading the primary texts and laying out the historical and contextual parameters of the research. The hypothesis that eschatology functioned as an authorizing hermeneutic for the ministry of women is then tested through primary sources and three case studies of prominent Pentecostal women: Maria Woodworth-Etter, Zelma Argue, and Aimee Semple McPherson. Through their writings, I contend that they privately overcame their doubts about women in the pulpit through biblical eschatological texts and images, which they then also used publicly to legitimize their ministries in the eyes of others. After the historical analysis, I defend the importance of considering Pentecostal origins for developing any significant contribution to Pentecostal belief and practice. One defining characteristic of the first few decades of Pentecostalism was the unprecedented increase of women leaders. After briefly sketching that history, I draw conclusions concerning how eschatological thinking led to egalitarian practices in the early Pentecostal movement, and how these findings might instruct the construction of a contemporary Pentecostal eschatological–egalitarian hermeneutic in the ensuing chapters.

## 2.1 Methodology and Parameters

My historical investigation of classical Pentecostalism uses what I term a feminist-functional interpretive approach.[2] My goal in proceeding in this manner is to read and analyze the historical material in a way that connects Pentecostalism with its power to liberate and empower through its eschatological message of hope that gave all—especially women—a sense of participation in the divine

---

2. See Augustus Cerillo Jr. and Grant Wacker, "Bibliography and Historiography of Pentecostalism in the United States," in *NIDPCM*, 397–405. They lay out four approaches (providential, genetic, multicultural, and functional). My approach combines the functional and multicultural (with feminist rather than racial emphases).

plan of God, which gave them new authority and purpose.³ The goal is not so much to trace the antecedents behind their eschatological egalitarian practices (although I briefly use this genetic approach), nor is it to determine whether or not the new empowerment women experienced was actually a part of the divine plan (a providential approach). A feminist-functional approach seeks to uncover the stories of women and how they and others interpreted and justified their newfound freedoms, in this case looking especially at how eschatology might have helped their cause. Therefore, we are looking for how early observers and participants interpreted what was happening and the role they saw women play in bringing about and participating in the *eschaton*. This historical approach stands up to scholarly scrutiny while still respecting and taking seriously the philosophy of history early Pentecostals themselves held.

Before investigating how the eschatological imagination fueled egalitarian practices in early Pentecostalism, we must first lay out the scope and parameters of the historical research and what is meant by "early Pentecostals." The focus of this chapter and this project is on North American classical Pentecostals, with emphasis on the Assemblies of God USA and the Pentecostal Assemblies of Canada (PAOC). The "early" or "formative" years of these movements include the period from the birth of Pentecostalism in 1901 to the end of the 1920s. Charles Barfoot and Gerald Sheppard describe two eras of Pentecostalism: "Prophetic Pentecostalism" (1901–20s), marked by increased equality for women, and "Priestly Pentecostalism" (1930–present), which saw the rapid decline of the influence of women.⁴ Similarly in his work on the Assemblies of God, Howard Kenyon argues that the "pre-organizational era" from 1901 to 1914 was the height of openness to women leaders and preachers. After organizations officially formed (1914 for the Assemblies of God, 1919 for the PAOC), Kenyon states the prophetic edge of the pioneer years that led to women in leadership was largely gone within ten years of their formation, and by the late 1920s more conservative and restrictive attitudes toward women began to form.⁵ Therefore, these first few decades provide the primary testing ground for the argument that eschatology significantly influenced the authorization of early egalitarian practices for Pentecostals.

---

3. Cerillo and Wacker, "Bibliography," 404–5.

4. Barfoot and Sheppard, "Prophetic vs. Priestly," 4–10. Barfoot and Sheppard call the 1927 General Council of the AG a "watershed" moment and "the discernible demarcation line between 'Prophetic' and 'Priestly' Pentecostalism" (11).

5. Howard N. Kenyon, "An Analysis of Ethical Issues in the History of the Assemblies of God" (PhD diss., Baylor University, 1988), 278–80. *After* my extensive reading of this unpublished dissertation from 1988 for my research, it was finally published in 2019 for Pickwick's Pentecostals, Peacemaking, and Social Justice series. See Howard N. Kenyon, *Ethics in the Age of the Sprit: Race, Women, War, and the Assemblies of God* (Eugene, OR: Pickwick, 2019). Although the newer work remains largely the same (but a bit shorter), the page numbers do not match. Therefore, the citations throughout my work correspond to the dissertation.

The most significant primary sources are the inaugural and earliest issues of the major Pentecostal periodicals in each country, primarily *The Apostolic Faith* of the Azusa Street mission and revival and *The Promise* of the early Toronto revival. These issues contain a high volume of reports about women preachers, leaders, and evangelists, and therefore contain the earliest indications of how leaders sought to articulate and legitimize the never-before-seen freedoms being given to women. The goal is not to conduct an exhaustive historical study, but to construct the patterns that will inform the approaches in the following chapters and to show whether they are in line with the historical heart of the movement, an important criterion for many Pentecostal scholars as explained in section 2.3. The only exceptions to the aforementioned parameters are when people under direct discussion (such as the case studies) are specifically mentioned in later periodicals. For the case studies, I widen my reading to include any autobiographies and select writings and sermons that specifically attempt to defend women's authority to preach. Because this chapter is part of a larger argument and not a comprehensive historical work, I limit myself to some of the more widely read sources from the time in order to establish what I believe was the dominant pattern for authorizing the ministry of women in the early years of the movement.

According to historian Grant Wacker, there are two primary methodological challenges when it comes to researching and telling the story of women in early Pentecostalism.[6] First, the question on women's place in the revival is anachronistic, often "wringing answers from data not designed to provide such answers [which] creates distortions." Although it is true moderns are more interested in gender issues than the earliest Pentecostals, I question Wacker's presupposition that the issue of women leaders "ranked fairly low" on the list of concerns of early writers. I hope to show that some of the earliest men and women leaders intentionally put the issue front and center, usually in celebration, and sought ways to legitimize biblically what they were experiencing in order to sustain and promote egalitarian practices. Second, Wacker suggests that men wrote most of the relevant texts. The question here is what is deemed to be the "relevant" texts? Wacker is referring to official denominational publications and published historical accounts. However, most of those texts are not from the first few decades and do not reflect the height of women's freedoms and the earliest attempts at authorizing their ministry; hence, they are outside of the historical parameters of this chapter. In addition, as evangelical historian Sarah Williams argues, focusing only on official statements or questions of authority and "who's in charge?" is limiting and distorts our understanding of gender history, for it downplays the "myriad and subtle ways in which influence is wielded."[7] What this chapter seeks to construct are the

---

6. See Wacker, *Heaven Below*, 158–9, for discussion of these two challenges and the proceeding quotations.

7. Williams, "Evangelicals and Gender," 272–3. Williams goes through five unhelpful underlying assumptions that often preoccupy historical works on gender, the first of which is "who is in charge?"

earliest patterns within the Pentecostal movement for explaining the newfound legitimization of women in ministry. In other words, what was the initial thrust that caused women to find a central place in the movement, even if that original pattern faded in later years when it came time for "official" statements? It is to that question we now turn.

## 2.2 Eschatology as Authorizing Hermeneutic for Women

### 2.2.1 Background: Nineteenth-Century Foundations

The seeds of eschatological authorization were planted in the Wesleyan and Holiness traditions, which laid the foundation for the Pentecostal movement of the early twentieth century.[8] Perhaps the most well-known justification for the ministry of women in the nineteenth century was Phoebe Palmer's *The Promise of the Father*. Palmer links the eschatological outpouring of the Spirit narrated in the Joel 2 and Acts 2 passages as an authorizing tool for the ministry of women and as a hermeneutical key for discussing the problematic passages that presumably limit women in the church.[9] A. J. Gordon, an early fundamentalist leader of the late 1800s who had a profound effect on early Pentecostal leaders, also used Joel's prophecy as his biblical basis and foundational text for the ministry of women.[10] Like Palmer, Gordon argued that all other Scripture, and particularly problematic passages regarding women, needed to be interpreted in light of this eschatological text.[11] He asserts that just "as in civil legislation, no law can be enacted which conflicts with the constitution, so in Scripture we shall expect to find no text which denies

---

8. For Wesleyan-Holiness roots of Pentecostalism, see Dayton, *Theological Roots*; Cerillo and Wacker, "Bibliography," 399; Griffith and Roebuck, "Women," 1203. For some examples of an emerging egalitarian (and eschatological) hermeneutic among women in the nineteenth century, see Chapter 5 in Joy A. Schroeder and Marion Ann Taylor, *Voices Long Silenced: Women Biblical Interpreters through the Centuries* (Louisville, KY: Westminster John Knox, 2022), 151–207, and esp. 158–62 for Wesleyan-Holiness interpreters.

9. Phoebe Palmer, *The Promise of the Father; or, A Neglected Specialty of the Last Days* (Boston: Henry V. Degan, 1859), 49–51. See also discussion in Schroeder and Taylor, *Voices Long Silenced*, 161.

10. See his article in *The Alliance Weekly*, reprinted over fifty years after his death in 1895: Adoniram Judson (A. J.) Gordon, "The Ministry of Women," *The Alliance Weekly*, May 1, 1948, 277–8, 286. Original publication: Adoniram Judson Gordon, "The Ministry of Women," *Missionary Review of the World* 7 (1894): 910–21. Subsequent citations refer to the reprint. I am indebted to Howard Kenyon, "Ethical Issues," 188–91 for some of these insights on Gordon.

11. See Gordon's discussion of the more problematic passages ("Ministry of Women," 278–86).

to woman her divinely appointed rights in the new dispensation."[12] Thus, without naming it, Gordon was using an eschatological hermeneutic to authorize the ministry of women. Recognizing this step is important because Gordon's thinking of Joel's prophecy as "the *Magna Carta* of the Christian Church" became a classic Pentecostal argument: the day of Pentecost ushered in equal privilege between men and women, a new eschatological age that rescinded former positions.[13]

The Wesleyan-Holiness groups of the nineteenth century laid the foundation for the Pentecostal movement and its eventual authorization of a new egalitarian paradigm. But despite the similarities, most scholars agree that the Holiness movement did not lead to the same prominence for women or same type of movement toward equality that early Pentecostalism had. What changed at the onset of the Pentecostal movement? The Pentecostal movement intensified these foundational beliefs and set them on a new trajectory through a heightened eschatological imagination.[14] Land specifically argues that although the ministry of women was a significant part of the Wesleyan-Holiness inheritance, it was the Pentecostal "eschatological intensification" of these restorationist themes that led to a complete paradigm shift.[15] Instead of only looking back to the restorationist texts of the New Testament (such as Acts 2), what gave Pentecostal practices their distinctiveness from other groups was how their practices were shaped by an eschatological orientation. In this way, says Land, certain practices were now "seen as readiness for and anticipations of the end" where "the believer is shaped for and expressed the foretaste of the kingdom."[16] This insight reveals a key point for the discussion of primary sources, namely, the eschatological dialectic of imagination and participation. More than being a movement that looked back to participate in a form of primitive Christianity, early Pentecostals imaginatively looked forward, which inspired their desire to participate now in the kingdom that is to come.[17] This line of thinking was key to how Pentecostals authorized the newfound freedoms of women. Whereas only looking *back* to the New Testament church eventually leads to hesitancy, hermeneutical uncertainty, and paradoxical messages regarding the role of women, early Pentecostals sought to look *forward* and prioritized eschatological texts to confidently authorize the ministry of women.

12. Gordon, "Ministry of Women," 277.

13. Gordon specifically calls the Pentecost proclamation the hermeneutical *Magna Carta* for understanding biblical admonitions on the work of women (Gordon, "Ministry of Women," 277–8). See Kenyon, "Ethical Issues," 189; Tackett, "Callings," 77.

14. See Payne, *Gender*, 7.

15. Land, *Pentecostal Spirituality*, 43, 89–90, 184; cf. 119. This is also the argument of Dayton, *Theological Roots*, and Faupel, *Everlasting Gospel*, 75–114. Both explore the nineteenth-century American Wesleyan-Holiness roots of Pentecostalism and argue that what birthed Pentecostalism as a new movement was its eschatological emphasis.

16. Land, *Pentecostal Spirituality*, 89, 173.

17. See 3.1.1 for my discussion on this development and the difference between restorationist and eschatological Pentecostalism.

## 2.2.2 Early Writings and Periodicals

Eschatology played a leading role in the initial egalitarian impulse of early Pentecostals. Some of the earliest circulated written materials sought to articulate and authorize the newfound freedoms of women through the lens of eschatological thought. At the turn of the century in Topeka, Kansas, where the Pentecostal movement in North America was essentially launched, Charles Parham expressed the purpose of his Bible school through the lens of eschatological urgency: "to fit men and women to go to the ends of the earth to preach," preparing the way for the return of the Lord.[18] At Parham's school, Agnes Ozman was the first person to be baptized in the Holy Spirit with the evidence of speaking in tongues. The Spirit baptism of this thirty-year-old woman preacher was seen as fulfilling the "all flesh" prophecy of Joel 2:28-29. In her autobiography, Ozman wrote that when she and some other women learned about the second coming of Jesus, "our hearts gladly responded to the call from the Word to be ready ourselves and also to preach to others."[19]

The very first issue of *The Apostolic Faith* out of Azusa Street spends most of its pages articulating the eschatological framework of the movement and how that eschatological imagination is informing their practices, particularly the sending out of women. People heard a messenger from God say that "Jesus is coming. Go forward in My name, preach the Gospel of the Kingdom, for the King's business demands haste. My people have only time to get on the beautiful garments, and prepare for the wedding supper in the Heavens."[20] The front page proclaims that

> many are the prophesies spoken in unknown tongues and many the visions that God is giving concerning His soon coming. The heathen must first receive the gospel. One prophecy given, in an unknown tongue was interpreted, "The time is short, and I am going to send out a large number in the Spirit of God to preach the full gospel in the power of the Spirit."[21]

The evidence suggests many, if not most, of this "large number" sent out were women.

Much of the first issue of *Apostolic Faith* spends time documenting the stories and testimonies of women being called by God to go preach the gospel.[22] Sister

---

18. From his tract "The Latter Rain," reprinted in his biography by Sarah E. Parham, *The Life of Charles F. Parham, Founder of the Apostolic Faith Movement* (1930; repr., New York: Garland, 1985), 51. See also David G. Roebuck, "Loose the Women," *Christian History* 17, no. 2 (1998): 58.

19. Agnes N. Ozman, *What God Hath Wrought: Life and Work of Mrs. Agnes N. O. LaBerge* (n.d.; repr., New York: Garland, 1985), 17-18.

20. Anna Hall, "Jesus is Coming," *AF* 1, no. 1 (September 1906): 4.

21. "The Old-Time Pentecost," *AF* 1, no. 1 (September 1906): 1.

22. Although this list is my own, Faupel also spends significant space documenting the number of women sent out in response to these eschatological prophecies (see *Everlasting Gospel*, 220-6).

Wettosh, a German sister of Pasadena, received the gift of tongues and "has gone out to carry this Gospel" to Reno, Nevada.[23] It is reported that there are "Christian workers who . . . having been called of God from other line of employment to devote their time in praying with the sick, preaching, working with souls at the altar, etc." are often working without pay. And the primary example given is of "a sister who was called to Oakland" and for whom the Lord miraculously provided funds.[24] Lucy Farrow is described as a messenger of the gospel and

> God's anointed handmaid, who came some four months ago from Houston, Texas, to Los Angeles, bringing the full Gospel, and whom God has greatly used as she laid her hands on many who have received the Pentecost and the gift of tongues, has now returned to Houston, en route to Norfolk, Va. This is her old home which she left as a girl, being sold into slavery in the south. The Lord, she feels, is now calling her back.[25]

These stories of women were interpreted as signs of "the last Pentecostal revival to bring our Jesus. The church is taking her last march to meet her beloved."[26] These women found their boldness to preach from the eschatological urgency that "Jesus is Coming," the title of the section that prints the "vision and revelation" of Anna Hall who came to Los Angeles to assist "in response to the call of God."[27]

Similarly in Canada, the inaugural issue of *The Apostolic Messenger* out of Winnipeg, Manitoba, contains articles and testimonies written by women (at least equal to the number of men) and stories of women being sent out urgently to preach the gospel.[28] Of the seven updates given of people sent out on mission, six involve women leaving their homes, including Sister T. McCloud who left to attend an apostolic missionary school in Alliance, OH, Sister R. Murdoch who has been "laboring" at the mission and is now "holding meetings" in Saskatchewan, Sister Lockhart who is "holding meetings at Oxbow, Calgary and other points in the West," and Sister Newsham "who has been preaching holiness for years" and is now leaving for Vancouver, British Columbia.[29] A testimony of being baptized in the Spirit at the Mission in Winnipeg at 501 Alexander Ave. is written by "Mrs.

---

23. "Tongues as a Sign," *AF* 1, no. 1 (September 1906): 2. The original actually says "Reno, Neb." but is likely a mistake and meant to say "Reno, Nev."

24. "Pentecostal Faith Line," *AF* 1, no. 1 (September 1906): 3.

25. "The Old-Time Pentecost," 1.

26. "Missionaries to Jerusalem," *AF* 1, no. 1 (September 1906): 4.

27. Hall, "Jesus is Coming," 4. See Estrelda Y. Alexander, *The Women of Azusa Street* (Cleveland, OH: The Pilgrim, 2005), 130–1.

28. *The Apostolic Messenger* 1, no. 1 (February/March 1908). See the articles on prayer on pages 1 and 3.

29. Untitled Testimonies, *The Apostolic Messenger* 1, no. 1 (February/March 1908): 2.

(Rev.) Maria E. North" from Whitewater, Manitoba.[30] Previous pages contain more testimonies from women, including from Sisters Saunders and Flett whom "God has been using to help many precious souls."[31] An article entitled "A Gentile's Pentecost in the 20th Century" is written by "Evangelist" Ella M. Goff.[32] These stories of women preaching, being sent out on their own, holding meetings, and pastoring souls take place in the context of and sometimes sandwiched between articles like "Jesus is Coming Soon," "What is Meant by the Latter Rain," "This is That," and "The Last Days."[33] Pentecostal eschatology opened new doors of ministry and new opportunities for spiritual leadership for women in Canada.

The remaining three *Apostolic Faith* issues from the 1906 inaugural year continue a similar pattern. After being baptized with the Spirit, Florence Reed Crawford became one of the most influential women of early Pentecostalism, even founding a denomination (Apostolic Faith Mission) and later becoming editor of *The Apostolic Faith*. Though she had no previous preaching experience, she drew large crowds on the revival circuit and was responsible for many people's first encounter with Spirit baptism, some of whom would later become important players at Azusa.[34] She proclaims,

> I *must* go out and tell this story. Souls are perishing far and near. The Lord told me yesterday to go into all the world and preach His Gospel. "The kingdom of heaven is at hand" and "Behold, I come quickly." What He says to me, He says to every baptized soul. He wants us to go out into the highways and hedges and declare this Gospel. He has anointed me to tell the story of Jesus and I can go alone for Jesus is with me. O, glory to God![35]

Though she wished to stay at "home" at Azusa, it was eschatological urgency that moved her to preach.

In that same October 1906 issue, in an article titled "Back to Pentecost," one of the signs of the inbreaking of the kingdom is that "a young sister, fourteen years old, was saved, sanctified, and baptized with the Holy Ghost and went out, taking a band of workers with her, and led a revival in which one hundred and ninety souls were saved."[36] There is also an update on the ministry of Lucy Farrow, a

---

30. Maria E. North, "A Testimony," *The Apostolic Messenger* 1, no. 1 (February/March 1908): 3.

31. Untitled Testimonies, *The Apostolic Messenger* 1, no. 1 (February/March 1908): 1-2.

32. Ella M. Goff, "A Gentile's Pentecost in the 20th Century," *The Apostolic Messenger* 1, no. 1 (February/March 1908): 2.

33. *The Apostolic Messenger* 1, no. 1 (February/March 1908): 3-4.

34. See Alexander, *Women of Azusa*, 65.

35. Untitled section but under "Letters from Bro. Johnson," *AF* 1, no. 2 (October 1906): 3; italics mine. See also Alexander's chapter on Florence Reed Crawford in *Women of Azusa*, 59-70.

36. "Back to Pentecost," *AF* 1, no. 2 (October 1906): 3.

black woman and one of the most important (although overlooked) figures of the early movement. She writes in her update entitled "The Work in Virginia": "God is making a short work in the earth today. He is soon coming to earth again. He said we should not get over the cities until the Son of Man should come, so we have not much time to lose."[37] In their mind, the "soon coming" return of Jesus led to an eschatological urgency that rescinded previous limitations on women. It is reported in the next month's issue that the Joel 2/Acts 2 outpouring of the Spirit at Azusa meant that "all were equal . . . No instrument that God can use is rejected . . . this is why God has so built up this work."[38] The last *Apostolic Faith* issue of 1906 unapologetically describes two women as "at present *in charge*" of the mission in Woodland, California.[39]

Over the course of 1907, the eschatological authorization of egalitarian practices continued. The January *Apostolic Faith* issue features a testimony from the Akron revival led by Ivy Glenshaw Campbell, which proclaims that "the burden of everyone that has received their personal Pentecost is 'Jesus is coming soon.'"[40] That burden and the eschatological imagination that came with it led to regular articles continuing to validate the full inclusion of women. The eschatological texts of Joel 2:28, Acts 2:17-18, and Galatians 3:28 are repeatedly used to authorize this new wave of women leaders, preachers, and messengers.[41] Under the main title "In the Last Days" and a quotation of Acts 2:17, the June to September issue features stories of "young women" and even a "little girl" boldly preaching to "unconverted" male skeptics and denouncers who are "visibly affected by the message" and confess they cannot refuse these women's demonstrations of the power of God.[42] A later quotation of Joel 2/Acts 2 concludes that just as the women in Acts "received the power along with the men. . . . So we women have a part in this Gospel. Hallelujah to my God!"[43] These affirmations, among others, are sandwiched between the eschatological inclusio of the main headline "In the Last Days" and the closing song sheet on the final page for "Jesus is Coming."

The September 1907 issue argues that Jesus qualified both men and women to minister and preach the gospel, concluding "In Christ Jesus there is neither male

---

37. "The Work in Virginia," *AF* 1, no. 2 (October 1906): 3. See Alexander's chapter on Lucy Farrow in *Women of Azusa*, 39–46.

38. "Bible Pentecost," *AF* 1, no. 3 (November 1906): 1.

39. "Pentecost in Woodland," *AF* 1, no. 4 (December 1906): 1; italics mine.

40. Pearl Bowen, "Akron Visited with Pentecost," *AF* 1, no. 5 (January 1907): 1. See Alexander's chapter on Ivy Glenshaw Campbell in *Women of Azusa*, 139–49.

41. See McQueen, *Pentecostal Eschatology*, 62n9. See 4.3 for why Galatians 3:28 is considered an eschatological text.

42. See "The 'Latter Rain' in Zion, Ill." and "In Minneapolis, Minn." under the heading of "In the Last Days," *AF* 1, no. 9 (June–September 1907): 1.

43. "The Promise of the Father and Speaking in Tongues in Chicago," *AF* 1, no. 9 (June–September 1907): 3.

nor female, all are one" (Gal. 3:28).[44] Early Pentecostals believed Pentecost initiated the new eschatological age where both men and women could be mouthpieces of the Lord. One of the defining articles is "Who May Prophesy," found in the January 1908 issue of *Apostolic Faith*. It conveys the idea that "before Pentecost" the Lord only spoke directly to men, but after the Spirit was poured out at Pentecost,

> God baptized them all in the same room and made no difference. All the women received the anointed oil of the Holy Ghost and were able to preach the same as the men . . . It is contrary to the Scriptures that women should not have her part in the salvation work to which God has called her. We have no right to lay a straw in her way . . . It is the same Holy Spirit in the woman as in the man.[45]

Women could now preach with the same authority as men because of the new eschatological age brought about by the Spirit.

Even this very brief survey of some of the earliest periodicals reveals a strikingly egalitarian movement that consistently authorizes the ministry of women in eschatological terms. One of the main signs of the new era of the Spirit of God and the last days was the leadership and preaching of women. Early issues of *The Apostolic Faith* equally reported on the ministry of women and men and included articles and testimonies written by both. Marie Griffith and David Roebuck even claim that early Pentecostal denominational periodicals contain far *more* contributions from women than men, especially in the testimonies sections.[46] Kenyon says that prior to 1914, *The Christian Evangel* rarely printed an issue without a report of some women's activity.[47] Within Azusa and outside of it as it spread, several early Pentecostal papers and periodicals were run, edited, and mostly written by women.[48] As both the American and Canadian histories highlight, the first and some of the earliest adopters and receivers of tongues-speech were women, which contributed to their centrality in the movement. And they often articulated their experience and authorized their leadership with the Joel 2/Acts 2 message that these are the last days and "Jesus is coming soon."

Although most of the writings and reports cited above are either anonymous or written by women, there is evidence that men also looked to eschatology as an authorizing hermeneutic for women in leadership. In his historical research, Wacker confirms that the earliest Pentecostal periodicals are quite evenly split between male and female authors, with men writing most of the official

---

44. "Pentecostal Notes," *AF* 1, no. 10 (September 1907): 3.
45. "Who May Prophesy," *AF* 1, no. 12 (January 1908): 2.
46. Griffith and Roebuck, "Women," 1206.
47. Kenyon, "Ethical Issues," 178.
48. For example, see evangelist and novelist Mae Eleanor Frey's *The Gospel Highway* out of Los Angeles.

publications, which mostly highlight the contributions of men to the movement.[49] But when men *did* talk about the central place of women in the movement, they authorized this new egalitarianism and rescinded previous limitations by using eschatological arguments. Their early endorsement of prophesying daughters was built on their eschatological commitment,[50] as evidenced by the writings of some the most well-known male figures.

From early on, Azusa Street mission pastor William J. Seymour defended women's involvement through eschatological texts such as Galatians 3:28.[51] Seymour's vision for equality was heavily based on eschatology and the outpouring of the Spirit in Acts 2.[52] One of the early documenters of the Pentecostal movement, Frank Bartleman, explains that one sign the Spirit was being poured out in these last days was that there was no need for hierarchy for God "might speak through whom He would. He had poured out His Spirit '*on all flesh*' (Acts 2:17), even on His '*servants and . . . handmaidens*' (verse 18)."[53] Several oft-cited quotes from male Pentecostal leaders in the mid-1910s justify the new ministry of women being experienced in terms of eschatological authorization. In *The Weekly Evangel*, A. G. Jeffries called the great movement of women in the early twentieth century a sign of the end times, writing that

> A marked feature of this "latter day" outpouring is the Apostolate of women. . . . They did not push themselves to the front, God *pulled* them. They did not take this ministry on themselves, God *put* it on them. Today more than one-half of the missionary force is composed of women. . . . preaching and working in every way conceivable.[54]

In his apology for women in ministry, Walter V. Grant claimed that twentieth-century women preachers are God-given signs that these are the last days.[55] Stephen Merritt, a wealthy New York City undertaker, makes a strong eschatological argument for the ministry of women in a magazine published by an Assemblies of God congregation in Manhattan:

---

49. Wacker, *Heaven Below*, 159.

50. Tackett, "Callings," 74.

51. The "Pentecostal Notes" section where this is articulated is usually attributed to Seymour. See *AF* 1, no. 10 (September 1907): 3.

52. Althouse, *Moltmann*, 34. For more on the eschatology of Seymour, including comparison with Parham's eschatology, see Althouse, *Moltmann*, 24–36.

53. Frank Bartleman, *Azusa Street* (New Kensington, PA: Whitaker House, 1982), 95; italics in the original.

54. A. G. Jeffries, "The Limit of Divine Revelation," *Weekly Evangel*, March 18, 1916, 6; italics in the original.

55. Walter V. Grant, *Putting the Women in Their Place* (Dallas: Grant's Faith Clinic, n.d.), quoted in David G. Roebuck, "Pentecostal Women in Ministry: A Review of Selected Documents," *Perspectives in Religious Studies* 16, no. 1 (Spring 1989): 38.

As the Holy Ghost takes sway and control, women rise in place, position and power.... In these days of promise, these 'latter days,' there is an overturning, an awakening, an enlargement of vision. Woman under the anointing and imbuing of the Holy Ghost is to be a great factor in the ... work of these latter days... . Every woman should receive and honor the Holy Ghost, as He is the Great Emancipator, and the blessed Equalizer, and as He controls, He brings in the equality of the sexes.[56]

The eschatological argument for egalitarianism was not a hermeneutic used only by women for women, but an important way of thinking for men as well.

Augustus Cerillo Jr. and Wacker explain that although Pentecostals believed in God's providential guidance of history, they simultaneously saw themselves as affecting the timing of God's actions in history, particularly in helping move things to their ultimate end.[57] Although the historian may look to other reasons for the rise of women's voices, it is important to unearth how these women and men themselves articulated what was happening, their own philosophy of history that included the eschatological latter rain narrative.[58] As Cerillo and Wacker state, the issue was not causation but consummation, not "Where did it all come from?" but rather "What did it all mean?"[59] And for early Pentecostals, the rise of women leaders in the church meant the inbreaking of God's kingdom was among them, and therefore the ministry of women was embraced as a sign of the last days.

### 2.2.3 Three Case Studies

The above investigation into early Pentecostal writings reveals that eschatology was one of the chief ways men and women sought to grant previously denied authority to women teachers and preachers. The arguments we have seen thus far have been general. The following three brief case studies close and hopefully solidify the argument that eschatology rescinded previous perceived limitations on early Pentecostal women by acting as an authorizing hermeneutic that legitimized their ministries.

The lives and ministries of Maria Woodworth-Etter, Zelma Argue, and Aimee Semple McPherson represent a broad spectrum to test the argument of this chapter within the historical and contextual parameters laid out. Together they represent examples of old, young, and middle-aged, married, single, and divorced women from rural and urban settings, all who were able to establish influential ministries in the first few decades of the movement in Canada and the United States. Their stories reveal a pattern of women who initially struggled with their call to ministry

---

56. Stephen Merritt, "Women," *Midnight Cry*, March 6, 1919, quoted in Blumhofer, *Restoring the Faith*, 171. See also Qualls, *Forgive Us*, 121.
57. Cerillo and Wacker, "Bibliography," 392.
58. Wacker, *Heaven Below*, 164.
59. Cerillo and Wacker, "Bibliography," 395.

but who overcame doubts concerning their legitimacy by appealing to the eschatological imagination. They cut through the prevailing gender limitations of the day by applying an eschatological hermeneutic to scriptural texts. These three women are significant studies because each of them rarely addresses the issue of women in leadership—usually preferring to let their lives speak—but when they do, they almost always use eschatological language to authorize their ministries. Each case study first briefly considers one or two primary sources written by the woman under study where they discuss the topic of women's roles. I then consult a contemporary study of the woman's work that (re)affirms how these women overcame previous limitations through an appeal to eschatology.

### 2.2.3.1 Maria Woodworth-Etter

Maria Beulah Woodworth-Etter (1844–1924) was already in her sixties when she embraced the Pentecostal message at the dawn of the Pentecostal revival.[60] She was known for her healing services and sometimes attracted as many as five thousand people per night to her revival meetings.[61] However, before that, despite receiving a call to ministry, she struggled greatly due to having been taught women belonged in the home and not in the pulpit.[62] After her conversion to Pentecostalism, what changed her mind and emboldened her ministry were the eschatological promises of Scripture and her belief she was participating in the last days described in those texts. Her post-Pentecostal conversion messages contain a constant sense of expectancy for Christ's return that broke down divisions among those present.[63]

In her sermon "Women's Rights in the Gospel" printed in her 1916 book *Signs and Wonders*, she gives a stirring defense of women in the New Testament and in Paul's ministry, quoting Galatians 3:28.[64] After her biblical defense of women in leadership, Woodworth-Etter turns her attention to the present day:

> "I will pour out in the last days of my Spirit"; that refers in a special manner to these last days in which we are now living. God is promising great blessings and power to qualify His handmaidens for the last great harvest just before the

---

60. For more on her life see Kenyon, "Ethical Issues," 179–88; Payne, *Gender*, 2–4.

61. For example, her five months of revival meetings in Dallas (see Faupel, *Everlasting Gospel*, 273).

62. Kenyon, "Ethical Issues," 180.

63. Faupel, *Everlasting Gospel*, 275.

64. Maria Woodworth-Etter, "Women's Rights in the Gospel," in *Signs and Wonders God Wrought in the Ministry for Forty Years* (Indianapolis: n.p., 1916). See also the reprint edition, *A Diary of Signs and Wonders: A Classic* (Tulsa, OK: Harrison House, 1980). The sermon is also reprinted in the chapter "Maria Beulah Woodworth-Etter," in *A Reader in Pentecostal Theology: Voices from the First Generation*, ed. Douglas Jacobsen (Bloomington: Indiana University Press, 2006), 24–30.

notable day of the Lord comes.... The Lord says we shall prophesy.... The Lord has promised this greatest gift to his handmaidens, and daughters.[65]

In *Signs and Wonders*, Woodworth-Etter consistently refers back to Joel's prophecy to argue for the ministry of women in the present.[66] She repeatedly cites the promise of Joel "in these last days, I will pour out my Spirit," saying, "Thank the Lord, those days are here."[67] In her later book *Marvels and Miracles* (1922), she recounts how she overcame her fear of being a woman preacher when she realized that the prophesying daughters of Joel was a necessary sign of the last days.[68]

In her recent study of Woodworth-Etter and McPherson, Leah Payne argues that neither of these women were very interested in debating the gender issue and mostly circumvented any of the problematic, restrictive texts.[69] However, they still had to find ways to overcome the gender binaries and biblical arguments used to deter women from ministry and had to find images of authority that legitimized their ministry.[70] Payne recounts how Woodworth-Etter repeatedly told stories of Deborah in the Old Testament as a warring "Mother in Israel."[71] Payne claims that this "warring mother" imagery "gave her credibility by tapping into the avid interest that holiness and Pentecostal revivalists of the era had in all things end times. She took a figure of relatively no eschatological value in the Bible, and put her at the fore of the epic battle for the fate of the world."[72] Woodworth-Etter, describes Payne, "was the Mother in Israel who would lead God's people to a final eschatological victory."[73] Woodworth-Etter was able to legitimize her calling and ministry by seeing herself as a key actor and participant in the divine eschatological drama.

---

65. Woodworth-Etter, "Women's Rights," in Jacobsen, *A Reader*, 25.
66. Woodworth-Etter, *Diary of Signs and Wonders*, 211. See also Kenyon, "Ethical Issues," 181.
67. Woodworth-Etter, "Women's Rights," in Jacobsen, *A Reader*, 28.
68. Maria Woodworth-Etter, *Marvels and Miracles: God Wrought in the Ministry of Mrs. M. B. Woodworth-Etter for Forty-Five Years* (Indianapolis: n.p., 1922); cited in Roebuck, "Pentecostal Women," 37.
69. Payne, *Gender*, 62.
70. Payne, *Gender*, 17, 35, 84.
71. See Payne, *Gender*, 44–51. For more on the significance of the Deborah story for Pentecostals and its use for empowering women, see Rick Wadholm Jr., "'Until I, Deborah, Arose' (Judges 4–5): A Pentecostal Reception History of Deborah Toward Women in Ministry," in *Receiving Scripture in the Pentecostal Tradition: A Reception History*, ed. Daniel D. Isgrigg, Martin W. Mittelstadt, Rick Wadholm Jr. (Cleveland, TN: CPT, 2021), 93–111.
72. Payne, *Gender*, 51.
73. Payne, *Gender*, 62.

## 2.2.3.2 Zelma Argue

On the other side of the border and age spectrum is Zelma Argue, a Canadian Pentecostal minister born in 1900 who started her evangelistic ministry in her late teens. Along with her younger sister Beulah, Zelma was a traveling evangelist, pastor, and prolific writer.[74] Although Zelma struggled less with doubts about the calling of women to preach, partly due to the encouragement and support of her well-known father,[75] Argue faced the unique challenge of being and remaining a single woman throughout her entire ministry. She was heavily influenced by Woodworth-Etter, and like her rarely addressed women's roles, despite being a young single woman.[76] But when she did, she typically went straight to eschatology and the last days texts of Joel 2/Acts 2 to make her argument.

In the very first issue of the *Canadian Pentecostal Testimony*, a magazine to which she would eventually contribute nearly two hundred articles,[77] Argue penned "Your Sons and Your Daughters," where she highlights "that dear familiar quotation" from Acts 2:17 to 2:18.[78] She states that the "latter rain" of the last fourteen or more years "is a sign of the last days" and that "on the strength of this passage, divinely anointed women, handmaidens of the Lord, are conceded the right to prophecy, to minister, under the power and the guidance of the Holy Spirit." She connects the authority of women to preach and lead to "spreading the last-day message" that "The Latter Rain is falling. Jesus is coming soon. Get ready to meet Him!" Regarding the response to this eschatological call, she says women can make either Eve's choice of disobedience or Mary's choice of obedience, "the choice that brought the SAVIOUR into the world."[79] She ends by encouraging all—young and old, men and women—to "Get the vision! Bear the message! Haste! 'For yet a little while and He that shall come will come, and will not tarry.'"

---

74. Argue wrote four books: *What Meaneth This?* (Later renamed *Contending for the Faith*), *The Vision and Vow of a Canadian Maiden*, *Garments of Strength*, and *Practical Christian Living*.

75. See Linda Ambrose, "Zelma and Beulah Argue: Sisters in the Canadian Pentecostal Movement," in *Winds from the North: Canadian Contributions to the Pentecostal Movement*, ed. Michael Wilkinson and Peter Althouse (Leiden: Brill, 2010), 105–7.

76. For Woodworth-Etter's influence see Ambrose, "Zelma," 105–7; Pamela M. S. Holmes, "Zelma Argue's Theological Contribution to Early Pentecostalism," in Wilkinson and Althouse, *Winds from the North*, 136.

77. See Peter D. Hocken, "Argue, Zelma," in *NIDPCM*, 331; Ambrose, "Zelma," 114. She contributed a similar amount to the Assemblies of God periodical *The Pentecostal Evangel*.

78. Zelma Argue, "Your Sons and Your Daughters," *Canadian Pentecostal Testimony* 1 (December 1920): 3. All quotes in this paragraph are from this article, which is all on a single page. The inaugural issue itself says it will "always be kept clean-cut from all contentious issues" (4), which makes the inclusion of this article all the more significant.

79. Capitalization in the original.

In a later front-page feature article entitled "Emergency Ministries: 'The Time Is Short,'" Zelma looks for an "explanation" for the "abnormal" and never-before-seen "army of 'handmaiden' witnesses who have mysteriously appeared." Her answer is that this is a sign of the "last days . . . revival" as prophesied in Joel 2:28.[80] She argues that "before the Lord comes, some women will *have* to preach the Gospel" and that such "women proclaimers are a *necessary sign* of the coming of the Lord."[81] The best explanation, according to Argue, for women suddenly being "chosen by the Spirit and thrust forth by the Spirit" is that they are "signs" of a last days "emergency."[82]

In some of the first published work on the Argue sisters, Linda Ambrose considers how their ministries reflected themes in the larger story of North American Pentecostal women during the first half of the twentieth century.[83] She wants to know how these women—one single and one married with children—took on such large public roles over an extended period despite the prevailing traditional female roles and gendered expectations in the church.[84] Although early on they ministered and traveled alongside their father, they later set out without him as featured speakers on the merit of their own ministries, first together as sisters and then each on their own (Beulah often without her husband). Ambrose suggests that the reason they were able to accomplish this feat, something rarely seen in church history up to that time, is due to the eschatological authority they found in the Bible. Zelma used the Joel 2/Acts 2 texts "as a means to stake her claim of legitimacy because she herself was young and female."[85] She was highly esteemed not despite her youth and gender, but precisely because of it, since those factors were seen as a fulfillment of last days prophecy. Ambrose argues that the legitimacy of a young female evangelist like Zelma was shored up by the people's eschatological sense of living in the last days, a hermeneutic that overcame previous limitations that would have prevented a young, single woman from ministering and traveling on her own.[86] Similarly in her work on Argue, Pamela Holmes argues that Zelma's egalitarian teaching was primarily motivated by her eschatology; for Argue, the main factor that validated her ministry was "the immediacy of the eschatological coming of Jesus."[87] Throughout her life and ministry, Zelma used eschatology as the cornerstone for women like her to minister freely without restriction.

---

80. Zelma Argue, "Emergency Ministries: 'The Time is Short,'" *The Pentecostal Evangel*, December 2, 1939, 1, 10.
   81. Argue, "Emergency Ministries," 11; italics mine.
   82. Argue, "Emergency Ministries," 11.
   83. Ambrose, "Zelma," 99.
   84. Ambrose, "Zelma," 100.
   85. Ambrose, "Zelma," 111.
   86. See Ambrose, "Zelma," 112.
   87. Holmes, "Zelma," 130–1; see also 139–46.

*2.2.3.3 Aimee Semple McPherson*

One of the reasons the Argue sisters' father encouraged their ministry and ordination was that he previously worked alongside the ministry of a young Canadian woman named Aimee Semple McPherson.[88] Born Aimee Kennedy on a small farm in 1890 in Ingersoll, Ontario, ten kilometers from the nearest town, Aimee's rise to celebrity American pastor is one of the most unlikely and well-documented stories ever of a Christian woman.[89] Raised in a Christian home, she seemed destined for a quiet life on a Canadian farm. That is, until she encountered the full gospel message of Pentecostalism at a revival meeting in town and was "converted" in 1907 at the age of seventeen.[90] Sometime shortly after her conversion, she felt God speak to her and call her to preach the gospel, a moment she recounts in her book *This Is That*.[91] Her incredible and rapid rise to celebrity status is hard to overstate as she became one of the most recognizable figures of her time: crisscrossing the continent, speaking nightly to often over ten thousand people, appearing weekly on the front page of America's biggest newspapers, and becoming the first woman to preach over the radio. She eventually set up her permanent headquarters in Los Angeles where she founded her own denomination (International Church of the Foursquare Gospel) and built and pastored what was for a time the largest church in America in both capacity and attendance.[92] She has been called the most heralded and prominent leader Pentecostalism has produced,[93] as well as the most important ordained woman in the history of Christianity.[94]

However, a less familiar part of the story is that, especially early on, McPherson regularly felt unsure about her calling in a day and culture where

---

88. See Ambrose, "Zelma," 106–7. The same December 1920 inaugural issue of the *Canadian Pentecostal Testimony* that Zelma Argue wrote her article in states on page 1 under "Current News": "Perhaps the greatest campaign in the history of the Pentecostal work in Canada has just closed at Montreal. Aimee Semple McPherson was in charge."

89. For brief life sketches see Payne, *Gender*, 4–6; Edith Blumhofer, *The Assemblies of God: A Chapter in the Story of American Pentecostalism* (Springfield, MO: Gospel Publishing House, 1989), 1:249–53; Wacker, *Heaven Below*, 32–3; Susan C. Hyatt, "Spirit-Filled Women," in *The Century of the Holy Spirit: 100 Years of Pentecostal and Charismatic Renewal, 1901–2001*, ed. Vinson Synan (Nashville: Thomas Nelson, 2001), 248–52; Barfoot and Sheppard, "Prophetic vs. Priestly," 5–7. Several full-length biographies exist including Matthew Avery Sutton, *Aimee Semple McPherson and the Resurrection of Christian America* (Cambridge, MA: Harvard University Press, 2007) and Edith Blumhofer, *Aimee Semple McPherson: Everybody's Sister* (Grand Rapids: Eerdmans, 1993).

90. Wacker, *Heaven Below*, 32.

91. Aimee Semple McPherson, *This Is That* (1919; repr., New York: Garland, 1985), 11.

92. See Wacker, *Heaven Below*, 145, 155; Synan, *100 Years*, 135, 250; Stephenson, *Dismantling*, 53.

93. Wacker, *Heaven Below*, 145; Cecil M. Robeck Jr., "McPherson, Aimee Semple," in *NIDPCM*, 858.

94. Synan, *100 Years*, 133.

only men could preach.⁹⁵ After tragically losing her first husband to malaria on the mission field, becoming a single mother at the age of nineteen, and then marrying a businessman, she says she resisted her call and attempted to take on the traditional role of a domestic housewife. McPherson describes this as the most miserable time in her life. She wrote in 1919: "Oh, don't you ever tell me that a woman cannot be called to preach the Gospel! If any man ever went through one-hundredth part of the hell on earth that I lived in, those months when out of God's will and work [when resisting God's call to preach], they would never say that again."⁹⁶ Part of what helped McPherson overcome her questioning of her calling and gave her authorization to preach was her emerging eschatological convictions.

An eschatological zeal was foundational to McPherson's thinking and spirituality.⁹⁷ As one of her biographers describes, she was "obsessed with being ready for Christ's coming . . . Aimee latched onto the notion [that Christ would return soon] and found that it reinforced her newfound resolve to live differently."⁹⁸ One of the four tenants of her "foursquare" gospel was Jesus as soon-coming king, and McPherson consistently emphasized the importance of this belief in her preaching and actions.⁹⁹ The architecture and artwork of Angelus Temple, which she helped design, is filled with eschatological reminders. She wrote in her autobiography that she chose the blue sky with white clouds on the domed ceiling "to remind us that Jesus is coming in the clouds of glory so that I and others might look up at it while preaching and wonder, 'Jesus are you coming during this service? Will I be ready to meet you with souls if you come right now?'"¹⁰⁰ Another window in the building pictured McPherson and the apostles anticipating the Second Coming as McPherson preaches. One of McPherson's favorite metaphors was picturing herself as the bride and Jesus as the coming bridegroom who was "near" and "at the door."¹⁰¹ She titled her publications *The Bridal Call* and at times dressed herself as a bride in preparation for his return.¹⁰² Although the eschatological drive behind McPherson's ministry is a worthy examination on its own, what is often overlooked is how she utilized the popular eschatological imagination and zeal of her time to authorize her ministry and to overcome her own and others' doubts about a woman in the pulpit.

---

95. Stephenson, *Dismantling*, 51.
96. McPherson, *This is That*, 76; information in brackets mine.
97. See Robert Cornwall, "Primitivism and the Redefinition of Dispensationalism in the Theology of Aimee Semple McPherson," *Pneuma* 14 (Spring 1992): 23–42.
98. Blumhofer, *Aimee Semple McPherson*, 64; information in brackets mine.
99. For examples, see Payne, *Gender*, 109–11.
100. Aimee Semple McPherson, *The Life Story of Aimee Semple McPherson* (Los Angeles: Foursquare Publications, 1979), 124.
101. See her sermon, "As a Bride Adorned: Glowing Sermon on the Glorious Second Coming of Christ," *The Bridal Call* 9, no. 9 (1926): 3.
102. See discussion in Payne, *Gender*, 62, 80.

McPherson is an interesting case study because she rarely addresses the issue of female preachers, but when she does, she almost always solely refers to eschatology and the eschatological texts of Joel 2/Acts 2 as the most convincing apology for her and other women's right to minister.[103] As a close reading of her books and messages reveals, McPherson was quite regularly plagued by doubts about the legitimacy of her ministry as a woman. But nearly every time, she turns to eschatology to overcome her uncertainty. In *This Is That*, the title itself based on the Acts 2/Joel 2 texts, she looks to the last days prophecy of Joel to confirm (and reassure herself) that women will prophesy when the Spirit is poured out.[104] In her baccalaureate message given January 7, 1930 to the "Watchmen Class," she begins with Joel 2:29 to affirm women's ministry and proclaims the Lord is calling "the daughters as well as the sons."[105] For those who argue that a woman's "lips should be sealed," McPherson claims that "this is not according to the Word of God. 'Your sons and your daughters shall prophesy.'" Although she expresses thankfulness for the men who have "paved the way" in the past, she calls on women to preach because "the time is short" and "WE ARE LIVING on the edge of time, nearing the coming of the Lord Jesus Christ."[106]

In a lengthier article entitled "Signs of the Times," McPherson documents several "Scriptural" signs of the last days, one of the main ones being women preachers. After quoting Acts 2:17, she recounts her own story as evidence of this Scripture being fulfilled: "When the Lord saved me, fifteen years ago, I was but a girl of seventeen. He . . . took me from a Canadian farm and sent me out to tell the story of Jesus."[107] A prophesying daughter such as herself, she says, "indeed, is a sign."[108] Like Argue, McPherson argues that women preachers are an absolute necessity for the Lord to return. In response to the Joel 2/Acts 2 passage, McPherson writes that "before the coming of the Lord takes place, there *must* be at

---

103. Susie Stanley, citing Estrelda Alexander's PhD dissertation, confirms McPherson rarely addressed the issue, but notes two exceptions, her teaching on Acts 2:17-18 and her quoting of Joel 2:28 ("Wesleyan/Holiness and Pentecostal Women Preachers: Pentecost as the Pattern for Primitivism," in Alexander and Yong, *Philip's Daughters*, 36). Blumhofer also makes this observation, which is likely why Blumhofer's biography of McPherson makes so little mention of the issue (*Aimee Semple McPherson*, 362).

104. McPherson, *This Is That*, 60.

105. Aimee Semple McPherson, "The Servants and the Handmaidens: Baccalaureate Sermon," *The Bridal Call Foursquare* 8, no. 9 (February 1930): 5-6. See Priscilla Pope-Levison, *Turn the Pulpit Loose: Two Centuries of American Women Evangelists* (New York: Palgrave Macmillan, 2004), 197-200.

106. McPherson, "The Servants and the Handmaidens," 5-6; capitalization in the original.

107. Aimee Semple McPherson, "Signs of the Times," *The Bridal Call Foursquare* 11, no. 2 (July 1927): 7.

108. McPherson, "Signs of the Times," 7.

least a few women preaching the Gospel—else the Scripture will not be fulfilled."[109] She similarly insisted at one of her rallies in Oakland that "women must preach to fulfill the Scriptures" and that their doing so was an important "sign of the times" in preparing the church for Christ's return.[110]

McPherson saw the eschatological vision of equality contained within the biblical text as a type of precondition for the Lord's return, heightening the urgency of egalitarian practices in the present. Therefore, the old arguments about women were no longer relevant, since the urgency of the moment demanded an "all hands on deck approach," including the hands of women.[111] McPherson also used her eschatological bridal paradigm (popular language among Pentecostals) to authorize her ministry. Payne shows extensively how McPherson used the language of her "bride of Christ" identity to authorize her ministry and the special position she held in the church to act on behalf of Christ.[112] Like Woodworth-Etter, McPherson used biblical eschatological images of authority to legitimize her ministry.[113]

McPherson is a complex figure with many contradictions. Scholars note that her actions at times seemed inconsistent with her egalitarian stance, often promoting more traditional roles for women or not supporting other women in leadership roles.[114] But it was her eschatological imagination that helped her to rescind doubts (including her own) about the role of women in the church and helped her persevere in the face of what was often strict opposition to women in the pulpit. Her eschatological imagination led herself and other women to participate more fully in the leadership of the church because they saw themselves as prophetic actors in the fulfillment of the last days prophecy of Joel 2/Acts 2.

Accounts of "great female leaders" such as these three women may not always tell the full story about actual women's roles,[115] but they do provide glimpses of what is possible and the potential trajectories the theological seeds of a movement might grow toward. The life stories of Woodworth-Etter, Argue, and McPherson reveal three women able to overcome their own and others' doubts about their ministry by applying eschatological metaphors and texts from the Bible to authorize and legitimize their actions. This eschatological authorization led to newfound freedoms for them as well as acceptance of their ministry by believers across North America. None of these women were overly interested in scriptural

109. McPherson, "Signs of the Times," 7; italics mine.
110. See Blumhofer, *Aimee Semple McPherson*, 195.
111. See Anderson, *Vision of the Disinherited*, 84. See also Scott Billingsley, *It's a New Day: Race and Gender in the Modern Charismatic Movement* (Tuscaloosa: University of Alabama Press, 2008), 19.
112. See Payne, *Gender*, 52–61.
113. Payne, *Gender*, 17.
114. Blumhofer regularly points this out in *Aimee Semple McPherson*, see for example 361–2. See also Stephenson, *Dismantling*, 54–5; Pope-Levison, *Turn the Pulpit Loose*, 197.
115. Griffith and Roebuck, "Women," 1203.

debates on women in leadership. They mostly avoided the issue, seeking instead to place their stories in the biblical story and in the unfolding eschatological drama taking place around them, for they saw this as the most effective way to overcome any previous or perceived limitations placed upon them.[116]

### 2.2.4 Outcomes of Historical Investigation

The above historical investigation reveals eschatology as potentially the cornerstone of the legitimization of the ministry of early Pentecostal women. Although some of the seeds of the egalitarian ethos were planted in the nineteenth century, it was the Pentecostal eschatological intensification that watered those seeds into a full-blown women's movement within Pentecostalism. The inaugural and earliest issues of the most influential Pentecostal periodicals in the United States and Canada repeatedly authorize the ministry of women using eschatological arguments. Both Pentecostal women and men of the first few decades of the movement appealed to the eschatological imagination when defending the right of women to preach. This general pattern of eschatology as authorizing hermeneutic was confirmed more specifically in the lives of three quite different, but influential, Pentecostal women.

My position and goal is not to paint early Pentecostal practices as *the* standard or some "golden age" to which we should return.[117] As Blumhofer says, only a "superficial survey" would portray a perfect, pristine past with regard to openness to women in ministry, and her (and some others') description of the history of women in Pentecostalism is certainly more somber and subdued.[118] Stephenson, following Blumhofer, has perhaps most notably made the argument that full equality of the sexes has never existed within Pentecostalism; rather, men to some extent have always monopolized authority in the movement.[119] These early

---

116. See Payne, *Gender*, 62.
117. Blumhofer, *Assemblies of God*, 1:141–2.
118. Blumhofer, *Assemblies of God*, 1:358, 367; Blumhofer, "Women," 6. See also Blumhofer's article "A Confused Legacy: Reflections of Evangelical Attitudes toward Ministering Women in the Past Century," *Fides et Historia* 22, no. 1 (Winter-Spring 1990): 49–61. See also Tackett, "Callings," 86–7. Wacker also describes the two competing narratives about women in early Pentecostalism, concluding "both views are partly right" (*Heaven Below*, 158). Vondey makes a similar argument that tensions have always existed in the movement, which he seeks to embrace (*Perplexed*, 2–3).
119. See Stephenson, *Dismantling*, particularly 9–22 (see 22n30). However, her evidence is sparse, only giving a few examples from Azusa, and citations are lacking. She does provide arguments to the contrary in a note on page 22. But Stephenson is not alone in her less than favorable picture of early Pentecostal attitudes toward women. For more, see Alexander, *Limited Liberty*, viii–xiv, 14, 26; Barfoot and Sheppard, "Prophetic vs. Priestly," 4; R. Marie Griffith, "Women's Aglow Fellowship International," in *NIDPCM*, 1211; David Roebuck, "Limiting Liberty: The Church of God and Women Ministers, 1886–1996" (PhD diss., Vanderbilt University, 1997).

sources do at times offer a "ritualized" version of history. While they are by no means invented, they are simplified accounts "designed to celebrate that which they thought should be celebrated."[120] But what and how they celebrate—in this case the ministry of women—is important and can inform our study and the present work's quest to find an appropriate theological method for resolving the Pentecostal gender paradox across various disciplines.

Early Pentecostalism was not as good for women as some portray and not as bad as others depict. The tensions of the gender paradox have always existed to some extent: there is no ideal past or golden age. To claim there was no initial "stained-glass ceiling" in the early days of the movement,[121] or to label early Pentecostals as "gender-blind,"[122] would be hyperbole at best. However, this does not mean we need to come to the conclusion, as Geoffrey Kirk does in his historical work on the issue of women in ministry, that all claims about the Christian past "are hopelessly optimistic" and that the past contains "no program for gender equality."[123] Most Pentecostal scholars, in fact, have argued the exact opposite: the past should play a central role in determining Pentecostalism's present and future. This idea of the importance of Pentecostalism's past for constructing its future is why this historical chapter must come first before constructing an eschatological–egalitarian hermeneutic and praxis.

### 2.3 The Early-Years Argument

A common, though at times contested, argument among Pentecostal scholars is that the early years of the movement represent the core of the Pentecostal identity.[124] Walter Hollenweger first argued that the formative years of Pentecostalism represent the "heart" and not just the "infancy" of the movement.[125] Land then

---

120. Cerillo and Wacker, "Bibliography," 397, 403. This is sometimes criticized as "the myth of Azusa Street." See Robby Waddell and Peter Althouse, "The Promises and Perils of the Azusa Street Myth," *Pneuma* 38, no. 4 (2016): 367–71; Qualls, *Forgive Us*, 152–3.

121. This *is* what English de Alminana says ("Introduction," 13). The term "stained-glass ceiling" is usually attributed to Susie C. Stanley, "Shattering the Stained-Glass Ceiling," in *The Wisdom of Daughters: Two Decades of the Voice of Christian Feminism*, ed. Reta Halteman Finger and Kari Sandhaas (Philadelphia: Innisfree, 2001), 83–6.

122. Wilkinson and Ambrose *do* use the term "gender-blind" to describe the early roots of Pentecostalism (*After the Revival*, 87).

123. Geoffrey Kirk, *Without Precedent: Scripture, Tradition, and the Ordination of Women* (Eugene, OR: Wipf & Stock, 2016), 115.

124. Cf. Vondey, *Beyond Pentecostalism*, who wants to move "beyond" the early years as the heart of the movement, arguing that global Pentecostalism is expanding beyond these roots (7, 182).

125. Walter Hollenweger, *The Pentecostals: The Charismatic Movement in the Churches*, trans. R. A. Wilson (Minneapolis: Augsburg, 1972), 551.

attempts to capture this heart and argues that the construction of an authentic Pentecostal theology must engage with the practices and reflections of early Pentecostals.[126] Following both Hollenweger and Land, Faupel contends that "for Pentecostalism to remain a vital force into the twenty-first century, it must look to its origins as a source for theological and spiritual renewal."[127] Other scholars have followed suit by attempting to ground their theological works fully in conversation with the heart of the early Pentecostal tradition.[128]

This historical approach is of course not exclusive to Pentecostalism, for the past is significant to the present identity of any group.[129] But the story of the beginnings of the Pentecostal movement may be uniquely privileged in Pentecostal spirituality because of the distinctive role experience and story play in the Pentecostal worldview and in recruiting the imagination.[130] As many have argued and shown, Pentecostal worship and theology begin with experience and then move to the text,[131] so much so that Kenneth Archer claims that "the Pentecostal story is the primary hermeneutical context for the reading of Scripture."[132] Therefore, knowledge of Pentecostal history must precede scriptural debates or any theologizing; Pentecostal epistemology is embedded in Pentecostal narrative and praxis. For Pentecostals, "story comes before propositions—imagination precedes intellection."[133] The early story of women in Pentecostalism is the seed from which the roots and shoots of scriptural interpretation, egalitarian theology, and ecclesiological practice are meant to grow. Conversely, any deviation from the heart and trajectory laid out in the early movement should fall under serious scrutiny—an analogous relationship should exist between past experiences and present practices.[134] This priority given to the origins of the Pentecostal story has led to a heightened interest among current Pentecostals in their own history.[135] And it is this interest that has led to the (re)discovery of the egalitarian and eschatological heart of the movement.

---

126. See Land, *Pentecostal Spirituality*, 47, as well as Stephenson's discussion of Land in *Types of Pentecostal Theology*, 38.

127. Faupel, *Everlasting Gospel*, 309.

128. Two examples would be McQueen, *Pentecostal Eschatology* and Green, *Lord's Supper*.

129. See Lonergan, *Method*, 182.

130. See Smith, *Imagining*, 20.

131. See Johnathan E. Alvarado, "Pentecostal Worship and the Creation of Meaning," in *Toward a Pentecostal Theology of Worship*, ed. Lee Roy Martin (Cleveland, TN: CPT, 2016), 232; Yong, *Renewing*, 23; Smith, *Thinking in Tongues*, 43–4.

132. Kenneth J. Archer, *A Pentecostal Hermeneutic: Spirit, Scripture and Community* (Cleveland, TN: CPT, 2009), 134.

133. Smith, *Tongues*, 43–4. For the importance of story for how we live our lives, see Smith, *Imagining*, 32–8.

134. See Green, *Lord's Supper*, 75, 244; Lonergan, *Method*, 225.

135. Yong, *Spirit-Word-Community*, 291.

## 2.3.1 The Egalitarian Heart of the Movement

In their introduction to their edited volume *Women in Pentecostal and Charismatic Ministry*, Margaret English de Alminana and Lois Olena say the achievements of American Pentecostal women have been "overlooked, marginalized, or rejected" despite the fact that it was women "who launched and carried Pentecostalism" in the early years.[136] This "androcentricity" of Pentecostal history has led to "testimonial injustice" and "epistemic violence" toward women.[137] Their book is a corrective effort from a female-centric perspective to hear the "overlooked feminine majority" from past and present within the movement.[138] In her well-received book on women in the Assemblies of God, Qualls argues that constantly omitting women from the story of Pentecostal history reinforces the current ambiguity women consistently face regarding their roles in the church.[139]

Pentecostal scholars wonder why, despite Pentecostals' treasuring of their spiritual experiences and telling of stories, the stories of the "foremothers" of the Pentecostal faith have failed to find a central place in the telling and writing of the Pentecostal story.[140] Just one example of this omission of women in popular Pentecostal literature is Keith Malcomson's book *Pentecostal Pioneers Remembered: British and Irish Pioneers of Pentecost*. Malcomson features twenty-six "Pentecostal Pioneers," only one of which is a woman (Eleanor Crisp), and the front cover is a black and white photo of fifteen men.[141] A different example is that while most histories of the Azusa Street revival consider Seymour the most influential and central figure, much of the primary evidence suggests Lucy Farrow may have been

---

136. English de Alminana, "Introduction," 1. Their context is American Pentecostalism. It is not just Pentecostals who have overlooked the contributions of Pentecostal women in the movement. Further adding to the inattention to women in Pentecostalism is the consistent absence of the Pentecostal story in the growing general literature on women's liberation in the church. This is the premise of Bernice Martin's previously mentioned influential article "The Pentecostal Gender Paradox" discussed in the Introduction. See the complaints of Ambrose, "Zelma," 101. In particular, Ambrose laments the little scholarship on Canadian Pentecostal women (101). See also Johns, "Conscientization," 161n2; Anne Motley Hallum, "Taking Stock and Building Bridges: Feminism, Women's Movements, and Pentecostalism in Latin America," *Latin American Research Review* 38, no. 1 (2003): 169-86; Roebuck, "Pentecostal Women," 30.

137. English de Alminana, "Introduction," 8, 10.

138. English de Alminana, "Introduction," 9-11. See also see David G. Roebuck, "'Cause He's My Chief Employer': Hearing Women's Voices in a Classical Pentecostal Denomination," in Alexander and Yong, *Philip's Daughters*, 38-60.

139. Qualls, *Forgive Us*, 17.

140. Cavaness, "Leadership Attitudes," 112.

141. Keith Malcomson, *Pentecostal Pioneers Remembered: British and Irish Pioneers of Pentecost* (n.p.: Xulon, 2008).

just as instrumental in bringing about the revival.[142] These kinds of works and images reinforce the faulty notion that the Pentecostal movement was and is a movement led and dominated by men. In their 2002 essay, Cerillo and Wacker lament the "paucity of scholarly work on women in the pentecostal and charismatic movements."[143] Although much progress has been made in the last twenty years, providing historical revision of patriarchal interpretations of the movement and the "naming" of women remains an important and necessary step for any work on gender.[144]

The full telling of the story of women's involvement and leadership in the early Pentecostal movement is well documented and beyond the scope of this chapter.[145] However, even a brief historical sketch quickly catapults women to the forefront of the Pentecostal story. Alexander argues that women indeed enjoyed their greatest liberty when the movement was in its "embryonic stages."[146] Johns claims that the Pentecostal story is "rich with symbols" of freedom and partnership between women and men.[147] In the United States, the events leading up to and including the Azusa Street revival prominently feature women. At Parham's Bible school, Ozman was the first person to speak in tongues[148] and Parham ordained women, commissioned them to ministry, and often left women in charge of meetings.[149]

Later at Azusa Street, Seymour did not see speaking in tongues as the main miracle of Pentecost or the Pentecostal revival; rather, it was the healing and

---

142. This is the famous portrait of Farrow and Azusa Street that "Mother" Emma Cotton paints in "Inside Story of the Outpouring of the Holy Spirit, Azusa Street, 1906," *Message of the Apostolic Faith* 1, no. 1 (April 1939): 1–3. See Cerillo and Wacker, "Bibliography," 396; Wacker, *Heaven Below*, 159.

143. Cerillo and Wacker, "Bibliography," 387.

144. Part of the premise of the title of Alexander and Yong's book *Philip's Daughters*, referring to the unnamed daughters of Philip.

145. For a helpful overview of the literature on American Pentecostal women pre-1960s, see Roebuck, "Pentecostal Women," 29–44. For the story of women in the Assemblies of God, see Qualls, *Forgive Us*, especially chapters 2–5; Kenyon, "Ethical Issues," 178–283. See also Chapter 1 of Alexander and Gause, *Women*; Hyatt, "Spirit-Filled Women," 244–52.

146. Alexander, *Limited Liberty*, 27.

147. Johns, "Conscientization," 161.

148. Pointing to Ozman as the one to usher in the movement has become (finally) a more common part of the Pentecostal narrative (see Wacker, *Heaven Below*, 162; Alexander and Gause, *Women*, 12; Hyatt, "Spirit-Filled Women," 233).

149. Roebuck, "Loose the Women," 38. Cavaness highlights the role women played in the success of both Parham and Seymour ("Leadership Attitudes," 114–22). See also Hyatt, "Spirit-Filled Women," 245–6. Of course, Parham changed his position as the years went on, even showing disgust at egalitarian behaviors. See Charles F. Parham, "Free Love," *Apostolic Faith* (Baxter Springs, AR) 1, no. 10 (December 1912): 4–5.

breaking down of divisions, including gender barriers.[150] Early on, his leadership style was considered to be radically inclusive and egalitarian.[151] The initial minimal institutional structure at Azusa was thoroughly egalitarian, consisting of a board of six women and six men.[152] In her work on the women of Azusa Street, Alexander argues that women were just as instrumental, if not more, in the events leading up to Azusa, the actual Azusa revival, and the spread of its message through preaching, writing, teaching, and organizing.[153] Wacker argues in his work on early American Pentecostal women that although gender distinctions were not eradicated, social barriers did quickly crumble and "striking equality prevailed" in Pentecostal worship.[154] Wacker gives evidence of outsiders' reports underscoring the prominence of women and showing them "approaching parity with men" early on.[155] Men shared their testimonies on how the Pentecostal experience helped them let go of their pride and subordinate themselves to women, sometimes even young girls, in spiritual matters.[156]

The Pentecostal story in Canada follows a similar storyline. Ellen Hebden is the first known person to speak in tongues in Canada, at the East End Mission in Toronto on November 17, 1906. In the first issue of *The Promise* paper out of Toronto in 1907, Hebden gives the full report of "How Pentecost Came to Toronto" and how she first received the baptism and tongues.[157] As she pursued the supernatural experience, "a little fear crept into my heart and I said, 'Lord, let my husband come.' I tried to speak to my husband but failed, and I found that God wanted me to go through alone."[158] The next night during the evening service, as she sat in the front row, Hebden says she

---

150. See Douglas J. Nelson, "For Such a Time as This: The Story of Bishop William J. Seymour and the Azusa Street Revival" (PhD diss., University of Birmingham, 1981), 201–5. For more on Seymour and the story of Azusa, see Faupel, *Everlasting Gospel*, 190–227, 257–8.

151. Cecil M. Robeck Jr., "William J. Seymour: An Early Model of Pentecostal Leadership," *Enrichment: A Journal for Pentecostal Ministry* 11, no. 2 (Spring 2006): 50–1. Like Parham, Seymour became more limiting in future years (see Alexander, *Limited Liberty*, 38).

152. Susie Stanley, "'Laying a Straw in Her Way': Women in Pentecostalism," *Enrichment: A Journal for Pentecostal Ministry* 11, no. 2 (Spring 2006): 112; Alexander, *Women of Azusa*, 12.

153. Alexander, *Women of Azusa*, 10, 179.

154. Wacker, *Heaven Below*, 103. Yong also argues egalitarianism was central to the Azusa movement (Yong, *Renewing*, 101).

155. Wacker, *Heaven Below*, 104.

156. Wacker, *Heaven Below*, 104. See the stories in Alexander, *Women of Azusa*, 12–13, 37.

157. Ellen Hebden, "How Pentecost Came to Toronto," *The Promise* no. 1 (May 1907): 2.

158. Hebden, "How Pentecost Came to Toronto," 2. Wacker reports that women receiving the baptism in the Spirit before their husbands was a common pattern (*Heaven Below*, 161).

knew that the time had come when God wanted me to declare to the people what He had done. Stepping upon the platform, and realizing all the time that the power of God was upon me mightily, I testified to all that God had done for me, telling them how I had received the Holy Ghost according to the Bible.[159]

Hebden then goes on to give testimony about how she led the movement early on as an evangelist.

The earliest reports of the movement in Canada are full of women called to preach, and it could be argued that women are featured more prominently than men in these early descriptions. In the second issue of *The Promise*, all four of the featured submitted testimonies are from women.[160] A later issue contains a quote from an eyewitness of the past six months who says,

> The early history of this work has been given so often that no mention need be made now except to say that Mrs. Ellen K. Hebden, who first received the Baptism of the Holy Ghost there, has been much used of God in the leading of the praise, worship, and prayer to God, and by giving great aid to those seeking the baptism.[161]

A later paper raves of the preaching of McPherson and how she "made the presence of God very manifest to all."[162] That same issue mentions that during the meetings "Mrs. Hebden gave a very beautiful message of great power and authority on the divinity and holiness of Jesus."[163] Early photographic evidence from Canadian Pentecostal Bible college yearbooks in the following decades repeatedly show that women equaled or outnumbered men in training for ministry.[164]

Similar narratives could be given for other Pentecostal denominations and the movement in general. Wacker reports that at the beginning, about one-third of official clergy, founding members, and church pastors were women in each of the three oldest and largest US Pentecostal bodies.[165] In the early years of the International Church of the Foursquare Gospel, eighteen of its fifty-five churches were *led* by women, and another sixteen were led by married co-pastors, meaning well over 50 percent of its churches had women in lead roles.[166] Wacker argues

---

159. Hebden, "How Pentecost Came to Toronto," 2.

160. "Correspondence," *The Promise* no. 2 (June 1907): 3–4. The women are M. Webb ("Your sister in Christ"), Ursula Lowther, Estella M. Willard, and Mrs. Phillips.

161. "Pentecostal Work in Toronto," *The Promise* no. 12 (February 1909): 2.

162. "God Appointed Convention," *The Promise* no. 15 (March 1910): 1.

163. "God Appointed Convention," 2.

164. Wilkinson and Ambrose, *After the Revival*, 87.

165. The Pentecostal bodies are the AG, Church of God, ICFG (Wacker, *Heaven Below*, 160). Kenyon says one-third of the clergy in the AG in 1914 were women ("Ethical Issues," 198).

166. Wacker, *Heaven Below*, 160.

that on the whole, "the primary evidence suggests that something like half of the traveling evangelists, divine healers, and overseas missionaries were women" and that women also made up a majority of members and worshippers in Pentecostal congregations at a percentage exceeding other denominations.[167] He concludes, "If any worried about the formalities of women in ministry, few let on."[168] Harvey Cox determines similarly that women played "a disproportionately prominent place in the Pentecostal movement" and were one of the primary reasons the movement spread so fast.[169] Women founded and led denominations, Bible schools, churches, and revival meetings, both large and small.[170] And as the movement grew and spread, it attracted more and more women to it partly due to the greater freedom it offered women to participate in ministry.[171]

The purpose of this brief history is to highlight the initial egalitarian heart of the early movement. The evidence shows that the early years of the movement do at least represent the *height* of women's influence in Pentecostalism, even if those years do not represent the ultimate ideal or a pristine past to return to. These stories have been often untold, overlooked, or forgotten. Agnes Ozman, the women of Azusa, and Ellen Hebden are hardly household names in the Pentecostal movement. However, only telling the story cannot resolve the current gender paradox within Pentecostalism; this history-only argument is where many works fall short. Understanding the first few decades of the movement as the height of women in ministry is important only if we can (re)discover what authorized this increased participation and articulate the theology behind it that helped rescind previous limitation on the ministry of women. What caused the initial egalitarian commitment in the early Pentecostal movement, freedoms afforded to women that were "never before seen in church history"?[172] It was primarily the Pentecostal eschatological imagination that informed this participation in egalitarian practices.

### 2.3.2 The Eschatological Heart of the Movement

In her research on early Pentecostal women, Qualls makes the important point that these female leaders were not motivated by women's rights, feminism, or overcoming oppression; rather, they were compelled to preach the gospel by eschatological urgency and saw themselves as participants in the "last days" plan

---

167. Wacker, *Heaven Below*, 160–1.

168. Wacker, *Heaven Below*, 162.

169. Harvey Cox, *Fire from Heaven: The Rise of Pentecostal Spirituality and the Reshaping of Religion in the Twenty-First Century* (Cambridge, MA: Da Capo, 1995), 121.

170. Barfoot and Sheppard, "Prophetic vs. Priestly," 2–3; Hyatt, "Spirit-Filled Women," 247–52; Faupel, *Everlasting Gospel*, 273.

171. Alexander, "Introduction," 3.

172. Hyatt, "Spirit-Filled Women," 234.

of God as laid out in the Joel 2/Acts 2 texts.[173] Alexander also asserts this was not a women's rights movement: "Rather, they played out a practical feminism in sharing with their brethren the singular understanding that Jesus was soon to return; what they, as well as their brethren, were called to do, they must do quickly and with all their heart."[174] Similarly, Johns suggests that the initial equality was not based on philosophic ideology nor totally upon critical reflection;[175] rather, the primary fuel for the sudden "scandalous" equality and liberation of women that challenged previous accepted norms for ministry was an "eschatological urgency" for the end-time harvest.[176] The early endorsement of prophesying daughters by Pentecostals was an extension of their eschatological commitment.[177] Perhaps more than any other factor, it was this eschatological urgency that gave women a crucial role within the movement.[178]

It is widely agreed that eschatology was central to, and perhaps even the *best* way to understand and explain, the rapid growth of the early Pentecostal movement and its beliefs and practices.[179] Pentecostal scholars describe eschatology as the integrating core, central theme, primary message, ultimate concern, most prominent feature, primary framework, hermeneutical key, and driving force of early Pentecostalism.[180] Eschatology "permeates" the pages of *Apostolic Faith*, often side by side or intermingled with stories of women.[181] Pentecostal scholars have argued that almost all experiences and expressions of early Pentecostal congregations were in anticipation of Christ's soon return and were interpreted within that framework.[182] Although Spirit baptism and tongues are sometimes

---

173. See Qualls, *Forgive Us*, 88; Alexander, *Limited Liberty*, 16.

174. Alexander, *Women of Azusa*, 179.

175. Johns, *Pentecostal Formation*, 69.

176. Johns, "Conscientization," 162–3.

177. Tackett, "Callings," 74.

178. This is the conclusion of Griffith and Roebuck, "Women," 1204.

179. See also the Introduction to this work. The list of scholars taking this position is long. For a sort of literature review of those who have argued this, see Althouse, "Pentecostal Eschatology," 205–31. Althouse argues that most models explaining the growth of the early movement contain and integrate an eschatological impulse (209).

180. The following works all feature eschatology as central for understanding early Pentecostalism (with some specific passages cited): Wacker, *Heaven Below*, 251–6; French L. Arrington, "Dispensationalism," in *NIDPCM*, 584–6; Thompson, "Eschatology," 189; Althouse, *Moltmann*, 21–2; Land, *Pentecostal Spirituality*, 29–41; Dayton, *Theological Roots*, 33, 143; Robert M. Anderson, *Vision of the Disinherited*, 4–5, 80, 97. Faupel uses tons of primary sources to make his argument that eschatology best explains early Pentecostalism (*Everlasting Gospel*, 18–21). See McQueen's discussion of Faupel in his *Pentecostal Eschatology*, 7–10.

181. Larry R. McQueen, "Early Pentecostal Eschatology in the Light of *The Apostolic Faith*, 1906–1908," in Althouse and Waddell, *Eschatologies*, 141.

182. Anderson, *Vision of the Disinherited*, 80; Blumhofer, *Assemblies of God*, 1:141.

considered the central component of early Pentecostalism, many argue eschatology was more important: the outpouring of the Spirit found its significance mainly as a sign of the "last days" and "latter rain," fueling the eschatological urgency of the movement.[183]

Intricately tied to the language of Joel 2/Acts 2 and its eschatological egalitarianism was the dominant "latter rain" storyline embraced by early Pentecostals.[184] The latter rain doctrine originated from the language and imagery of Joel 2:23-29 and James 5:7-8, based on an analogy of the rainfall patterns of Palestine. Whereas the "former rain" was considered the outpouring of the Spirit at Pentecost that birthed the church, this even greater "latter rain" of the modern outpouring of the Spirit was now meant to prepare the church for the end-time harvest and Christ's return.[185] This latter rain motif helped Pentecostals articulate what they were experiencing in eschatological language.[186] As Dayton describes, the role of women had been in a "drought" since the time of the apostolic church, but the Joel/Acts 2 equality was being restored and carried forward through this latter rain.[187] The new freedoms being experienced by women were both a renewal and ultimate fulfillment of the day of Pentecost.

In order to propose an eschatological argument for the equal role of women and equal access to leadership positions for women in Pentecostalism, it is important to show that both eschatological and egalitarian tendencies were foundational to the early heart of the movement. The brief sketch above and overall historical evidence presented in this chapter opens the door for the potential of an eschatological resolving of the Pentecostal gender paradox because it proves an eschatologically authorized egalitarianism is consistent with the early heart of the movement. What was lacking for early Pentecostals, and what eventually contributed to the decline of both the prominence of women and eschatology, was the development and articulation of a hermeneutic that reflected this early eschatological authorization of women leaders.

---

183. See Smith, *Tongues*, 44; Wacker, *Heaven Below*, 255–7; Arrington, "Dispensationalism," 585; Dayton, *Theological Roots*, 144; Gerald T. Sheppard, "Pentecostals and the Hermeneutics of Dispensationalism: The Anatomy of an Uneasy Relationship," *Pneuma* 7 (Fall 1984): 7. Anderson calls speaking in tongues "subordinate" to eschatology (*Vision of the Disinherited*, 80). The strong link between pneumatology and eschatology is discussed more in 3.4.2.

184. For the development of the latter rain doctrine, see Daniel D. Isgrigg, "The Latter Rain Revisited: Exploring the Origins of the Central Metaphor in Pentecostalism," *Pneuma* 41, no. 3-4 (2019): 439–57; Althouse, *Moltmann*, 1, 18–25.

185. See Dayton, *Theological Roots*, 27; Larry R. McQueen, *Joel and the Spirit: The Cry of a Prophetic Hermeneutic* (1995; repr., Cleveland, TN: CPT, 2009), 77.

186. See Archer, *Pentecostal Hermeneutic*, 136–8. See 136–56 for his full discussion of the latter rain development.

187. See Dayton, *Theological Roots*, 28.

## 2.4 The Function(s) of Eschatology

The evidence in the previous sections from early Pentecostal writings indicates that the eschatological authorizing hermeneutic used by early Pentecostals kept at bay the later hermeneutical uncertainty and inconsistency that suppressed the role of women. This chapter has sought to show that the rise of women in leadership corresponded with the centrality of eschatology in the early movement. The next chapter, therefore, seeks to argue that the decline of women leaders was potentially concomitant with a shift in the function of eschatology which led to its waning in the movement: the loss of eschatological urgency resulted in the loss of Pentecostalism's egalitarian impulse.[188] As time went on and "less favorable theologies" began to place limitations on women,[189] Pentecostal women continued to seek to legitimize their ministries in different ways—through personal calling,[190] biblical exegesis, marriage to male ministers, abstaining from marriage, revivalist methods, Spirit baptism,[191] and more—but they had very limited success compared to their predecessors who relied on an authorizing hermeneutic of eschatology.[192] Therefore, understanding the functions of eschatology is a necessary step in presenting eschatology as a solution to the Pentecostal gender paradox.

The critical and constructive functions of eschatology in history, theology, and Christian practice are wide and varied and often times debated.[193] There are both individual and social (collective) aspects to eschatological thought, often relating to the otherworldly and this-worldly domains of eschatological ideas respectively.[194] Eschatology is both ultimate in its otherworldliness, illuminating the insufficiency of earthly human efforts alone (its critical function), and penultimate in its this-worldly impact of empowering action in the present (its constructive function).[195] As Wolfhart Pannenberg argues in his essay on the functions of eschatology, it is nearly impossible to separate the two fully,[196] which is part of the reason for the dialectic of imagination and participation proposed in this work. The feminist-

---

188. See my Introduction for more on the decline of Pentecostal women in ministry.

189. Hyatt, "Spirit-Filled Women," 247, see 252–62 for her summary.

190. Many others have promoted this argument of the importance of calling or the call narrative to legitimize the ministry of women. See Payne, *Gender*, 12–15; Powers, "Pentecostal Hermeneutics," 319–20; Barfoot and Sheppard, "Prophetic vs. Priestly," 4; Elaine Lawless, *Handmaidens of the Lord: Pentecostal Women Preachers and Traditional Religion* (Philadelphia: University of Pennsylvania Press, 1988), 76–84.

191. See Stanley, "Laying a Straw," 111.

192. For examples, see Payne, *Gender*, 1–2, 34–7.

193. See Wolfhart Pannenberg, "Constructive and Critical Functions of Christian Eschatology," *The Harvard Theological Review* 77, no. 2 (April 1984): 119–39.

194. See Pannenberg, "Constructive and Critical," 119–23.

195. See Pannenberg, "Constructive and Critical," 124.

196. Pannenberg, "Constructive and Critical," 125. For a similar perspective, see Bauckham and Hart, *Hope Against Hope*, 129, 181, 184, 193.

functional investigation of select primary sources in this chapter shows that early Pentecostals used an eschatological program for empowering women that functioned both critically and constructively. Eschatology worked critically in passing on other theological or purely secular programs for gender equality and instead inspiring an otherworldly egalitarian imagination. It functioned constructively as an authorizing hermeneutic that liberated the ministry of Pentecostal women by inspiring eschatological egalitarian participation. The eschatological dialectic of imagination and participation authorized the ministry of women both on paper theologically and in practice ecclesiologically, with each informing the other.

This work adopts a transformational eschatology that is in line with both early Pentecostalism and recent developments in Pentecostal eschatology.[197] The goal is a new critical contribution to resolve the Pentecostal gender paradox using the method and heuristic tool of transformational eschatology. Eschatologies varied widely among early Pentecostals, and there is no definitive consensus with regard to a particular eschatology they employed.[198] Despite the "multiplicity of views" regarding early Pentecostal eschatology, states Yong, "what is undeniable is the overall eschatological orientation [of] early pentecostal believers."[199] No matter the type of eschatology—whether defined as premillennial pessimism,[200] postmillennial optimism, latter rain, or some other eschatology[201]—the early Pentecostal eschatological worldview functioned similarly on the ground when it came to acting as an authorizing hermeneutic that liberated women to lead. Therefore, using a feminist-functional interpretive approach to the material, this

---

197. See my Introduction chapter as well as the next chapter. See Yong, *Spirit Poured Out*, 96–7; Vondey, *Pentecostal Theology*, 139–43; Althouse, *Moltmann*, 61, 196.

198. For the wide range of Pentecostal eschatology, see Althouse and Waddell, *Eschatologies* (notice the plural in the title), including the "three stages" of latter rain, dispensational millennialism, and proleptic eschatology (210–11); Thompson, *Kingdom Come*, 49–50; Warrington, *Pentecostal Theology*, 310–13. McQueen also argues immense variety existed within early Pentecostal eschatology, calling it perhaps the "most significant conclusion" of his exhaustive study (*Pentecostal Eschatology*, 122, 140–1). For an extensive review and survey of the scholarly literature on Pentecostal eschatology, see McQueen, *Pentecostal Eschatology*, 5–59. For select various writings on Pentecostal eschatology from its pre-beginnings to more modern voices, see chapter 3, "Pentecostal Eschatology," in William K. Kay and Anne E. Dyer, eds., *Pentecostal and Charismatic Studies: A Reader* (London: SCM, 2004), 25–46. For an analysis of early periodical literature on Pentecostal eschatology, see McQueen, *Pentecostal Eschatology*, 60–199.

199. Yong, *Renewing*, 33–4.

200. For a discussion of premillennialism's prominence in the early movement, see Isgrigg, *Imagining the Future*, 4–8; Blumhofer, *Assemblies of God*, 1:22–6; Wacker, *Heaven Below*, 251–6; Faupel, *Everlasting Gospel*, 91–114.

201. Often there was a combination of several—a simultaneous sense of doom and sense of hope (see Wacker, *Heaven Below*, 251).

chapter has sought to prove that a thoroughly eschatological orientation to faith and life influenced the authorization of early Pentecostal egalitarian practices.[202] Although Pentecostalism and its beliefs and practices such as newfound freedoms for women did not emerge out of nowhere, what gave it its explosion of growth and lasting significance was the eschatological intensification of these inherited practices.

## 2.5 Conclusion

At a time in history when women were often restricted in their leadership roles in the church, Pentecostal female ministers had to find biblical grounds to signal and legitimize their authority.[203] The argument of this chapter is that eschatology functioned as an authorizing hermeneutic that legitimized the ministry of women in the first few decades of Pentecostalism because it helped rescind previous perceived limitations concerning the role of women. Using a feminist-functional interpretive approach, the chapter discovered through primary sources and biographical case studies how the eschatological imagination encouraged this egalitarian participation and functioned as a liberating agent for Pentecostal women. The evidence suggests an interdependence between eschatology and women's equality: eschatological intensification inspired egalitarian practices and the Spirit-led ministry of women inspired feelings of participation in the eschatological inbreaking of God's future kingdom. The historical materials reveal that many Pentecostal male and female leaders in the United States and Canada did not just tolerate women leaders but excitedly embraced female ministers as the eschatological signs of God's Spirit being poured out.

Focusing on the first few decades of the movement is important because these early years are considered the "heart" of the movement that laid out a trajectory for Pentecostal belief and practice. Although (as the next chapter argues) the ministry of women began to wane as eschatological fervor diminished, the "dangerous corporate memory of its revolutionary roots" still exists,[204] which this chapter has sought to unearth. These early decades do not represent a golden age to be duplicated, but rather contain the seeds for an egalitarianism that is faithful to the heart of the movement: seeds that need to be continually watered and nourished by the eschatological imagination. The preceding investigation into primary sources reveals that early Pentecostalism contained at least two defining characteristics that separated it from its antecedents: a robust eschatological imagination that led to a thoroughly eschatological orientation to faith and life, and an emerging egalitarianism fueled by the latter rain paradigm that saw the ministry of women as an essential way to participate in and bring about the *eschaton*. As both Argue

---

202. See McQueen, *Pentecostal Eschatology*, 200; Land, *Pentecostal Spirituality*, 55.
203. Payne, *Gender*, 35–7, 84.
204. Johns, "Conscientization," 165.

and McPherson articulated, women are a necessary sign of the last days and *must* preach in order to fulfill the Scriptures. Eschatology functioned both critically and constructively and led to a belief that last days prophecy could not be fulfilled if women were not preaching, which led to the urgent call for the active participation of women.[205] However, as the eschatological imagination dissipated, the desire for participation in eschatological realities—such as gender equality—did the same.

Although some have briefly pointed to the eschatological convictions of early Pentecostals and the Joel 2/Acts 2 texts as the main impetus behind the newfound freedoms for the ministry of women,[206] few (if any) have sought to articulate how eschatology might provide a comprehensive, unified solution to the gender paradox across several disciplines. This chapter has provided an initial step toward a consistent and convincing authorizing hermeneutic for the ministry of women, namely, to test whether eschatology influenced the initial egalitarian trajectory of Pentecostalism and whether an eschatological orientation to a hermeneutical-theological problem is faithful to the historical heart of the movement. The Pentecostal story is the primary hermeneutical context for reading the Scriptures, and the story that emerges from this chapter is that the eschatological–egalitarian promises of Scripture led to increased participation in those promises in the here and now. The next step is to test whether any change, shift, or decline in the function of eschatology fueled the well-documented waning of women leaders in the movement. If that concomitance can be established, then an eschatological–egalitarian hermeneutic and praxis can be (re)developed, safely building upon the eschatological–egalitarian heart of early Pentecostalism. For eschatology to convincingly resolve the gender paradox and once again become a cornerstone for the legitimization of the unrestricted ministry of women, it must also prove it can solve the hermeneutical, theological, and ecclesiological questions surrounding the gender debate. These areas are the focus and challenge of the remaining chapters.

---

205. Barfoot and Sheppard, "Prophetic vs. Priestly," 9.

206. See Barfoot and Sheppard's three factors for equality, the third of which is eschatology. However, although several pages are spent on the first two factors, curiously eschatology is only given two paragraphs and mostly only discusses McPherson's comments on Joel 2:28 ("Prophetic vs. Priestly," 4). Tackett follows a similar pattern in "Callings." See also Roebuck, "Loose the Women," 39; Blumhofer, *Assemblies of God*, 1:355-9.

## Chapter 3

## THE LOSS OF ESCHATOLOGY AS AUTHORIZING HERMENEUTIC

The previous chapter has revealed that women's equality in early Pentecostalism was motivated and authorized by eschatological concerns. However, early Pentecostals failed to articulate deliberately an intellectual basis for how their eschatology authorized the newfound freedoms for women.[1] This lack of a defined authorizing hermeneutic opened the door for significant changes to eschatology and its corresponding liberating hermeneutic. The result was the concomitant waning of the eschatological hermeneutic and egalitarian practices. The purpose of this chapter is to investigate the historical reasons for this waning and then to move toward developing and defending a constructive eschatological hermeneutic that is in line with the heart of the movement and with current developments in Pentecostal eschatology and hermeneutics. Hence, this chapter acts as a transition between the previous chapter's historical findings of the eschatological–egalitarian origins of the movement and the constructive chapters that follow. The current lack of an authorizing hermeneutic for women, caused by historical shifts that removed eschatology from the center of Pentecostal praxis, led to the gender paradox that has become symptomatic for the movement. Instead of a consistent authorizing hermeneutic based on their eschatological imagination, Pentecostals embraced hermeneutical inconsistencies that slowly led to restrictions concerning the leadership and authority of women.[2]

The argument of this chapter is that the loss of eschatology as an authorizing hermeneutic contributed significantly to the waning of Pentecostal women in ministry leadership. A strong interdependence exists between the role of eschatology and the role of women within Pentecostalism, which reflects my dialectic of imagination and participation. In other words, as eschatology

---

1. This is not so much a critique of early Pentecostals as it is historical fact. It is not surprising Pentecostals struggled to articulate a theology of gender equality since experience often comes first for Pentecostals (see 3.4.4). As Vondey suggests, Pentecostal theology is playful and experiential rather than propositional and prescriptive; therefore, theology "*cannot* proceed without being practiced but *can* proceed without being articulated as doctrine" (*Pentecostal Theology,* 28; italics in the original; see Vondey, *Pentecostal Theology,* 8–29).

2. See Powers, "Pentecostal Hermeneutics," for a critique of these inconsistencies (317).

shifted and became less central to Pentecostal practices, egalitarian participation decreased; as women were restricted, the eschatological imagination dissipated. Eschatology has been an oft-overlooked component in the development of and changes to Pentecostal hermeneutics, and its (re)construction is essential to (re)discovering a liberating hermeneutic for Pentecostal women.

The first part of this chapter articulates how the Pentecostal gender paradox historically has been primarily a hermeneutical issue. Pentecostals slowly shifted the way they sought to answer the gender question. Early Pentecostals looked to the eschatological *future* of Scripture and its present *inbreaking* (as evidenced by their latter rain language) to justify the prominent role of women in the movement. However, later Pentecostals looked to the historical *past* of the biblical text and its present *restoration* for direction on women's roles. This approach led to a more literal reading of Scripture which led to reservations or even outright rejection concerning the ministry of women. As Pentecostals shifted their participatory hermeneutical model from eschatological to restorationist, it led them to exchange their imaginative latter rain eschatology for a more literal dispensationalist view, a move that had far-reaching impact on the role of women in the movement. The more Pentecostals stopped looking forward to inform their present practices (an eschatological hermeneutic) and instead started searching for a pristine past (a restorationist hermeneutic), the more women's influence waned. Just as it was an eschatological authorization that initially freed women to minister in new ways, it was a change in or even removal of eschatology as a methodological hermeneutic that began to restrict women.

The above hypothesis is tested by investigating changes to interpretations of biblical texts on gender among North American Pentecostals after the Azusa Street revival, beginning with the formation of the Assemblies of God in 1914.[3] The chapter critiques these later hermeneutical developments that led to a change in attitude toward women leaders in the movement. I then engage with modern Pentecostal developments in eschatology and hermeneutics to show that my proposed eschatological hermeneutic of imagination and participation provides a constructive framework which pairs current hermeneutical strategies of the movement with its eschatological–egalitarian origins. The chapter concludes with an assertion of the need for a consistent authorizing hermeneutic to resolve the gender paradox and why eschatology provides the best way forward.

## 3.1 Historical Developments: The Shifting of Eschatology and Hermeneutics

As Chapter 2 demonstrated, the liberating and authorizing hermeneutic of eschatology gave urgency and agency to women preachers, teachers, and leaders. Their biblical

---

3. Most mark 1914 as the beginning of the decline for women's involvement in Pentecostal leadership. See Alexander, *Women of Azusa*, 151; Kenyon, "Ethical Issues," 197–202. The Azusa mission held services until the 1930s, but most consider 1914 to be the end of the revival.

eschatological authorization intensified their egalitarian practices and vice versa. While this dialectic existed, women remained at the forefront of leadership in the movement. However, two interrelated developments occurred post-1914 that led to the eventual gender paradox. First, Pentecostals replaced their eschatological hermeneutic with a restorationist orientation to Scripture that caused them to look back in time instead of forward. Second, this development led to dispensational eschatology becoming the dominant way of thinking, replacing latter rain eschatology. As the rest of this section explains, both these changes were problematic for women, as they promoted a literalist approach to Scripture that resulted in inconsistency and confusion over women's leadership and weakened their authority in the church.

### 3.1.1 Hermeneutics: From Eschatological to Restorationist

The authorizing hermeneutic of eschatology used by early Pentecostals (even if never deliberately articulated as such) led to never-before-seen freedoms for women. As Qualls states in her study of women in the Assemblies of God USA, due to the strong connection between the eschatological outpouring of the Spirit depicted in Acts 2/Joel 2 and the ministry of women, "for the first time in Church history, women had a scriptural and doctrinal basis for their inclusion in the ministry of the church."[4] It was the eschatological framework of early Pentecostals that led to the initial overcoming of previous barriers and limitations for women.[5] Just like the early church, Pentecostals were challenged in new ways to open themselves up to the ministry of women through the understanding that they were living in the last days.[6] Incorporating women at all levels of leadership energized and expanded their eschatological vision as they sought a "lived reality" of the coming kingdom promised in Scripture, one that leaned toward the inclusion rather than exclusion of women.[7] Texts that were previously assigned to the future began to have present applicability due to the eschatological Spirit's outpouring upon the people.[8]

Applying their eschatological hermeneutic to biblical texts enabled early Pentecostals to cut through any existing scriptural uncertainty concerning women's leadership: the powerful eschatological promises of God held hermeneutical priority over other supposedly limiting texts, and early Pentecostals were more than willing to act accordingly.[9] As Land argues, "a discerning reflection upon

---

4. Qualls, *Forgive Us*, 122. This point has already been argued in the previous chapter, but see English de Alminana, "Introduction," 15; Tackett, "Callings," 81.

5. See McQueen, *Joel*, 83; Land, *Pentecostal Spirituality*, 209.

6. See Alexander, "Introduction," 3; Land, *Pentecostal Spirituality*, 43.

7. McQueen, *Pentecostal Eschatology*, 95.

8. McQueen makes this argument specifically for the events at Azusa (McQueen, *Pentecostal Eschatology*, 74, 100–1).

9. For similar arguments, see Powers, "Pentecostal Hermeneutics," 323, and Mary McClintock Fulkerson, *Changing the Subject: Women's Discourses and Feminist Theology* (Minneapolis: Fortress, 1994), 289–98.

the living reality of the outpouring of the Spirit upon sons and daughters led the Pentecostals to see that the Scriptures concerning 'silence' of women in the church had to be reinterpreted."[10] Early men and women leaders of the movement interpreted eschatological texts on gender *and their experience of them* as biblical endorsement for female ministerial authority. The eschatological hermeneutic they applied to the Scriptures allowed them to confidently circumvent more restrictive texts and mainline-fundamentalist ways of reading them.[11] In the words of revivalist minister Alma White, the eschatological texts such as Joel 2/Acts 2 "forever settles the question as to woman's ministry."[12] However, although White's assessment may have been convincing to Pentecostals in 1912, the question was apparently far from settled.

The initial rise of women's leadership was eventually followed by a continuous decline of women's involvement and a consistently inconsistent message on what the Scriptures say about the role of women in the church.[13] But what caused a conviction that was once so clear to become so convoluted? Qualls states perceptively the reason:

> During the earliest years of the Pentecostal movement, validation of women's roles in ministry were based on the eschatological Pentecostal proclamation found in Acts 2 and the prophecy found in Joel 2. A *hermeneutical shift* developed in which the Pauline limitations in the Corinthian and Timothy letters were emphasized more with less regard for how women were perceived in other New Testament writings.[14]

Due to hermeneutical changes, the Bible was now both an authoritative resource for the liberation of Pentecostal women *and* a restrictive tool of limitation upon them: the Pentecostal gender paradox was born. Although Qualls's observation is on-target, she does not clearly name or describe this hermeneutical shift or its causes.[15] Therefore, determining what this hermeneutical shift was and the reasons behind it may hold the key to resolving the current paradoxical impulses of freedom for and constraint upon women ministers.

In her research on early Pentecostal women leaders, Alexander highlights part of the reason and irony of why the initial egalitarian thrust did not continue.

---

10. Land, *Pentecostal Spirituality*, 43.
11. Payne, *Gender*, 39.
12. Alma White, *The New Testament Church* (Bound Brook, NJ: The Pentecostal Union, 1912), 223, quoted in Payne, *Gender*, 41.
13. See my Introduction and 3.2 below.
14. Qualls, *Forgive Us*, 182–3; italics mine.
15. Qualls does refer to some rhetorical events and shifts, including shifts in terminology for offices within the church (*Forgive Us*, 123) as well as the shift from Spirit-empowered servanthood to positional authority (183). Following Barfoot and Sheppard, she also describes the shift from prophetic to priestly (126–9).

The women who led exemplary lives of leadership did not engage in developing theologies to encourage the leadership of women to continue. Therefore, their legacy eventually expired.[16] As the three case studies in the previous chapter showed, women leaders usually preferred to live out their calling rather than spend time defending it.[17] One of the reasons for this neglect was because they genuinely expected Christ to return soon, so that "the luxury of reflection and writing" about women's issues could not be afforded.[18] Herein lies a great irony: the eschatological urgency that authorized women's leadership was never fully articulated or developed for the very reason that it was eschatological!

The eschatological authority that helped women in the short term ended up hurting them in the long term; when the eschatological urgency faded, so did its authorizing hermeneutic. This decline left a hermeneutical vacuum for the next generation of Pentecostal leaders, particularly regarding texts on gender—which is why the current task is to develop and articulate a hermeneutic that reflects the early heart of the movement. Because an intellectual basis for the ministry of women was never established, the eschatology and hermeneutic that initially authorized their ministry was pushed aside and replaced with "less favorable" ways of reading Scripture that were not in line with the first few decades of Pentecostalism.[19] The result was that biblical texts that seem to restrict gender roles, which previously did not trouble eschatologically minded Pentecostals, suddenly came into conversation as Pentecostals changed their hermeneutic due to their shift in eschatological thinking.[20]

One of the "less favorable" ways of reading biblical texts on gender was the shift toward a restorationist hermeneutic. Despite the evidence that early Pentecostals used a hermeneutic heavily influenced by the latter rain motif, which inspired them to be a forward-looking eschatological movement,[21] they slowly moved toward and became known for being a restorationist or "throwback" movement.[22] The problem with this shift, as Alexander confirms, is that these two ways of thinking were competing impulses that "complicated the status of women ministers."[23] Pentecostals had to decide whether the goal was to move imaginatively beyond the New Testament toward the eschatological–egalitarian trajectory of the Scriptures, or to go back and imitate a culturally bound New Testament ecclesiology, including its Pauline restrictions on women.

16. Alexander, *Limited Liberty*, 152.
17. See Alexander, *Limited Liberty*, 155, 159.
18. Alexander, *Limited Liberty*, 154.
19. Hyatt, "Spirit-Filled Women," 247.
20. Kenyon, "Ethical Issues," 281.
21. See Archer, *Pentecostal Hermeneutic*, 136–8.
22. See Martin, "Gender Paradox," who disagrees with the majority scholarly opinion of describing Pentecostalism as a "regressive," "fundamentalist," or "conservative throw-back" (61–2).
23. Alexander, "Introduction," 4.

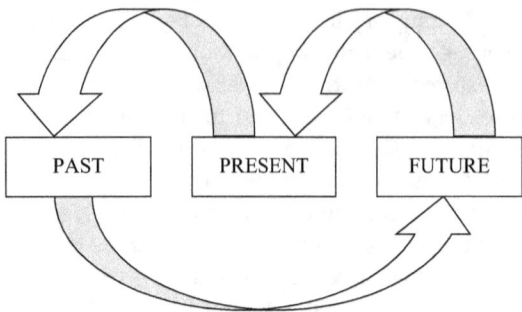

**Figure 1** The eschatological hermeneutic.

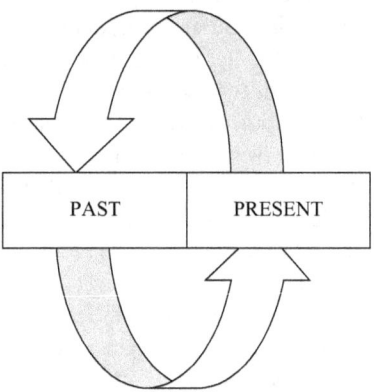

**Figure 2** The restorationist hermeneutic.

The above illustrations (Figures 1 and 2) of the two hermeneutics demonstrate the distinction. The "past" represents the biblical text (and its reading), the "future" denotes the eschatological trajectory of the text, the "present" the practices resulting from the text, and the arrows the imaginative movement in time.

Land explains this movement in time like this: "The Spirit acts as a kind of 'time machine' via the Word, enabling the believer to travel backward and forward in salvation history and to imaginatively participate in the events that have been and are yet to be."[24] It was this eschatological hermeneutic and movement in time that liberated women in new ways and authorized their ministries in early Pentecostalism. Early Pentecostals looked to the past biblical text, not to imitate its practices in the present (Figure 2), but to imagine its future eschatological promises and then put those promises into practice in the here and now (Figure 1).

Restoration of New Testament Christianity (Figure 2) was not the goal of early Pentecostals, for they did not consider it the full expression of God's eschatological

---

24. Land, *Pentecostal Spirituality*, 92.

kingdom. To merely "re-experience" the text, as some have argued,[25] is insufficient and causes ambiguity concerning women's roles. Rather, the goal is to reimagine what the text might mean in the present based on its eschatological trajectory. As argued below, the absence of this future eschatological orientation in the restorationist hermeneutic led over time to the eventual loss of an authorizing hermeneutic for women.

Several scholars have argued that restorationism indeed was (or still is) the dominant hermeneutic for reading Scripture among Pentecostals (post-1914). Although some believe it is the best way to understand *early* Pentecostals—a notion my previous chapters refute—their work is revealing in that their argument indicates the incredible traction this restorationist mindset eventually had as it replaced the early eschatological mindset. Blumhofer is the most notable to argue for restorationism as the leading paradigm for understanding Pentecostals. She argues that the restorationist mindset of Pentecostals was the "driving force" of the movement and was and still is what makes Pentecostals who they are.[26] Blumhofer defines restorationism as "the attempt to recapture the presumed vitality, message, and form of the Apostolic Church. . . . Based on a nostalgic sense of the pristine experience of the first Christians, restorationism articulates a yearning for the return of 'the good old days.'"[27] She depicts Pentecostals as looking for a full restoration of the New Testament experience and believing that restoring the true church of the New Testament would bring about the *eschaton*.[28]

What is significant is Blumhofer's argument that these restorationist tendencies created a "restorationist ambiguity" surrounding the role of women.[29] A restorationist reading of Scripture, suggests Blumhofer, inevitably led to "a New Testament warrant for regulating women's participation."[30] She traces the ambiguities about women in ministry to a restorationist hermeneutic that could be used to either support or restrict the ministry of women depending on which New Testament Christianity one is seeking to restore.[31] In a separate work, Blumhofer describes well the hermeneutical tension a restorationist perspective brings:

---

25. Joseph Byrd, "Paul Ricoeur's Hermeneutical Theory and Pentecostal Proclamation," *Pneuma* 15, no. 2 (Fall 1993): 205.
26. Blumhofer, *Assemblies of God*, 1:15.
27. Blumhofer, *Assemblies of God*, 1:18.
28. Blumhofer, *Assemblies of God*, 1:20–1.
29. Blumhofer, *Restoring the Faith*, 177. Again, Blumhofer believes this became the dominant paradigm earlier than I do. There are certainly seeds of restorationism in early Pentecostalism, but I have argued that an eschatological mindset was much more prominent in the first few decades. However, the point is restorationism *did* eventually become the primary hermeneutic used by Pentecostals.
30. Blumhofer, *Assemblies of God*, 1:15.
31. Blumhofer, *Assemblies of God*, 1:358–9.

The issues raised by restorationism were complex. On the one hand, the restorationist reading of the New Testament backed the appeal for new power in the Holy Spirit. Early Pentecostals took metaphors such as latter rain with restorationist seriousness and thus challenged accepted practices and traditions, including appropriate roles for women. On the other hand, restorationists noticed the apparently overwhelming preponderance of texts that narrowed women's sphere. The liberationist and the patriarchal exegesis, then, were rooted in ambiguities in the restorationist reading of Scripture, for taking everything in the New Testament literally gives us both daughters speaking their visions and women keeping silence.[32]

In other words, seeking to imitate the New Testament through restorationist readings creates an inescapable and paradoxical tension concerning the role of women. Which roles for gender are to be restored: the eschatological-egalitarian community of the Spirit or the institutionalized hierarchical order of some of the epistles?[33]

Others have argued similarly that it was the restorationist or primitive impulses of Pentecostals that eventually led to the simultaneous affirmation and exclusion of women.[34] Susie Stanley argues that the "primitivist emphasis" of Pentecostals "reflected a restorationist perspective with the goal of restoring the practices of the early church."[35] Stanley interprets this more positively, arguing this restorationist impulse led to what she calls "egalitarian primitivism," meaning Pentecostals' desire to imitate the early church led to an egalitarian praxis.[36] However, her assessment that this primitivism reflects an *early* Pentecostal reading of Scripture is inaccurate or at best anachronistic; rather, it was an eschatological impulse that fueled the early egalitarianism. If early Pentecostals did use primitivist concerns, it was subservient to and used to fuel their eschatological imaginations.[37]

As the restorationist impulse of early Pentecostals led to an eschatological impulse, they realized the New Testament was incomplete in that it proposed an eschatological way of living that was not yet fully realized within the text. Said another way, the Bible—and particularly its eschatological texts—was the right place to begin for it laid out the trajectory (Figure 1), but the wrong place to end (Figure 2). Restorationist thinking was not meant to *be* a hermeneutic but *lead to* a hermeneutic. The later restorationist impulse described by Stanley is what caused initial egalitarian practices to come under scrutiny. This misreading of early Pentecostalism is potentially disruptive for women's equality, for it perpetuates the restorationist myth which in turn perpetuates the gender paradox. As Archer

---

32. Blumhofer, *Restoring the Faith*, 176.
33. See Blumhofer, *Assemblies of God*, 1:355–72.
34. See, for example, Wacker's chapter on women in *Heaven Below*.
35. Stanley, "Pentecostal Women Preachers," 19, 28.
36. Stanley, "Pentecostal Women Preachers," 29.
37. A point made by Land, *Pentecostal Spirituality*, 46, 51–2.

comments, reading any later literalistic hermeneutic back into early Pentecostal hermeneutics is a "sweeping pejorative generalization."[38]

But even if anachronistic, historians such as Blumhofer are right to highlight the ambiguity that a restorationist way of thinking eventually brought to the gender question. Early Pentecostals used a forward-looking eschatological hermeneutic. What authorized women was not looking back, but ultimately looking forward, for the cry "Back to Pentecost" was really a cry of "forward to the coming kingdom."[39] Ironically, looking back to the biblical past throws us into the future.[40] As illustrated in Figure 1, early Pentecostals looked back to the biblical text, which caused them to look forward in imaginative eschatological anticipation and ultimately led them to look to the present to participate in the eschatological future. Women were not just seen to be restoring the biblical status of women (the later restorationist hermeneutic, Figure 2), but to be ushering in a *new* eschatological age of the Spirit. Therefore, restorationist and eschatological ways of reading Scripture are two competing impulses that led (and lead) to different results for Pentecostal women. A restorationist hermeneutic or return to primitive Christianity will not capture the egalitarian thrust of early Pentecostalism and the eschatological hermeneutic they used. But as Pentecostals replaced their eschatological imagination with restorationist imitation, the clarity and conviction of the eschatological authorization for women in leadership was replaced with restorationist reservations. The next section exposes how these restorationist tendencies also caused Pentecostals to change their eschatology and privilege a literal reading of Scripture, all of which began to invert the egalitarian trajectory of early Pentecostalism.

### 3.1.2 Eschatology: From Latter Rain to Dispensational

Pentecostals of the first few decades of the twentieth century looked more forward than backward to determine their present practices, as evidenced by the imaginative latter rain language used by early Pentecostals. The early rain was Pentecost, and the latter rain was the movement they were experiencing. The early rain established the church, and the latter rain was ripening it for the end-time harvest.[41] The goal was not to go back to the "former rain" of Acts 2, not to recover the primitive "good old days" as Blumhofer and others argue. Rather, early Pentecostals looked forward beyond the text, believing "they would experience within their communal life the reality of the age to come."[42] Early Pentecostals saw

---

38. Archer, *Pentecostal Hermeneutic*, 90; see 89–93.

39. Not directly quoting, but playing off Land, *Pentecostal Spirituality*, 46, 51–2. Land calls the movement "simultaneously restorationist and eschatological" (6). See also Faupel, *Everlasting Gospel*, 304.

40. Shields, *Eschatological Imagination*, 2.

41. See Faupel, *Everlasting Gospel*, 30–5.

42. Faupel, *Everlasting Gospel*, 43.

themselves as "Pentecost continued" and moving toward "the final Pentecost" that would close out the present age.⁴³ They were not satisfied with simply restoring New Testament practices as later Pentecostals emphasized. Rather, in the words of Azusa participant Joseph Grainger, this new movement was "a foretaste of the glad millennial day" to come.⁴⁴

However, the latter rain eschatology of early Pentecostals was slowly replaced with a dispensational eschatology.⁴⁵ This change was problematic as dispensationalists rejected the connection between the "latter rain" Pentecostal outpouring with the "early rain" Joel 2/Acts 2 outpouring.⁴⁶ The ideas of dispensationalism trace their roots back to British theologian John Nelson Darby (1800–1882) and found their way into mainstream conservative Christianity through Cyrus Scofield's influential *Scofield Reference Bible* (1909).⁴⁷ Scofield's Bible eventually led to more popular works such as Hal Lindsey's *The Late Great Planet Earth* and more recently the *Left Behind* novels by Tim LaHaye and Jerry Jenkins at the end of the century. Dispensational beliefs vary, but a basic conviction is that the current dispensation will soon end and be followed by the "rapture" of the saints.⁴⁸

---

43. See Faupel, *Everlasting Gospel*, 187–8, who is quoting early participants of the movement such as H. A. Ironside and G. Campbell Morgan.

44. Joseph A. Grainger, "Testimonies," *AF* 1, no. 12 (January 1908): 4.

45. For the differences between the two and evidence that dispensationalism was a later development and at odds with the heart of early Pentecostal eschatology (a consensus opinion), see Craig Keener, *Spirit Hermeneutics: Reading Scripture in Light of Pentecost* (Grand Rapids: Eerdmans, 2016), 53–4; L. William Oliverio Jr., *Theological Hermeneutics in the Classical Pentecostal Tradition: A Typological Account* (Leiden: Brill, 2012), 29, 114–16; McQueen, *Pentecostal Eschatology*, 60–199, particularly 57, 74, 101, 142; McQueen, "Early Pentecostal Eschatology," 139–54; Vondey, *Beyond Pentecostalism*, 62–6; Thompson, *Kingdom Come*, ix–x, 2–3, 23–58; Frank D. Macchia, "Baptized in the Spirit: Towards a Global Theology of Spirit Baptism," in Kärkkäinen, *Spirit in the World*, 11; Althouse, *Moltmann*, xii, 1–16, 35–60; Arrington, "Dispensationalism"; Dayton, *Theological Roots*, 145–6. For a slightly different take, one that questions the assumption the AG fully adopted fundamentalist dispensationalism and that sees more similarities than differences between the latter rain eschatology and dispensationalism, see Isgrigg, *Imagining the Future*, esp. 5, 81–3, 95–8.

46. Oliverio, *Theological Hermeneutics*, 114.

47. For more on "Scofieldian dispensationalism" and the hermeneutical and eschatological system it promoted, see Thompson, *Kingdom Come*, 3, 7, and especially his chapter, "Strange Bedfellows: An Analysis and Critique of the Pentecostal Adoption and Adaptation of Scofieldian Dispensationalism," 49–58.

48. For some history on dispensationalism and a summary of it as an eschatological system and hermeneutic see Yong, *Days of Caesar*, 318–23. See also John A. Bertone, "Seven Dispensations or Two-Age View of History: A Pauline Perspective," in Althouse and Waddell, *Eschatologies*, 61–94; Peter Prosser, *Dispensationalist Eschatology and Its Influence on American and British Religious Movements* (Lewiston, NY: Edwin Mellen, 1999).

Therefore, dispensational eschatology relegates many of the prophetic promises of Scripture to future times or "dispensations" until Christ returns. This type of eschatology tends to tolerate inequalities such as gender hierarchy until "the end" rather than to transform them in the present. Why Pentecostals would uncritically adopt such a paradigm that seems at odds with their history is a question that has perplexed Pentecostal scholars,[49] but its approval has had tremendous impact on the movement and the role of women in it.

As the imaginative and participatory latter rain eschatology of early Pentecostals gave way to the literalistic and reserved-only-for-the-future fundamentalist dispensationalism, the role of women waned. This shift and its impact on hermeneutics are best summarized by Larry McQueen in his analysis of Pentecostal eschatology:

> It may be concluded that the trajectories of eschatology that apply these texts solely to the future are most often associated with a hermeneutic that does not incorporate the movement's [early] spirituality into the interpretive process, but rather focuses on reasoned principles of interpretation. These trajectories of thought lean *toward* classical dispensationalism. Conversely, the trajectories that allow for contemporary application of these biblical texts are most often associated with a hermeneutic that incorporates the dynamic spirituality of the [early] movement... These trajectories of thought lean *away from* classical dispensationalism.[50]

McQueen concludes that later Pentecostal eschatologies such as classical dispensationalism lacked continuity with the historical heart of the movement and removed eschatology from informing Pentecostal hermeneutics and present practice.[51] That is to say, as Pentecostals shifted away from the eschatological dialectic of imagination and participation, they decided to adopt more literalistic ways of reading Scripture. The key is not to try to recapture a specific *type* of eschatology, for there were many, but to employ the early Pentecostal eschatological methodology that led to greater opportunity and freedom for women in Pentecostal churches.[52]

Other prominent Pentecostal scholars have connected the rise of dispensationalist eschatology (and its methodology) with hermeneutical literalism.[53] Some of that story is discussed and critiqued below (see 3.3.1). However, my immediate

---

49. In *Kingdom Come*, Thompson explains some of the historical circumstances that caused Pentecostals to adopt dispensational thinking (49–59 and elsewhere). Most attribute it to the "historical pressures" of the day and desire to gain credibility with other fundamentalist and evangelical groups (Althouse, *Moltmann*, 39–41).
50. McQueen, *Pentecostal Eschatology*, 142; brackets mine, italics in the original.
51. See McQueen, *Pentecostal Eschatology*, 142, 200–1.
52. See previous discussion on eschatology as a methodology in the Introduction and 2.4.
53. See Thompson, *Kingdom Come*, 26–8, who also suggests dispensationalism is more than an eschatology but is also a hermeneutic (43). See also Yong, *Days of Caesar*, 5–6, 318–23.

focus is eschatology's impact on gender and how dispensational ways of thinking and corresponding literal readings of Scripture led to the waning of present eschatological passion and participation,[54] all of which had negative impact on the ministry of women.[55] Warrington and Alexander conclude that it was the demise of early Pentecostal eschatological intensity that caused hierarchical structures to emerge, which limited the ministry of women.[56] Griffith and Roebuck argue that a loss of eschatological urgency led to "an increasingly male ministry,"[57] and Margaret Poloma states that as the eschatological intensity of Pentecostalism waned so too did the leadership of women.[58] Kenyon concludes that as the eschatological vision of the Assemblies of God was lost, so too was its message of liberation for women. As eschatological promises came to be reserved only for the future, says Kenyon, preservation of the status quo replaced the desire for prophesying daughters.[59]

Although I subscribe to the assessment by these Pentecostal scholars of the concomitant waning of eschatology as Pentecostal centerpiece for hermeneutics and praxis and the waning of women in leadership, a problem is that they tend to make these observations only in passing; most, if not all, are lacking historical evidence to back up their claims and end up turning their attention to other reasons for the decline of women.[60] Instead, we must test the hypothesis of the

54. An argument with wide scholarly consensus. See Allan Heaton Anderson, *An Introduction to Pentecostalism: Global Charismatic Christianity*, 2nd ed. (Cambridge: Cambridge University Press, 2014), 233; Land, *Pentecostal Spirituality*, 193; McQueen, *Joel*, 89; Dayton, *Theological Roots*, 33n44; Kenyon, "Ethical Issues," 402. Daniel Castelo claims eschatological fervor has been diminishing for some time and "Pentecostal eschatological expectancy is in tatters" ("Patience as a Theological Virtue: A Challenge to Pentecostal Eschatology," in Althouse and Waddell, *Eschatologies*, 234). See also Peter Althouse, "The Landscape of Pentecostal and Charismatic Eschatology: An Introduction," in Althouse and Waddell, *Eschatologies*, 1–21. Althouse elsewhere argues that it not so much waned as was replaced with less urgent eschatologies influenced by fundamentalism, which were less in line with the liberating social ethic of early Pentecostalism (see Althouse, *Moltmann*, 1–16). McQueen also critiques contemporary Pentecostal eschatology based on his analysis of early Pentecostal eschatology (*Pentecostal Eschatology*, 207–14).

55. As noted and concluded by Alexander, *Limited Liberty*, 26; Johns, "Conscientization," 165; Land, *Pentecostal Spirituality*, 187, 210.

56. Warrington, *Pentecostal Theology*, 148, alluding to Barfoot and Sheppard, "Prophetic vs. Priestly," 2–17; Alexander, *Limited Liberty*, 25–6. Similar conclusions are found in Land, *Pentecostal Spirituality*, 180, 187; Tackett, "Callings," 78; Peter Althouse, "The Landscape," 15.

57. Griffith and Roebuck, "Women," 1205.

58. Margaret Poloma, "Charisma, Institutionalization and Social Change," *Pneuma* 17, no. 2 (1995): 245.

59. Kenyon, "Ethical Issues," 403.

60. This goes back to the initial claim in my Introduction and Chapter 1, namely, that many have hinted at a relationship between eschatology and gender, but no one has consistently tested it as a constructive method.

### 3. The Loss of Eschatology as Authorizing Hermeneutic

correlation between the waning of eschatology as authorizing hermeneutic and the waning of the ministry of women. The next section investigates the impact this shift in eschatology and the loss of its authorizing hermeneutic had on women as previously accepted egalitarian practices came into question, both on paper and in practice. The section takes a similar historical approach with the same geographical parameters as the previous chapter, except now looking at the "post-organizational era" of so-called "Priestly Pentecostalism" rather than the "pre-organizational era" of "Prophetic Pentecostalism."[61] As the Azusa Street revival came to an "end" in 1914 and official denominations and decisions came into being, the inverse of the eschatological–egalitarian trajectory began. The "unifying thread" between eschatology and women's equality was slowly being severed.[62]

### 3.2 The Impact: The Loss of Eschatology as Authorizing Hermeneutic

The shift from an imaginative eschatological latter rain hermeneutic to a more literal-restorationist dispensational hermeneutic was catastrophic for women. The changing center of Pentecostal hermeneutics from an experiential, Spirit-driven hermeneutic to a more literalistic and fundamentalist approach[63] eventually led to two related developments that hindered the ministry of women. First, gender texts that were previously used to validate and authorize women leaders were reinterpreted sans an eschatological hermeneutic. Second, this shifting hermeneutic allowed a separate set of more literally interpreted texts to begin to dominate, putting them equal with and at times superior to the eschatological texts that were so prominently featured in the early years. This section provides historical and contemporary examples to illustrate the loss of the authorizing hermeneutic of eschatology and its impact on Pentecostal women. These developments support my proposal concerning the need to construct an interpretive lens and hermeneutic that is true to the historical heart of the movement and its eschatological–egalitarian thrust.

As Chapter 2 discovered, texts such as Galatians 3:28 and especially Joel 2/Acts 2 were read as eschatological texts that authorized the ministry callings of women, whom early Pentecostals celebrated as signs of the inbreaking of God's kingdom. Therefore, it would be shocking for early Pentecostals to read these words in 1973 from the largest Pentecostal denomination in the United States: "the Church of God in Christ cannot accept the following Scriptures as a mandate to ordain women preachers: Joel 2:28; Gal 3:28-29; Matt. 28:9-11."[64] In its section on women, that *Official Manual* of COGIC goes on to privilege texts such as 1 Timothy 3:2-7

---

61. The two similar eras laid out by Kenyon and Barfoot and Sheppard. See 2.1.
62. Grant, "Merchandised Women," 282.
63. See Alexander and Gause, *Women*, 15–16; Thompson, *Kingdom Come*, 53–7.
64. *Church of God in Christ Official Manual* (Memphis: Church of God in Christ Publishing, 1973), quoted in Ware, "Spiritual Egalitarianism," 224.

and Titus 1:7-9 to argue for male-only ordained ministry. The COGIC statement is not an isolated example but, rather, the culmination of the slow inverse of the early egalitarian trajectory due to the loss of eschatology as an authorizing hermeneutic.

A significant example is the largest Pentecostal denomination in the world, the Assemblies of God, and its US branch. As early as its formation in 1914, a hermeneutical inconsistency and ambiguity begins to emerge that departs from the early hermeneutical certainty and boldness concerning women leaders.[65] In a fascinating juxtaposition of texts in the section "Rights and Offices of Women" from its inaugural 1914 *General Council Minutes*, the Conference Committee asserts the right for women to preach while at the same time limiting their roles. The exact wording and ordering of the first half of the section is worth reproducing in full as it appears in the minutes.

> The Conference Committee recommended to the GENERAL COUNCIL that whereas the hand of God is mightily upon many women to proclaim and publish the "good tidings of great joy" in a wonderful way, that the GENERAL COUNCIL of the ASSEMBLIES OF GOD submit the following Scriptures for consideration.
>
> 1. In Christ, that is in the matter of salvation, the lines of sex are blotted out. Gal. 3:28.
> 2. Women are commanded to be in subjection and not to usurp authority over the man. 1 Tim. 2:11-15.
> 3. They are called to prophesy and preach the gospel. Acts 2:17.[66]

Early publications such as *The Apostolic Faith* often allowed the two texts of Galatians 3:28 and Acts 2 to stand alone together (without mentioning other texts) in support of women in ministry.[67] In contrast, the tension and ambiguity concerning the role of women is exemplified in the Assemblies of God statement in two ways. First, the layout is significant. The eschatological texts of Galatians 3:28 and Acts 2:17 are "interrupted" by 1 Timothy 2:11-15 and the call to be under the authority of men. Second, the commentary on Galatians 3:28 is important and decisive. The disclaimer that the text applies primarily to "the matter of salvation"

---

65. For 1914 as the beginnings of the slow loss of egalitarian boldness, see 2.1. The story of the Church of God (Cleveland, TN) shows a very similar, and perhaps even quicker, "devolution" of women's leadership due to a new selectivity of texts. See Alexander, "Persisting and Worshipping through Brokenness," 141–4.

66. *Combined Minutes of the General Council of the Assemblies of God* (St. Louis: Gospel Publishing House, 1914), 7, in The Flower Pentecostal Heritage Center Archives, accessed on May 11, 2021, at: https://archives .ifphc.org/DigitalPublications/USA/Assemblies%20of%20God%20USA/Minutes%20General%20Council/Unregistered/1914/FPHC/1914_04_11.pdf.

67. See 2.2.2 for examples.

is a definitive break from earlier eschatological interpretations of Galatians 3:28 that were used to authorize the ministry of women,[68] a shift in thinking recognized by several scholars and historians.[69]

Perhaps no one represents (or influenced) the above shift more than E. N. Bell, the chairman of the first General Council of the Assemblies of God in 1914.[70] Unlike many of his Pentecostal predecessors who viewed women leaders and preachers as signs of the last days and a new era of the Spirit of God, Bell declared there was no precedent "either in example or by direct teaching" for women to hold positions of authority and "no scriptural precept or example for such independent leadership by women."[71] Bell's desire for a "direct teaching" and "scriptural precept" represents the move toward a literal-restorationist hermeneutic that would have been foreign to some early Pentecostals. Although the Assemblies of God early statements are not as definitive as the 1973 COGIC position, they mark the beginnings of a shift within the movement from eschatological to restorationist understandings, which resulted in the authorizing latter rain hermeneutic being swallowed up by literalistic interpretations of Scripture.

Further distinctions between the ministry of men and women continued over the next two decades.[72] The 1931 General Council resolution on the ordination of women begins with the statement, "Inasmuch as the scriptures *clearly teach* that there is a difference in the prerogative of the ministry of men and women in the church," and then goes on to regulate their ordination to that of an evangelist and restricts their ability to perform funerals, weddings, and administer the ordinances of baptism and the Lord's Supper.[73] Commenting on this resolution, Griffith and Roebuck claim that it silenced "the argument that women should do these pastoral functions in the last days because of the urgency of the times" and instead created a new "pattern of limitation."[74] A slight improvement to the 1931 resolution was offered at the 1935 General Council but still extended different requirements for

68. Such as William Seymour and Maria Woodworth-Etter (see 2.2.2).

69. For example, see the "Women in Ministry" section in Edith L. Blumhofer and Chris R. Armstrong, "Assemblies of God," in *NIDPCM*, 335.

70. For more on Bell, see Qualls, *Forgive Us*, 15–16, 102–7; Blumhofer, *Assemblies of God*, 1:206–7.

71. E. N. Bell, "Women Elders," *The Christian Evangel* 15 (August 1914): 2; E. N. Bell, "Some Complaints," *Word and Witness* 10, no. 1 (January 20, 1914): 2. See also quotes in Stephenson, *Dismantling*, 42–3.

72. For an extensive overview of the changing positions of the AG on women, see Kenyon, "Ethical Issues," 219–77.

73. *Constitution and By-Laws of the General Council of the Assemblies of God* (1931), 17–18, accessed on May 11, 2021, at: https://archives.ifphc.org/DigitalPublications/USA/Assemblies%20of%20God%20USA/Minutes%20General%20Council/Unregistered/1931/FPHC/1931.pdf; italics mine.

74. Griffith and Roebuck, "Women," 1205.

female ordination and represented little more than a "technical improvement" that did not address underlying reservations about women in ministry.[75]

Questions of women's authority and place in the church began to dominate in the post-organizational era. Practices that went unquestioned at the beginning, such as single women going out to the mission field (à la Zelma Argue), were now coming under scrutiny and having limitations placed upon them.[76] The early Pentecostal call for prophesying daughters to go out in boldness was now replaced with the cry for Spirit-filled men to take the reins of leadership in the movement.[77] Double standards for women increased as the amount and influence of women in visible leadership decreased.[78] For example, despite several women speaking at the Assembly of God's General Conference in the first seven years, including the keynote address in 1917, not a single woman preached an evening service at General Council in the sixty years between 1921 and 1981, and from 1933 to the late 1970s only three women appeared as speakers of any kind at General Council services.[79]

The Pentecostal Assemblies of Canada shows a similar pattern to the Assemblies of God. In their study of the PAOC, Ambrose and Michael Wilkinson tell the story of the "marked contrast" in women's roles between the first three decades of the PAOC and what followed.[80] They document the "surprising departure" from the early Joel 2/Acts 2-inspired egalitarian practices to a highly gender-specific ministry where women were pushed to the sideline, taught to shun visible leadership, and confined to minister solely to other women.[81] What Wilkinson and Ambrose find most surprising is how this complementarian thinking was not only accepted by women but even promoted by female leaders.[82] Instead of Galatians 3:28 or Acts 2 as central texts for women, the pages of postwar PAOC publications feature texts that are interpreted as teaching women not to challenge male authority figures and to instead be a "help-meet" and "support" to male leaders.[83] The end result was the PAOC not allowing the ordination of women until 1984 or women to

---

75. Blumhofer, *Assemblies of God*, 1:368–9.

76. For examples see Wacker, *Heaven Below*, 172; Qualls, *Forgive Us*, 129.

77. Qualls, *Forgive Us*, 129. For more on the shift toward the call for more male leaders, see Qualls, *Forgive Us*, 134–5.

78. See Wacker, *Heaven Below*, 171–5 for lots of examples; see also Tackett, "Callings," 79–85; English de Alminana, "Introduction," 16.

79. Wacker, *Heaven Below*, 166; Kenyon, "Ethical Issues," 229, 278.

80. Wilkinson and Ambrose, *After the Revival*, 88 (see 86–94 for their full discussion).

81. Wilkinson and Ambrose, *After the Revival*, 90, 92. They attribute this mostly to Pentecostalism reflecting postwar Canadian society and culture (see 86–8).

82. See the three examples given from the *Pentecostal Testimony* in Wilkinson and Ambrose, *After the Revival*, 88–94.

83. Wilkinson and Ambrose, *After the Revival*, 92–3 (see also 89–90).

hold district or national leadership positions until 1998.[84] In light of continued practices that privilege men over women for leadership roles, Ambrose concludes that the PAOC's more recent commitments to gender equality "ring hollow."[85]

Similar stories can be told of other Pentecostal denominations or leaders. Whereas early on Seymour passionately defended the involvement and equality of women with the eschatological passages of Galatians 3:28 and Acts 2:17,[86] it was his later rigid determination for a literal reading of Scripture to settle all controversial matters that led him in a different, less egalitarian, direction.[87] Pentecostal movements founded by women, such as the International Church of the Foursquare Gospel (McPherson) and the Apostolic Faith Church (Crawford), were succeeded by men.[88] During McPherson's life, about three-quarters of all ordinations were female, a number that has steadily declined since her death.[89] In the Church of God (Cleveland, TN), women have been continually restricted from ministry and even serving on church councils (boards), and the percent of credentialed ministers who are women has consistently hovered below 5 percent.[90] Similar to Bell in the Assemblies of God, the Church of God suffered from the literalistic interpretation of Scripture by A. J. Tomlinson who initiated the "Tomlinsonian" limitations on women.[91] And the situation is largely similar in countries outside of North America where many Pentecostal women currently may teach but not preach, must ensure male authority over them, cannot be ordained, are instructed to remain silent, must adhere to specific dress codes, are forced to embrace a separate sphere of ministry because of their gender, and are underrepresented in formal leadership.[92] Knowing Pentecostalism's egalitarian beginnings and history,

---

84. For more of the PAOC story on women, see Holmes, "Canadian," 185–7; Pamela Holmes, "The 'Place' of Women in Pentecostal/Charismatic Ministry Since the Azusa Street Revival," in *The Azusa Street Revival and Its Legacy*, ed. Harold Hunter and Cecil M. Robeck Jr. (Eugene, OR: Wipf & Stock, 2006), 301–4; Cavaness, "Leadership Attitudes," 126–7.

85. Linda M. Ambrose, "Shaming the Men into Keeping Up with the Ladies: Constructing Pentecostal Masculinities," in Alexander et al., *Sisters, Mothers, Daughters*, 69.

86. See 2.2.2. See also Cecil M. Robeck Jr., *The Azusa Street Mission and Revival* (Nashville: Thomas Nelson, 2006), 31, 99.

87. See Robeck, *Azusa Street*, 114–15, 125; Wacker, *Heaven Below*, 170–1.

88. In her research on Afro-Christian churches, Crumbley found that "a female founder guarantees neither gender egalitarian structures nor a female successor" ("Sanctified Saints," 115–34).

89. See Payne, *Gender*, 132–3; Barfoot and Sheppard, "Prophetic vs. Priestly," 15.

90. Alexander and Gause, *Women*, 20.

91. Alexander and Bowers, *What Women Want*, 24. See examples in Alexander, "Persisting and Worshipping Through Brokenness," 146–8.

92. For just a sampling of these stories, see J. Ma, "Changing Images," 203–14, esp. 211; Crumbley, "Gender, Race and the Body," 89–108; Crumbley, "Sanctified Saints"; Jacob K. Olupona, "Africa, West," in *NIDPCM*, 19–20; Paul Lewis, "Indonesia," in *NIDPCM*, 129–30. Many situations would be like Jamaica where the Pentecostal church "is a community of

one might ask, what happened?[93] How did the question of women's ministry go from being "forever settled"[94] by eschatological texts such as Joel 2/Acts 2 to being a debated and controversial issue in Pentecostal churches? Why did the egalitarian trajectory of the early years reverse, seemingly unchecked?

Scholars have attempted to give many reasons for the decline.[95] Cultural accommodation and institutionalization,[96] the "lure of acceptance" from evangelicals,[97] economic and cultural factors,[98] and fear and suspicion of liberalism or feminism[99] are just a few of the frequent reasons given. What is rarely stated as a reason is the loss of the eschatological authorizing hermeneutic, despite the evidence in the last chapter that this was a (if not *the*) primary factor in establishing the credibility of women leaders in the first few decades. In their research on contemporary Pentecostal attitudes toward women in ministry, Alexander and Bowers found the primary reason given by their respondents for not fully affirming the ministry of women was a desire to be faithful to the Scriptures.[100] Hermeneutical concerns are at the core of the gender paradox and must therefore be a part of resolving it. In order to close out this section and argument, three brief examples from three different and diverse North American Pentecostal circles will help give a summary of the current majority view and status on the ground with regard to the gender question. These contemporary examples are chosen to

---

women, seemingly led by men. Women do most of the inconspicuous work of the church, while men take center stage" (William Wedenoja, "Jamaica (I)," in *NIDPCM*, 144).

93. A question Wacker poses in *Heaven Below*, 166, concerning the waning of the role of women.

94. See Alma White quote above in 3.1.1.

95. See my Introduction.

96. For a review of institutionalization, see Michael Wilkinson and Peter Althouse, *Catch the Fire: Soaking Prayer and Charismatic Renewal* (Dekalb, IL: NIU Press, 2014), 133–5; Qualls, *Forgive Us*, 182; Vondey, *Beyond Pentecostalism*, 183–9; Margaret Poloma and John Green, *The Assemblies of God: Godly Love and the Revitalization of American Pentecostalism* (New York: New York University Press, 2010), 98; Powers, "Pentecostalism 101," 133–51; Grenz and Kjesbo, *Women in the Church*, 2, 28.

97. Martin W. Mittelstadt, "My Life as a Mennocostal: A Personal and Theological Narrative," *Theodidaktos: Journal for EMC Theology and Education* 3, no. 2 (September 2008): 16. For more, see Qualls, *Forgive Us*, 124–6, 135–40, 183.

98. Wilkinson and Ambrose, *After the Revival*, 86–7; Blumhofer, *Assemblies of God*, 1:357, 366; David G. Roebuck and Karen Carroll Mundy, "Women, Culture, and Post-World War Two Pentecostalism," in *The Spirit and the Mind: Essays in Informed Pentecostalism*, ed. Terry L. Cross and Emerson B. Powery (Lanham, MD: University Press of America, 2000), 191–204.

99. Griffith and Roebuck, "Women," 1208; Griffith, "Women's Aglow," 1209–10. See also Qualls, *Forgive Us*, 140–3, 182; Clifton, "Sexism," 51–70; Yong, *Spirit Poured Out*, 192–3; Alexander and Bowers, *What Women Want*, 39–43.

100. Alexander and Bowers, *What Women Want*, 58–9.

represent both written and behavioral evidence in the United States and Canada of how literal interpretations of texts on gender have replaced the previous priority given to eschatological texts, representing the current need to establish a consistent and liberating hermeneutic.[101]

In her research on Appalachian Pentecostal women leaders of the early 1990s, Mary McClintock Fulkerson discovered women's particular struggle to accept God's call to preach due to the existing gender restrictions. She found that all but one of the Pentecostal women preachers she interviewed accepted the supposed biblical injunction for women to submit to their husbands and to the male leaders of the church.[102] Many insisted their ministering was "always appropriately submissive to the fully ordained male ministers."[103] In a move reminiscent of the 1931 Assemblies of God decision, most of these women were not allowed to baptize, perform weddings, or preside at the Lord's Supper.[104] Despite expressing extreme confidence in their own ability to preach, they considered public speaking to be *the* forbidden territory for women in order to stay faithful to the prohibitive texts.[105] These women chose to embrace "a limited strategy of freedom from male authority," which Fulkerson struggles to see as any kind of freedom at all but rather as evidence of gender oppression.[106]

In *Spiritual Gifts*, a widely read and consistently reprinted book in classical Pentecostal circles, David Lim seeks to give a "Pentecostal Perspective" on the gifts.[107] Of note is his section on women in ministry and their use of the gifts "from a Pentecostal point of view."[108] Lim emphasizes that women must minister in a "humble manner," should "not assume a position for her own prestige and power or covet a position that should be released to others," and should not seek

---

101. Similar stories could be given for other parts of the world. For example, Jenkins suggests the biggest "problem" regarding equality for Pentecostal Christians in the global South is that "contradicting the straightforward words of the biblical text is intolerable" (*Next Christendom*, 235).

102. Fulkerson, *Changing the Subject*, 266. See the chapter, "Joyful Speaking for God: Pentecostal Women's Performances," 239-98.

103. Fulkerson, *Changing the Subject*, 266.

104. Fulkerson, *Changing the Subject*, 267.

105. Fulkerson, *Changing the Subject*, 269, 286.

106. Fulkerson, *Changing the Subject*, 265-6n52, 293. She is also using Elaine Lawless's observations from *Handmaidens of the Lord*.

107. David Lim, *Spiritual Gifts: A Fresh Look; Commentary and Exhortation from a Pentecostal Perspective* (Springfield, MO: Gospel Publishing House, 1991). For a time, this book was often used by or introduced to students at Pentecostal schools and Bible colleges. Lim still speaks on the book frequently and was the featured speaker at a 2018 Pentecostal gathering of pastors in the PAOC that I attended, where he mostly used the book to outline his talks.

108. Lim, *Spiritual Gifts*, 176-8; mostly dealing with 1 Corinthians 14:34-35.

"personal glory."[109] Furthermore, she should understand that "submission does not mean suppression" and her "primary responsibility [is] to her husband and family" as "she is the heart and he is the head of the home."[110] *If* she does all this, then "God opens the doors" for ministry for her.[111]

Some may argue that it is the more traditional, larger Pentecostal denominations that lean toward hierarchical structures and interpretations of Scripture. However, in their study of charismatic Toronto fellowship Catch the Fire (John and Carol Arnott) and its soaking prayer ministry, Wilkinson and Peter Althouse discovered that the heavily restorationist tendencies of apostolic networks like Catch the Fire also lead to male-dominated leadership.[112] They document how in these movements "authority has shifted from a more egalitarian view of the 'the Spirit falling on all flesh' to favor men as apostles and to imbue the network with authority."[113] In other words, they have moved from an eschatological latter rain reading to a restorationist reading of imitating apostolic New Testament structures. Part of the difficulty for women, Wilkinson and Althouse argue, is that the focus among modern charismatics on impartation and release as a form of authority can lead to gender inequality in formal leadership.[114] They conclude that "while women are by far the ones who pray, have a passion for prayer, and have been responsible for the growth of soaking prayer, they are not granted the same kind of authority as men" and no women are officially acknowledged as apostles.[115] Any of the women who are prominent in leadership often are so only as partners with their husbands.[116]

These examples of how gender roles are being taught and practiced in three different Pentecostal groups all have in common the desire to be faithful to the biblical texts and its supposed prohibitions on women. Britt Peavy, an Ordained Bishop in the Church of God (Cleveland, TN), is an example of this majority position among Pentecostals. In a 2010 interview in *The Christian Century* he states:

> This has nothing to do with women not being smart enough or good enough or qualified enough . . . The issue is, did God know what he was talking about? And whether we like it or don't like it . . . if our rules, our standard, is biblical text,

---

109. Lim, *Spiritual Gifts*, 177.
110. Lim, *Spiritual Gifts*, 177, 178.
111. Lim, *Spiritual Gifts*, 177.
112. Wilkinson and Althouse, *Catch the Fire*, 122–6. Wilkinson and Althouse primarily use the term institutionalization to describe the reason for the shift away from egalitarianism (133–5). However, restorationism goes hand in hand with institutionalization and is one of its main causes.
113. Wilkinson and Althouse, *Catch the Fire*, 115.
114. Wilkinson and Althouse, *Catch the Fire*, 121.
115. Wilkinson and Althouse, *Catch the Fire*, 130.
116. Wilkinson and Althouse, *Catch the Fire*, 133.

3. *The Loss of Eschatology as Authorizing Hermeneutic* 111

then we have to be faithful to the biblical text even in contemporary society that sees it as bigoted or old-fashioned.[117]

What is noticeably lacking here and in all the above examples is reference to any of the eschatological texts that were consistently featured in the early Pentecostal movement. The hermeneutical shift to biblical literalism, influenced by dispensational thinking, and the corresponding loss of the eschatological authorizing hermeneutic for women caused these future-oriented texts to be ignored, replaced, or demoted in their priority or authority.[118] As a result, many Pentecostal churches and denominations are *less* open to the ministry of women than they were one hundred years ago.[119] Any increased roles given to women or emphasis on women's equality is now often seen as a "worldly" development rather than a Spirit-inspired eschatological development as it was with the early Pentecostals.[120]

There have been a few promising signs that a return to an eschatological hermeneutic holds the key to reaffirming and elevating the role of women. The 1990 Assemblies of God position paper "The Role of Women as Described in Holy Scripture" (reaffirmed at the 1991 General Council) makes a marked turn from earlier positions such as the 1914 and 1931 statements. It addresses the "problematic" texts used to restrict women in the 1914 resolution and uses an eschatological argument of "the fields ripe for the harvest" to authorize the ministry of women.[121] Most notable is that Galatians 3:28 is no longer taken to apply only to matters of salvation. It also introduces new arguments such as positioning gender inequality as a result of the Fall and claiming there is no hierarchy in Genesis 1–2 (an eschatological text, as argued in the next chapter). In a statement that sounds like a purposeful rebuke of E. N. Bell's previous position that there is no scriptural precedent for the ministry of women, the document concludes that "we cannot find convincing evidence that the ministry of women is restricted according to some sacred or immutable principle."[122] In an insightful comment on the position paper, Qualls highlights how it "reaches back to the earliest arguments" for the equality of women, which she does not name, but which I argue are eschatological arguments.[123] Yet, despite the positive hermeneutical developments in the

---

117. Religious News Service, "Church of God says Women Can't be Bishops," *The Christian Century* (August 27, 2010), https://www.christiancentury.org/article/2010-08/church-god-says-women-can-t-be-bishops.

118. See Thompson, *Kingdom Come*, 26–8.

119. The conclusion of Powers, "Pentecostalism 101," 149.

120. Roebuck and Mundy, "Post-World War Two Pentecostalism," 193.

121. "The Role of Women as Described in Holy Scripture," in *Where We Stand: The Official Position Papers of the Assemblies of God* (Springfield, MO: Gospel Publishing House, 2001).

122. "The Role of Women as Described in Holy Scripture," 189.

123. Qualls, *Forgive Us*, 176, 178.

1990 position paper, the majority of evidence is that an egalitarian position is not the norm within today's Pentecostalism. The lack of a consistent authorizing hermeneutic for women and literalistic interpretations of Scripture still plague the movement.

The historical investigation of the previous chapter and the first half of this chapter have sought to illustrate how contemporary Pentecostal positions or behaviors are often "all out of sorts with the views and practices of early Pentecostals."[124] The more Pentecostals stopped looking forward to inform their present practices and instead started searching for a biblical pristine past, the more women's influence has waned. Early Pentecostal women and men saw themselves as participating in the eschatological work of God's Spirit, which was evidenced by radical egalitarianism.[125] But as this eschatological emphasis faded, Pentecostals drifted into biblical literalism and searched for prototypes from the past rather than promises for the future. As a result, words like "submission," "covering," and "headship" that are rarely, if ever, mentioned in the early periodicals, slowly began to take over the discussion on women's place in the movement.[126] Therefore, women went from being scripturally justified by eschatological texts such as Galatians 3:28 and Joel 2/Acts 2 to being scripturally unqualified by other texts; the focus shifted from Joel's prophesying daughters to Paul's prohibitive directives as their eschatological freedom was replaced with biblical restrictions. The initial egalitarian trajectory of the movement gradually waned as eschatology—and its impact on reading Scripture—waned as well and was replaced with a more historical, literal reading of the Bible. However, there has been a resurgence and rethinking of both eschatology and hermeneutics in modern Pentecostal scholarship. These developments pave the way for a potential new critical hermeneutical approach to the gender paradox.

## 3.3 Modern Developments: The Re-Visioning of Eschatology and Hermeneutics

The gradual shift in eschatological beliefs and hermeneutical approaches among Pentecostals has not gone unnoticed, and a counter movement has arisen that seeks to reflect more closely the eschatology and hermeneutics of the early years of the movement. These historians and theologians are not naively promoting that Pentecostals duplicate uncritically the way things were, for, as previously stated, there is no "golden age" that simply needs to be rediscovered and repeated. Their goal is not to go back to the ways of the Azusa Street mission and revival or the early years, for that only represents the initial trajectory of Pentecostal

---

124. Green, *Lord's Supper*, 244. Johns attributes this to an inferiority complex among Pentecostals that causes them to borrow ill-fitting paradigms (*Pentecostal Formation*, 7).

125. Tackett, "Callings," 86.

126. Hyatt, "Spirit-Filled Women," 254–5.

egalitarianism inspired by the eschatological imagination.[127] As Alexander comments, "the gender line was strongly bent, but not broken" at Azusa—there was always more work to be done.[128] But, in the words of Archer, there is a growing desire among Pentecostals "to retrieve the praxis-driven spiritual ethos of the early Pentecostal movement and re-present it from a contemporary post-critical and Pentecostal perspective."[129] This desire among Pentecostal scholars has led to significant changes in Pentecostal eschatology and hermeneutics,[130] both of which open the door for a new or re-visioned eschatological hermeneutic for texts on gender.

### 3.3.1 Eschatology: From Dispensational to Transformational

The participatory, lived, and materialized eschatology of early Pentecostals slowly gave way to a speculative, otherworldly, end-times dispensational eschatology. This shift caused eschatological fervor to wane because it removed eschatological praxis from the center of Pentecostal life, which led to the diminishing role of women.[131] However, this shift in eschatology has more recently been critiqued by Pentecostal scholars, and a counter-hermeneutic has emerged. Those who study the movement are recognizing that dispensational thinking is at worst anti-Pentecostal and at best not in line with the heart and ethos of the movement.[132] It is outside the scope of this work to offer a full discussion or critique of dispensational eschatology,[133] but in summary the wedding of dispensational thinking to Pentecostalism has

---

127. See Waddell and Althouse, "The Promises and Perils," 367–71. See Althouse's three stages of eschatological thought from latter rain eschatology to fundamentalist dispensationalism to inaugurated eschatology ("Pentecostal Eschatology," 210–11). See also Althouse, *Moltmann*, 1–2.

128. Estrelda Y. Alexander, "The Role of Women in the Azusa Street Revival," in Hunter and Robeck, *Azusa Street*, 66. See also Land, *Pentecostal Spirituality*, 190; Blumhofer, *Assemblies of God*, 1:141.

129. Archer, *Pentecostal Hermeneutic*, 3. This shift in hermeneutics often includes an appreciation for the "pre-critical commonsense" interpretive methods of early Pentecostals (Archer, 125) as well as premodern patristic and mystic interpreters. See discussion of pre-critical models in 5.4.1.

130. For more on the interconnected relationship between the two, see Marius Nel, *African Pentecostalism and Eschatological Expectations: He Is Coming Back Again!* (Newcastle upon Tyne, UK: Cambridge Scholars, 2019), esp. Chapters 3 and 4 (104–31), on a new Pentecostal hermeneutics and its influence on eschatology.

131. See Land, *Pentecostal Spirituality*, 193, 210.

132. See Warrington, *Pentecostal Theology*, 310.

133. This work has already been done extensively. See McQueen's lengthy analysis and critique in his *Pentecostal Eschatology*. See also Isgrigg, *Imagining the Future*, 22–7; Sheppard, "Hermeneutics of Dispensationalism."

been called "disastrous" and "unfortunate,"[134] "alien" and "inimical" to Pentecostal thinking,[135] and at best an "uneasy" relationship.[136] Therefore, there has been a call from prominent Pentecostal scholars to rediscover, rethink, and then re-vision Pentecostal eschatology in a way that does justice to the heart and early character of the movement.[137]

The influential eschatologically driven works of Land, Althouse, and others, which call for a re-visioned Pentecostal eschatology, have led to a renewed focus on this task among Pentecostal scholars.[138] For example, in the final chapter of his work dedicated to developing a Pentecostal political theology, Yong argues for a participatory eschatological politics of hope based on the eschatological imagination.[139] Throughout the work and particularly in the last chapter,[140] Yong is critical of dispensational eschatology, primarily for three reasons: (1) it does not fit well with central and early Pentecostal commitments; (2) it lacks a pneumatological emphasis; and (3) it promotes "escapist" tendencies which lead to social inaction.[141] Yong concludes that dispensational ways of thinking are "misguided" and "counterintuitive to pentecostal spirituality," and he claims they are "uncritically borrowed from other Christian traditions, are inconsistent with the ethos, intuitions, and sensibilities of pentecostalism, and should be either rejected or severely revised."[142] He then seeks to articulate and construct a "counter-eschatology" that can be summarized as: (1) in line with the intuitions of the Pentecostal imagination; (2) pneumatological; and (3) transformational or

---

134. Thompson, *Kingdom Come*, 3, 48. Thompson's rebuke of dispensational thinking is scathing in *Kingdom Come* (see x, 3, 7, 43–58; Thompson, "Eschatology," 189–90).

135. Sammy Alfaro, "'*Se fue con el Señor*': The Hispanic Pentecostal Funeral as Anticipatory Celebration," in Althouse and Waddell, *Eschatologies*, 340–60; Thompson, "Eschatology," 189.

136. From Sheppard's title "Pentecostals and the Hermeneutics of Dispensationalism: The Anatomy of an Uneasy Relationship." See also Oliverio, *Theological Hermeneutics*, 113–16; Warrington, *Pentecostal Theology*, 309–10; McQueen, "Early Pentecostal Eschatology," 154; Althouse, *Moltmann*, 36–60; Land, *Pentecostal Spirituality*, 53–5; Arrington, "Dispensationalism"; Dayton, *Theological Roots*, 145–6. For a more positive treatment of premillennial dispensationalism in Pentecostalism, see James J. Glass, "Eschatology: A Clear and Present Danger—A Sure and Certain Hope," in *Pentecostal Perspectives*, ed. Keith Warrington (Carlisle, England: Paternoster, 1998), 120–46.

137. A big part of Althouse, *Moltmann*, Chapter 2 (see 61); Thompson, "Eschatology," 190; Alfaro, "Hispanic Pentecostal Funeral." Isgrigg reviews the key contributions of Althouse and Yong in this "revisioning" of Pentecostal eschatology in *Imagining the Future*, 29–35.

138. See my Introduction for more discussion of these scholar's works and of the recent revival of eschatology in Pentecostalism and its transformational nature.

139. See Yong, *Days of Caesar*, 316–58.

140. The work begins with a rebuke of dispensationalism (*Days of Caesar*, 4–6).

141. Yong, *Days of Caesar*, 317.

142. Yong, *Days of Caesar*, 325, 317–18.

"performative," meaning it has practical consequences in the social dimensions of the present age.[143] Yong claims this shift away from a futuristic dispensationalism (while still preserving the central commitment to the imminent return of Christ) is more in line with a Lukan eschatology that emphasizes the eschatological outpouring of the Spirit "on all flesh" in order to bring about the kingdom of God "in the last days" (Acts 2:17).[144] This kind of eschatology "affirms the Spirit's past, present, and future breaking into and redemption of history's times and places."[145]

Yong, while prominent, is neither the only nor the first Pentecostal scholar to call for a renewed Pentecostal eschatology that is pneumatological and transformational. Althouse puts the revisionist eschatologies of Pentecostal theologians Land, Macchia, Eldin Villafañe, and Miroslav Volf in conversation with the pneumatological eschatology of Moltmann. Althouse concludes that each of these scholars "argue for transformational eschatologies and thereby reject the fundamentalist vision of world destruction and passive resignation."[146] Much, if not most, of this "transformational ethic," as he calls it, has been lost in the middle years of Pentecostalism. However, Althouse observes that a strong movement exists toward a re-visioning of Pentecostal eschatology that recaptures the prophetic elements and social engagement of the early movement, "which have been displaced by an apocalyptic vision of the world's destruction."[147] Vondey also perceives that Pentecostal eschatology is changing. He argues it is moving away from classical dispensational thought toward emphasizing present transformation through the inbreaking of the last days as patterned by the eschatological activity of the Holy Spirit on the day of Pentecost.[148] In recovering the transformative dimensions of early Pentecostal eschatology, Vondey suggests that "a more socially and ethically responsible eschatology" is emerging.[149] Pentecostal scholars from other countries are echoing similar sentiments, calling for a more holistic African Pentecostal eschatology,[150] highlighting the interconnection of social and

---

143. This is my summary, based on Yong's argument throughout the chapter, including on 316–17 and 327–9. Yong makes similar arguments elsewhere (*Renewing*, 59).

144. Yong, *Days of Caesar*, 323, 330–2.

145. Yong, *Days of Caesar*, 338.

146. Althouse, *Moltmann*, 196. Moltmann is well known for his transformational eschatology. For Macchia's ethical eschatology as influenced by Moltmann, see *Baptized*, 91–112. See also Isgrigg's short section on "transformationalist eschatology" (*Imagining the Future*, 192–4).

147. Althouse, *Moltmann*, 1–2, 157.

148. Vondey, *Pentecostal Theology*, 138–44.

149. Vondey, *Pentecostal Theology*, 144. For example, see his remarks on creation care, 171–4.

150. J. Ayodeji Adewuya, "Constructing an African Pentecostal Eschatology: Which Way?" in Althouse and Waddell, *Eschatologies*, 361–74.

theological-eschatological issues in Latin America,[151] and recognizing the link between eschatology and social ministries around the world.[152]

Dispensational eschatology led to the reinterpretation or dismissal of eschatological texts on gender that once empowered women; it also introduced a literalist-restorationist hermeneutic that resulted in prioritizing restrictive texts from the Bible concerning the role of women. Therefore, (re)discovering and re-envisioning eschatology as a liberating approach may provide the key to resolving the gender paradox. In his article on the eschatological dialogue between the disciples and Jesus in Acts 1, Blaine Charette shows that the disciples' eschatological assumptions prevented them from recognizing the work of God in their midst and the role they were to play in that work, and even in some cases caused them to oppose God's work.[153] Charette concludes that "Luke can be read as a cautionary tale on the dangers that attend an overconfident attachment to a faulty eschatological perspective," and specifically mentions that a dispensationalist eschatology has blinded Pentecostals from recognizing God's eschatological activity in their midst.[154] The evidence suggests this change in eschatological thinking caused later Pentecostals to abandon their previous egalitarian impulse that led to a liberative praxis in favor of a restorationist approach that limited women.

Since eschatology and hermeneutics are interrelated, a renewed eschatology alone cannot overcome the gender paradox. Re-visioning Pentecostal eschatology requires and leads to re-visioning hermeneutics as well. A transformational eschatology that centers on the pneumatological imagination is interconnected with a Spirit-centered hermeneutic. Thompson makes the connection that a faulty eschatological way of thinking can cause Pentecostals to adopt questionable hermeneutics that downplay their pneumatology.[155] He concludes that the adoption of dispensational eschatology by Pentecostals is above all a pneumatological problem, which in turn makes it a hermeneutical problem.[156] But similar to recent developments in eschatology, Pentecostals are recapturing the pneumatological center of their hermeneutic that originally led to a dynamic way of reading Scripture that embraced the ministry of women. This (re)new(ed) hermeneutic provides an

---

151. Néstor Medina, "The New Jerusalem versus Social Responsibility: The Challenges of Pentecostalism in Guatemala," in Althouse and Waddell, *Eschatologies*, 339. For the relationship between liberation theology, popular in the South, and eschatology, see Hans Schwarz, *Eschatology* (Grand Rapids: Eerdmans, 2000), 152–62.

152. Miller and Yamamori, *Global Pentecostalism*, 59, 213; Rice, "Practicing the Passion of Pentecost," 69.

153. Blaine Charette, "Restoring the Kingdom to Israel: Kingdom and Spirit in Luke's Thought," in Althouse and Waddell, *Eschatologies*, 49–60.

154. Charette, "Restoring the Kingdom," 60.

155. Thompson, *Kingdom Come*, 127.

156. Thompson, *Kingdom Come*, 56.

opportunity to reappropriate in a critical fashion the liberating hermeneutic of early Pentecostals.

### 3.3.2 Hermeneutics: From Scripture-Centered to Spirit-Centered

Pentecostals desire both to be faithful to the Scriptures and to be led by the Spirit. These desires have sometimes led to competing or even conflicting impulses when it comes to the role of women in the church, which has led to the gender paradox. But is there a way to be Scripture-centered and Spirit-centered and still to promote the full inclusion of women in the ministry of the church? Proposing a viable way forward, Kenyon tells a story from the 1983 General Council where C. David Gable, a pastor from Fresno, California, brought a discussion to the floor about whether decisions about women in ministry were being made in a way faithful to the Pentecostal tradition. Using Acts 15 as his example, Gable argues that understanding what the Spirit is doing in churches may change one's interpretations of Scripture. Kenyon summarizes Gable:

> Gable explained to the Council that this was what the early Pentecostals and holiness people did regarding women preachers. They did not just follow the lead of other traditions. They examined the Word in light of what the Spirit was doing. Paul's restriction on women in authority had been enough for others, but those Spirit-led pioneers could not forget Joel's prophecy. And the same Paul who talked about women keeping silent had also said there is neither male nor female in Christ. The pioneers did not ignore the Word; they simply were determined to discover *a consistent application* predicated on the Work of the Spirit.[157]

Gable's argument is noteworthy in that it aligns with the early Pentecostal approach of prioritizing eschatological texts on gender (he alludes to Joel 2/Acts 2 and Galatians 3:28) over literal readings of more contextualized biblical texts. His call for a consistent application of the Word predicated on the work of the Spirit could not be more relevant to the eschatological hermeneutic and methodology I am proposing.

Kenyon contends the two eras of the movement—the pre-organization era, which encouraged the ministry of women, and the later era that restricted women—can be marked by two hermeneutics or ways of reading Scripture: "the age of the Spirit" and "strict allegiance to Scripture."[158] The first perspective, which

---

157. Kenyon, "Ethical Issues," 409; italics mine.

158. Kenyon, "Ethical Issues," 280. Kenyon's argument, one of the earliest, reflects a growing consensus on the evolution of Pentecostal hermeneutics from privileging the Spirit to a more evangelical privileging of a literal reading of the Bible as the "final word." See Oliverio, *Theological Hermeneutics*, who describes the same shift as moving from a "classical Pentecostal hermeneutic" to an "Evangelical-Pentecostal hermeneutic" hybrid (84–5).

mostly had popularity during the pioneer years, links the day of Pentecost with Joel's prophecy to give greater freedom for women to preach, ushering in "a whole new era for women."[159] Thus, "the age of the Spirit" did not dismiss Scripture, but appealed to experience to help interpret it and gave hermeneutical priority to eschatological texts that reflected the new age. Fulkerson makes this exact point about early Pentecostals. It was their eschatological beliefs and impulse that helped them instinctively to feature texts that promoted the egalitarian vision over more restrictive texts.[160] They sought to move beyond the text toward the eschatological vision to which the text points. However, the age of "strict allegiance to Scripture" abandoned these imaginative Spirit-led eschatological readings and led Pentecostals mostly to restrict the ministry of women.[161] Hollingsworth and Browning argue that the "egalitarian Spirit-space" of liberating passages has been replaced by literalist interpretations of texts that silence women, and therefore it is time to consider a new way forward.[162]

The eschatological hermeneutic of imagination and participation I propose promotes faithfulness to the biblical text *and* an unrestricted egalitarian vision. Some feminist scholars have argued that the only way to achieve full equality for women is to abandon Scripture because egalitarianism is simply too different from the biblical world.[163] On the other end of the spectrum, some complementarians claim the Scriptures become "uncomfortable territory" for those seeking a full egalitarian position.[164] However, neither of these positions represents the approach of early Pentecostals. Early Pentecostals emphasized the authority of Scripture, so much so that Land claims they were "suspicious of anything which did not

---

Roebuck also explores the tension between the Spirit versus the Word and the impact on women ("Pentecostal Women," 38–40, 44), as does Pamela M. S. Holmes, "Acts 29 and Authority: Towards a Pentecostal Feminist Hermeneutic of Liberation," in Wilkinson and Studebaker, *Liberating Spirit*, 186, 198, 200–1. See also discussion in Archer, *Pentecostal Hermeneutic*, 177–208.

159. Kenyon, "Ethical Issues," 280.

160. Fulkerson, *Changing the Subject*, 254. In the women Fulkerson studied, however, she found this egalitarian vision was often limited in its application to preaching and did not apply to governance.

161. Kenyon, "Ethical Issues," 281. See also Barbara Brown Zickmund who makes a similar point in "The Struggle for the Right to Preach," in *Women and Religion in America*, vol. 1, *The Nineteenth Century*, ed. Rosemary Radford Ruether and Rosemary Skinner Keller (San Francisco: Harper & Row, 1981), 193.

162. Hollingsworth and Browning, "Daughters," 30.

163. See, for example, Naomi R. Goldenberg, *Changing of the Gods: Feminism and the End of Traditional Religions* (Boston: Beacon, 1979), 3–10. Goldenberg is critical of a proposal like mine of taking a single strand of neglected themes from the Bible and expanding it toward a picture of "real Christianity" (14).

164. Kirk, *Without Precedent*, 18. For a popular example, see Kathy Keller, *Jesus, Justice, and Gender Roles: A Case for Gender Roles in Ministry* (Grand Rapids: Zondervan, 2012).

have direct biblical precedent," and they believed "if it was not in Scripture, then it should not be enacted."[165] They were also unapologetically egalitarian, primarily due to how their experience of the Word (especially eschatological texts) as guided by the Spirit led them in new directions. The waning of women's leadership in Pentecostalism had nothing to do with Pentecostals' desire to take the Bible more seriously or to interpret it more accurately, but it had everything to do with the type (or lack) of hermeneutic they used to read the Scriptures.

The supposed competing traditions of taking the Bible seriously, on the one hand, and the Spirit's empowerment of women, on the other, have kept Pentecostals stuck in a cycle of "scriptural ambiguity."[166] But, as Cox proclaims, "Wherever the original Pentecostal fire breaks through the flame-extinguishing literalist theology, women shine."[167] For Pentecostals, Scripture does not stand on its own, a statement that sounds more controversial than it really is. Pentecostal hermeneutics involves the interplay between the Sprit, the Word, and experience in community.[168] This emerging consensus on an authentic Pentecostal hermeneutic is nothing new. It was the early Pentecostals' experience of the Spirit through biblical texts that led them initially to embrace egalitarian practices in community. Land summarizes well this early Pentecostal hermeneutic.

> Salvation history was an ongoing history of revelation. The Bible was a closed canon but revelation continued because God was not yet all in all. Nothing revealed would be unbiblical, but it was beyond the Bible because salvation history had progressed beyond the first century. All that the Spirit spoke was scriptural, but not all that he spoke was in the Bible. It was not the role of the Sprit only to repeat Scripture.[169]

Early Pentecostals were not just "readers" or "interpreters" of the Bible but involved participants who engaged their imagination with the text and participated in community.[170] The task now for Pentecostals, and for the rest of this work, is to retrieve the early eschatological hermeneutic that led to the initial egalitarian thrust of the movement and present and apply it in a more critical, contemporary form.[171]

---

165. Land, *Pentecostal Spirituality*, 7, 66. Payne makes a similar argument (*Gender*, 137).
166. Yong, *Spirit Poured Out*, 191.
167. Cox, *Fire from Heaven*, 125.
168. This interpretative triad has become the definitive and dominant model among Pentecostal scholars. See Archer, *Pentecostal Hermeneutic*; Yong, *Spirit-Word-Community* (a theological, not biblical, hermeneutic, but still applicable); John Christopher Thomas, "Women, Pentecostals and the Bible: An Experiment in Pentecostal Hermeneutics," *JPT* 5 (1994): 41–56. See below for more detailed discussion.
169. Land, *Pentecostal Spirituality*, 113.
170. I am summarizing here Vondey, *Beyond Pentecostalism*, 59.
171. The call from Archer in *Pentecostal Hermeneutic*, 2–3.

## 3.4 The Need for an Eschatological Authorizing Hermeneutic

The gender paradox in Pentecostalism is primarily a hermeneutical issue: denominational statements, modern and historical stories of women, an appeal only to the Spirit, and other approaches, while helpful, are not enough to solve the gender paradox.[172] The much-overlooked loss of eschatology as an authorizing hermeneutic has left Pentecostal women of the last one hundred years without a way of reading Scripture that makes sense of their experiences and what the Spirit of God seems to be doing. However, recent developments in Pentecostal scholarship have opened the door to (re)construct the forward-thinking eschatological hermeneutic used by early Pentecostals. In the words of Christopher Stephenson, "The way forward [for Pentecostalism] is in some respect backward, not along the path of an attempted uncritical reduplication of the early spirituality but a reappropriation of it that is essentially faithful to the original vision, especially its apocalyptic tenor."[173] Pentecostal scholars are beginning this quest to reappropriate an eschatological approach to life and the Scriptures.[174] However, the gender issue thus far has received little eschatological attention, leaving Pentecostals without an authorizing hermeneutic for the ministry of women.

Early Pentecostals were far from imitators. As Daniel Castelo suggests, "they 'did not understand' what they were doing (cf. Jn 13:7), but at present we are coming to understand more and more the way the Spirit was leading this fellowship.... They improvised in a holy way as they caught a glimpse of God's kingdom."[175] The task of this and the previous chapter has been to articulate and understand what early Pentecostals perhaps did not, namely, how an eschatological hermeneutic authorized the ministry of women and how the loss of that authorizing hermeneutic led to the decline of women in leadership. As Pentecostals struggled with the practical implications of their radical eschatological gospel of inclusion,[176] a full eschatological basis for the ministry of women that was true to the heart of the movement never fully materialized. Therefore, the egalitarian trajectory laid out in the early years of the movement did not continue and in fact reversed, at least partly due to the shifting of eschatological beliefs among Pentecostals. As

---

172. Stephenson, *Dismantling*, 72; Nordling, "Gender," 505; Cavaness, "Leadership Attitudes," 128; Stanley, "Laying a Straw," 115. See Stephenson, *Dismantling*, 59–86, for the different approaches to and accounts of Pentecostal women and why they fall short on their own.

173. Stephenson, *Types of Pentecostal Theology*, 38, commenting on Land.

174. For example, see Marius Nel and his chapter "The Eschatological Lens that Pentecostals Use When They Read the Bible" in his *An African Pentecostal Hermeneutics: A Distinctive Contribution to Hermeneutics* (Eugene, OR: Wipf & Stock, 2018), 197–225.

175. Daniel Castelo, "The Improvisational Quality of Ecclesial Holiness," in Thomas, *Pentecostal Ecclesiology*, 103.

176. Tackett, "Callings," 85.

eschatology became more of a formal doctrine than a liberating social ethic,[177] the early eschatological impulse of Pentecostals that embraced the ministry of women was eventually replaced with scriptural debates and theological controversies that looked back toward the text rather than forward to the *eschaton*.[178] What is needed is a unified eschatological approach to the gender debate that can connect the imaginative hermeneutics and latter rain eschatology of early Pentecostals with the transformational eschatology and pneumatological hermeneutics of contemporary Pentecostalism.

### 3.4.1 The Eschatological Hermeneutic

The construction of an eschatological hermeneutic of imagination and participation—by which I mean a hermeneutic that utilizes the dialectical relationship between eschatological thinking (imagination) and eschatological doing (participation)—would fill a tremendous void in the Pentecostal gender debate: the articulation of a hermeneutic that is distinctly Pentecostal and deliberately egalitarian.[179] The quest for an authentic Pentecostal hermeneutic has become a significant task for Pentecostal scholars. The goal here is not to provide an extensive overview of that literature,[180] but rather to show that the hermeneutic proposed in this section and applied in the following chapters fits

---

177. Anderson, *Vision of the Disinherited*, 96.

178. See Faupel, *Everlasting Gospel*, 228–9, 308–9.

179. For discussions on reading the Scriptures in a way that is distinctly Pentecostal, see Jacqueline Grey, *Three's a Crowd: Pentecostalism, Hermeneutics, and the Old Testament* (Eugene, OR: Pickwick, 2011); Matthew S. Clark, "An Investigation into the Nature of a Viable Pentecostal Hermeneutic," (DTh diss., University of Pretoria, 1997); Thomas, "Women, Pentecostals and the Bible."

180. For some detailed summaries, historical surveys, or lists of the literature on Pentecostal hermeneutics see Nel, *African Pentecostal Hermeneutics*, 47–91, and Lee Roy Martin, *Pentecostal Hermeneutics: A Reader* (Leiden: Brill, 2013), which traces the development of the field through mostly reprinted articles from the *JPT*. For history and developments, particularly within the pages of the journal *Pneuma*, see the editorial "The Pentecostals and Their Scriptures" by Peter Althouse and Robby Waddell in *Pneuma* 38, no. 1–2 (2016): 115–21. For more overviews and bibliographies see Jacqueline Grey, "Biblical Hermeneutics: Reading Scripture with the Spirit in Community," in *The Routledge Handbook of Pentecostal Theology*, ed. Wolfgang Vondey (New York: Routledge, 2020), 129–39; Oliverio, *Theological Hermeneutics*; Grey, *Three's a Crowd*, 36–61; Vondey, *Beyond Pentecostalism*, 71–7; John Christopher Thomas, "'Where the Spirit Leads': The Development of Pentecostal Hermeneutics," *Journal of Beliefs & Values: Studies in Religion & Education* 30, no. 3 (December 2009): 289–302; Warrington, *Pentecostal Theology*, 187n37; Thomas, "Women, Pentecostals and the Bible," 43n4.

firmly within current developments in the field.[181] Although articulated with variations, there is an emerging consensus that a Pentecostal hermeneutic involves the dynamic interplay of three theological necessities: the Holy Spirit, the Word of God, and experience (in community).[182] In this triadic model,[183] no single part functions alone: none is subordinate or superior to the other and all depend on and include each other for interpretation.[184] Therefore, it is often referred to as an "ongoing spiral," hermeneutical circle, trialectic, or dialectic of the Spirit and the Word in community.[185] Most scholars argue this approach is contained in the New Testament itself,[186] is true to the way early Pentecostals interpreted and applied the Scriptures,[187] and exposes the inadequacy of other (particularly evangelical) models often used by Pentecostals.[188] In addition, those specifically concerned with resolving the Pentecostal gender paradox insist that any proposed hermeneutical model or methodology must incorporate the triadic interplay of being pneumatological, biblical, and experiential.[189]

181. Other Pentecostal hermeneutics for reading texts on gender have been proposed, at least in part, and are discussed throughout this work. See Stephenson's Isaianic New Exodus hermeneutical framework for reading Luke-Acts (*Dismantling*, 89–113) and some of Johns's work in "Conscientization" and "Grieving, Brooding, and Transformation."

182. Thomas specifically applies this hermeneutic to the issue of women in "Women, Pentecostals and the Bible." See also Johns, "Grieving, Brooding, Transformation," 148; Vondey, *Beyond Pentecostalism*, 66, 71; McQueen, *Pentecostal Eschatology*, 200–3; Archer, *Pentecostal Hermeneutic*; Yong, *Spirit-Word-Community*. Jacqueline Grey, in a bit of a departure from her previous *Three's a Crowd*, separates experience and community in "Biblical Hermeneutics," 134–7.

183. For the use of "models" in theological work, see discussion below in 5.2.

184. See Yong, *Spirit-Word-Community*, 8–9, 18. Yong's work is about more than biblical hermeneutics and by "Word" he sometimes means *Logos* and not solely Scripture. That said, he still has a lot to say about interpreting the Bible. See discussion in Stephenson, *Types*, 83, 109. For more on the triadic interplay, see Thomas, "Women, Pentecostals and the Bible," 50; Land, *Pentecostal Spirituality*, 28; Rickie D. Moore, "Canon and Charisma in the Book of Deuteronomy," *JPT* 1 (Oct 1992): 91. This interplay likely disputes any arguments for "epistemic primacy," including that of Scripture (but see Keener, *Spirit Hermeneutics*, 104–5).

185. Yong uses all these terms (*Spirit-Word-Community*, 7–14).

186. Thomas, "Women, Pentecostals and the Bible," 55.

187. Archer, *Pentecostal Hermeneutic*, 2.

188. Grey, *Three's a Crowd*, 42; Holmes, "Acts 29," 187.

189. Powers, "Pentecostal Hermeneutics," 324–5, 331; Kenyon, "Ethical Issues," 281. Plenty of hermeneutics have been proposed by feminist scholars for reading texts, most notably by Elizabeth Schüssler Fiorenza (see *Bread Not Stone* and *In Memory of Her*). For summaries or typologies of different types of readings by feminists, see Joseph Abraham, "Feminist Hermeneutics and Pentecostal Spirituality: The Creation Narrative of Genesis as a Paradigm," *Asian Journal of Pentecostal Studies* 6, no. 1 (2003): 6–10; Carolyn Osiek, "The

Therefore, the hermeneutic I propose is thoroughly eschatological while still following the hermeneutical triad of Spirit, Word, and experience (in community). What is unique in my approach is the application of an eschatological lens to each part of the triad in order to develop an eschatological hermeneutic for reading biblical texts on gender. The eschatological hermeneutic of imagination and participation emphasizes the three-way interplay or "trialectical spiral" between the eschatological Spirit, the eschatological Word (imagination), and eschatological experience in community (participation).[190] There is cross-pollination between the three, and it is important to remember the spiraled or circular nature of this hermeneutic (and this work as a whole).[191] Although they are discussed in an intentional order below, the order is non-linear. The same rule applies to this project and its overall procedure: the historical chapter corresponds to the work of the eschatological Spirit, the hermeneutical chapter to the eschatological Word,[192] and the final praxis chapters to the eschatological experience in community. However, one could justify beginning or ending with any of the three elements: the work of the eschatological Spirit enters a dialectical dance between the eschatological imagination (through the Word) and eschatological participation (in community). Although these terms and their relationship have already been discussed, the following briefly explains each of these necessary components of the consensus hermeneutical triad of Spirit-Word-community and eschatologically rearticulates them in order to move toward developing a consistent Pentecostal reading of biblical texts on gender.

### 3.4.2 The Eschatological Spirit

The Holy Spirit is the eschatological Spirit, and the Spirit's work is eschatological work.[193] Therefore, an eschatological hermeneutic is by necessity a pneumatological hermeneutic. McQueen affirms that "Pentecostal eschatology finds its source

---

Feminist and the Bible: Hermeneutical Alternatives," in *Feminist Perspectives on Biblical Scholarship*, ed. Adela Yarbro Collins (Chico, CA: Scholars, 1985), 97–105. The purpose here, however, is a distinctly Pentecostal hermeneutic for gender texts in the Bible, and these other approaches have their limitations for Pentecostals (see Johns, "Grieving, Brooding, and Transformation," 151).

    190. Yong, *Spirit-Word-Community*, 23.
    191. See my Introduction.
    192. By "Word" I am referring to the Bible, a set of Scriptures that inspire the eschatological imagination.
    193. See Andrew K. Gabriel, "Pneumatology: Eschatological Intensification of the Personal Presence of God," in Vondey, *Routledge Handbook*, esp. 212–13; Daniela C. Augustine, *The Spirit and the Common Good: Shared Flourishing in the Image of God* (Grand Rapids: Eerdmans, 2019), 7–9; J. Rodman Williams, "The Holy Spirit and Eschatology," *Pneuma* 3, no. 2 (Fall 1981): 54–8; Gordon Fee, *God's Empowering Presence: The Holy Spirit in the Letters of Paul* (Grand Rapids: Baker Academic, 2009), 816.

in the presence of the eschatological Spirit."[194] Therefore, to interpret texts eschatologically is to engage with and experience the eschatological Spirit.[195] Through eschatological texts, the Spirit begins "calling forth new worlds," including a world of gender equality.[196] As Pentecostals read the Bible eschatologically, they realize that to live "according to the Spirit" (Rom. 8:4-5, 13) is to live to the fullest extent possible according to one's eschatological existence.[197] Therefore, there is an interdependent relationship between pneumatology and eschatology.[198]

If the triadic interplay of the Pentecostal hermeneutic privileges any one area, it is the Spirit, for the Spirit drives all the movements in the hermeneutical circle.[199] Without a Spirit-led dynamic reading of the text,[200] one cannot fully interpret or experience the Word. This is especially true of the eschatological hermeneutic and its dialectic of imagination and participation proposed in this work. The same Spirit that inspired the eschatological texts also inspires the eschatological imagination in reading them and the call to participate presently in eschatological realities. This triple inspiration of the Spirit[201] shows "that a vital pneumatology is indispensable for a truly healthy dialectic in that it drives the to-and-fro movement."[202] Daniela Augustine hints at this triple inspiration when she describes her socio-transformative pneumatology as a "Spirit-filled vision to inspire redemptive daydreaming and reenvisioning of the world," which leads to a "pneumatic embodiment of the world's eschatological future."[203] Because of the interdependence between pneumatology and eschatology, it is no surprise eschatological texts would feature prominently in the Spirit's repertoire for speaking to complex social issues, including gender roles. The Spirit enables the reader to imaginatively "think from the other end" through the text[204] and then invites the reader to participate in that "end" in the here

---

194. McQueen, *Joel*, 93.

195. See Keener, *Spirit Hermeneutics*, 53.

196. Johns, "Grieving, Brooding, and Transformation," 145.

197. See Fee, *God's Empowering Presence*, 817. See practical application in my Chapter 6.

198. See Isgrigg, *Imagining the Future*, 8–9.

199. See Yong on this point in *Spirit-Word-Community*, 7; *Renewing*, 339. See also Warrington, *Pentecostal Theology*, 199–200; Archer, *Pentecostal Hermeneutic*, 264.

200. Clark H. Pinnock with Barry L. Callen, *The Scripture Principle: Reclaiming the Full Authority of the Bible*, 2nd ed. (Grand Rapids: Baker Academic, 2006), 261.

201. Playing off Clark Pinnock who calls it a "double inspiration" in "The Work of the Holy Spirit in Hermeneutics," *JPT* 2 (1993): 4.

202. Yong, *Spirit-Word-Community*, 14.

203. Augustine, *Spirit and the Common Good*, 7. She further explains this pneumatology in her first chapter and then applies it in the remaining chapters of the book to create a picture of an eschatological-pneumatic theological vision of the common good.

204. Russell, *Household*, 60, 67. See 1.1.3 for discussion.

and now, causing the old order of sexism and patriarchy to give way to the new egalitarian order.²⁰⁵

### 3.4.3 The Eschatological Word: Imagination

To read the biblical text pneumatologically necessitates allowing the Spirit to recruit the eschatological imagination, which becomes a primary vehicle for God's transforming activity in the world.²⁰⁶ However, this is not just one's own imagination but rather a "Spirit-driven" divine imagination that is rooted in the biblical text and more specifically (for our purposes) eschatological texts.²⁰⁷ Therefore, a Pentecostal reading of biblical texts on gender rejects any reading that emphasizes a passive posture of merely receiving information. Rather, a three-way eschatological interplay between Spirit, Word, and experience in community causes the reader to be imaginatively "taken up" into the eschatological world of the text and then become (trans)formed by that world.²⁰⁸ As Hart pronounces, "God makes himself and his purposes and promises known not by downloading a body of digitized factual data, but by taking our imagination captive, lifting us up through Spirit-filled reading to 'see' and 'taste' the substance of things lying way beyond our natural purview, and calling us responsibly to imagine further."²⁰⁹ As Pentecostals read eschatological texts on gender with a Spirit-driven imagination, they are challenged to imagine further a world of complete equality as well as how they might participate in bringing about that world.²¹⁰

---

205. See Johns, "Grieving, Brooding, and Transformation," 153.

206. See Hart, "Imagination," 62, 76. See also Rausch's chapter "The Eschatological Imagination" in his *Eschatology*, where he traces the diminishing eschatological imagination since the early church due to increased emphasis on judgment and hell and an increasingly individualistic understanding of eschatology. For previous discussion on the imagination, see my Introduction and elsewhere. The focus here is specifically on imagination as it relates to the Word.

207. See Vondey, *Pentecostal Theology*, 13; Vondey, *Perplexed*, 37–8, 44. For more on the pneumatological dimensions of the imagination, see Yong, *Spirit-Word-Community*, 12–13, 133–42, among other places.

208. For more, see David Tracy, *The Analogical Imagination: Christian Theology and the Culture of Pluralism* (New York: Crossroad, 1981), 114; Eugene Peterson, *Eat This Book: A Conversation in the Art of Spiritual Reading* (Grand Rapids: Eerdmans, 2009), 24, 41. For further discussion of the eschatological dimensions of Tracy's *Analogical Imagination*, see Shields, *Eschatological Imagination*, 87–121.

209. Hart, "Eschatology," 264.

210. Several feminist scholars have mentioned the significant role of the imagination in interpreting Scriptures on gender and for equality in the church. See Schüssler Fiorenza, "Emancipative Reading," 90, 100; Aida Irizarry-Fernández, "A Communal Reading. See—Judge—Act: A Different Approach to Bible Study," in An and Darr, *Engaging the Bible*, 62.

The role of the pneumatological-eschatological imagination in reading biblical texts (and theological reflection) has become an important and unique part of Pentecostal hermeneutics.[211] A leading example of this emphasis is the work of Vondey, who sees a "revival of the imagination" among Pentecostals, which he ties closely to renewed eschatological and pneumatological pursuits.[212] In *Beyond Pentecostalism*, Vondey calls for the centrality of the (eschatologically inspired) imagination and the role of the Holy Spirit in order to participate biblically in the Christian story.[213] Vondey argues not for a performed re-enactment of a biblical script, but rather a more imaginative "playful" approach that is in tune with the biblical script yet also able to improvise as inspired by the pneumatological-eschatological imagination.[214] He suggests that "for Pentecostals, there exists an inherent narrativity in the sanctified, eschatological imagination, which emerges from the spirit of the biblical texts, and yet is carried by that spirit beyond the text."[215] Vondey concludes that "the Pentecostal imagination is the pneumatological, eschatological, and ethical pursuit of God," and then goes on to discuss how this imagination might impact the reading of the biblical text.[216] For Vondey, the goal of the pneumatological imagination "is a transformation of the present crisis in light of the eschatological future breaking open the present conditions for the renewing work of God's Spirit."[217] In other words, the pneumatological-eschatological imagination leads to present eschatological participation through the experience

---

211. See discussion in Isgrigg, *Imagining the Future*, 199–209; Oliverio, *Theological Hermeneutics*, 78–83, 160, 195–6; Yong, *Spirit-Word-Community*, 222–4. See also Roger Stronstad, "Pentecostal Experience and Hermeneutics," *Paraclete* 26, no. 1 (Winter 1992): 14–30, esp. 25–8.

212. Vondey, *Beyond Pentecostalism*, 31–9, 45. It is a revival of the imagination because it reflects the origins of Pentecostalism (26). Vondey is following and builds on Yong's pneumatological imagination to an extent, but Yong's emphasis is a bit more on theological hermeneutics and the theological imagination, although he certainly engages biblical hermeneutics (see previous note 184).

213. Vondey, *Beyond Pentecostalism*, 35–40. Vondey is engaging with, and critiquing, the work of Vanhoozer and specifically his work *The Drama of Doctrine*. For Vondey, Vanhoozer's description of imagination is overly dependent on cognitive performance and contains a "pneumatological deficit" (38). Vondey prefers the language or metaphor of "play" over performance (see 40–6). He discusses the pneumatological imagination in his other works as well (for example, see *Pentecostal Theology*, 156; *Perplexed*, 44–6).

214. Vondey, *Beyond Pentecostalism*, 43–4, 66.

215. Vondey, *Beyond Pentecostalism*, 38. Therefore, Vondey argues in his next chapter that Pentecostals move "beyond Scripture" to the "dynamic concept of revelation as the interplay of Spirit, Word, and community" (71). Although I am still emphasizing the "Word" as biblical text here, my emphasis on eschatological imagining still goes well with Vondey's ideas, even if he sees the Word as a slightly more limited element.

216. Vondey, *Beyond Pentecostalism*, 39 (see also 34), 47–62.

217. Vondey, *Beyond Pentecostalism*, 42.

## 3. The Loss of Eschatology as Authorizing Hermeneutic

of the Spirit's activity. Scripture, including eschatological texts that point to a world beyond the text, is not meant to be only read or heard, but also experienced.[218] Through the biblical text, the eschatological Spirit helps one to "imagine the world otherwise."[219] However, stopping there would make an eschatological hermeneutic primarily an intellectual (and potentially individual) exercise of otherworldly speculation about gender, which would betray the Pentecostal emphasis on experience in community in its triadic hermeneutical model. As Archer asserts, Pentecostals "desire to *live* as the eschatological people of God," not just imagine it.[220] Appealing to the authority of the future leads to present participation in that future.

### 3.4.4 Eschatological Experience (in Community): Participation

As engaging the Word causes the readers or hearers to imagine the world otherwise, the Spirit then invites them to participate now in ways consistent with that future-imagined world. Experience and Scripture are dialectically related, with the Spirit maintaining their relationship by inspiring both the insights into eschatological realities of a text and the creativity and empowerment needed to participate in those eschatological realities.[221] Therefore, in order to close the "dissonance gap" between the now and not yet in Scripture, the way things are and the way we long for them to be, we must employ an eschatological hermeneutic that is experiential and praxis-driven.[222]

This emphasis on experience in the hermeneutical journey is where Pentecostal theology and feminist concerns for women's equality work well together,[223] for both emphasize the importance of experience as an authoritative source for theological reflection.[224] Russell argues that the Bible functions most authoritatively when it is read and practiced imaginatively, as we respond to the Spirit's invitation through the Word to participate in the struggle for justice, including gender equality.[225] For Russell, the "scripture" becomes an open-ended "script" that is a "prompting for life" and invitation to participate now in God's eschatological work of

---

218. For more on going beyond Scripture to carry out its intentions and the role of experience, see Pinnock with Callen, *Scripture Principle*, particularly the Appendix "The Inspiration and Authority of the Bible: Thoughts since 1984," 253–72, esp. 259.

219. Smith, *Tongues*, 84.

220. Archer, *Pentecostal Hermeneutic*, 134; italics mine. Cf. Middleton, *New Heaven*, 17.

221. See Holmes, "Acts 29," 208; Vondey, *Perplexed*, 45; Peterson, *Eat this Book*, 27; Yong, *Spirit-Word-Community*, 133, 139; Johns, *Pentecostal Formation*, 85–6.

222. Deryck Sheriffs, *The Friendship of the Lord: An Old Testament Spirituality* (Carlisle, England: Paternoster, 1996), 10–11, 25. This applies to Pentecostal scholarship as well, which is to be experiential (Vondey and Mittelstadt, "Introduction," 9).

223. See Holmes, "Acts 29," 188, 204.

224. See Copeland, "Journeying," 32.

225. Russell, "Authority," 141. See also discussion of Russell in Copeland, "Journeying," 30.

restoration.[226] Pentecostals value both the authority of Scripture and the authority of experience,[227] and they both influence each other in a necessary dialectical tension.[228] Therefore, the next chapter on reading eschatological texts on gender should be read in dialectical tension with the ensuing chapters on eschatological-egalitarian participation in the church.

Participation in the eschatological future inspired by the biblical text takes place in the context of community. For Pentecostals, the "experience of God in community is indispensable to the interpretive process,"[229] as is the participation of the community in that process,[230] a tradition dating back to the earliest years of the movement.[231] This communal, experiential part of the interpretive process is communicated in a variety of ways such as the performative or performance aspect of Scripture,[232] an ongoing drama or story of God's unfolding plan,[233] or as "play."[234] Whatever the terminology (and there are differences between them), the consensus is that a Spirit-led experience of the text through community praxis offers a hermeneutical key for interpreting texts as well as a hermeneutical goal.[235]

A Pentecostal reading of biblical texts on gender must incorporate the interpretive interplay of Spirit-Word-community. The advantage of the proposed eschatological hermeneutic of imagination and participation as a consistent way of reading biblical texts on gender is that it necessitates a biblically based eschatological imagination, eschatological participation in community, and the guidance of the eschatological Spirit for both. Reading the Bible with an eschatological lens draws the reader into the dialectic of imagination and participation, a continuous back-and-forth of participating in eschatological promises amid the worshipping community in order to imagine more deeply the meaning of eschatological

---

226. Russell, "Authority," 138–9.

227. See Stronstad, "Pentecostal Experience and Hermeneutics."

228. Archer, *Pentecostal Hermeneutic*, 87; Ware, "Spiritual Egalitarianism," 230.

229. Green, *Lord's Supper*, 186.

230. See Holmes, "Acts 29," 197–8.

231. See Oliverio, *Theological Hermeneutics*, 356; Vondey, *Beyond Pentecostalism*, 58–60; Althouse, *Moltmann*, 10.

232. See Yong, *Renewing*, 351–4; Kevin J. Vanhoozer, "Scripture and Hermeneutics," in McDermott, *Oxford Handbook*, 47–8.

233. Clark, "Viable Pentecostal Hermeneutic," 295, which is similar to Joseph Byrd, "Paul Ricoeur's Hermeneutical Theory," 203–14. Both argue for Scripture as an ongoing story of God's purposes. Grey adopts this "ongoing" model as an attractive reading model for Pentecostal communities (*Three's a Crowd*, 156–8). For the importance of the drama (of salvation history), which is key for Pentecostals, see Vondey, *Beyond Pentecostalism*, 59; Smith, *Tongues*, 69; Land, *Pentecostal Spirituality*, 71.

234. Vondey, *Pentecostal Theology*, 12–14; Vondey, *Beyond Pentecostalism*, 40–6. Vondey is more critical of "performance" language (see *Beyond Pentecostalism*, 69–74).

235. See Arden C. Autry, "Dimensions of Hermeneutics in Pentecostal Focus," *JPT* 3 (1993): 44.

texts—a hermeneutical circle of eschatological knowing and eschatological doing. The next chapter assembles a proposed set of texts for the former, while the closing chapters construct how the latter might work for the gathered church.

## 3.5 Conclusion

The previous chapter and this chapter have argued that the rise and decline of women in leadership in Pentecostalism was concomitant with the rise and decline of eschatology as an authorizing hermeneutic. In an interconnected descent, the waning of eschatology as authorizing hermeneutic led to the waning of egalitarian practices. Due to their shifting hermeneutics and eschatology, Pentecostals adopted restorationist and dispensationalist ways of thinking that betrayed their eschatological way-of-being in the world that had initially elevated the status of women. The shift from a latter rain eschatological hermeneutic to a dispensationalist literal hermeneutic gave texts such as "women are to be silent in the churches" more authority than "Your sons and daughters will prophesy." This loss of eschatology as an authorizing hermeneutic resulted in increased reservations over the role of women in Pentecostal churches and placed growing restrictions upon them. Therefore, the (re)discovery and critical reappropriation of an eschatological hermeneutic may hold the key to recapturing the egalitarian thrust of the first few decades.

Recent developments in Pentecostal eschatology and hermeneutics have opened the door to develop a thoroughly eschatological approach to the gender problem. The proposed eschatological dialectical hermeneutic of imagination and participation corresponds to the current Pentecostal landscape as examined in this chapter and aligns with the historical heart of the movement as investigated in Chapter 2. The construction of an eschatological–egalitarian hermeneutic promises to fill the void left by early Pentecostals, namely, the articulation of a conscious hermeneutic that is distinctly Pentecostal and leads to the unrestricted right of women to lead and minister. What is necessary now is to apply this hermeneutic in the areas of biblical theology and practical theology in order to construct a thoroughly eschatological basis for the full flourishing and unhindered inclusion of women in all parts and at all levels of church life and ministry. These areas of eschatological knowing (Chapter 4) as well as eschatological doing and being (Chapters 5 and 6) form the remainder of my work. The methodological potential of an eschatological resolution to the gender paradox must be tested to see whether it can overcome the theological and hermeneutical indecision and inconsistency that has perpetuated the paradox and plagued the movement for decades. One way to recapture the egalitarian heart and trajectory of early Pentecostalism is to recover, (re)construct, and formally articulate the eschatological hermeneutic that early Pentecostals used. It is to this challenge the next chapter now turns.

**Chapter 4**

IMAGINING THE *ESCHATON*

(RE)CONSTRUCTING THE ESCHATOLOGICAL
AUTHORIZING HERMENEUTIC

The goal of this chapter is to address the hermeneutical inconsistency surrounding the Pentecostal gender paradox by establishing a unified eschatological–egalitarian narrative thread in Scripture that acts as a hermeneutical guide for interpreting other texts on gender. This eschatological approach seeks to establish the central eschatological texts on gender and argues for their hermeneutical priority over supposed problematic (and non-eschatological) texts used to restrict women. The previous chapter demonstrated that eschatological and hermeneutical shifts in Pentecostalism led to the loss of eschatology as an authorizing hermeneutic for the ministry of women. The lack of an appropriate Pentecostal hermeneutic for reading biblical texts on gender led to hermeneutical inconsistencies that created indecision and paradoxical messages concerning the role of women in church leadership. Janet Powers argues that as long as this hermeneutical inconsistency remains, so too will the gender paradox.[1] The argument of this chapter is that recovering, (re)constructing, and formally articulating the eschatological authorizing hermeneutic that previously empowered Pentecostal women provides a consistent way of reading biblical texts on gender, which overcomes the uncertainty created by other biblical passages that perpetuate the gender paradox. Reading biblical texts on gender through an eschatological lens contains promise for Pentecostals, for it is in line with the early heart of the movement (Chapter 2), recent developments in Pentecostal scholarship (Chapter 3), and Pentecostalism's emphasis on experience and pragmatic praxis presented in the next chapters.

The (re)construction and application of the eschatological authorizing hermeneutic requires that we identify the central biblical texts on gender that orient the eschatological hermeneutic. I propose three texts for discussion, all of which are integrated into key biblical narratives: Genesis 1–3 (creation), Galatians 3:28 (the ministry of Jesus), and Acts 2:17-18 (Pentecost). These three texts and their surrounding or connected narratives are chosen for three main reasons: (1) they already hold a prominent place in feminist theology, affirming

---

1. Powers, "Pentecostal Hermeneutics," 317.

their potential for hermeneutical priority in the gender debate; (2) they are a part of the central biblical story of creation, fall, redemption, and restoration, thus establishing them as already foundational texts; (3) they are interconnected thematically and narratively, moving from creation to new creation, with the two New Testament texts potentially alluding to the eschatological–egalitarian trajectory of Genesis 1–2. Key to the argument is that these eschatological texts form a unified overarching egalitarian narrative that has the potential to hold hermeneutical priority and theological authority over more contextual and less universal texts and can therefore provide a consistent method for reading other texts on gender. The task is to establish the validity of these texts as hermeneutical guides—due to their narratively connected universal eschatological vision—for interpreting more ambiguous passages about women. This eschatological way of reading texts on gender presents an interpretive model for resolving the gender question that is faithful to the biblical text, Pentecostal ways of reading Scripture, and an unrestricted egalitarian vision. Moving toward a scriptural consensus on gender equality is an essential step for moving beyond a century of inconsistent conclusions about the place and role of women in Pentecostal life and ministry.[2]

A majority of biblical and hermeneutical studies on feminist concerns ignore the potential of an eschatological approach to gender.[3] Similarly, most works on eschatology's ethical and practical implications for the church omit gender equality as a potential sign of the *eschaton*.[4] Some scholars even contend that arguments for gender equality in church leadership stem only from "anxiety about relevance" and have no biblical grounds.[5] Others have argued for redemptive threads[6] in the Bible that may be "faint or even hidden,"[7] "hint" at greater equality,[8] or contain "limited moves" toward greater equality.[9] But what often happens is the promise of these potential threads gets tangled up in discussions of the problem of prohibitive texts in the Bible that limit the role of women.

---

2. See Cavaness, "Leadership Attitudes," 129.

3. As already argued in previous chapters (see 1.1). To restate just one example, in her "feminist ways of reading Scripture" section, Natalie Watson does not mention eschatological readings (*Feminist Theology*, 4–15).

4. See 5.3.4 in the next chapter. Examples of omission: Schwarz, *Eschatology*; Gladd and Harmon, *Inaugurated Eschatology*; Rausch, *Eschatology*, 116.

5. Kirk, *Without Precedent*, 134.

6. See especially William Webb's influential "redemptive-movement hermeneutic" in *Slaves, Women, and Homosexuals: Exploring the Hermeneutics of Cultural Analysis* (Downers Grove, IL: InterVarsity, 2001), esp. 21–41. For a more popular treatment of the redemptive-movement hermeneutic applied to feminism, see Bessey, *Jesus Feminist*, 25–31, and carried throughout.

7. Johns, "Grieving, Brooding, Transformation," 150.

8. Stackhouse, *Finally Feminist*, 54.

9. Webb, *Slaves, Women, and Homosexuals*, 31; see also Johns, "Grieving, Brooding, Transformation," 145, 149–50.

This chapter does not intend to interpret the New Testament "problematic passages" concerning the prohibition of women in leadership such as 1 Corinthians 14:34-35 and 1 Timothy 2:11-15[10] or the Old Testament so-called "texts of terror."[11] These texts have received an abundance of convincing, helpful, and in-depth treatment by Pentecostal and other scholars, demonstrating that the texts neither prohibit the ministry of women nor condone inequality.[12] What is lacking in these treatments is a constructive and consistent hermeneutic that is distinctly Pentecostal and reflects the early (eschatological) heart of the movement.[13] The

---

10. Other texts commonly treated include 1 Cor. 11:3 and the *Haustafeln* or "household codes" of Eph. 5:21–6:9, Col. 3:18–4:1, and 1 Pet. 2:18–3:7.

11. The title of Phyllis Trible's well-known work *Texts of Terror: Literary-Feminist Readings of Biblical Narratives* (Philadelphia: Fortress, 1984). However, suggestions for how churches can teach on some of these passages are discussed in 6.3.2.

12. For some Pentecostal treatments or summaries see Melissa L. Archer, "Was the Spirit Poured out on Women to Remain Silent in the Church? Reading 1 Corinthians 14.34–35 and 1 Timothy 2.11–15 in the Light of Pentecost," in Johns and Stephenson, *Grieving, Brooding, and Transforming*, 123–34; Melissa L. Archer, "Women in Ministry: A Pentecostal Reading of New Testament Texts," in English de Alminana and Olena, *Women*, esp. 38–49; Stephenson, *Dismantling*, 12n21; Warrington, *Pentecostal Theology*, 148–51; Craig Keener, "Luke's Perspective on Women and Gender," in his *Acts: An Exegetical Commentary*, vol. 1 (Grand Rapids: Baker Academic, 2012), 597–638; Craig Keener, *Paul, Women, & Wives: Marriage and Women's Ministry in the Letters of Paul* (Peabody, MA: Hendrickson, 1992); Deborah M. Gill and Barbara Cavaness, *God's Women Then and Now* (Springfield, MO: Grace & Truth, 2004); R. Hollis Gause, "Does the New Testament Prohibit Women Leaders?," in Alexander and Gause, *Women*, 77–107; Thomas, "Women, Pentecostals and the Bible," 53; Lim, *Spiritual Gifts*, 168–78. For just a sample of other (non-Pentecostal) works and treatments on these texts, see Philip B. Payne, *Man and Woman, One in Christ* (Grand Rapids: Zondervan, 2009); Catherine Clark Kroeger and Mary J. Evans, eds., *The IVP Women's Bible Commentary* (Downers Grove, IL: InterVarsity, 2006); Stackhouse, *Finally Feminist*, 51–62; R. T. France, *Women In The Church's Ministry: A Test Case for Biblical Interpretation* (Grand Rapids: Eerdmans, 1997); Grenz and Kjesbo, *Women*, esp. 123–34; Ben Witherington III, *Women and the Genesis of Christianity* (Cambridge: Cambridge University Press, 1990); Ben Witherington III, *Women in the Earliest Churches* (Cambridge: Cambridge University Press, 1988); Bonnidell Clouse and Robert G. Clouse, eds., *Women in Ministry: Four Views* (Downers Grove, IL: IVP Academic, 1989); Ruth A. Tucker and Walter Liefeld, *Daughters of the Church: Women and Ministry from New Testament Times to the Present* (Grand Rapids: Zondervan, 1987); Mary J. Evans, *Woman in the Bible: An Overview of All the Crucial Passages on Women's Roles* (Downers Grove, IL: InterVarsity, 1984); William Swartley, *Slavery, Sabbath, War, and Women: Case Issues in Biblical Interpretation* (Scottdale, PA: Herald, 1983). An online resource would be Christians for Biblical Equality, https://www.cbeinternational.org/.

13. Randall Holm calls for a more "sophisticated" hermeneutical approach for Pentecostals, one that is more than a strict exegesis of Pauline literature. See the closing

hermeneutical energy in these works is spent on the passages of prohibition that are heavily influenced by historical context.[14] The church and Pentecostal communities can appreciate these necessary and thorough works on these complex texts, but their approach alone cannot resolve the Pentecostal gender paradox. What proved effective for the early Pentecostals was looking to eschatological texts to authorize the ministry of women. Only when discussion of other texts entered the Pentecostal gender debate did the authority of these eschatological texts and the eschatological imagination wane. Therefore, (re)discovering and (re)constructing the hermeneutical power of imaginative eschatological passages on gender that are more universal in application may provide a better way forward. Before seeking to identify the central biblical texts on gender that establish the eschatological-egalitarian narrative thread, I explain the methodology of hermeneutical priority that allows certain (in this case eschatological) texts to act as hermeneutical guides for other (non-eschatological) texts.

### 4.1 The Hermeneutical Priority of Eschatological Texts on Gender

The Pentecostal gender paradox has persisted because eschatological passages that challenge gender hierarchy are compared equally—and considered equally instructive hermeneutically—to other passages that seem to support or at least concede accommodation to male hierarchy, patriarchy, and male-dominated leadership. Is the tension of the gender paradox therefore canonized, scripturally justified, and destined to continue if these other texts exist and if Pentecostals wish to live by "all scripture" (2 Tim. 3:16)? This section seeks to defend the idea of hermeneutical priority and proposes that reading the Bible eschatologically is a way of reading Scripture that is especially conducive to Pentecostals and should be the primary hermeneutical approach for solving the gender paradox. To arrive at that conclusion, the premise of hermeneutical priority in general is briefly defended, including its use by Pentecostals and its application in feminist works. The promise of a more specific *eschatological* hermeneutical priority is then proposed, arguing that it is congenial to current Pentecostal hermeneuts as well as other similar interpretive approaches in feminist works. The section concludes by proposing a set of unified eschatological texts on gender and outlining the procedure for examining them.

---

remarks in his article "Pentecost: Women's Emancipation Day?" *Eastern Journal of Practical Theology* 5, no. 2 (1991): 27–34.

14. That is not so say these are wasted efforts. These works are helpful because, as Keener argues, understanding the cultural contexts help us move toward, not away from, an egalitarian reading (many of his works emphasize this, but see his summary in "Refining Spirit Hermeneutics," *Pneuma* 39, no. 1–2 [2017]: 220–2, 239).

### 4.1.1 *The Premise of Hermeneutical Priority*

The hermeneutical wisdom that some texts are more fundamental than others and may be used as interpretive guides goes back at least to Jesus, who encourages interpreting all the Law and the Prophets through a select group of texts (see Matt. 7:12, 22:34-40).[15] In the fourth century, Augustine argued that obscure passages should be interpreted in light of less difficult passages in order to "remove the uncertainty of ambiguous [passages]."[16] Luther appealed to this tradition of interpreting confusing passages based on clear passages in his influential argument that Scripture interprets itself.[17] Although in no way original or exclusive to Luther, this inner-biblical interpretation and eventual maxim that "Scripture interprets Scripture" became a principle feature of the Reformation and much of the biblical hermeneutics that followed.[18]

This interpretive strategy that the plain of Scripture should help illuminate the difficult has been adopted by many groups over the centuries, including Pentecostals who have consistently privileged Luke-Acts and Pentecost as hermeneutical guides for approaching issues in Pentecostalism.[19] Stephenson claims an advancement in Pentecostal theology and hermeneutics has been the move from a "Bible doctrines" methodological approach, which aims for topical arrangement of biblical texts that gives equal weight to all statements in the Bible, to a schema that allows certain biblical texts to be more formative in one's theology and take "interpretive authority over other texts."[20] Yong claims that "approaching

---

15. For more on the hermeneutics of Jesus and Jesus as a hermeneutical model see Keener, *Spirit Hermeneutics*, 207–18.

16. See Saint Augustine, *On Christian Teaching*, trans. R. P. H. Green (Oxford: Oxford, 2008), 37. See also David Steinmetz, "The Superiority of Pre-Critical Exegesis," *Theology Today* 37, no. 1 (April 1980): 30.

17. Usually attributed to the phrase *Scriptura sui ipsius interpres* found in *Assertio Omnium Articulorum* or *An Assertion of All the Articles of Martin Luther Which Were Quite Recently Condemned by a Bull of Leo x*, article 36. See translation and discussion by David I. Starling in *Hermeneutics as Apprenticeship: How the Bible Shapes Our Interpretive Habits and Practices* (Grand Rapids: Baker Academic, 2016), 11–12. Luther makes similar arguments in other places, most notably in his section on the clarity of Scripture in *On the Bondage of the Will*, trans. and ed. Philip S. Watson, in *Luther and Erasmus: Free Will and Salvation*, ed. E. Gordon Rupp and Philip S. Watson (Philadelphia: Westminster, 1969), 109–13.

18. See Michael Graves, *How Scripture Interprets Scripture: What Biblical Writers Can Teach Us about Reading the Bible* (Grand Rapids: Baker Academic, 2021). Cf. James K. A. Smith, *The Fall of Interpretation: Philosophical Foundations for a Creational Hermeneutic* (Downers Grove, IL: InterVarsity, 2000), 17.

19. Dayton, *Theological Roots*, 23; Mittelstadt, "Reimagining Luke-Acts," 29; Yong, *Spirit Poured Out*, 201.

20. Stephenson, *Types*, 8, 107. Examples of the "Bible doctrines" approach from Pentecostals would be E. S. Williams and French L. Arrington. Yong would be an example of the latter approach Stephenson mentions.

the whole of Scripture through a part of the whole" is not only acceptable but unavoidable.[21] John Christopher Thomas argues that this approach is itself biblical. Using Acts 15 as his example, he illustrates how the witness of the Spirit helps the church prioritize some texts over others when making decisions on crucial issues in which the Bible seems to teach two possible outcomes.[22] Giving equal weight to all biblical texts when seeking to solve a theological dispute such as the woman-man relationship will always lead to a "text-jam" or "bitter stalemate."[23] The quote-war between biblical texts has led to what this work has summarized as the so-called gender paradox within Pentecostalism, fueled by a constant sense of scriptural indecision. Therefore, a different (hermeneutical) solution must be offered.

The argument that some texts hold more importance or authority over other texts is also a common approach among those arguing for the full equality of women. These biblical scholars and theologians see within the Bible "control texts,"[24] "timeless" passages,[25] "window" texts,[26] "inbreaking" moments,[27] "prophetic" or "critical" norms,[28] "golden threads,"[29] a "liberating tradition,"[30] and "trajectory" movements,[31] all of which signal the "hermeneutical priority" of some texts over others.[32] In this approach, the "timeless" or "golden thread" passages on gender hold more authority than historically bound patriarchal texts and can therefore

---

21. Yong, *Spirit Poured Out*, 27.
22. Thomas, "Women, Pentecostals and the Bible," 50, 54.
23. Kevin Giles, *The Trinity and Subordinationism: The Doctrine of God & the Contemporary Gender Debate* (Downers Grove, IL: InterVarsity, 2002), 3.
24. Stackhouse, *Finally Feminist*, 29.
25. Schüssler Fiorenza, *Memory of Her*, 33.
26. David Scholer, "Galatians 3:28 and the Ministry of Women in the Church," in *Theology, News and Notes* (Pasadena: Fuller Theological Seminary, June 1998), 20.
27. Defined as a passage "which confounds cultural expectations and raises human sights to possibilities that are rooted in God's vision and will for humankind" (Mary Aquin O'Neill, "Anthropology: The Mystery of Being Human Together," in LaCugna, *Freeing Theology*, 142).
28. Ruether, *Sexism*, 24, 31–4; Cahill, *Sex, Gender*, 143.
29. Hampson, *Theology and Feminism*, 25.
30. Letty M. Russell, "Authority and the Challenge of Feminist Interpretation," in *Feminist Interpretation of the Bible*, ed. Letty M. Russell (Philadelphia: Westminster, 1985), 138–9. See also Copeland, "Journeying," 30.
31. Webb, *Slaves, Women, and Homosexuals*, 30–4. Archer also uses a trajectory argument ("Women in Ministry," 53). For a less scholarly but helpful approach to the trajectory argument and forward movement in Scripture, see Glen G. Scorgie who uses "the trajectory of the Spirit" in *The Journey Back to Eden* (Grand Rapids: Zondervan, 2005).
32. Grenz and Kjesbo, *Women*, 106. For more examples, see Gordon Fee and Douglas Stuart, *How to Read the Bible for All Its Worth*, 3rd ed. (Grand Rapids: Zondervan, 2003), 72; Stackhouse, *Finally Feminist*, 23.

be used to interpret passages that are less clear or to deem them as less important for understanding God's plan for gender.[33] The premise of hermeneutical priority is where Pentecostal hermeneutics and feminist hermeneutics can work together to address the gender paradox.[34] Some have argued a weakness of feminist-liberationist readings and part of its failure to produce adequate results is that they have inspired no *telos*, no eschatological hope.[35] As an eschatological movement, Pentecostals may want to consider the priority of eschatological texts when attempting to discern God's plan for God's church, especially when the biblical text is unclear on an issue. The Scriptures can appear to be "irredeemably patriarchal or unequivocally egalitarian" depending on the hermeneutic used.[36] The question for Pentecostals is whether there is a hermeneutic that is faithful to the Bible, the early heart of the movement, and an egalitarian vision.

### 4.1.2 The Promise of an Eschatological–Egalitarian Hermeneutical Priority

This project uses an eschatological lens or hermeneutic to interpret Scripture, an approach this chapter seeks to justify. By eschatological–egalitarian hermeneutic I mean using passages on gender that clearly state or imply an eschatological trajectory for equality in order to help interpret other passages on gender. Therefore, all texts on gender are read with an eschatological lens, with explicitly eschatological passages providing hermeneutical priority over passages on gender that are without direct eschatological reference. Eschatological passages hold this priority because of the "authority of God's new creation" over the one that is passing away.[37] In the words of Deborah Sawyer, "The 'end time' gives permission to biblical writers to explode expectations and transgress given boundaries."[38] This "permission" allows biblical writers to override cultural constraints as the author communicates the ultimate divine intention, rendering other texts that impede that intention as less hermeneutically instructive.[39] In short, an eschatological

---

33. Hampson, *Theology and Feminism*, 25.

34. But see Abraham, "Feminist Hermeneutics and Pentecostal Spirituality," 3–21, who has a mostly negative assessment of feminist hermeneutics and believes it poses a challenge to Pentecostal spirituality.

35. The observation of Susan Frank Parsons, cited by Rees, "Sarah Coakley," 301. Bernice Martin describes the "irony" of Pentecostalism doing what liberation theology and left-leaning development specialists could not do in Latin America ("Gender Paradox," 62). It is why Miller and Yamamori see Pentecostalism as the potential successor to Liberation Theology (*Global Pentecostalism*, 4).

36. Abraham, "Feminist Hermeneutics and Pentecostal Spirituality," 4. See also Stackhouse, *Finally Feminist*, 128, 135. As Schüssler Fiorenza mentions in *Bread Not Stone*, use of the Bible can lead to liberation or oppression depending on how it is used (67).

37. Russell, *Household*, 20.

38. Deborah F. Sawyer, *God, Gender and the Bible* (London: Routledge, 2002), 152.

39. See Russell, "Authority," 138–9.

hermeneutic argues that interpretation from this historical place in time should be influenced by another (future) historical place in time. It looks to future visions of human flourishing contained in the text to understand the possibilities of flourishing in the present.

Reading and interpreting the Bible through an eschatological lens is a hermeneutic with growing support from Pentecostals.[40] Craig Keener argues that in the new age of the Spirit, the disciples and Paul were learning to use an eschatological framework for understanding Scripture, which "demands that we read Scripture from this eschatological perspective as well."[41] Yong suggests there is an "eschatological horizon" to Scripture and its interpretation must have an eschatological dimension.[42] Clark Pinnock makes a few proposals in his article "The Work of the Holy Spirit in Hermeneutics," one being that we should recognize the eschatological dynamic in the interpretive process.[43] And Johns argues that Scripture is to be interpreted within its teleological framework.[44] Being a narrative people—and therefore understanding that the ending of a story is perhaps the most crucial element in determining the meaning of a story—Pentecostals "often determine the meaning of biblical passages and their own experience in the light of the coming kingdom of God."[45] As my historical investigation unearthed, Pentecostals instinctively used an eschatological hermeneutical priority approach at the beginning of the movement, even if they did not formally articulate it as such.

A few feminist and Pentecostal scholars have at least indicated the promise of a specifically eschatological hermeneutic for reading texts on gender.[46] Johns argues the Bible is mainly a book of hope for women when read eschatologically, for it points to a future which the Spirit is already actualizing.[47] Jobling sees eschatology as the potential "hermeneutical key" for reading texts on gender.[48] Russell consistently promotes thinking "from the other end," appealing to the authority of the future, and searching for a "usable future" when determining

---

40. And support from non-Pentecostals as well. See discussion of Russell in 1.1.3. Wolfhart Pannenberg sees eschatology providing the key to understanding the NT (*Systematic Theology*, 2:218).

41. See Keener, *Spirit Hermeneutics*, 49–51 (quote from 51).

42. Yong, *Renewing*, 350, 352.

43. Pinnock, "Holy Spirit in Hermeneutics," 17.

44. Johns, "Conscientization," 163.

45. Powers, "Pentecostal Hermeneutics," 317.

46. See previous works already discussed in 1.1.3 and 1.2.

47. Johns, "Conscientization," 157.

48. Jobling, *Feminist Biblical Interpretation*, 139. See also Jobling's chapter "Towards an Eschatological Hermeneutic" in the same work (99–115), although the chapter does surprisingly little to develop this hermeneutic, instead discussing the hermeneutic of remembrance of Schüssler Fiorenza and Trible.

gender practices from Scripture.[49] And Chris Green implies that the *eschaton* should have the first and last word when considering the question of women in the church and interpreting relevant passages.[50] What these authors hint at is that the eschatological–egalitarian thread of the Bible is the norm through which to view all other passages on gender. Instead of trying to hold together in tension the limiting and liberating elements of the biblical text, an eschatological hermeneutic elevates the liberating elements above the limiting ones.

A helpful approach for interpreting other (non-eschatological) passages about women as well as applying the hermeneutical priority of eschatological texts on gender is John Stackhouse's "holy pragmatism" paradigm.[51] Stackhouse argues that to get the gospel to as many people as possible as effectively as possible, God temporarily accommodates God's self to work within current culturally conditioned human limitations, including the pervasiveness of a patriarchal culture. God was willing to forgo secondary objectives (such as eradicating hierarchy) to make sure the primary objective of getting the gospel to people was accomplished, with the hopes that the latter would eventually and gradually accomplish the former. The Bible is realistic about the global reality of patriarchy and where the eschatological trajectory of gender equality stood in history at the time. This accommodative stance of God (and by extension the biblical authors) explains, Stackhouse suggests, why one seems to get two messages on gender in Scripture (which has led to the gender paradox in Pentecostalism). However, the message of eschatological texts on gender recruits the eschatological imagination and offers a glimpse of what can and should be in the present, pending the changed social circumstances that passages like Galatians 3:28 point toward.[52] The eschatological–egalitarian texts were limited in their application in the first century, even if there was forward movement in the trajectory. But if these texts did not exist, there would be no clear instruction on God's ultimate plan for gender for the time when the cultural circumstances no longer require patriarchal systems.

Reading the Bible with an eschatological lens allows one to read the more "problematic" texts without completely dismissing them or spending all one's energy trying to explain them away. Trying to explain away the patriarchal tendencies of the Bible or its authors through lengthy, technical exegesis—even if creative and at times helpful—will not solve the gender paradox.[53] As Yong astutely observes, "no amount of sophisticated re-reading of the biblical texts can do away

---

49. Farley and Jones, "Introduction," xii.

50. Chris E. W. Green, "Does (Not) Nature Itself Teach You? Pentecostal Reflections on a Troubled and Troubling Text," *Pneuma* 38, no. 4 (2016): 474.

51. Stackhouse, *Finally Feminist*, 38–54. Similar is the "missionary principle" of Swartley in *Slavery, Sabbath, War, and Women*, 188–9.

52. Stackhouse does not specifically mention eschatological texts, but more broadly texts that affirm the equality of men and women.

53. Archer, "Was the Spirit Poured out on Women," 132.

with the patriarchal bias of the biblical authors themselves."[54] We can come to grips with the reality that the biblical authors *do* temporarily accommodate themselves to a patriarchal and androcentric culture, while understanding that these passages do not communicate God's ultimate plan for gender the way eschatological texts do.[55] Stackhouse, summarizing William Webb, states that although we do not learn timeless teachings on gender from patriarchal passages, we can learn a lot about God pastorally, pedagogically, evangelistically, redemptively, and soteriologically.[56] In short, God's eternal purposes could not all be accomplished entirely at once in the early church. Although sinful structures and human nature are not reformed quickly, God set out an eschatological plan that was and is to be realized more fully in time. An eschatological–egalitarian hermeneutic prioritizes texts on gender that reveal the liberating activity of the Spirit and that "work towards the liberation which [the] Christian narrative offers as a real and therefore plausible possibility."[57] These eschatological texts on gender hold hermeneutical priority over other gender texts that temporarily conceal or concede the eschatological ideal for pragmatic purposes.

Early Pentecostals used an eschatological hermeneutic as a commonsense approach.[58] They valued all of Scripture but realized that the eschatological outpouring of God's Spirit in these last days took priority over teachings relegated to past situations. The obvious nature of the hermeneutical priority of eschatological texts was in a way part of its downfall: a formal, well-rounded hermeneutic was never developed or articulated. Stanley observes that most Pentecostals did not expand their argument for equality in ministry past the example of Pentecost because they felt their experience and the validation from Acts 2 was enough.[59] Emphasizing a Pentecost-only or Lukan-only hermeneutical approach to the gender problem maintains (or adds to) the ambiguity:[60] Pentecostals will rightly desire to consider "all Scripture" useful (2 Tim. 3:16) for knowing the "whole purpose of God" (Acts 20:27). Reading the Bible through an eschatological lens provides a more comprehensive, convincing, and defensible approach to empowering Pentecostal women. Although still grounded in Acts 2, it understands Pentecost as a part of a larger eschatological–egalitarian narrative trajectory begun at creation and continued in the ministry of Jesus, all compactly connected thematically and grammatically in Paul's eschatological vision in Galatians 3:28. The eschatological–egalitarian trajectory is not confined to one Testament, one text, or one member of the Trinity. When the eschatological imagination is alive—even in the cultural context of patriarchy—egalitarian ideals

---

54. Yong, *Spirit-Word-Community*, 307 (see 308 as well).
55. See O'Neill, "Anthropology: The Mystery of Being Human Together," 142, 147.
56. Stackhouse, *Finally Feminist*, 40.
57. Shields, *Eschatological Imagination*, 7.
58. For Pentecostals' commonsense approach to Scripture, see Archer, *Pentecostal Hermeneutic*, 125–6.
59. Stanley, "Laying a Straw," 112.
60. See Yong, *Spirit Poured Out*, 27; Stephenson, *Dismantling*, 11.

rise to the forefront. The equality of men and women is a crucial part of the biblical story of creation, fall, redemption, and restoration.

*4.1.3 The Procedure for Constructing the Hermeneutic*

To establish the central eschatological texts on gender and validate their hermeneutical priority, we must construct a unified eschatological-egalitarian narrative trajectory within the biblical text. The rest of the chapter proposes three passages that both inspire eschatological imagining and call for present participation in egalitarian practices to the fullest extent possible: Genesis 1–3, Galatians 3:28, and Acts 2:17-18. These three texts—integrated into the narrative points in history of creation, fall, redemption in Christ, and Pentecost—are frequently mentioned together in Pentecostal literature as texts supporting gender equality.[61] In addition, the latter two were heavily used in the early Pentecostal movement as texts for authorizing women in ministry.[62] However, although their eschatological dimension is often recognized and agreed upon, a constructive hermeneutic birthed from these texts that convincingly presents their theological and hermeneutical priority due to their eschatological vision has never been articulated.[63] If the Christian faith in general and the Pentecostal movement in particular are primarily forward looking and forward moving,[64] then mining the Scriptures for their eschatological-egalitarian yield is vitally important to the gender debate.[65]

The texts of Genesis 1–3, Galatians 3:28, and Acts 2:17-18 are chosen for three main reasons: their already prominent place in feminist theology; their core role in the biblical narrative of creation, fall, redemption, restoration; and their interconnectedness thematically and through potential allusions that tie them together as a part of a single narrative.[66] These reasons heighten their importance and possibility to be used as hermeneutical guides for other texts on gender as they provide a comprehensive narrative thread. In order to establish their eschatological significance and argue for their hermeneutical priority, each of these interconnected passages is examined as follows: (1) tracing briefly their *importance* in feminist theology and in the gender debate; (2) identifying the

---

61. For example, see Stephenson, *Dismantling*, 79–86, and her grouping of *imago Dei, imago Christi, imago Spiritus*; Gill and Cavaness, *God's Women*; Hyatt, "Spirit-Filled Women," 238; Powers, "Pentecostal Hermeneutics," 318; Alexander and Gause, *Women*, 29. See also Ruether, *Sexism*, 195.

62. As established in 2.2.2.

63. See Schüssler Fiorenza, *Memory of Her*, 33.

64. See previous discussion in my Introduction and Bauckham and Hart, *Hope against Hope*, 82.

65. Playing off Studebaker's quest to mine the biblical narratives of the Spirit for their Trinitarian yield (Studebaker, *From Pentecost to the Triune God*, 3).

66. Additionally, these three texts nicely incorporate the ministry of the Father, Son, and Holy Spirit.

*relevant background* and *context* (and exegetical arguments when necessary) for understanding the egalitarian nature of the text; (3) locating their *eschatological significance*; (4) establishing the case for their *hermeneutical priority* in the gender debate; (5) assessing their recruitment of the eschatological *imagination* and call to *participation* in eschatological realities.

There is by necessity overlap between some of the five sections as some discussions of the text could fit within multiple sections. For example, some of the relevant background and context of the passage may be additionally discussed in sections three and four to accomplish the goals of those sections. Overall, the third and fourth parts for each textual discussion are the most important task for the goal and argument of this chapter. They move us toward establishing a set of eschatological texts that can be formally articulated as a Pentecostal eschatological authorizing hermeneutic, which overcomes the perpetual inconsistency and uncertainty surrounding the gender debate. Despite the vast amounts of literature concerning the gendered aspects of the texts in sections one and two, I offer only summaries of necessary information that help to support the case for sections three and four. Part five offers hints of how the texts inspire action, some of which has already been documented in the previous chapters concerning how early Pentecostals interpreted and applied these texts. The next chapters will also expand upon and apply the assessments in part five. Although Pentecostal scholars are featured prominently in the discussion—especially for the Acts 2 passage—feminist theologians from other traditions are incorporated when appropriate or when providing a leading or important interpretation, as has been the approach throughout my work. Some texts or specific sections receive longer discussions when warranted due to do the debated status of the text as it pertains to my argument. For example, the eschatological significance of Galatians 3:28 is widely and contentiously debated and therefore some detailed assessment is needed to support its inclusion in the proposed unified eschatological-egalitarian biblical narrative thread. Lastly, the end of the Galatians examination necessarily branches out into the ministry of Jesus in the Gospels for reasons that will become clear after the initial discussion of the text.

### 4.2 In the Beginning Is the End: Genesis 1–3 and Creation

#### 4.2.1 Importance

The argument for equality in the *end* finds its starting point "in the beginning" (Gen. 1:1). The Genesis creation narrative is an appropriate place to begin, not least because it teaches that hermeneutics itself is a prelapsarian good, an original aspect of creation and human life.[67] But more than that, as the "*locus classicus*" of

---

67. See Smith, *Fall of Interpretation*, 23. Smith cites the beginning of hermeneutics as "Did God really say?" in the garden of Eden (Gen. 3:1).

feminist interpretation, it is one of the most frequent areas of feminist investigation over the last few decades.[68] Despite so-called malestream interpretations of Genesis 1–3 dominating for millennia,[69] feminist theologians (and others) have begun challenging those interpretations and providing alternative readings based on the historical and literary context and on exegetical analysis. For example, they challenge interpretations of 2:18-23 that imply the man being created before woman or the woman being called "helper" (v. 18) indicate subordination of any kind, highlighting that animals are created before humans without hierarchical significance and "helper" is often used of God in the Bible.[70] Revised feminist readings of the creation account demonstrate how any implied hierarchy of the text could easily be interpreted in favor of the woman.[71] As woman is created last and fashioned from the superior material of Adam's rib (2:21) rather than the lowly dust (2:7), she becomes the pinnacle "crowning achievement" of creation, rescuing man from his loneliness (2:18), as he leaves his family and is appended to her life (2:24), in which he finds his significance.[72]

A prelapsarian understanding of gender has emerged as a "critical norm" against passages that subordinate women.[73] Although the entire narrative is important

---

68. See Abraham, "Feminist Hermeneutics and Pentecostal Spirituality," 5, 13. Other OT passages also receive attention, just not to the same extent. For examples of women leaders in the OT, see Mimi R. Haddad, "Examples of Women's Leadership in the Old Testament and Church History," in English de Alminana and Olena, *Women*, 59–69; Alexander and Gause, *Women*, 47–58.

69. See Rebecca Chopp, "Eve's Knowing: Feminist Theology's Resistance to Malestream Epistemological Frameworks," in *Feminist Theology in Different Contexts*, ed. Elisabeth Schüssler Fiorenza and M. Shawn Copeland (London: SCM, 1996), 116–23. For some examples and critiques of these kinds of malestream interpretations, see Ruether, *Sexism*, 166–70.

70. There is nothing to indicate that the woman being created "out of man" implies subordination (see Hampson, *Theology and Feminism*, 71). It is less clear in the second creation story whether the *adam* ("human/man") of 2:7-21 was a sexed being before the division into male and female (2:22; see Stackhouse, *Finally Feminist*, 66). The Hebrew word 'ēzer ("helper") in 2:18 is never used of a subordinate in the Bible and is most frequently used of God—certainly no subordinate—as our helper and strength. See Grenz and Kjesbo, *Women*, 164–5; Gretchen Gaebelein Hull, *Equal to Serve: Women and Men in the Church and Home* (Old Tappan, NJ: Fleming H. Revell, 1987), 182. For more on 2:18 and 'ēzer, see Haddad, "Examples," 60; Johns, "Conscientization," 154–5n2. The naming of Eve by Adam, for some a sign of authority, happens in 3:20 after the Fall and not here.

71. An interpretive move many feminists consider equally unfair, but simply use to make a point. For an insightful satire that does just that, see Alvera Mickelsen's humorous essay in Hull, *Equal to Serve*, 245–50.

72. For summary of some of these arguments, see Schroeder and Taylor, *Voices Long Silenced*, 271; Grenz and Kjesbo, *Women*, 161.

73. Cahill, *Sex, Gender*, 143.

and brought into the proceeding discussion, central attention here is given to Genesis 1:26-28 and specifically verse 27 below, partly due to its (eschatological) connection with Galatians 3:28:

> So God created humans in his image,
> in the image of God he created them;
> male and female he created them.

This verse has received an "astonishing range of interpretations."[74] Therefore, some contextual background to the first few chapters of Genesis is important to make an eschatological case.

### 4.2.2 Relevant Background

The first three chapters of Genesis are crucial for interpreting passages on gender throughout the rest of the Bible. The current focus on Genesis 1–3 is less about the literal historicity of the story and more on the theological points being presented through the literary text.[75] Whether the creation narrative establishes a hierarchal pattern of authority or whether that pattern is a result of sin and the Fall has significant hermeneutical implications.

The two creation accounts (Gen. 1:26-28, 2:4-25) contain no hint of subordination, hierarchy, or authority structures.[76] Male and female are created equal and equally share in the "image of God" (1:27).[77] The way "male and female" structurally corresponds to "image of God" makes gender an essential attribute of humanity's likeness to God, rather than a limitation in reflecting God's likeness.[78] Additionally, both male and female are blessed by God as coequal rulers and royal representatives with shared partnership, dominion, and vocational responsibility in the cultural mandate of 1:26, 28.[79] The scene is one of full equality and mutuality

---

74. Christopher Noble, "Biblical Literalism and Gender Stability: A Christian Response to Gender Performance Theory," in Jule and Pedersen, *Being Feminist*, 187.

75. This is a common approach, particularly among feminist theologians. See Karras, "Eschatology," 251. See also Yong, *Renewing*, 284.

76. For discussion, including the importance of and reasons for reading Genesis 2 through the lens of Genesis 1, see Archer, "Was the Spirit Poured out on Women," 124–5.

77. This is a standard argument. See Alexander and Gause, *Women*, 30–9, for summary.

78. See Phyllis Trible, *God and the Rhetoric of Sexuality* (Philadelphia: Fortress, 1978), 17. See also Noble, "Biblical Literalism," 188–9. Some argue "humankind" (Hebrew *adam*) refers to an androgynous being (see discussion in 4.3.3). Many see the image of God in this passage as mainly relational, not individual (Grenz and Kjesbo, *Women*, 170–1). Consequently, later sin is more of a relational event than individual (see Yong, *Renewing*, 273).

79. Carmody, *Feminist Theology*, 89; Stephenson, *Dismantling*, 118, 121. However, many eco-feminists prefer a diminished emphasis on dominion in the text as the degradation of

between man and woman in their commission to care for the earth, containing no defined roles based on gender,[80] with the later indication that ruling alone without equal partnership would be inadequate (Gen. 2:18).[81]

God's original intention for shared leadership and complete equality in Genesis 1–2 has profound implications for interpreting what happens in Genesis 3 (and much of the rest of the biblical story).[82] The account of the Fall is a shocking departure from the creation narrative of mutuality, as it portrays subordination, hierarchy, and role distinction as direct results of sin entering the world.[83] The husband's "rule" over his wife and the wife's "desire" for her husband (3:16) are signs of the disruption of God's good creation and egalitarian order.[84] The gender inequality of 3:16 is a symptom of separation from God and therefore "should not be regarded as an eternally valid norm";[85] in fact, like any sinful system, it should be fought against. Genesis 3 is descriptive, not prescriptive, explaining how the Fall tainted God's original creation design for men and women to be coequal rulers in the world: sexism and patriarchy are distortions of the original gender plan.[86] Because gender hierarchy is a result of the Fall, we can conclude that gender-based discrimination runs counter to God's intention for creation and we should "anticipate that the new creation will include the reshaping of male-female relationships."[87]

### 4.2.3 Eschatological Significance

There are several reasons for interpreting the narrative of Genesis 1–2 as an eschatological text. Although the world of Genesis 1, with its indications of equality, is called "very good" (1:31), it is not a perfect or ideal world with perfect relationships or people. Rather, it is a world in need of cultivation and growth (1:28-30), an incomplete world moving toward an ultimate goal or *eschaton*.[88] There is no utopian paradise to return to, but there are the "basic ingredients" that

---

nature is seen as an extension of the degradation of women (Carmody, *Feminist Theology*, 91–100, 230–4).

80. Some interpret the text as more about mutuality and community than marriage. See Claus Westermann, *Creation*, trans. John Scullion (Philadelphia: Fortress, 1974), 86–8.

81. Haddad, "Examples," 68.

82. See here Grant, "Merchandised Women," 280–2.

83. Grenz and Kjesbo, *Women*, 160–2, 209.

84. "Desire" is sometimes interpreted as overdependence. See Ruth Tucker, *Women in the Maze: Questions and Answers on Biblical Equality* (Downers Grover, IL: InterVarsity, 1992), 50–1. Cf. Song of Sol. 7:10.

85. Westermann, *Creation*, 101.

86. Tucker, *Women*, 51; Ruether, *Sexism*, 37, 61; Stackhouse, *Finally Feminist*, 93.

87. Grenz and Kjesbo, *Women*, 177, 169.

88. See Simon Oliver, *Creation: A Guide for the Perplexed* (London: Bloomsbury T&T Clark, 2017), 84–8.

lay the eschatological trajectory for a world of equality.[89] The prelapsarian *imago Dei* is incomplete and still in process; it is the eschatological seed for the eventual completion of humanity's "likeness" (1:26) to God in the new creation.[90] And it is the Bible's connection of Genesis 1–2 with the new creation that has convinced most biblical scholars and theologians to interpret creation as an eschatological event. As G. K. Beale states, "Genesis 1–3 lays out the basic themes for the rest of the OT, which are essentially end-time or 'eschatological' themes."[91] In other words, there is a natural or dialectic relationship between origin and *eschaton*: creation is ultimately about consummation.[92]

Finding the end in the beginning (and vice versa) is a biblical idea. Thomas Rausch argues that the "tendency to separate creation and eschatology, pushing both to opposite margins, to the beginning and end of time" causes us to lose sight "of their essential connectedness" within the Bible.[93] The dictum "*Endzeit* (end-time) corresponds to *Urzeit* (primal time)" positions eschatology as the completion of creation.[94] There is a noticeable and strong link between the first few chapters of the Bible (creation) and the last few (new creation).[95] Revelation 20–22 is not a return to the original creation, not simply a picture of the restoration or reformation of Eden's garden; more than that, it is a heavenly city depicted as the completion and transformation of the eschatological vision that began at creation that is now finally complete (see Rev. 21:22–22:5).[96] There is a distinct continuity between the original creation and the new creation, but also a newness as the "very good" of creation is now enhanced (but not abolished).[97] For example, in Revelation 20:4-6 the faithful saints will now *fully* rule and reign over God's creation as co-regents with Christ, an eschatological fulfillment of Genesis 1:26-28.[98] The eschatological

---

89. Ruether, *Sexism*, 254.

90. The Eastern tradition distinguishes between the likeness and image of Gen. 1:26-27. See Augustine, *Spirit and the Common Good*, 16-19; Karras, "Eschatology," 252.

91. G. K. Beale, "The End Starts at the Beginning," introductory chapter in Gladd and Harmon, *Inaugurated Eschatology*, 5.

92. See Augustine, *Spirit and the Common Good*, 8.

93. Rausch, *Eschatology*, 20. Cf. Russell: "we cannot ignore the fact that 'myths of origin' and 'myths of *eschaton*' are interrelated" (Russell, *Future*, 45).

94. Bauckham and Hart, *Hope Against Hope*, 149; Rausch, *Eschatology*, 121.

95. Or "echoes" (Bauckham and Hart, *Hope Against Hope*, 149).

96. There is strong consensus for this way of thinking about Genesis 1–2 and Revelation 21–22. See Yong, *Renewing*, 75; Karras, "Eschatology," 245; Bauckham and Hart, *Hope Against Hope*, 149; Luke Timothy Johnson, *The Writings of the New Testament: An Interpretation*, rev. ed. (Minneapolis: Fortress, 1999), 588.

97. Wright, *Surprised by Hope*, 259; Van Leeuwen, *Gender*, 215; Richard Bauckham, "Eschatology," in *The Oxford Companion to Christian Thought: Intellectual, Spiritual, and Moral Horizons of Christianity*, ed. Adrian Hastings, Alistair Mason, and Hugh Pyper (Oxford: Oxford University Press, 2000), 209.

98. McQueen, *Pentecostal Eschatology*, 272.

orientation of Genesis 1–2 also influences how one interprets the Fall and Genesis 3. The postlapsarian world of gender hierarchy and "rule" (3:16) is a world moving in the opposite direction of the *eschaton* (even as the judgment of the man and woman in Genesis 3 is an eschatological act, in that it is meant to move them—and all humanity—toward redemption[99]).

Genesis 1–2 represents the beginning of the eschatological-egalitarian narrative thread in the Bible. It represents an eschatological trajectory that, although at times stifled or stalled by accommodation to patriarchy in the Old Testament, persists throughout the biblical narrative. The eschatological-egalitarian seeds planted in creation survive and are later watered and brought to life through the ministry of the eschatological Christ and his eschatological Spirit (see texts below). The creation story is the beginning of an egalitarian narrative that points toward the eschatological renewal of male and female relationships as depicted in Genesis 1–2.

### 4.2.4 Hermeneutical Priority

The hermeneutical priority of Genesis 1–2 is clear in its context. The original—and eventually redeemed—order of creation in the first two chapters of Genesis holds priority over the fallen order of Genesis 3. Therefore, Scriptures that are in the service of restoring the creation trajectory should be prioritized over ones that uphold the fallen order. Russell suggests the image of a mended creation should function "as a hermeneutical key for interpretation of scripture and tradition."[100] Paul Jewett makes the argument that the New Testament authors' mistake was sometimes to follow the rabbinical tradition of understanding gender relationships according to the Fall in Genesis 3 rather than the preceding creation narrative,[101] a mistake Jesus himself exposes.

Jesus provides an example of reading from the vantage point of eschatological texts on gender, particularly Genesis 1–2, for solving gender questions. In his teaching about divorce in Matthew 19:1-12, Jesus sought to break the power men used over women in divorce practices, which demeaned and disadvantaged women in the first century.[102] The Pharisees quote Scripture and assume its

---

99. See Alexander and Gause, *Women*, 42. For redemption as communal rather than "a socially disembodied personal experience," see Augustine, *Spirit and the Common Good*, 43.

100. Russell, *Household*, 71. Russell, however, does not give any indication or examples of how this might work.

101. Paul K. Jewett, *Man as Male and Female: A Study in Sexual Relationships from a Theological Point of View* (Grand Rapids: Eerdmans, 1975). Jewett discusses how the apostle Paul reflects this tension in his letters, reflecting his Jewish background and training (as reflected in 1 Cor. 11:9) in contrast with the "new insight" he had through Christ displayed in passages such as Galatians 3:28 (see 111–28, esp. 112).

102. I am summarizing some of Murray Dempster in this paragraph but adding my own insights on Jesus' eschatological hermeneutical priority (see Dempster, "Eschatology," 185).

authority to defend the patriarchal practice of divorce (v. 7). However, Jesus uses the hermeneutical strategy that some texts offer a clearer picture of God's intentions than others. He uses the eschatological passage of Genesis 1:27 to argue that "from the beginning it was not so" (vv. 4, 8). Jesus claims that more culturally specific commands were temporary concessions that had more to do with the hardness of (specifically men's) hearts than with God's ultimate vision for male-female relations (v. 8). Jesus' respect for the equality of male and female (Gen. 1:27) and the protection of women supersedes other quotations from Scripture used to legitimate oppression and social practices that support male domination. Despite a scriptural "command" (v. 7) that justified postlapsarian concessions to human fallenness, Jesus' ethics of male-female relationship is not predicated on such concessions, even if canonized. Rather, Jesus' understanding of gender and prescribed practices was based on a prelapsarian eschatological understanding. Jesus encourages practices in the present world that are in line with the eschatological plan laid out "at the beginning" (v. 4).

In her feminist-pneumatological reading of Genesis 1–3, Stephenson also sees an egalitarian thread present from the beginning of creation that informs the rest of the biblical narrative and its interpretation.[103] She argues the Spirit is at work from the very beginning (cf. Gen. 1:2), bringing life and vocational equality and mutuality between the genders. Stephenson then proposes that any hint of subordination or supremacy in gender relations is a perversion of the original creation, a trajectory moving in the opposite direction of the intention of creation. Like the narrative approach of this chapter, Stephenson then connects the foundational egalitarian narrative of Genesis to the ministry of Jesus (Gal. 3:28) and the ministry of the Spirit in Acts 2. The same Spirit that brought to life the egalitarian world of the original creation is now also bringing to life the egalitarian world of the new creation.[104]

### 4.2.5 Imagination and Participation

If the equality of male and female is a feature of the original creation, and the new creation is an enhancement of that creation, a robust eschatological imagination must include the full equality and partnership of women and men in all parts of the new creation. An eschatological reading of Genesis 1–3 exposes subordination and male domination not only as perversions of creation and sinful temptations, but also distorted visions of God's eschatological intent.[105] Both men and women can participate in these distortions by assuming male dominion is God-ordained and accepting it as a part of social order (even if fallen).[106] Rather than participation in distortions of creation, an eschatological reading of Genesis 1–3

---

103. See discussion in Stephenson, *Dismantling,* 118–22.
104. See Stephenson, *Dismantling,* 128.
105. See Stephenson, *Dismantling,* 122; Van Leeuwen, *Gender,* 44–6.
106. See discussion by Van Leeuwen, *Gender,* 46–50.

calls a community to participation in co-equal rulership that gives equal voice to both women and men.[107] As "new creation people," followers of Jesus are to bring the "signs and symbols of the kingdom" on earth as in heaven, including full gender equality.[108]

As a "memory of the future" type of text,[109] Genesis 1–2 causes the reader to look back in order to look forward, which then inspires one's practice in the present. Pentecostals must live in the "in between" time with a dual focus: looking back in an attempt to live as we would have lived if the Fall had not occurred, and looking forward to glean inspiration for how to live in the present.[110] The new creation transcends the old and we should expect even more at the end than the beginning.[111] An eschatological reading of the creation story reveals that one's ache for Edenic equality is actually an eschatological ache. The goal is not to go back to Eden or to restore the original state.[112] Rather, "the end starts at the beginning."[113] We look back to what was "very good" in the beginning (Gen. 1:31) in order to look forward to what will be even better in the end. The eschatological seeds of an egalitarian world are firmly planted in the creating work of God in Genesis 1–2. In Galatians 3:28, those seeds are brought to life in the redeeming work of Christ as the effects of the Fall begin to be reversed and overcome as humanity is put back on the original trajectory of God's eschatological plan for women and men.

## 4.3 In the End Is the Beginning: Galatians 3:28 and the Ministry of Jesus

### 4.3.1 Importance

Galatians 3:28 has been called "the most quoted piece of Scripture in the gender debate," receiving attention from both egalitarian and complementarian advocates to promote their biblical stance.[114] The passage is considered by most scholars to be the climax of Paul's letter and his theological teaching in it, and the verse's implications for gender roles and status are considered momentous and

---

107. Van Leeuwen, *Gender*, 46.
108. Wright, *Surprised by Hope*, 209.
109. A key phrase in Russell, *Household*.
110. Alexander and Gause, *Women*, 45. However, this recommended eschatological praxis is not applied or fleshed out in any way in their work.
111. See Russell, *Future*, 46.
112. This is contra some arguments for gender equality, such as Gause, *Women*, 26.
113. The title of Beale's introductory chapter in Gladd and Harmon, *Inaugurated Eschatology*.
114. Linda Woodhead, "God, Gender and Identity," in *Gospel and Gender: A Trinitarian Engagement with Being Male and Female in Christ*, ed. Douglas A. Campbell (London: T&T Clark, 2003), 101.

foundational by feminist theologians.[115] The text reads, "There is no longer Jew or Greek; there is no longer slave or free; there is no longer male and female, for all of you are one in Christ Jesus." Books on gender equality in the church often place Galatians 3:28 as central to their argument.[116] It functions as an epigraph to Christian feminist publications,[117] has been a foundational text for equality during renewal movements in the church,[118] and is considered by most to be Paul's clearest and most radical statement on gender identity and roles.[119] It is also important because, perhaps more than any other passage, it links the original creation (through allusion to Gen. 1:27) to the new creation through Christ and calls the believer into present participation in that new life.[120]

*4.3.2 Relevant Background*

Galatians is an important study for any inquiry into potential trajectory passages on gender, for it is where Paul, in the face of opposition, "pushes the scandalous implications of the gospel to their limits."[121] Rather than the common depiction of it being a letter of raw emotion and random thought, it is a carefully constructed argument that is rooted heavily in eschatological and egalitarian thinking.[122] Paul's primary concern is the Galatians "turning to a different gospel" (1:6), one that looks back toward living under the old ways and curse of the law (represented by circumcision) rather than forward toward the new eschatological life and promises they are called to in Christ (represented by the Spirit). Paul distinguishes these two trajectories as a choice between the life of the "flesh" and the life of the "Spirit" (5:16-26), the former being "foolish" (3:1, 3) and the latter leading to freedom (4:28–5:1). Fundamental to Paul's passionate argument is that the way of the law and the flesh upholds traditional hierarchical status boundaries, boundaries that were eliminated by the inauguration of the "new creation" begun at Christ's crucifixion (6:14-16).

Paul lays out his ultimate vision of a new eschatological social order most clearly in Galatians 3:28. The three couplets in the text (Jew/Gentile, slave/free, male/female) represent a (re)defining of the people of God in light of the redeeming

---

115. See Sheila Briggs, "Galatians," in *Searching the Scriptures: A Feminist Commentary*, vol. 2, ed. Elizabeth Schüssler Fiorenza (New York: Crossroad, 1994), 219; Stephenson, *Dismantling*, 123.

116. For example, see Schüssler Fiorenza, *Memory of Her*, 160–99.

117. For example, see Jule and Pedersen, *Being Feminist*.

118. See 2.2.2 for its importance in the initial egalitarian thrust of the Pentecostal movement.

119. Judith M. Gundry-Volf, "Beyond Difference? Paul's Vision of a New Humanity in Galatians 3.28," in Campbell, *Gospel and Gender*, 8.

120. See Grenz, *Moral Quest*, 226.

121. Johnson, *New Testament*, 327.

122. Johnson, *New Testament*, 328.

work of Christ: "for all of you are one in Christ Jesus." For Paul, salvation through Christ involves the inauguration of the age to come, which includes the eradication of hierarchical structures and the liberation of the oppressed.[123] The possible baptismal formula (see 3:27) of Galatians 3:28 represents the overthrowing of the previous privileged status of Jew over Greek, free over slave, and male over female.[124] Whereas the old social order of the desires of the flesh leads to rivalry, dissensions, and factions between these groups (5:16-21), the new social order of the Spirit ushers in the age of equality (5:24-26).

Despite the context of Galatians 3:28 and its placement in the letter, some scholars see no significance for a new understanding of gender in the passage, claiming that the text is quoted from somewhere else or is exclusively soteriological in meaning.[125] Some complementarians also point to other similar unification statements in 1 Corinthians 12:13 and Colossians 3:9-11 and their lack of male-female implications. In addition, a few feminist scholars dismiss the letter to the Galatians, seeing it as a "phallocentric" document addressing primarily male problems with androcentric solutions.[126] However, in her literary analysis of Galatians, Brigitte Kahl refutes these various positions and argues that Galatians 3:26-28 is the organizational center of Paul's argument and signifies the complete elimination of all hierarchies and inequalities, including gender.[127] She demonstrates how other parts of Galatians fit the egalitarian ethic of 3:28. Although she agrees the letter is mostly about the restructuring of national and social identity (Jews and non-Jews), Kahl argues that Paul shows consistent awareness of how that restructuring has fundamental effects on the male-female hierarchy.[128] Paul understood that "the symbolic superiority of male over and against female, which is marked by circumcision, loses theological foundation and dignity."[129] The entire letter (especially Chapters 3–6) contains an ethics of mutuality (5:13, 6:2). Paul strategically dismisses previous gender ideas by rereading the Genesis story in non-patriarchal categories (Gal. 3–4), rethinking genealogies and the male line of descent (4:21-31), and regularly incorporating female and motherly imagery throughout the letter, including himself as a mother in labor (4:19). Kahl concludes that Galatians is a "nightmare" for anyone interested in orderly patriarchal categories or practices and that Paul's purposeful confusing of gender

---

123. See N. T. Wright, *The New Testament and the People of God* (Minneapolis: Fortress, 1992), 300.

124. See Ruether, *Sexism*, 26, 33; Stephenson, *Dismantling*, 146.

125. Most notably Wayne Meeks's influential article cited in the next section.

126. For a review of this literature, see Brigitte Kahl, "Gender Trouble in Galatia? Paul and the Rethinking of Difference," in Sawyer and Collier, *Feminist Theology*, 57–8. See also Beverly Gaventa, "Is Galatians Just a 'Guy-Thing'? A Theological Reflection," *Interpretation: A Journal of Bible and Theology* 54, no. 3 (July 2000): 267–78.

127. Kahl, "Gender Trouble," 59.

128. Kahl, "Gender Trouble," 60.

129. Kahl, "Gender Trouble," 71.

and identities throughout the letter serves his transformational purposes, as most clearly stated in Galatians 3:28.[130]

### 4.3.3 Eschatological Significance

What is often overlooked in Paul's argument—even by those who affirm the egalitarian significance of Galatians 3:28—is the eschatological thrust of his egalitarian position. Galatians 3:1–5:1 has been called "one of the clearest" passages of the New Testament regarding the church as the eschatological people of God, with 3:28 as its centerpiece.[131] Verses 27 and 29 communicate one's eschatological standing before God and verse 28 applies that to the right-now ethnic, social, and gender ramifications of that eschatological standing.[132] Galatians 3:28 is a statement both of what *should be* in the *eschaton* and what is *already* beginning to happen as eschatological promises (v. 29) become reality through Christ (v. 27).[133] For example, several scholars point to the full inclusion of Gentiles into the people of God as an eschatological event fulfilling promises predicted throughout the Old Testament (see Gen. 12:3; 18:18; Isa. 49:5-6).[134] Therefore, the passage has been called "deeply apocalyptic" in that it fleshes out the ideal for the new creation (6:15) in contrast to the diminishing old world order (1:4).[135] The removal of hierarchical orders such as Jew over Greek, free over slave, and male over female, is a sign that the old order is passing away and a new social order is breaking forth in the new age of the Spirit.

Fundamental to establishing the validity of an eschatological–egalitarian interpretation of Galatians 3:28, and therefore its ability to function as a hermeneutical guide, is its relationship with Genesis 1:27. A primary reason to interpret Galatians 3:28 as the inauguration of the new creation is its reference to the old creation. There is abundant evidence that the "no longer male and female" of Galatians 3:28 is a direct allusion to the "male and female" of Genesis 1:27.[136]

---

130. See Kahl, "Gender Trouble," 72–3.

131. Gladd and Harmon, *Inaugurated Eschatology*, 24. For an opposing view, see Kirk, *Without Precedent*, who claims eschatology does not determine Paul's stance here at all (62–4).

132. See Hans Dieter Betz, *Galatians: A Commentary on Paul's Letter to the Churches in Galatia* (Philadelphia: Fortress, 1979), 184–5; Stephenson, *Dismantling*, 124.

133. Hampson, *Theology and Feminism*, 27; Russell, *Household*, 38.

134. Richard Hove, *Equality in Christ? Galatians 3:28 and the Gender Dispute* (Wheaton: Crossway, 1999), 47; T. David Gordon, "The Problem at Galatia," *Interpretation* 41 (1987): 38–9.

135. Kahl, "Gender Trouble," 67–8.

136. So much so that N. T. Wright suggests we should understand the phrase "male and female" in scare-quotes. See his "Women's Service in the Church: The Biblical Basis" (paper presented at the symposium, "Men, Women and the Church," St John's College, Durham, September 4, 2004), posted July 12, 2016, https://ntwrightpage.com/2016/07/12/

Richard Hove demonstrates that when the Greek phrase used in Galatians 3:28 is used in biblical and extrabiblical literature it nearly always refers to Genesis 1:27.[137] Paul purposely seems to alert the reader to his Genesis allusion by disrupting the parallelism of "Jew *or* Greek," "slave *or* free," with "male *and* female."[138] The Greek words for male and female are also not what one would expect, but Paul uses them to indicate his allusion to Genesis (using the words from the Septuagint translation of Gen. 1:27).[139] Paul's main emphasis in Galatians 3:28 is that to be "one in Christ Jesus" as the eschatological people of God is to abolish all previous hierarchical orders that are a part of the old age and the Fall.[140] A new trajectory is being born or restored, and in a subtle yet powerful grammatical move, Paul brings to mind the prelapsarian eschatological–egalitarian trajectory of the co-equal rule and reign of men and women. But the significance of Galatians 3:28 is not only in its looking back—finding eschatological hints in the original creation—but in its looking forward in eschatological hope and to the present implications of that future reality. Linking eschatological promises with the trajectory of creation is nothing new for Paul (see Rom. 8:19-22), and the promised gender equality is one of the primary features of that trajectory.

Two primary counterarguments stand in the way of an eschatological–egalitarian interpretation of Galatians 3:28: the soteriological argument and the androgynous argument. Although both arguments often see eschatological significance in the passage, their interpretation leaves little room for participation now in eschatological realities.[141] Most complementarians argue the primary application of Galatians is in its theology, not sociology. Therefore, the significance of 3:28 is its soteriological statement that salvation is open to all regardless of race, class, or gender—there is no distinction regarding being heirs to the promise of God.[142] This is a powerful statement and of course is part of what Paul is communicating. But to limit the scope of this passage to primarily Jews and Gentiles and to a theological change in status before God is to rob it of its eschatological vision that is filled with immediate social implications. Paul uses the Jew/Gentile divide as

---

womens-service-in-the-church-the-biblical-basis/. See also discussion in Craig S. Keener, *Galatians: A Commentary* (Grand Rapids: Baker Academic, 2019), 308–9.

137. Hove, *Equality*, 66–7. Examples: Matt. 19:4; Mark 10:6; Gen. 5:2 (LXX). Although I disagree with Hove's overall conclusions, his book is a valuable examination of the context and exegetical issues.

138. The Greek text transitions from *or* (οὐδὲ) in the first two couplets to *and* (καὶ) in the last.

139. Hampson, *Theology and Feminism*, 71.

140. See Kahl, "Gender Trouble," 68.

141. For example, Hove defends gender role distinctions, but does see eschatological significance in the passage, even if only in the Jew/Gentile couplet (*Equality*, 47).

142. "No distinction" (not nonexistence) is the consensus reading for the figure of speech "there is neither." The question then is what this "no distinction" means. See Hove, *Equality*, 80–2.

an occasion to announce that a new period of redemptive history has dawned, one in which the old social divisions created by the Fall are being replaced by a (re)new(ed) social order (thus his powerful allusion to Gen. 1:27) as inaugurated by the life, death, and resurrection of Christ. Elsewhere, the letter is less concerned with gender because apparently no one was suggesting that one must be male (or free) to become a Christian.[143] Paul would not have included the slave/free or male/female couplets if he did not have in mind more than only salvific equality in Christ. There is a radical "newness" proclaimed in Galatians 3:28, so much so that Klyne Snodgrass calls it "the most socially explosive text in the New Testament."[144] To interpret the text as primarily or exclusively about one's standing before God seems not only disembodied but also antithetical to the social implications and eschatological vision of the gospel Paul lays out.

Of larger concern for establishing an eschatological–egalitarian reading of Galatians 3:28 and its implications for gender practices is the androgynous argument. The androgynous interpretation goes back to at least Gregory of Nyssa in the fourth century and was made popular by Wayne Meeks's influential article "The Image of the Androgyne."[145] These authors and others argue that an eschatology of gender according to Galatians 3:28 is that all gender or sex differences will cease to exist as believers become genderless, sexless beings in the *eschaton*. Therefore, gender hierarchy is not abolished in the present, but remains as a temporary, but good, placeholder on this side of the *eschaton* until a genderless humanity is achieved. The new creation is either a restoration of the original androgynous divine-image humanity (an interpretation of Gen. 1:27 and 2:21-22) or a purposeful contrast to or transcendence of the sexual differentiation of "male

---

143. Klyne Snodgrass, "Galatians 3:28—Conundrum or Solution?" in *Women, Authority, and the Bible*, ed. Alvera Mickelsen (Downers Grove, IL: InterVarsity, 1996), 179.

144. Snodgrass, "Galatians 3:28," 161, 167–8.

145. Wayne A. Meeks, "The Image of the Androgyne: Some Uses of a Symbol in Earliest Christianity," *History of Religions* 13, no. 3 (February 1974): 165–208. See Gregory's works such as *On the Soul and the Resurrection* and *The Life of Macrina*. Whether or not Gregory's contribution was positive or negative for women is debatable. See discussion in Michael Nausner, "Toward Community Beyond Gender Binaries: Gregory of Nyssa's Transgendering as Part of his Transformative Eschatology," *Theology & Sexuality* 16 (2002): 55–65. According to Nausner, restored humanity transcends gender for Gregory (61). See also Sarah Coakley's chapter, "The Eschatological Body: Gender, Transformation and God" in her book *Powers and Submissions: Spirituality, Philosophy and Gender* (Oxford: Blackwell, 2002), 153–67, esp. 163. Gregory has received quite of a bit of attention in works on gender and his eschatological orientation to that subject. See the two influential articles by Verna Harrison, "Male and Female in Cappadocian Theology," *Journal of Theological Studies* 41 (1990): 441–71; "Gender, Generation, and Virginity in Cappadocian Theology," *Journal of Theological Studies* 47 (1996): 38–68. Others have noted the relationship between asceticism and gender equality in the patristic era. See Elizabeth Clark, *Women in the Early Church* (Wilmington, DE: Glazier, 1983), 17.

and female."¹⁴⁶ Either way, to be fully in God's image is to transcend gender and to one day erase the differences between man and woman. Until the solution of sameness is achieved, differences in gender necessitate a system of hierarchy. What these scholars get right is seeing Galatians 3:28 as an eschatological text. But is androgyny the appropriate interpretation of its eschatological edge?

Several scholars have refuted the androgynous hypothesis. Samuel Terrien claims that to conclude that androgyny is what Paul envisioned when he described male and female becoming "one in Christ" (v. 28) "is completely out of order."¹⁴⁷ Interpreting Galatians 3:28 as the eradication of sexual distinction is a poor interpretation that disregards the mutuality of the sexes extolled in other passages, including the clear allusion to the "very good" (Gen. 1:31) creation of male and female in Genesis 1:27.¹⁴⁸ Rather, the "all of you are one in Christ Jesus" of verse 28 extolls unity and equality amid diversity, not the eradication of diversity.¹⁴⁹ Keener also affirms that Paul's precise terminology of "no longer male and female" has nothing to do with a return to some primeval androgyny, but rather represents the unity of male and female that flourished before the Fall, now being restored through new creation in Christ.¹⁵⁰

In a technical and thorough exegetical analysis of Galatians 3:28, Judith Gundry-Volf similarly refutes the position that Paul in any way envisioned an abolition of gender difference in the new creation.¹⁵¹ She argues that an undifferentiated humanity misses the context of Galatians itself, and particularly the broader argument of Galatians 3:6-29. Paul does not explain in Galatians what he means by "no longer male and female" but he *does* explain what he means by "no longer Jew or Greek," and it is certainly not the erasure of difference—that is, to stop being Jews or Gentiles in this new age.¹⁵² Gundry-Volf sees a strong

---

146. See discussion in Gundry-Volf, "Beyond Difference?," 9-10, 16; Sawyer, *Gender and the Bible*, 133-5; Middleton, *New Heaven*, 276n16. However, the majority opinion is that "male and female" in Genesis 1:27 structurally seems to be only a restatement of "humankind," not a development from non-sexed to sexed beings (see Pannenberg, *Systematic Theology*, 3:390).

147. Samuel Terrien, *Till the Heart Sings: A Biblical Theology of Manhood and Womanhood* (Grand Rapids: Eerdmans, 1985), 173. For more on androgyny and the eschatological being, see Terrien, 206-10.

148. Terrien, *Heart Sings*, 206; cf. 1 Cor. 7:3-4.

149. Terrien, *Heart Sings*, 207.

150. Keener, *Galatians*, 308-9.

151. Gundry-Volf, "Beyond Difference?" She argues against two major discussions that reflect the "abolition of differences" interpretation of 3:28: Antoinette Clark Wire, *The Corinthian Women Prophets: A Reconstruction through Paul's Rhetoric* (1990) and Daniel Boyarin's *A Radical Jew: Paul and the Politics of Identity* (1994). She claims they make "controversial exegetical moves" (9).

152. In fact, Paul elsewhere prohibits this line of thinking of the erasure of difference (1 Cor. 7:18-19). See Gundry-Volf, "Beyond Difference?," 20-1.

relationship, both thematically and grammatically, between Galatians 3:28 and Galatians 5:6 and 6:15, with similar double negations followed by a contrasting positive assertion. Paul transitions the identity marker of circumcision from religious to ethnic marker so that neither circumcision nor uncircumcision counts for anything (5:6, 6:15); there is no advantage or disadvantage in relation to God or others. "The point is not that fleshly differences do not persist in the eschatological community," argues Gundry-Volf, "but that they do not and should not 'count.'"[153] Unity and equality does not come through the erasure of physical differences between Jew and Gentile, and the same applies to gender: androgyny is not the goal. The eschatological transformation of being "clothed" with Christ (3:27) breaks down hierarchies of Jew over Greek, free over slave, and male over female, and any advantages previously held because of those markers.

One weakness of Gundry-Volf's article is that she focuses mostly on the soteriological and hamartiological significance of the passage and does not expand the eschatological application of the text into the present. One scholar who does hint at present eschatological–egalitarian participation is Douglas Campbell. Like Gundry-Volf, he presents a detailed exegetical analysis, interpreting "no longer male and female" in light of the letter's argument and what Paul means by "no longer Jew or Greek."[154] He concludes that the "oneness" of the text (3:28b) has nothing to do with an undifferentiated metaphysical unity referring to androgynous or genderless beings. Although Paul's main argument in the book is about the distinction (or new lack of) between Jew and Gentile, Paul intentionally adds the abolition of class and gender distinctions in order to indicate "the cosmic sweep" of his Jew/Gentile argument.[155] Binaries such as the ones listed in 3:28 between ethnicities, class, and gender were well known in both Hellenistic ideology and Jewish life.[156] And although Galatians (and the New Testament) are primarily preoccupied with the distinction between Jew and Gentile, Galatians 3:28 provides a window into the present implications of eschatologically being "one in Christ." To be "in Christ," states Campbell, is to have died to distinctions that belong to the old created order: "Paul's abolitions of created dimensions is complemented by eschatological expectations of another creation."[157] A common argument from complementarians on this text is that because the rest of the letter emphasizes the Jew/Gentile issue, to "read in context" is to prioritize that couplet; to interpose

---

153. Gundry-Volf, "Beyond Difference?," 21.

154. Douglas A. Campbell, "The Logic of Eschatology: The Implications of Paul's Gospel for Gender as Suggested by Galatians 3:28a in Context," in Campbell, *Gospel and Gender*, 58–83. For more exegetical analysis, see also Gordon D. Fee, "Male and Female in the New Creation: Galatians 3:26–29," in *Discovering Biblical Equality: Complementarity without Hierarchy*, ed. Ronald W. Pierce and Rebecca Merrill Groothuis (Downers Grove, IL: InterVarsity, 2005), 172–85.

155. Campbell, "Logic of Eschatology," 66.

156. Campbell, "Logic of Eschatology," 61–2.

157. Campbell, "Logic of Eschatology," 67.

implications for gender equality as having equal meaning to the Jew/Gentile issue would be to distort the intent of the passage. However, what Campbell and others convincingly argue is that Galatians 3:28 is the climax of Paul's argument and the ultimate outworking or application of his Jew/Gentile (non)distinction and the eschatological social vision to which it leads.

Campbell therefore argues for a realized eschatological aspect to Paul's argument, claiming that otherwise Paul's principal goal in composing Galatians, namely, negating the benefit of Jewish law-observance, would be compromised and would "open the door for a certain validity to be attached to ethnic behavior in the old age . . . I cannot see Paul granting such concessions here."[158] Just as any return to law-observance by Gentile converts would be "a betrayal of the way Easter has effected reality at is most fundamental levels," so a return to hierarchy and distinction in gender is acting as if the new age has not begun.[159] Based on Campbell's arguments, it is not a stretch to say that Galatians 3:28 is perhaps the most realized eschatological text in the New Testament. As he argues:

> There is little eschatological nuancing. We do not receive here an account of the degree to which Christians participate in the new creation because any admission of partiality will also mute Paul's contentions [in the letter]. So we should not expect detail concerning eschatological inauguration or remaining futurity from Galatians 3:28a in context; merely statements of its actual realization—which we are nevertheless irrevocably committed to in some sense.[160]

To be "in Christ" (3:27) is to follow the new (eschatological) social order his death and resurrection inaugurated.

The contextual analysis of Galatians 3:28 and its eschatological significance leads to several conclusions relevant to my proposal of a unified eschatological-egalitarian narrative thread: (1) the verse involves more than just man and woman's salvific standing before God; (2) the text is not about the erasure of differences (including physical), but rather the abolition of hierarchical structures; (3) the grammatical structure, the allusion to Genesis 1:27, and other contextual factors prohibit an androgynous interpretation of "no longer male and female"; (4) both the immediate (vv. 27, 29) and surrounding (Chapters 3–6) context support the eschatological nature of the passage and its centrality to Paul's argument; (5) Paul's intention was for a realized participation in eschatological realities to the fullest extent possible, including gender equality, as the old order is replaced with "new creation" (6:15) trajectories, including (re)instituting the eschatological trajectory of Genesis 1:27. Galatians 3:28 in context is an eschatologically inspired egalitarian text that draws part of its inspiration from the biblical creation narrative and seeks the ultimate fulfillment of God's original intention for male and female.

---

158. Campbell, "Logic of Eschatology," 68.
159. Campbell, "Logic of Eschatology," 69n23.
160. Campbell, "Logic of Eschatology," 71.

### 4.3.4 Hermeneutical Priority

The eschatological hermeneutical priority of Galatians 3:28 for interpreting other passages (especially Pauline) and informing Christian practice has been argued by several,[161] and was applied by early Pentecostals and Holiness women alike without much argument.[162] Tackett discovered among early Pentecostals a hermeneutic that said all Pauline limitations need to be interpreted in light of the eschatological egalitarian gospel.[163] It was only when later Pentecostal readings began to suppress the eschatological content of Galatians 3:28, claiming it was not about gender equality but rather about access to salvation, that other Pauline teachings on women began to play a larger role in the movement.[164] Although Paul writes about (and to) both the present and new age, his vision of the new supersedes the present even while he attends to the present as necessary.[165] Campbell summarizes the hermeneutical implications of an eschatological reading of Galatians 3:28:

> In Gal. 3.28a Paul boldly negates three standard bifurcations of society [Jew/Greek, slave/free, male/female] that include gender on the grounds of the eschatological existence of Christians in Christ; negations that he intends radically and seriously *and that his gospel is intrinsically committed to. That is, we now have a theological criterion from Paul's own hand of the (correct) ethical implications of his gospel* (and not merely of a putative early church confession), here specifically for questions concerning ethnicity, slavery and/or gender.[166]

Interpreting Paul on gender entails starting where he starts, not with isolated passages about isolated situations, but with his grander eschatological vision of a new creation.

Like Campbell, Hampson uses Galatians 3:28 as her example of a "golden thread" passage, which she defines as a statement fundamental to the biblical outlook on gender equality that can be used as a criterion to measure other passages.[167] And it is specifically the eschatological significance of Galatians 3:28 on which she builds her case. She believes Paul had an eschatological breakthrough where he realized "the ultimate implications of the Christian message." She posits that "it

---

161. For example, Grenz and Kjesbo who use the term "hermeneutical priority" in relation to Galatians 3:28.

162. For historical examples, see 2.2 as well as Schroeder and Taylor, *Voices Long Silenced*, 160–1.

163. Tackett, "Callings," 93.

164. See my previous chapter (3.2); Blumhofer, *Assemblies of God*, 1:364; Blumhofer and Armstrong, "Assemblies of God," 335.

165. See Yong, *Renewing*, 32–3, for a summary of Paul's apocalypticism.

166. Campbell, "Logic of Eschatology," 76n29; italics in the original, brackets mine.

167. Hampson, *Theology and Feminism*, 25–6. Despite explaining this concept quite convincingly and being a former proponent of this approach, Hampson explains that she has now abandoned it for a post-Christian approach (25–9).

may well be a statement as to what should be the case in the eschaton."¹⁶⁸ When comparing Galatians 3:28 to the apparently prohibitive passages that deal with particular social situations, Hampson argues that Paul "would surely want to be judged in terms of the highest [good] that he knew."¹⁶⁹ In a contemporary example of applying this eschatological hermeneutical priority, Stephen Cottrell, in a video from 2012, calls Galatians 3:28 the "mountain peak" of biblical passages and "the one through which we then interpret many others." He claims it took the church about twenty years to work out what "no longer Jew or Greek" meant. "No longer slave or free" took about eighteen hundred years. Working out the implications of no longer male and female, he challenges, is the task of this generation.¹⁷⁰

### 4.3.5 Imagination and Participation (the Ministry of Jesus)

Paul's eschatological imagination is perhaps most alive in Galatians, which leads him to his passionate plea in 3:28 for present participation in eschatological realities. It would not shock original readers, nor should it shock us, when Paul sometimes follows the Hellenistic and Jewish norms of male authority and restricts women in some cases.¹⁷¹ What *is* shocking is when Paul departs from that model, allowing his eschatological imagination to overrule previous held ideas. As believers put on the eschatological clothing of Christ through the eschatological act of baptism (v. 27), they imagine the eschatological "oneness" (v. 28b) of the kingdom. Through the allusion to Genesis 1:27, Paul emphasizes that our eschatological calling as God's image bearers has been reconstituted through the work of Christ (Col. 3:10).¹⁷² The eschatological G/genesis of gender equality in Galatians 3:28 awakens and restores our prelapsarian ability to recognize each other as equals and recapitulates it through the work of Christ, the second Adam. The fulfillment of history hinted at in creation becomes possible in Christ as new possibilities emerge through the ministry of the eschatological Spirit.

Although Paul at times recognizes the hierarchical social structures of his world and is at times constrained by them despite their lack of correspondence to God's eschatological kingdom, he also recognizes that hierarchy does not and will not belong in the ideal eschatological community.¹⁷³ Interpreting Paul as legitimizing the social structure is to miss completely Paul's intention and the priority he gave to eschatological thinking.¹⁷⁴ Because of the eschatological orientation of Paul's argument in Galatians, Stanley Grenz argues that the conflict between "the Spirit"

---

168. Hampson, *Theology and Feminism*, 26–7.
169. Hampson, *Theology and Feminism*, 27; brackets mine.
170. Cited and quoted in Kirk, *Without Precedent*, 48–9. Kirk actually quotes Cottrell in order to heavily critique his comments. Cottrell is of the Diocese of Chelmsford.
171. Again, see Jewett, *Man as Male and Female*, 111–28.
172. See Stephenson, *Dismantling*, 126.
173. Johnson, *New Testament*, 400–1, 418–19.
174. Johnson, *New Testament*, 401.

and "the flesh" in Galatians is best understood through an eschatological lens.[175] To follow the old social order and its gender hierarchy is to be conditioned by the present age that is passing away and to "gratify the desires of the flesh" (Gal. 5:16; cf. 1:4). On the contrary, to "live by," be "led by," and "guided by" the Spirit (5:16, 18, 25) is to embrace one's new existence through union with Christ by the Spirit and to live within the believing community according to the eschatological ideal(s) of equality.

The ministry of Jesus is intricately connected with the eschatological ideals of Galatians 3:28 and its imaginative call to participate in egalitarian action. The phrase "in Christ Jesus" directly before verse 27 and repeated at the end of verse 28 forms an inclusio around the promises in between.[176] The eschatological–egalitarian ideal of Galatians 3:28 finds its origin in the ministry of Jesus and the new kingdom he inaugurated. Although some scholars believe the idea of a feminist Jesus is "inventive,"[177] the Gospels (and an eschatological reading of them) provide a firm foundation for Paul's radical Jesus-centered egalitarian claim in Galatians 3:28. The ministry of Jesus represents the dawn of all eschatological hope, the ushering in of a new created order.[178] He himself is the beginning of (and/or the coming of) the new creation.[179] He is the quintessential eschatological prophet,[180] emphasizing both the present and future aspects of the eschatological kingdom and what present participation looks like now in light of the imagined *eschaton*.[181] Jesus' ministry provides the first fruits of the eschatological inbreaking of the kingdom, beginning trajectories that beckon those who receive his Spirit "into a still unrealized future."[182] Jesus announces God's reign (Mark 1:15), a reign that has its fullness in the future but that is now breaking into the present.[183] Therefore, what Jesus accomplished had a future-orientation with present implications, an eschatological imagination coupled with eschatological participation. More specifically for our purposes, the

---

175. Grenz, *Moral Quest*, 120–2.

176. This inclusio is more obvious in the Greek text (ἐν Χριστῷ Ἰησοῦ) and its order of words.

177. Such as Kirk, *Without Precedent*, 21, who goes through all of Jesus' encounters with women to come to this conclusion (27–47).

178. See Johns, "Conscientization," 159.

179. Col. 1:15. See Augustine, *Spirit and the Common Good*, 29, 33.

180. See Roger Stronstad, *The Prophethood of All Believers: A Study in Luke's Charismatic Theology* (Sheffield: Sheffield Academic, 1999), 36–9. For the trend in NT studies and theology of the thoroughly eschatological nature and character of Jesus and his ministry, see Shields, *Eschatological Imagination*, 2.

181. See Grenz, *Moral Quest*, 111. Dempster goes through groups of texts that show this. Some examples of present aspects: Mark 2:18-22; Luke 4:18-19, 7:28-35, 11:20. Some examples of future aspects: Matt. 8:11-12, 12:32, 24:42, 25:13; Luke 12:35-40. See Dempster, "Eschatology," 164.

182. Ruether, "Letty Russell," 22.

183. See Grenz, *Moral Quest*, 110–11. See also Wolfgang Schrage, *The Ethics of the New Testament*, trans. David E. Green (Philadelphia: Fortress, 1988), 18.

actions he exhibited toward women, in an age where the inferiority and "dangers" of women were universally accepted in the Mediterranean world, hold great significance for determining God's eschatological plan for gender equality.

A sometimes glaring omission from arguments for gender equality is any mention of the ministry of Jesus.[184] For example, the Assemblies of God position paper affirming the role of women in ministry mentions the creation account, Galatians 3:28, and Acts 2:16-18, but makes no mention of Jesus' interactions with women and the implications of those interactions.[185] An exhaustive overview of Jesus and women is not intended here, nor is it the goal of this section.[186] The intent is rather to show the connection between the egalitarian trajectory of the ministry of Jesus to Paul's Jesus-centered eschatological–egalitarian imagining in Galatians 3:28. The actions of Jesus toward women are aimed toward eschatological fulfillment, the hope of full equality for women that inspired Paul and the early believers in Acts.[187]

Jesus never directly addresses the subject of women's equality. There is no discourse on women from Jesus; rather, we have actions.[188] Jesus gave to women the privilege of being the first Samaritan and Gentile convert (John 4, Matt. 15:21-28), the first to receive insight into resurrection (John 11:21-27), the first to perceive the sacrificial nature of the cross (Mark 14:1-9), and the first to witness the resurrection and testify about it (Matt. 28:1-10).[189] Jesus also engages women in theological discussion (John 4, 11:21-27), something nearly unheard of in the first century. All these actions were a part of the prophetic vision of Jesus that pointed to a new and eschatological reality, one that challenged hierarchical and patriarchal systems and restored all people to equal status.[190] The value Jesus placed on women "was revolutionary for his time"[191] and "radically altered the position of women."[192] Although Jesus was working within the hierarchical systems of the day, his counter-cultural radical eschatological vision and actions pointed to a new trajectory.[193] Through his actions and choices, Jesus unleashed a liberating praxis that creates new possibilities for an egalitarian world moving forward.[194] Jesus

---

184. But see Richard Bauckham, *Gospel Women: Studies of the Named Women in the Gospels* (Grand Rapids: Eerdmans, 2002).

185. "The Role of Women in Ministry," Assemblies of God Position Papers, version adopted August 11, 2010, https://ag.org/Beliefs/Position-Papers/The-Role-of-Women-in-Ministry.

186. But see Alexander and Gause, *Women*, 59–75.

187. See Ben Wiebe, *Messianic Ethics: Jesus' Proclamation of the Kingdom of God and the Church in Response* (Waterloo, ON: Herald, 1992), 166.

188. This insight is by Gause, *Women*, 65.

189. I am partially indebted to Professor Barbara Mutch for this list.

190. See Ruether, *Sexism*, 135–6.

191. Cahill, *Sex, Gender*, 125; see Grant, "Merchandised Women," 281.

192. Grenz and Kjesbo, *Women*, 78.

193. See Grenz and Kjesbo, *Women*, 71–3.

194. Elizabeth A. Johnson, "Christology: Redeeming the Name of Christ," in LaCugna, *Freeing Theology*, 123.

embodies in his person and praxis the dawn of a new age that discards gender privilege, hierarchy, and status. Jesus therefore becomes the hermeneutic for interpreting biblical passages that have rendered woman inferior.[195]

As eschatological prophet par excellence, Jesus' actions on gender matter, and it is his ministry and its eschatological trajectory that allowed Paul to imagine that "in Christ" there is no distinction between male and female in authority, status, or privilege. Jesus never said "do this" in relation to women or gender dynamics.[196] However, it would be hard to explain the sudden boldness of the New Testament writers on the role of women, including Paul's egalitarian vision in Galatians 3:28, outside of Jesus' behavior.[197] It would be nearly impossible for the gospel writers or early Christians to understand fully the equal status of women Jesus was pointing to with his actions.[198] As inaugurator of the new creation, Jesus set the eschatological trajectory of imagining a world of equality. He took measured, realistic steps against the gender expectations of his culture, leaving room for "much more" eschatological imagining of the full inbreaking of his kingdom (John 16:12-15).[199] Therefore, as we read the Gospels with an eschatological imagination, we are invited into participatory action that is analogous but not necessarily identical to Jesus.[200] The goal is not to replicate the practices of Jesus or the New Testament, but to imagine further their ultimate trajectory and put them into practice in a way that transforms human relationships to reflect God's eschatological plans and purposes.[201] And the story of the early church in Acts gives examples and evidence of just how the eschatological-egalitarian trajectory of the ministry of Jesus was meant to be carried forward. As the eschatological Spirit of Jesus was poured out on his early followers, one of the key distinguishing marks was the expansion and continuation of Jesus' egalitarian ministry.

### 4.4 The Beginning of the End: Acts 2:17-18 and Pentecost

#### 4.4.1 Importance

Acts 2:17-18 has been consistently used throughout history and in feminist theology to justify women's equal right to preach and lead.[202] Mary Stewart Van Leeuwen refers to Pentecost as "women's emancipation day" and a significant event

---

195. See Pedersen, "Christian Feminist," 29.
196. Wright, *New Testament*, 77.
197. Alexander and Gause, *Women*, 66. Contra Kirk, *Without Precedent*, 47.
198. See Mittelstadt, "Reimagining Luke-Acts," 35, 42–3.
199. See Stackhouse, *Finally Feminist*, 40, who is working from Webb.
200. Cahill, *Sex, Gender*, 121, 128.
201. Cahill, *Sex, Gender*, 122.
202. See Ruether, *Sexism*, 198.

for understanding gender.²⁰³ She argues that the other events in the biblical drama with regard to gender—creation, fall, redemption—should be read through the lens of Pentecost (and so she begins her discussion on gender there). The central role Pentecost plays for women's equality is significant for a Pentecostal approach to gender and is where the concerns of feminist theology and Pentecostal theology align most closely. Acts 2 functions as "the defining narrative" for the Pentecostal movement²⁰⁴ and also the primary basis for supporting women in ministry.²⁰⁵ Pentecost is the key to approaching any issue in Pentecostal theology, with prominent Pentecostal scholars arguing that it is the central interpretive lens for all other Scripture and the unifying event of the movement.²⁰⁶ Therefore, it is no surprise that the main theological justification among Pentecostals for challenging gender distinctions was and is the outpouring of the Spirit in Acts.²⁰⁷ Although perhaps obvious, it needs to be stated that any Pentecostal reading of biblical texts on gender must include and be informed by the Pentecost event.

### 4.4.2 Relevant Background

Reading Acts 2 in the context of Luke-Acts is important for understanding the eschatological significance of Pentecost and its promises concerning the unrestricted ministry of women.²⁰⁸ Eschatological themes are prominent in Luke-Acts, and Lukan eschatology is well known for its this-worldly implications and strong link with pneumatology in accomplishing eschatological promises.²⁰⁹ Furthermore, Pentecostal scholars generally accept that there is a paradigmatic relationship between the life of Jesus in Luke and the life of the church in Acts.²¹⁰ From the importance of the empowerment of the Spirit (Luke 3:21-22; Acts 2:1-4) to parallel prayers at death (Luke 23:34, 46; Acts 7:59-60) to the similarity between Jesus' and Paul's journeys, a "patterning" emerges in Luke-Acts to show that Jesus' followers are meant to carry forward his work.²¹¹ Luke's thesis for Luke-Acts is that

---

203. Van Leeuwen, *Gender*, 34–5. See also Holm, "Pentecost: Women's Emancipation Day?"

204. Mittelstadt, "Reimagining Luke-Acts," 29.

205. See Stanley, "Pentecostal Women Preachers," 29.

206. Keener, *Spirit Hermeneutics*, 66; Vondey, *Pentecostal Theology*, 38, 226–7; Yong, *Spirit Poured Out*, 201.

207. See Petersen, "Moral Imagination," 57; Wacker, *Heaven Below*, 163; Yong, *Spirit Poured Out*, 39–41; Stanley, "Laying a Straw," 110; Vondey, *Perplexed*, 114–15.

208. For the importance and priority of Luke-Acts in Pentecostal theology and hermeneutics, see Mittelstadt, "Reimagining Luke-Acts," 25–43.

209. Yong, *Renewing*, 44–8, esp. 48; McQueen, *Joel*, 38–40; Dayton, *Theological Roots*, 151.

210. See Martin W. Mittelstadt, *Reading Luke-Acts in the Pentecostal Tradition* (Cleveland, TN: CPT, 2010), particularly 168–9. See also Yong, *Renewing*, 57.

211. See Stephen C. Barton, *The Spirituality of the Gospels* (London: SPCK, 1992), 94–100.

if the Spirit of God who anointed Jesus now dwells in the church, then that same Spirit will inform and enable the church to do the same works that Jesus did—in fact, "greater works."[212] The church in Acts becomes the outworking of the kingdom life Jesus inaugurated in his actions, and through the Spirit even intensifies the eschatological "nearness" (Mark 1:15) of the kingdom.[213] Aided by the power of the Spirit, Jesus sought to liberate the poor, marginalized, and oppressed, and to break down social, economic, racial, and gender barriers as signs of the inauguration of his rule in the world (Luke 4:18-19; 7:22-23). At Pentecost and in the subsequent works of the church in Acts, Jesus' earliest followers reproduce and expand upon his actions. The prototype of the inauguration and ministry of Jesus anticipated and laid out the trajectory for the "greater works" of the church, namely, the breaking of barriers and liberation of all peoples through works of justice, equality, inclusion, and demarginalization.[214]

Understanding Acts as the Spirit-empowered eschatological church continuing and expanding the eschatological intentions of what Jesus began to do and teach (Acts 1:1) helps the reader interpret the actions of Jesus toward women as eschatological acts.[215] Yong elaborates on the consistency in the Spirit's work through Jesus in Luke and the church in Acts: "the last days ministry of the Spirit upon and through all flesh—sons and daughters, young and old, slave and free (Acts 2:17-18)—had been anticipated in Jesus' Spirit-anointed accomplishments [and] his Spirit-filled life."[216] This Spirit-Christology brings together the eschatological ministry of Jesus with the eschatological outpouring of the Spirit.[217] As Michael Wilkinson and Steven Studebaker highlight, Pentecostals have often focused on the charismatic manifestations of Acts 2/Joel 2 at the expense of the social message and liberating work of the Spirit in the text.[218] What Jesus started for women as "the proto-feminist" in Luke, the Pentecostal outpouring continued as the disciples become "witnesses" (Acts 1:8) to the eschatological kingdom that is breaking in.[219] The actions of Jesus toward women "project a springboard for envisioning"

---

212. This is Roger Stronstad's "transfer of the Spirit" argument. See Roger Stronstad, *The Charismatic Theology of St. Luke* (Peabody, MA: Hendrickson, 1984), 49. See John 14:12.

213. See Vondey, *Pentecostal Theology*, 278-9.

214. Yong defines this relationship between Luke and Acts as the transition from Spirit Christology to Spirit soteriology (*The Spirit Poured Out*, 83-91). See also Murray W. Dempster, "Evangelism, Social Concern, and the Kingdom of God," in *Called and Empowered: Global Mission in Pentecostal Perspective*, ed. Murray W. Dempster, Byron D. Klaus, and Douglas Petersen (Peabody, MA: Hendrickson, 1991), 22-43.

215. See Dempster, "Eschatology," 162-5.

216. Yong, *Renewing*, 45.

217. See Vondey, *Perplexed*, 46, 74.

218. Michael Wilkinson and Steven M. Studebaker, "Pentecostal Social Action: An Introduction," in Wilkinson and Studebaker, *Liberating Spirit*, 9.

219. See Amos Yong's *Who Is the Holy Spirit? A Walk with the Apostles*, and his chapter "Jesus the Proto-feminist," which is based specifically on Luke's description of

a community of equality, a community that begins to emerge post-Pentecost.[220] After Pentecost, new eschatological realities begin to restructure relationships in light of renewed understanding of what Jesus did, and any discriminatory practices or oppression based on race, class, or gender are now seen as a part of the old order that is passing away.[221] Reading the Pentecost narrative in the context of Luke-Acts and the eschatological ministry of Jesus suggests an eschatological interpretation of the event.

### 4.4.3 Eschatological Significance

Acts 2—and specifically 2:17-18—is considered one of the most explicitly eschatological texts in the New Testament, and interpreting Pentecost as an eschatological event has wide consensus among prominent Pentecostal scholars as well as other theologians.[222] Land claims that "the outpouring of the Spirit at Pentecost constituted the church as an eschatological community,"[223] and Augustine similarly argues that Pentecost is the beginning of the "Spirit-conceived transfiguration of the world."[224] Joel 2:28-29, the reference point for Acts 2:17-18, is itself an eschatological promise that anticipates the removal of privileges based on age, class, or gender at the outpouring of the Spirit.[225] But Peter (and/or Luke), quoting the Septuagint, takes Joel's "inclusive image of eschatological renewal" and intensifies and expands the eschatological framework of the promise with a few significant changes or additions.[226] First, he changes the "afterward" of Joel 2:28 to "in the last days" (quoting Isa. 2:2) to heighten the eschatological significance of what is happening.[227] Pentecost signals the arrival of the eschatological age of the restored people of God constituted by the eschatological Spirit as prophesied in

---

Jesus' interaction with women (Brewster, MA: Paraclete, 2011), 146–8. See Mittelstadt, "Reimagining Luke-Acts," 24, for examples. See also Yong, *Spirit-Word-Community*, 33.

220. Yong, *Renewing*, 241, 247.
221. Dempster, "Eschatology," 186–7.
222. This is a central argument in Daniela C. Augustine, *Pentecost, Hospitality, and Transfiguration: Toward a Spirit-inspired Vision of Social Transformation* (Cleveland, TN: CPT, 2012), but see specifically 15–42, 133–48. See also Vondey, *Pentecostal Theology*, 251. For non-Pentecostal interpretation of Pentecost as eschatological event, see Lee-Barnewall, *Neither Complementarian nor Egalitarian*, 98–100.
223. Land, *Pentecostal Spirituality*, 52.
224. Augustine, *Pentecost*, 141.
225. See McQueen, *Joel*, 33, and specifically the chapter "Themes of Joel and the Promise of the Spirit" where McQueen discusses the eschatological framework of Joel's text and its uses in the NT (37–67). See also Vondey, *Perplexed*, 115–17.
226. Sawyer, *Gender and the Bible*, 141.
227. See discussion by Craig Keener, *Acts: An Exegetical Commentary*, vol. 1, *Introduction and 1:1–2:47* (Grand Rapids: Baker Academic, 2012), 877–81.

Isaiah.²²⁸ Second, he restates a second time the promise "they shall prophesy" (v. 18), making emphatic the real-time participation in these eschatological realities and their universal application.²²⁹ These changes and Luke's overall presentation of the events of Acts 2 indicate that he interprets what is happening as eschatological events and the outpouring of the Spirit as an eschatological sign.²³⁰

Pentecostal eschatology has always thrived on the fulfillment of the promises of Pentecost as signs of the coming kingdom.²³¹ For Pentecostals, the day of Pentecost is not just a historical event, it is also an eschatological event—a "symbol of both the historical beginning and the eschatological purpose of the church."²³² Interpreting Pentecost as an eschatological event makes it a transformational happening meant to be (re)experienced as the eschatological destiny of humanity unfolds.²³³ The experience of Pentecost directs all of life forward toward a future (not past) event (Acts 2:20) and a continued and evolving participation in the eschatological realities and trajectories of Pentecost.²³⁴ And one of the marks of the eschatological community, as determined by the eschatological Spirit, is gender equality.²³⁵

### 4.4.4 Hermeneutical Priority

Interpreting Pentecost as an eschatological event adds to its hermeneutical significance and potential for hermeneutical priority over other non-eschatological texts on gender. Using Pentecost as an interpretive lens for approaching the rest of Scripture is already a common Pentecostal approach. Yong calls Pentecost the "point of entry" and the scripturally authorized "starting point" for Christian life and theology.²³⁶ In *Spirit Hermeneutics*, Keener proposes reading all of Scripture from the "vantage point of Pentecost," including its eschatological vision.²³⁷ Dayton

---

228. Stephenson, *Dismantling*, 109 (see Isa. 32:14-17; 42:1; 44:1-4); McQueen, *Joel*, 66; Yong, *Spirit Poured Out*, 96.

229. See McQueen, *Joel*, 66.

230. McQueen, *Joel*, 42-3. See 42-8 for discussion of the changes (McQueen closely follows the argument of Robert Menzies).

231. See 2.2; Vondey, *Pentecostal Theology*, 133, 277.

232. Vondey, *Pentecostal Theology*, 250, 276-7; see also Yong, *Renewing*, 45.

233. See Augustine, *Pentecost*, 35.

234. This future-orientation of and present participation in Pentecost is a consistent theme in both Vondey and Augustine (Vondey, *Pentecostal Theology*, 4, 17, 251, 279-80, 285; Augustine, *Pentecost*, 17, 145-7).

235. Augustine, *Pentecost*, 17-18; Macchia, *Baptized in the Spirit*, 210, 218.

236. Yong, *Renewing*, 19. Yong, *Spirit Poured Out*, 27, proposes a Lukan hermeneutical approach for Pentecostals.

237. Keener, *Spirit Hermeneutics*, 66. See his Chapter 1 for the importance of experience and eschatology in hermeneutics. For more, see the essays on Keener's *Spirit Hermeneutics* in *Pneuma* 39 (2017): 126-240. For a good overview from that issue, see L. William Oliverio, "Reading Craig Keener: On Spirit Hermeneutics; Reading Scripture in Light of Pentecost,"

states that elevating Pentecost to "the hermeneutical key by which the whole of Scripture is read" was a natural fit for Pentecostals because of the strong link between eschatology and pneumatology in Acts.[238] As James K. A. Smith suggests, Pentecost *is* a hermeneutic and offers a fresh hermeneutical framework.[239] Smith argues that Peter's understanding of the eschatological significance of the moment led to a newfound hermeneutical courage, even if not all welcomed his message (2:41). Peter was able to signal that the outpouring of the Spirit conveyed that a new day and new creation was unfolding, which revolutionized the church's understanding of the world and God's plan for it, including the role of women.[240]

The Pentecostal emphasis on Acts 2 as a hermeneutical priority text has led several scholars to propose reading potentially limiting passages on women through the lens of Pentecost.[241] Fulkerson discovered among contemporary rural Pentecostals that the Spirit baptism narratives of Acts "provide hermeneutical controls over the New Testament prohibitions to women speaking,"[242] an approach used by early Pentecostals (as discovered in Chapter 2). Both Melissa Archer and Tackett argue that Acts 2:17-18 provides the primary hermeneutical support for affirming the full and unrestricted inclusion of the ministry of women in the church.[243] But Powers offers the closest approach to the one proposed in this work regarding the importance of reading Pentecost through an eschatological lens for empowering women.[244]

Powers argues it was the Pentecostal insistence on the doctrine of Spirit baptism that empowered and allowed women to minister. Because of the distinctiveness of this doctrine, Powers asserts that past Pentecostal women developed a unique and sophisticated hermeneutic to defend it, which included four distinct elements: (1) it affirmed the vital role of experience in interpretation; (2) it insisted on the value of narrative texts in developing theology; (3) it refused to accept that teaching passages were more authoritative than narrative passages; and (4) "It saw the significance of the eschatological dimension of Pentecost—that the church was meant to be a community being transformed by the power of the age to come which would reflect the reality of the coming kingdom."[245] Although she does not state it

---

*Pneuma* 39 (2017): 126-45. For a critique of Keener's approach, see Kenneth J. Archer in the same issue, "Spirited Conversation about Hermeneutics: A Pentecostal Hermeneut's Response to Craig Keener's Spirit Hermeneutics," *Pneuma* 39 (2017): 179-97, esp. 191-6.

238. Dayton, *Theological Roots*, 151.

239. Smith, *Tongues*, 23.

240. Smith, *Tongues*, 23.

241. See Archer, "Was the Spirit Poured out on Women," 132-4; Macchia, *Baptized in the Spirit*, 219-20.

242. Fulkerson, *Changing the Subject*, 255.

243. Archer, "Women in Ministry"; Tackett, "Callings."

244. But a critique of her approach is she is less concerned with empowering women culturally; spiritually is more important (see Powers, "Pentecostal Hermeneutics," 331).

245. Powers, "Pentecostal Hermeneutics," 324-5.

as clearly or forcefully as this, Powers argues that women should not ground their new status in the baptism of the Holy Spirit but in what that baptism represents, the new eschatological community of people.[246] The problem, states Powers, is that Pentecostals never applied this hermeneutic to passages about women, continuing only to utilize the first element of affirming the role of experience. She then briefly applies the hermeneutic to Mark 5:21-43 and 1 Corinthians 11:2-16 as examples and "to show how an eschatological understanding of the text can lead to transformations in the Christian community."[247] Although her proposal is brief, what Powers highlights is the need for a thoroughly Pentecostal hermeneutic that emphasizes reading the Bible with an eschatological imagination,[248] which has the potential to overcome the supposed scriptural ambiguity that creates indecision or reservations concerning women's authority to lead.

### 4.4.5 Imagination and Participation

The outpouring of the Spirit in Acts represents a canonized case study for the eschatological hermeneutic of imagination and participation and its dialectic. The more believers experienced and participated in eschatological egalitarianism, the more they understood their role in continuing the eschatological trajectory of the ministry of Jesus. Luke continues the story and actions of Jesus (Acts 1:1) by showing that the historical Jesus is not separated from the ongoing eschatological work of the Spirit in the church. The Christian community continues through the Spirit what Jesus started. This work of the Spirit discloses the future so that a more complete reality of Jesus' inaugurated kingdom can be disclosed in the present.[249] In the words of C. K. Barrett, the Holy Spirit is "the eschatological continuum in which the work of Christ, initiated in his ministry and awaiting its termination at his return, is wrought out."[250] It was and is the Spirit-filled ministry of Jesus that represents a paradigm for a new egalitarian movement, one begun in the early church.[251]

According to Acts 2, a prominent sign of the eschatological reign of God is equality between the sexes. But, following the pattern of Jesus, this is not a proposition to be taught but rather an invitation to participate in eschatological realities. As the believers in Acts participated in eschatological mysteries, their imaginations were stirred, asking "What does this mean?" (2:12). The experience

---

246. Powers, "Pentecostal Hermeneutics," 327. For more on the ideology of Spirit empowerment not being enough for women, see Johns, "Spirited Vestments," and 6.2.2.

247. Powers, "Pentecostal Hermeneutics," 325.

248. She suggests this over against a feminist hermeneutic (Powers, "Pentecostal Hermeneutics," 331).

249. Ruether, *Sexism*, 131. See also Ruether, 138.

250. C. K. Barrett, *The Gospel According the St John* (London: SPCK, 1956), 74.

251. Vondey, *Perplexed*, 113.

of the community led to insight into the meaning of the Joel 2 text, often explained as a "this-is-that" (2:16) hermeneutic.[252] But it is perhaps more accurately a "this-is-that—which points to that!" hermeneutic, representing a three-way, rather than two-way, movement in time (see Figures 1, 2, in 3.1.1). A this-is-that hermeneutic is often described as when "the distance between the present and the past is seemingly eliminated as the present reality is redefined in terms of the past ... The present participates in the biblical events by fulfilling the past, which now redefines the present."[253] But an eschatological hermeneutic looks back to eschatological promises in order to peer into the future—God's eschatological heart—and then to bring as much of that future into the present as possible.

The story of Pentecost offers a foundational theological vision for an egalitarian ethic. The egalitarian "good work" begun by Jesus was transferred to the church and is meant to be brought to completion (Phil. 1:6). The Pentecostal community is meant to be a continuation and expansion of what Tackett calls "the eschatological Pentecost Proclamation," of which the implication for praxis is "a radical, egalitarian gospel" in the present while looking forward to its fullness in the future.[254] Pentecost offers a glimpse and invites us into "the future form of the Church," empowering us to "be the world's future within the present."[255] This dialectic of imagining and participating in the future of the church, which eschatological texts such as Acts 2 present as an *egalitarian* church, forbids any form of gender exclusion in church life. Rather, it invites the actions and equal voice of women in the faith community. In the already-not yet eschatological tension, the kingdom is "already" present in Christ's interaction with women,[256] even "more already" in the Spirit-filled prophesying daughters of Pentecost and Acts,[257] and "most already" in the continuing eschatological–egalitarian community.[258]

## 4.5 The Eschatological–Egalitarian Narrative as Hermeneutical Guide

By tracing their importance in the gender debate, identifying the relevant background for understanding their egalitarian nature, and locating their

---

252. See Vondey, *Pentecostal Theology*, 16; Warrington, *Pentecostal Theology*, 189–90.
253. Vondey, *Pentecostal Theology*, 16.
254. Tackett, "Callings," 73, 95; See also Vondey, *Pentecostal Theology*, 2, 133.
255. Augustine, *Pentecost*, 145–6.
256. Luke 1:40; 2:36-38; 8:1-4; 11:27-28. For a review of the women in Luke-Acts and the many works on women in Luke, see Yong, *Spirit Poured Out*, 191–4.
257. Acts 1:14, 2:17-18, 9:32-42 (Dorcas), 16:11-15, 40 (Lydia), 17:34 (Damaris), 18:18-19, 26 (Priscilla), 21:8-9 (Philip's daughters).
258. The "already" and "more already" insight is from Vondey (but not applied to women as it is here), but I have added the "most already" (see *Pentecostal Theology*, 278). See also Mittelstadt, "Reimagining Luke-Acts," 42–3, who says the vision of Luke could only be partially fulfilled and understood within the text.

eschatological significance, we can say the interconnected texts of Genesis 1–3, Galatians 3:28, and Acts 2:17-18 tell a unified story of God's eschatological plan for the full equality of women and men in life and ministry. These three texts and their corresponding narratives of creation, the ministry of Jesus, and Pentecost establish a unified eschatological–egalitarian narrative thread that holds hermeneutical priority over other (non-eschatological) texts on gender. Galatians 3:28 directly alludes to the original egalitarian trajectory of Genesis 1:26-27 while also echoing the promise of Joel 2's abolishing of the postlapsarian gender binary.[259] Through the ministry of Jesus—represented by the "in Christ" inclusio in Galatians 3:26-28—a (re)new(ed) social order is instituted, a work then carried forward by the Spirit at Pentecost.[260] At Pentecost, creation and new creation collide as the Spirit revives the egalitarian intent for humanity (Gen. 1–2) that was restored through Jesus (Gal. 3:28) and is now moving toward its eschatological end.[261] Pentecost is the redemptive eschatological recovery of Eden, as the equality of "one flesh" (Gen. 2:24) is expanded to "all flesh" (Acts 2:17)[262] and the egalitarian "first commission" gives way to the "last commission" in anticipation of the *eschaton*.[263]

The eschatological presence of the Spirit, also present at creation,[264] reverses the effects of the Fall and brings God's eschatological intentions to the forefront.[265] The outpouring of the Spirit and fulfillment of eschatological promises awakens humanity's (fallen and suppressed) imagination of the initial equality of the created order and actualizes those memories into a desire for eschatological participation.[266] Instead of being "clothed" with old creation garments of skin as reminders of the destroyed egalitarian ideal (Gen. 3:21, LXX), we are now "clothed" with new creation garments through Christ and His Spirit (Gal. 3:27; Luke 24:49) as we await our final eschatological clothing (2 Cor. 5:2-4). Through being baptized into Christ and His Spirit, we can put on egalitarian garments sown and held together by these eschatological threads.

A unified biblical narrative thread that teaches gender barriers will be dissolved in the *eschaton* means Pentecostals need not abandon faithfulness to the Bible to adopt a radical egalitarian position; indeed, it was faithfulness to the Bible—and its eschatological vision—that initially led Pentecostals to embrace the ministry

---

259. McQueen, *Joel*, 50, 53.

260. See Stephenson, *Dismantling*, 131.

261. Archer, "Women in Ministry," 37–8; see Althouse, "Ascension," 233.

262. See Vigen Guroian, "Fruits of Pentecost: The Christian Gardener," *The Christian Century* 113, no. 21 (July 3, 1996): 684–6; Augustine, *Pentecost*, 142; Vondey, *Pentecostal Theology*, 164–5.

263. Archer, "Was the Spirit Poured out on Women," 128–9.

264. See Stephenson, *Dismantling*, 120, 128. For Pentecostals and a pneumatological account of creation, see Vondey, *Pentecostal Theology*, 157–60.

265. See John Michael Penney, *The Missionary Emphasis of Lukan Pneumatology* (Sheffield: Sheffield Academic, 1997), 121–2 (discussed in Mittelstadt, *Reading Luke-Acts*, 94).

266. See Johns, "Conscientization," 157–8.

of women. Many modern Pentecostal leaders say they oppose full ministerial equality for women because they believe it "violates God-ordained order" found in Scripture.[267] Simply setting aside and rejecting some aspects of the Bible, as some propose,[268] will not work for Pentecostals who believe all Scripture is God-breathed (2 Tim. 3:16). An eschatological hermeneutic does not need to ignore, be afraid of, or seek to explain away patriarchal texts, most of which make sense for their time. Rather, an eschatological hermeneutic is able to highlight how "the biblical texts simultaneously communicates an alternative reality which can be reappropriated in a critical, historical hermeneutic fed by the New Testament's inclusive social vision."[269] When the Bible is at its clearest, that is, painting the ultimate vision of the highest good, it reveals a determined eschatological trajectory of advocacy for equality between women and men. Therefore, arguments over more controversial, convoluted, or historically influenced texts such as 1 Timothy 2:11-15, 1 Corinthians 11:3, or Ephesians 5:22-23 take the attention away from the Bible's eschatological plan for equality begun at Eden and fulfilled in the *eschaton*.[270] We need not be troubled by Paul's specific advice that Corinthian women keep quiet in the church (1 Cor. 14:34) when we know Paul's ultimate eschatologically inspired desire for egalitarianism (Gal. 3:28).[271] The persistent echo of restrictive texts and the restorationist hermeneutic that perpetuates the gender paradox is silenced by the eschatological echo of these liberating narratives and the eschatological hermeneutic that resolves the paradoxical messages concerning women's ecclesiastical roles and practices.

An eschatological hermeneutic that incorporates the hermeneutical priority of eschatological texts can move beyond cultural accommodations in the Bible that were never meant to be maintained moving forward. Due to their universal eschatological orientation and prominent role in the biblical story of creation, fall, redemption, and restoration, these texts hold hermeneutical priority over more culturally specific passages that may appear to limit the full participation of women. Identifying the eschatological–egalitarian trajectory of the biblical text allows us to move beyond isolated passages to broader theological and eschatological themes. Even if one affirms that the intent of some texts was to restrict women in those situations (and that conclusion is tentative at best), they play a secondary role

---

267. From the research of Alexander and Bowers, *What Women Want*, 44–6.

268. See Ruether, *Sexism*, 23, although she is likely right that theologies realistically "never consider all parts of the Bible equally authoritative" (23).

269. Cahill, *Sex, Gender*, 141.

270. See Archer, "Was the Spirit Poured Out on Women," 133; Nordling, "Gender," 505. However, applying an eschatological lens to these texts may still be helpful as in Chris Green's eschatological reading of and wrestling with 1 Corinthians 11:2–16 ("Troubled and Troubling Text," 456–75).

271. Keener believes Paul would have more clearly stated the eradication of gender hierarchy in a different social situation (Keener, *Acts*, 884n231).

to the eschatological texts that act as broader instructive guides in determining women's roles now.[272]

An eschatological hermeneutic leaves a choice regarding our point of reference for gender roles: do we choose to follow the temporary, pragmatic patriarchal pattern or the eternal, eschatological egalitarian paradigm? Do we determine praxis based on historically bound recommendations or eschatologically inspired realities?[273] Eschatological passages on gender offer no indication that hierarchy, patriarchy, or restrictions on women are a part of God's eschatological plan. The indication from eschatological texts on gender is that *gender inequality has no future*. As Augustine asserts, "What we see in the present that we do not see in the vision of the Kingdom has no future—it shall come to an end."[274] In contrast, eschatological texts that mention gender point consistently to an egalitarian ethic. In the words of Gordon (for a second time), "we shall expect to find no text which denies to woman her divinely appointed rights in the New Dispensation."[275] Despite some ambiguity in the Bible on gender roles, an eschatological reading reveals that "its main thrust is toward the leveling, not the maintenance, of birth-based status differences."[276] In order to be true to the s/Spirit of the text, we must "choose the better part" of the Scriptures,[277] what I argue are the eschatological parts, which invite readers into an egalitarian way of living.

## 4.6 Conclusion

The Pentecostal gender paradox is partly, and perhaps primarily, fueled by hermeneutical inconsistency and indecision. The initial egalitarian thrust of Pentecostalism was supported by an eschatological hermeneutic that began freeing women to practice their God-given callings in these last days. Early Pentecostal men and women used eschatological texts, which inspired their eschatological imagination, to authorize the ministry of women. However, as the eschatological imagination waned, so too did the power of these texts to inspire egalitarian practices. This led to the loss of eschatology as an authorizing hermeneutic, which opened the door for non-eschatological texts to influence Pentecostal attitudes on women occupying positions of authority. The result was a century of paradoxical messages and practices concerning women's roles as Pentecostals wrestled with their egalitarian past without a consistent hermeneutic to support it. Therefore, the goal of this chapter was to establish a way of reading texts on gender that

---

272. See Yong, *Spirit Poured Out*, 41–2.
273. See Ruether, *Sexism*, 33.
274. Augustine, *Pentecost*, 140. See also her *Spirit and the Common Good*, 9.
275. Gordon, "Ministry of Women," 277. See 2.2.1.
276. Van Leeuwen, *Gender*, 235.
277. Playing off Luke 10:42 and the work and title of Barbara Reid, *Choosing the Better Part? Women in the Gospel of Luke* (Collegeville, MN: Liturgical, 1996).

Pentecostals can confidently embrace. Recovering, (re)constructing, and formally articulating the eschatological authorizing hermeneutic of early Pentecostals results in a consistent Pentecostal way of reading Scripture that leads to the full flourishing of Pentecostal women. (Re)appropriating this strategy—reading texts on gender with an eschatological lens—overcomes the crippling hermeneutical inconsistency that has perpetuated the Pentecostal gender paradox.

What I have presented in this chapter is that the eschatological vision for gender equality in creation (Gen. 1-3), the ministry of Jesus (Gal. 3:28), and Pentecost (Acts 2:17-18) establishes a unified eschatological–egalitarian narrative that holds hermeneutical priority over non-eschatological passages on gender. Men and women were equal rulers in God's original creation, equal partners in Christ's redemption, and should now be equal participants in the Spirit's work in the church so that we might become a foretaste of God's eschatological–egalitarian community that is to come. A restorationist hermeneutic (see Figure 2, in 3.1.1) is insufficient because the goal is not to go back to Paradise or Pentecost, nor is it to replicate the actions of Jesus. Rather, these narratives cause us to imagine a world that is otherwise and then to focus those eschatological longings for equality toward present participation as the present is redefined in light of the future (see Figure 1, in 3.1.1), a future that is radically inclusive and egalitarian.

The eschatological hermeneutic of imagination and participation involves a dialectical dance, directed by the Spirit, between a Scripture-based imagination and community-based participation. This chapter is only one part of the proposed hermeneutical circle. Eschatological thinking leads to eschatological doing and vice versa. These narrative texts imaginatively invite participation in eschatological equality more than they cognitively inform about equality; eschatological possibilities are preferred over dogmatic propositions, experience over rational inquiry. To interpret Scripture in light of the end, we must also *live* in light of the end, including the yet-unrealized trajectories for God's plan regarding women's equality. The difficulty in dialectics is avoiding privileging one part over the other, which breaks down the dialectic.[278] The specific biblical hermeneutic of this chapter must be put into play with the broader and more comprehensive theological hermeneutic proposed in this work. Eschatological texts do not just cause us to imagine what *might* happen in the new creation; they invite us to participate in and expand upon those eschatological realities *now* as the imagined world critiques the present world. The eschatological imagining of the coming egalitarian age inspired by the biblical narratives of creation, the ministry of Jesus, and Pentecost prompts eschatological participation in those egalitarian realities in the current age. The strategy for that present participation is the concern of the final chapters.

---

278. See Yong, *Spirit-Word-Community*, 12.

## Chapter 5

PRE-ENACTING THE PROMISE

SOLVING THE GENDER PRAXIS PROBLEM

The previous chapter argued for the hermeneutical priority of eschatological texts on gender, recovering a hermeneutical strategy used by early Pentecostals and (re)constructing and formally proposing it as an authorizing hermeneutic for the unrestricted ministry of women. The unified eschatological–egalitarian narrative trajectory of the biblical text leads to imagining a world of equality between the genders, one free from hierarchy and vocational limitations. With a biblical foundation in place, one that recruits the eschatological imagination, the task of the remaining chapters is to develop an ecclesial praxis for present participation in eschatological realities based on the trajectory of and fidelity to the eschatological–egalitarian biblical narrative. The hermeneutical priority of the eschatological–egalitarian narrative thread creates the possibility for prioritizing an eschatologically inspired Pentecostal gender praxis: biblical visions of gender equality encourage present egalitarian practices due to the strong connection between eschatology and praxis, imagination and participation.

The goal of these final two chapters is to construct a Pentecostal eschatological–egalitarian praxis that frees women to act out fully their God-given callings and frees men to fully support women in their ecclesiological callings.[1] These closing chapters wrestle with how Pentecostals might practically participate in the eschatological egalitarianism that has been demonstrated historically (Chapter 2) and biblically (Chapter 4). The purpose of this chapter is to create and justify a conceptual framework or model[2] for an eschatologically oriented praxis that frees Pentecostal women from role restrictions, whereas the next chapter proposes what an eschatological–egalitarian praxis might look like in ecclesiological worship and leadership in Pentecostalism. Proposing a more conceptual chapter that distinguishes a praxis "model" from the actual practices may seem odd or even antithetical to the point of praxis. However, this chapter is a necessary bridge for connecting the proposed eschatological authorizing

---

1. The important role of *both* men and women for an eschatological–egalitarian praxis is discussed in the next chapter and in the Conclusion.
2. See 5.2 for what I mean by "model."

hermeneutic with a corresponding ecclesial praxis. The initial eschatological authorization for the ministry of women in early Pentecostalism did not last because the link between the imaginative hermeneutic and participatory practices was not properly argued or articulated, leading to a vacuum that eventually led to substantial changes in Pentecostal gender praxis. Therefore I seek to construct a solid foundation and justification for proposing how an eschatological praxis might provide a promising solution to decades of paradoxical gender attitudes in Pentecostalism.

Pentecostal ecclesiology suffers from what I call the "Pentecostal gender praxis problem": the disconnect between affirmative theological and hermeneutical arguments for gender equality in the church and the limitations and reservations women continue to experience when attempting to live out their God-given callings. The argument of this chapter is that an eschatological praxis model, primarily defined as the pre-enactment of eschatological promises, solves the Pentecostal gender praxis problem by authorizing a fully liberating egalitarian praxis that overcomes the inconsistency of re-enactment praxis models. Central to this argument is that an eschatological praxis prioritizes the pre-enactment of biblical eschatological promises over the re-enactment of past biblical events or prescriptions. Specifically applied to gender, a re-enactment praxis model—influenced by restorationist tendencies as outlined in Chapter 3—perpetuates the Pentecostal gender paradox. On the contrary, a pre-enactment model prioritizes eschatological texts on gender and their clear, yet open-ended, call to liberate women and men to participate in the promise of gender equality.

Four main tasks must be accomplished in order to suggest how an eschatological praxis model of pre-enactment has the potential to solve the gender praxis problem: (1) to identify and define the Pentecostal gender praxis problem and the need for an authorizing praxis model; (2) to introduce the concept of pre-enactment as the preferred praxis model for an eschatological praxis over against re-enactment; (3) to defend the necessity of developing a praxis in Pentecostal theological works, provide support for a specifically eschatological Pentecostal praxis, and critique some praxis gaps in current eschatologically oriented works; (4) to formulate the key features of an eschatological pre-enactment praxis model and to demonstrate how the proposed model and its features help solve the praxis problem(s). The first three sections comprise the first half of the chapter and lay the foundation for the argument of the last section, which moves toward the next chapter's task of presenting an eschatological–egalitarian praxis that authorizes women to live out their calling fully and freely in the areas of Pentecostal leadership, education, and worship.

## 5.1 *The Pentecostal Gender Praxis Problem*

Research of modern Pentecostal movements reveals a serious gap or disconnect between official doctrine, statements, and policy concerning women leaders and actual practice within Pentecostal groups.³ Just because women *can* hold senior leadership positions does not mean they do. A glaring contradiction exists between "official dogma and polity" that is egalitarian and the "unofficial tradition" of male-only leadership.⁴ Furthermore, having official statements "creates a false sense of well-being while not making a lot of difference in the practice of women being hired or allowed to fulfill their calling."⁵ In most North American Pentecostal denominations, such as the Assemblies of God and the PAOC, autonomy lies in the local church. Therefore, what is believed or articulated at the national level is not always practiced at the local level.⁶ Despite advances on paper, women continue to find restrictions in almost all leadership positions and "a remnant of male dominance" still remains.⁷

Pentecostals and others have presented hermeneutical and theological arguments for the unrestricted participation of women in all leadership roles, but women continue to be severely underrepresented in Pentecostal leadership in proportion to their numbers in the pews.⁸ Because of a lack of women in visible church leadership positions (despite an increase in women holding credentials⁹), the numbers of women in the pews are also dropping, and especially educated and professional women are leaving churches at a faster rate than men due to sexism in the church, their own painful experiences, and greater opportunities for them outside the church.¹⁰ Women continue to face "insurmountable obstacles" to finding the freedom to practice the biblical authority they are given on paper.¹¹

The gender praxis problem is simple: historical arguments, exegetical analysis, official position papers, and church polity in favor of women in leadership have not translated into a liberating praxis for women leaders. However, solving the praxis problem and the reasons behind it is more complicated. Pentecostal theological works arguing for women's equality often fail to develop an authoritative praxis model that is connected to the theological argument. A Pentecostal gender praxis, when developed at all, is often disconnected from the theological arguments or methodology being used, acting more as an appendix than as an integrated

---

3. See discussion in my Introduction for more, but see Ambrose, "Shaming the Men," 79–81; Crabtree and Qualls, "Women," 298; Catford, "Women's Experiences," 26–7; Blumhofer, "Women in American Pentecostalism," 20.

4. Alexander, "Introduction," 3. See also Cavaness, "Leadership Attitudes," 126.

5. Qualls, *Forgive Us*, 178–9.

6. Qualls, *Forgive Us*, 197, 217.

7. Qualls, *Forgive Us*, 193. See also Hyatt, "Spirit-Filled Women," 261.

8. See John G. Stackhouse Jr., *Evangelical Landscapes: Facing Critical Issues of the Day* (Grand Rapids: Baker Academic, 2002), 126–7.

9. Crabtree and Qualls, "Women," 296.

10. Crabtree and Qualls, "Women," 301–4.

11. Hollingsworth and Browning, "Daughters," 164.

part of the argument.¹² Conversely, some works that focus primarily on gender praxis in Pentecostal churches are often unable to support their praxis model with a developed and authoritative theological hermeneutic.¹³ The result is that praxis, the supposed goal of biblical-theological egalitarian arguments, has no methodologically connected authoritative basis. This gap between theory and praxis leads to confusion, inconsistency, or hesitancy on how to apply theoretical egalitarian arguments on the ground. Without an authoritative praxis model integrated into a consistent theological hermeneutic, Pentecostal churches are unable to escape the paradoxical gender practices that have plagued the movement for a century. The gender paradox becomes a lived and repeated reality as women are simultaneously encouraged to re-enact the prophesying daughters of Acts 2 and the silent and submissive women of 1 Corinthians 14:34-35,¹⁴ without any (hermeneutical) guide as to which passage holds greater priority for praxis.

A number of scholars have noticed this Pentecostal gender praxis problem. Stephenson observes that isolating or favoring Acts 2 and the message of Spirit baptism as the main (or only) argument for women in leadership "has never really translated into a fully liberating praxis for Pentecostal women."¹⁵ Johns argues that models focused on Spirit-empowerment of women and prophetic gifting, while sounding liberating, have not been enough, for they uphold a hierarchical structure where women are "ghettoized into the prophetic while men are free to be both prophetic and priestly."¹⁶ Shane Clifton similarly realizes that Pentecostal openness to the message of equal Spirit-empowerment for both genders has remained in tension with gender-based assumptions about the functional role of women.¹⁷ By not addressing the underlying uncertainty about the role of women in the church, these supposedly liberating models have not translated into freedom for women to live out their callings in the church without restriction. Re-enacting biblical texts, even the Pentecostal *magna carta* of Acts 2, has not materialized into the fully liberating praxis many women (and men) desire. A convincing, methodologically connected, liberative and authoritative praxis model that necessitates actual change(s) on the ground must be developed for any attempt to fully resolve the gender paradox. For such a task, I propose a pre-enactment praxis model as the preferred (eschatological) model over against a re-enactment model.

---

12. Some examples are given in Chapter 1 (1.2.1), such as the critique of Stephenson, *Dismantling*, who only gives a few pages in her conclusion for practical suggestions for churches. See also my conclusion (5.5) below.

13. For example, see Gill and Cavaness, *God's Women*; Alexander and Bowers, *What Women Want*.

14. As summarized in the title of Hollingsworth and Browning's article "Your Daughters Shall Prophesy (As Long as They Submit)."

15. Stephenson, *Dismantling*, 2. Tackett, "Callings," 92–3.

16. Johns, "Spirited Vestments," 171; cf. 182. See Barfoot and Sheppard, "Prophetic vs. Priestly."

17. Clifton, "Sexism," 54, 57–8.

## 5.2 Pre-Enactment and Re-Enactment Praxis Models

Pre-enactment is a recent concept in academic contexts and originally found its way into academic discourse through the artistic disciplines of theatre and performance practice.[18] Simple re-enactment in its most narrow sense aims "to faithfully reproduce historical events and promise an authentic re-experience" of those events.[19] In contrast, pre-enactment—while (importantly) still oriented to the past and the original historical event—experiments with and moves toward "an imagined future" which "opens up a realm of possibilities" for present performance.[20] Therefore, pre-enactment features an "entanglement of past, present, and future" in which present practice links the past and the future together in dynamic, experimental, and embodied ways.[21] The use of pre-enactment models is quickly transitioning from purely aesthetic disciplines to real-world situations in the social or political arenas as well as everyday life, as the transformative potential of pre-enactment and its future-oriented actions gain attention.[22] As "anticipations" of desired change, pre-enactment offers transformative experiences that are realizations of possible futures.[23] Work on pre-enactment is new and scholars are still developing the full range of the concept and its theoretical foundation,[24] but a

---

18. Other spellings appear in different works as preenactment, P/Re/Enactment, or (P)reenactment. Pre-enactment has gained traction mainly among a group of German scholars who have recently published books and articles on the topic, originating from a 2017 interdisciplinary international conference examining the concept. See "P/Re/Enact! Performing in Between Times," (conference, Institute for Cultural Inquiry, Berlin, October 27–8, 2017), https://doi.org/10.25620/e171027. See Adam Czirak et al., eds., *Performance zwischen den Zeiten: Reenactments und Preenactments in Kunst und Wissenschaft* (Bielefeld, De: transcript Verlag, 2019). Most of the book is written in German, but five chapters are in English, including the introduction by Friederike Oberkrome and Verena Straub, "Performing in Between Times," 9–22. The same group of editors (Adam Czirak et al.) wrote the chapter "(P)reenactment," in *Affective Societies: Key Concepts*, ed. Jan Slaby and Christian von Scheve (New York: Routledge, 2019), 200–9.

19. Czirak et al., "(P)reenactment," 200; Oberkrome and Straub, "Performing," 9–10.

20. Czirak et al., "(P)reenactment," 200, 201. Czirak et al. see a "fundamental interconnectedness and interdependence" between the two, thus preferring the term "(P)reenactment" (201).

21. Czirak et al., "(P)reenactment," 201–3 (quote from 201).

22. Czirak et al., "(P)reenactment," 207.

23. Oberkrome and Straub, "Performing," 10.

24. Oberkrome and Straub, "Performing," 9; Czirak et al., "(P)reenactment," 208. *Performance zwischen den Zeiten* is the first full work in this direction. To my knowledge, it has yet to be specifically applied to theological ideas or Christian practice. However, dramatic theory is already popular within Christian theology and hermeneutics. There are many works, but a good start is Kevin J. Vanhoozer, *The Drama of Doctrine: A Canonical-linguistic Approach to Christian Theology* (Louisville, KY: Westminster John Knox, 2005).

key development is its increasing application to political and social activism due to its potential emancipatory effects.[25]

Pre-enactment, while still having a retrospective dimension, seeks to move beyond the limitations of re-enactment. I have adopted these two terms as a way to distinguish my proposed eschatological praxis model (pre-enactment) from previously offered Pentecostal gender praxis models (re-enactment) and to critically evaluate them. Therefore, these terms make their way into each discussion to show the inadequacies of re-enactment models, which uphold the Pentecostal gender paradox, and why adopting an eschatological pre-enactment model can move toward solving the specific problem of this chapter and the next, the Pentecostal gender praxis problem. Pre-enactment is an exploratory rather than an explanatory model, which is important for any theological argument attempting to recruit the imagination and provide creative space for continued revelation.

In his work on models of the church, Avery Dulles argues for the value of the "method of models" and a model's heuristic use for theological and specifically ecclesiological work.[26] Models provide "conceptual tools and vocabulary" that help point toward the reality under consideration.[27] Importantly, an "exploratory" model like the one proposed here, as opposed to a more "explanatory" model, leaves room for development and the possibility of experimental verification.[28] A model will never be perfect, but certain models are more adequate than others for a particular theological discussion.[29] The argument here is that my proposed eschatological–egalitarian praxis requires a new and exploratory model due to its dialectical, experiential, and experimental features.[30] Therefore, when referring to an eschatological praxis "model" in this chapter, I mean a distinctive (eschatological) mindset that helps to address imaginatively a theological problem (here the gender praxis problem). The features of an eschatological pre-enactment praxis model enable it to move beyond the problems and limitations of re-enactment models, which have contributed to the Pentecostal gender paradox.[31]

---

25. Oberkrome and Straub, "Performing," 10; Czirak et al., "(P)reenactment," 206–7.

26. Avery Dulles, *Models of the Church*, exp. ed. (New York: Image Books, 2002), 4–5, 16–18.

27. Dulles, *Models*, 15.

28. Dulles, *Models*, 15–16. This experimental nature of an exploratory model is why I choose this term over other terms like paradigm. As Dulles explains, a model must first be shown to succeed repeatedly and in different situations to become a paradigm, which is less questioned (21). No term is perfect, but I believe "model" best captures the functional consequences of this new way of thinking (see Dulles, *Models*, 15).

29. Dulles, *Models*, 17, 21. However, the pluralism of models is inevitable (21).

30. See 5.4.1.

31. See Dulles, *Models*, 4–5.

The most common model for gender praxis in modern Pentecostalism is re-enactment. When applying this model for establishing egalitarian praxis, Pentecostal groups seek to imitate biblical texts that promote the equal participation of women in ecclesial worship and leadership. However, this model maintains the gender paradox and its hermeneutical inconsistency for two main reasons. First, a re-enactment approach to practicing Scripture must decide which texts are to be re-enacted. Do Pentecostals follow the biblical exhortations for women to keep silent in church (1 Cor. 14:34-35) or the encouragements for women to publicly prophesy (Acts 2:17-18; cf. 1 Cor. 11:5)? Second, even when re-enacting more egalitarian texts, the model does not offer a fully liberating praxis because, as argued in the last chapter, these texts are a part of an eschatological–egalitarian *trajectory*. They are imaginative eschatological texts that *point to* the full and equal participation of women and men in all aspects of church life and society, without directly prescribing such practices (which were not yet possible in their historical situations). Therefore, re-enacting even the most promising of texts such as Acts 2:17-18 falls short of a fully egalitarian praxis because the full meaning for praxis is not contained solely within the text or a linear interpretation-application explanatory model.

An eschatological pre-enactment praxis model has the potential to solve the gender praxis problem because it offers the opportunity to move beyond the limitations of re-enacting the text and move toward exploring and experimenting with the text's eschatological trajectory. An eschatological praxis based on the unified eschatological–egalitarian narrative thread of the Scriptures, prioritizes the pre-enactment of biblical promises over the re-enactment of biblical prescriptions. Before formulating the key features of this preferred praxis model, the following section briefly reviews and discusses the important function of praxis in Christian eschatology and Pentecostal theology in order to defend the inclusion of developing a robust praxis in any Pentecostal theological work, despite the lack of works that do so.

## 5.3 Pentecostal Eschatology and Praxis: Potentiality and Problem

Pentecostalism's change in convictions over the last century concerning what the Scriptures teach about women in ministry—driven by hermeneutical shifts and choices—has led to uncertainty on the ground regarding praxis. Approaching the gender problem eschatologically not only restores the biblical convictions and imagination of early Pentecostals about female leaders but also addresses uncertainty over gender practices in the church due to the strong connection between eschatology and praxis. This section reviews and further evaluates the vital role of praxis in both Christian eschatology and Pentecostal theology in order to assess the ability of my proposed praxis model to overcome both the gender praxis problem and what I term the "eschatological praxis problem." If eschatology is a praxis-driven discipline, and Pentecostal theology is praxis centered, then a Pentecostal eschatology (of gender) must contain a robust and thoroughly developed praxis that works on the ground.

### 5.3.1 Eschatology as Praxis-Driven Discipline

There is an emerging consensus that eschatology is a practical theological discipline,[32] so much so that Moltmann refers to Christian living as "nothing other than practical eschatology."[33] In her essay on the eschatological body, Sarah Coakley speaks of "practices of transformation that start now but have their final goal in the future: they create the future by enacting its possibilities."[34] The transformative practical benefits of eschatology and its this-worldly relevance means that "the adjective 'eschatological' does not refer just to things which lie as yet in the remote future, but equally to the significance and impact of those same things for the present moment."[35] For example, an eschatological basis for the practice of Sabbath has been presented by Moltmann, arguing it anticipates eschatological rest. What inspires Sabbath-keeping is not that it is a re-enactment of an ancient Jewish practice, but that it is a pre-enactment and sign of the eschatological equal participation in rest regardless of race, class, gender, or ability.[36]

Modern theologians refer to eschatology as "the presence of the future,"[37] "a guiding light" for present practice,[38] key to "a praxis consistent with the reign of God,"[39] and as having "clear and strong implications" for social praxis.[40] Trutz Rendtorff argues that eschatology "makes ethics possible and demands that it be practiced," for it provides a future reference point of the ultimate good that inspires present ethical living.[41] These scholars claim that belief in the eschatological

---

32. See Volf, "After Moltmann," 252–3. See previous discussion on developments in eschatology, including Moltmann's influence, in my Introduction. The goal here is not to repeat that more general discussion but to zero in on the emergence of eschatology as a praxis-driven discipline.

33. Moltmann, "Liberating," 190. See also Grenz, *Moral Quest*, 224.

34. Coakley, "Eschatological Body," 64. She is, somewhat ironically, alluding to postmodern secular feminist Judith Butler's work on the body.

35. See Bauckham and Hart, *Hope Against Hope*, 194. See also 129, 181, 184, 193; Hart, "Eschatology," 263.

36. Moltmann, "Liberating," 199; Jürgen Moltmann, *God in Creation: A New Theology of Creation and the Spirit of God*, trans. Margaret Kohl (Minneapolis: Fortress, 1993), 294–5. For more on the eschatological anticipations represented by Sabbath, see Augustine, *Spirit and the Common Good*, 133–5.

37. George Eldon Ladd, *The Presence of the Future: The Eschatology of Biblical Realism*, rev. ed. (Grand Rapids: Eerdmans, 1974).

38. Schwarz, *Eschatology*, xiii.

39. Beverly Wildung Harrison, *Making Connections: Essays in Feminist Social Ethics*, ed. Carol S. Robb (Boston: Beacon, 1985), 225.

40. Gutiérrez, *Theology of Liberation*, 122.

41. Rendtorff, *Ethics*, 1:187. The importance of a *telos* or reference point in relation to practices dates to Aristotle and is used extensively by Alasdair MacIntyre in his *After Virtue: A Study in Moral Theory*, 2nd ed. (Notre Dame, IN: University of Notre Dame Press, 1984). It is picked up for ecclesiological practice by J. R. Wilson in *Why Church Matters: Worship,*

transformation of the world has more to do with living that reality in the present than it does with waiting for that future reality to come.[42] Thus, they often refer to the actions of the people of God as living, historical, or concrete "parables" of the coming kingdom of God[43] or "the metaphorical birthpangs of the reign of God."[44] Because at certain times and places "God gives his future of the kingdom *in advance*" as foretastes of the redeemed world to come, eschatology has practical consequences for Christian living.[45] There is such a thing as an eschatological lifestyle, a present way of living and practicing one's eschatological hopes and beliefs.[46]

A helpful example of the development of the marriage between eschatology and praxis is Grenz's argument for living an ethical life firmly grounded in eschatology. "The moral life," he states, "is eschatological living: it involves living now as those who belong to the age to come."[47] Grenz argues that we must live in a manner consistent with our eschatological hope and allow that vision of God's future intention to "shape the way we live in the here and now."[48] Living in a way appropriate to our eschatological expectations, suggests Grenz, might even contribute to the present realization of those eschatological ideals.[49] Thus, when we understand the Christian life eschatologically, we begin to think differently about praxis.[50]

### 5.3.2 Pentecostal Theology as Praxis Centered

Pentecostal theology in general, like eschatology in specific, is praxis-centered. Therefore, it is no surprise that Pentecostal scholarship frequently argues for a praxis-based model for constructing theology. There is growing consensus among Pentecostal scholars that any theology or hermeneutical theory devoid of praxis

---

*Ministry, and Mission in Practice* (Grand Rapids: Brazos, 2006), see 12–14. For more on how actions are determined by a *telos*, see Smith, *Imagining*, 6–7.

42. See Gerhard Lohfink, *Jesus and Community*, trans. J. P. Calvin (Philadelphia: Fortress, 1984), 85.

43. Respectively: Harrison, *Making Connections*, 225; Hart, "Eschatology," 267; Moltmann, "Liberating," 204–5.

44. Rosemary P. Carbine, "'Artisans of a New Humanity:' Re-visioning the Public Church in a Feminist Perspective," in *Frontiers in Catholic Feminist Theology: Shoulder to Shoulder*, ed. Susan Abraham and Elena Procario-Foley (Minneapolis: Fortress, 2009), 192; Moltmann, "Liberating," 205.

45. Moltmann, "Liberating," 198; italics in the original.

46. Schwarz laments our "*non*eschatological lifestyle" (*Eschatology*, 4; italics mine).

47. Grenz, *Moral Quest*, 125.

48. Grenz, *Moral Quest*, 272. See also 119. Grenz uses both OT and NT examples for his argument.

49. Grenz, *Moral Quest*, 105.

50. Grenz, *Moral Quest*, 272.

is incompatible with a Pentecostal worldview. For the Pentecostal, to construct a praxis is to construct a theology for the two are intertwined, with praxis often preceding theological articulation. Vondey argues that this Pentecostal praxis theology finds its origins in the biblical event of Pentecost, which for Pentecostals "is a praxis rather than a doctrine."[51] Like those first believers at Pentecost, Pentecostals have always preferred to *live* a theology rather than *have* a theology.[52] Articulating doctrine, asserts Vondey, is not the primary task of Pentecostal theology for "certain doctrines rely much more on Pentecostal experience than on the power of explanation."[53] This praxis-based, lived theology is how early Pentecostals developed their theological positions, including on the role of women in leadership.[54] Their Spirit-led experience of greater gender equality led to theological articulations about it.[55] Only as those experiences dwindled and were less encouraged did the theology begin to change.[56]

For most Pentecostal scholars, praxis-derived knowledge comes prior to theological articulation of beliefs,[57] so that even Pentecostal scholarship is based on experience.[58] In this way, experiences and practices led by the Holy Spirit "become a source of theological insight."[59] For example, although the conventional story of early Pentecostalism is that students read Acts 2 and then sought the baptism in the Spirit with the evidence of speaking in tongues, more recent historical evidence and research suggests it was the other way around: students first spoke in tongues and then searched the Scriptures to help articulate their experience and develop their theology.[60] Therefore, some Pentecostal scholars consider Pentecostal

---

51. Vondey, *Pentecostal Theology*, 28.

52. See Vondey, *Pentecostal Theology*, 14.

53. Vondey, *Pentecostal Theology*, 17. Vondey, like Yong, is not saying articulation is not needed, just that it comes second (17–18; see Yong, *Renewing*, 26, 229).

54. See Chapter 2.

55. For the role of the Holy Spirit in Pentecostal praxis, see Mark J. Cartledge, "Practical Theology: Attending to Pneumatologically-driven Praxis," in Vondey, *Routledge Handbook*, 163–72.

56. See 3.1–3.3.

57. See Smith, *Tongues*, 27, 31, and 31n35. See also 48–50. Smith is influenced by Land here. For the role of experience in Pentecostal theology, see Peter D. Neumann, "Experience: The Mediated Immediacy of Encounter with the Spirit," in Vondey, *Routledge Handbook*, 84–94.

58. See Vondey and Mittelstadt, "Introduction," 9.

59. Studebaker, explaining Yong's approach (Steven M. Studebaker, "Toward a Pneumatological Trinitarian Theology: Amos Yong, the Spirit, and the Trinity," in Vondey and Mittelstadt, *Amos Yong*, 100). See also here Kenneth Archer, "A Pentecostal Way of Doing Theology: Method and Manner," *International Journal of Systematic Theology* 9, no. 3 (July 2007): 301–14.

60. Cerillo and Wacker, "Bibliography," 397. See the early test "experiments" in San Antonio, TX and Pittsburgh, PA (Gary B. McGee, "Initial Evidence," in *NIDPCM*, 786).

theology a "second-order set of reflections" arising out of praxis.[61] At the very least, theology and praxis have a dialectical or reciprocal relationship where they mutually inform each other.[62] As Johns summarizes, "Pentecostal theology is largely what a Pentecostal does. It is an ongoing exercise of praxis inasmuch as reflection arises out of experience, put into dialogue with Scripture and the witness of the community, and then flows back into concrete action."[63] In other words, theology does not lead to practice as much as practice leads to theology.

Eschatology is increasingly considered a practical discipline that grounds its imaginative theology in participatory action. Similarly, Pentecostal theology is centered on and informed by practices. Additionally, Pentecostalism is an eschatologically oriented movement. Therefore, bringing Pentecostal praxis into conversation with eschatology (and vice versa) is not only a commonsense approach but also a promising and vital step in any comprehensive attempt at solving a Pentecostal issue.

### 5.3.3 Pentecostal Eschatology as (a) Praxis

Incorporating praxis into Pentecostal eschatology (and vice versa) is an appropriate, if not necessary, development, and there is a growing consensus that Pentecostal eschatology should be praxis-centered. For Pentecostals, theological inquiry involves empowering praxis.[64] Consequently, Pentecostal eschatology is not (and cannot) be a purely speculative endeavor of future events.[65] Rather than escapist withdrawal from the world, Pentecostal eschatology is beginning instead to focus on active participation in eschatological realities.[66] Pentecostal scholars are increasingly adopting an eschatological basis for social action,[67] ethics,[68]

---

For a different take on the role of experience in Pentecostal theology, see Chang-Soung Lee, "In the Beginning There Was a Theology: The Precedence of Theology over Experience in the Pentecostal Movement," Asia Center for Pentecostal Theology (website articles), posted August 27, 2019, at: https://pentecost.asia/articles/in-the-beginning-there-was-a-theology-the-precedence-of-theology-over-experience-in-the-pentecostal-movement/.

61. Yong, *Renewing*, 229; Yong, *Days of Caesar*, 91. See also Vondey, *Pentecostal Theology*, 19; Vondey, *Beyond Pentecostalism*, 110.

62. See Stephenson, *Types*, who sees "a mutually informing process" between doctrine and praxis (116) and an overall interplay between worship and beliefs (see his chapter, "'Regula Spiritualitatis, Regula Doctrinae': A Contribution to Pentecostal Theological Method," 111–30). See also Studebaker, "Pneumatological Trinitarian Theology," 99.

63. Johns, *Pentecostal Formation*, 82–3.

64. Yong, *Renewing*, 26.

65. For speculation in Pentecostal theology see Vondey, *Pentecostal Theology*, 15–16.

66. Augustine, *Pentecost*, 147.

67. See Dempster, "Christian Social Concern"; Dempster, "Eschatology," 166; Augustine, *Pentecost*.

68. Kenyon, "Ethical Issues," 402–21.

mission,[69] ecclesiology,[70] and spirituality,[71] realizing that biblical eschatology demands participatory action. Some of the more influential Pentecostal scholars have placed eschatology at the center of Pentecostal praxis, joining together these two core markers of Pentecostal life.

Yong encourages discovery of "eschatological beliefs *and* practices" so that the church becomes "an eschatological sign" of what is to come.[72] Rather than a re-enactment of past events, Yong asserts Pentecostal praxis is more of a participation in the ongoing, unfinished, eschatological drama. He suggests Pentecostal life is like a twenty-ninth chapter of Acts, an "open book" for the continuation of the eschatological inauguration begun by Jesus and the apostles.[73] Yong emphasizes the performative nature of eschatology and how the eschatological future inspires present practices that open up and anticipate God's eschatological rule and reign.[74] Instead of spending our eschatological energy on date setting, timetables, and awaiting the future, Yong argues that eschatological doctrines should order one's practical life and urges Pentecostals to live out their eschatological faith.[75]

Similarly, Vondey argues that Pentecostal eschatology is not a "mere belief system" about the end; rather, it leads to action and is "the motivation for Christian life."[76] Using the narrative and image of Pentecost,[77] Vondey advances "a fundamentally praxis-oriented eschatology" in which the experience of the Spirit reshapes practices of the church into eschatological actions.[78] Like others, Vondey believes the eschatological horizon of the coming kingdom leads to present eschatological participation in transformative practices.[79] The church, as the eschatological community, not only *announces* the future to the present but through its actions *becomes* the future already present.[80] More than eschatological heralds

---

69. Smith, *Thinking in Tongues*, 31.

70. Althouse, "Ascension," 227.

71. Stephenson, *Types*, 119–20.

72. Yong, *Renewing*, 49, 184; italics mine.

73. Yong, *Renewing*, 342. See also Holmes, "Acts 29," for a similar idea.

74. See Yong, *Renewing*, 323–4. For the relationship between the eschatological and performative nature of renewal theology, see Yong, *Renewing*, 193, 252, 349.

75. Yong, *Days of Caesar*, 348. See also 317 and Yong, *Renewing*, 15, 49–52.

76. Vondey, *Pentecostal Theology*, 132, 150. Vondey argues for a comprehensive apocalyptic eschatology.

77. Pentecost as the root image is key to Vondey's eschatological argument. See *Pentecostal Theology*, 133–4, 200. He regularly speaks of a "perpetual Pentecost" as key to Christian praxis (151). Similarly, see Augustine's work *Pentecost*, esp. 139–48.

78. Vondey, *Pentecostal Theology*, 134, 137.

79. Vondey, *Pentecostal Theology*, 222–3, 193.

80. Vondey, *Pentecostal Theology*, 223.

who repeatedly *proclaim* the coming kingdom, Pentecostals are "eschatological signposts" who persistently *live* the coming kingdom.[81]

This evaluation of the importance of praxis in both Pentecostal theology and eschatology leads to two important conclusions. First, any theological or hermeneutical approach to a Pentecostal issue, such as an eschatological approach to gender, must include, lead to, or even start with praxis.[82] Applying an eschatological methodology to the gender problem would be incomplete without creating and applying an eschatological praxis model for the ministry of women in Pentecostal churches. Second, experience through praxis is not secondary to biblical interpretation or theological articulation, and in fact is a valid form of both. Therefore, to work toward an eschatological-egalitarian praxis—and to uncover early Pentecostal eschatological gender practices (Chapter 2)—is to work toward an eschatological-egalitarian theology. The vital role of praxis in Pentecostal theology necessitates the incorporation of praxis into a comprehensive approach to an issue such as gender. A historical, hermeneutical, or theological argument alone is not enough to make an impactful contribution. Praxis must play a significant role, and eschatology is a necessary partner for developing an authoritative Pentecostal praxis model due to the emerging eschatological center of Pentecostal praxis that features the theological authority and transformational nature of eschatology for praxis. However, a difficulty in applying an eschatological praxis to a concern such as women's equality is that there are so few examples of an eschatological praxis being applied to actual issues. Just as many theoretical works on gender fall short on praxis (the gender praxis problem), many works on eschatology do the same.

### 5.3.4 *The Eschatological Praxis Problem*

To embrace an eschatological orientation to praxis as a way to solve the gender praxis problem, there must be a strong relationship between theory and actualization. Although the praxis implications of eschatology have been widely embraced in the academic world, eschatological beliefs have yet to make a significant impact in the life and ministry of the church.[83] At least part of the reason for eschatology's lack of impact on the ground is that the literature on eschatology often theorizes an eschatological praxis with very few specific suggestions on actualizing the praxis.

---

81. Vondey, *Pentecostal Theology*, 253. See also 250-2. The importance of *living* rather than *proclaiming* the full gospel is central to Vondey's thesis and thinking in *Pentecostal Theology* (224).

82. See Kenneth Archer, "Early Pentecostal Biblical Interpretation," *JPT* 9, no. 1 (2001): 43; Archer, *Pentecostal Hermeneutic*, 228, 261. Thus, the spiraled nature of the order of this project (see my Introduction and 3.4.1).

83. See assessment in Gladd and Harmon, *Inaugurated Eschatology*, xii.

For example, J. Richard Middleton spends the last part of his book attempting to answer the "so what" question of his eschatology, but there are surprisingly few concrete applications.[84] Markus Mühling ends his lengthy *Handbook of Christian Eschatology* by concluding "Christian hope therefore drives us to action in the everyday life in the here and now," but offers little description of what those actions might be.[85] Shields's attempted construction of the eschatological imagination is to be commended; however, despite his intention to conclude with a "praxis oriented" chapter that answers the "how" of living eschatologically, he delays until the final few pages and even then offers no actual concrete examples.[86] Even Gustavo Gutiérrez's lauded work on liberation theology, which relies heavily on eschatological thinking, falls short of his stated goal to integrate critical-theological reflection with Christian praxis.[87] Eschatologically oriented theological works rightly encourage that eschatological truths "must be lived out concretely on earth"[88] and that God's people are to be "conformed to the standards of the promised coming age,"[89] but they often lack clear ideas on how that might happen.[90] Theorizing must lead to actualizing, imagination to participation.[91] Scholars of eschatology and theological ethics believe the eschatological imagination leads to social change,[92] but what is needed are examples of how the eschatological imagination translates into participation in eschatological realities on the ground: how does one (pre)enact the preferred possibilities of the future?[93] Thus, although these closing two chapters are specifically meant to solve the Pentecostal gender praxis problem through an eschatological approach, they also contribute to the general field of eschatology by providing a thorough and integrated example of an eschatological praxis for a social issue.

Pentecostal scholars have fared a bit better in providing examples of how an eschatological praxis works on the ground. Recent works in Pentecostal eschatology have attempted to (re)discover the transformational eschatology of early Pentecostals and apply it to current social issues—even calling for "the necessity of an eschatological orientation" for all matters surrounding Pentecostal

---

84. Middleton, *New Heaven*, 241–82.

85. Mühling, *Handbook of Christian Eschatology*, 368.

86. Shields, *Eschatological Imagination*, 5, 172. See 175-7 for attempted "practical strategies."

87. Gutiérrez, *Theology of Liberation*. Praxis is often mentioned, but few examples are given (see 5, 11, 122) and the scope is limited (79).

88. Middleton, *New Heaven*, 276; Shields, *Eschatological Imagination*, 175.

89. Keener, *Spirit Hermeneutics*, 50.

90. Even Gladd and Harmon's work surprisingly gives few implications of their inaugurated eschatology and repeatedly skirts the issue of application.

91. Procter-Smith, "Feminist Ritual Strategies," 511.

92. See Reginald Stackhouse, *The End of the World? A New Look at an Old Belief* (New York: Paulist, 1997), 26–7.

93. See Shields, *Eschatological Imagination*, 176, as well as 170–5.

spirituality and theology.[94] However, few have paid attention to the potential role eschatology might play for gender praxis and in solving the gender problem, representing the (unfortunate) amalgamation of the gender praxis problem with the eschatological praxis problem. Vondey lists five social action practices that a renewed eschatology has impacted within Pentecostalism (politics, race, pacifism, economic justice, and ecology) but does not mention gender.[95] Similarly, Daniel Isgrigg assesses numerous times throughout his work how an eschatological lens has influenced Pentecostals' approaches to social issues over time, including in the areas of peacemaking, politics, the environment, and economic and racial inequality, without a reference to gender.[96] McQueen reviews the Pentecostal literature calling for a renewed focus on eschatology in various topics within Pentecostalism including glossolalia, evangelization, social concern, spirituality, pneumatology, ecology, and ecumenism, but does not mention women's equality.[97] Pacifism, anti-nationalism, racial healing, and creation care occasionally get pulled into Thompson's discussion of eschatological signs of the inbreaking of the kingdom in *Kingdom Come*, but gender is never brought up.[98] The essays in Althouse and Waddell's work on Pentecostal eschatologies address questions of Pentecostal eschatology from biblical, theological, and contextual perspectives, including several chapters on social issues, but there are no mentions of eschatology's potential for furthering equality for Pentecostal women.[99] Yong mentions the political implications of eschatology in *In the Days of Caesar* and also states how it might impact concerns for the environment,[100] but there is no discussion on gender.[101] If, as James Glass argues, eschatology is a "stimulus to Pentecostal practice" and has the "power to control and influence almost every aspect of Pentecostal faith and life,"[102] why not apply it to an area struggling to find an authoritative praxis? The time seems right for an eschatological–egalitarian praxis that can authoritatively navigate the Pentecostal gender paradox and its praxis problem.

---

94. McQueen, *Joel*, 91. For an example, see Paul Alexander, *Peace to War: Shifting Allegiances in the Assemblies of God* (Telford, PA: Cascadia, 2009), where he connects a transforming eschatology to a radical commitment to nonviolence (337).

95. Vondey, *Pentecostal Theology*, 138, 144, 171–4. But Vondey does elsewhere hint at the potential difficulty or tension in bringing eschatology into conversation with gender (179; see also Vondey, *Perplexed*, 111).

96. Isgrigg, *Imagining the Future*, 27–9, 118–22, 134–6, 163–4, 192–3, 244–8.

97. McQueen, *Joel*, 91–100.

98. Thompson, *Kingdom Come*, see 129–34, 144–6.

99. See Althouse and Waddell, *Eschatologies*.

100. Yong, *Days of Caesar*, 344.

101. Many examples of the same problem could be (and already have been) given. See Chapter 1.

102. Glass, "Eschatology," 133–4, 145. It should be noted he considers this a *weakness* of Pentecostal eschatology, but most scholars and myself argue the opposite.

Pentecostals are eschatologically driven, praxis-oriented people with a passion for the coming kingdom.[103] However, as Warrington points out, current Pentecostal praxis in the pew indicates that many Pentecostals' view of how they experience the coming kingdom through the Spirit is narrowly focused and therefore more infrequent than it could be.[104] Eschatological participation in the Spirit is often limited to tongues-speech, divine healing, spiritual gifts, prophecy, and other signs and wonders as the main foretastes of the age to come.[105] It is time to expand the repertoire of eschatological practices, and considering the clear alignment and interdependent relationship between gender equality and eschatology as argued in the last chapter(s), egalitarian participation is a prime candidate. A purely theoretical approach to the gender problem through denominational statements or policy modifications has not changed actual practice on the ground. As Smith asserts, this theoretical approach is a flawed model that fails to recruit the imagination. Therefore, he argues, a better solution is to change first our practices to ones that embody and "enact a vision of the coming kingdom of God."[106] To inspire real change for Pentecostal women, an eschatological approach to the gender problem must include a robust praxis. The second half of this chapter moves toward formulating the key features of a Pentecostal eschatological–egalitarian praxis model, with an eye toward the next chapter's suggestions for closing the gender praxis gap in Pentecostal leadership, education, and worship.

### 5.4 Solving the Praxis Problem(s): Eschatological–Egalitarian Praxis as Pre-Enactment

Based on and continuing the above analysis of the strong relationship between eschatology and praxis, including within Pentecostalism, this section argues that an eschatological pre-enactment praxis model has the potential to solve the Pentecostal gender praxis problem by providing an appropriate conceptual tool and vocabulary for a liberating egalitarian praxis. An eschatological praxis frees women from all ecclesial restrictions by prioritizing the liberating pre-enactment of biblical promises over the ambiguous re-enactment of biblical prescriptions. In this section, I propose three intersecting features of an eschatological pre-enactment praxis that help overcome the gender praxis problem. First, it is a dialectical (as opposed to linear) exercise. Second, it uses experience as a part of the ongoing dialectical process of biblical interpretation and application. Third, it

---

103. This is basically a one-sentence summary of Land's *Pentecostal Spirituality*.

104. Warrington, *Pentecostal Theology*, 130. See Cartledge's assessment that the future challenge of a pneumatologically driven Pentecostal praxis is to broaden its scope to include anthropological issues ("Practical Theology," 167–8).

105. Cf. Frank D. Macchia, "Sighs Too Deep for Words: Toward a Theology of Glossolalia," *JPT* 1 (1992): 70–2.

106. Smith, *Imagining*, 40.

is therefore an experimental, rather than dogmatic, form of praxis. The experiential and experimental nature of eschatological praxis does not mean it considers every practice as potentially legitimate, for it is still grounded in the biblical authority of the ongoing eschatological drama and its egalitarian trajectory. In short, an eschatological praxis model creates a dialectical, experiential, experimental pre-enactment of the eschatological–egalitarian promises of the biblical narrative. These interrelated features of a pre-enactment praxis, when applied to gender and coupled with the eschatological and praxis-oriented heart of the Pentecostal movement, can lead to the possibility of a fully liberating praxis for Pentecostal women in all parts and at all levels of church life and ministry. Due to their intersecting nature, these features of a pre-enactment praxis are discussed together (but still in a loose order), as each mutually informs parts of the other. I conclude this section by revisiting early Pentecostalism as a potential prototype of the proposed pre-enactment praxis and by discussing potential limitations or critiques of an eschatological praxis model.

### 5.4.1 Pre-Enactment: Dialectical, Experiential, Experimental

Pentecostal gender praxis as pre-enactment of biblical eschatological–egalitarian promises recognizes the dialectical (or circular) nature of the hermeneutical process. Pre-enacting eschatological promises is not the result of a linear progression from biblical interpretation to definitive practices (an explanatory model); rather it is an integral part of an *ongoing* dialectical process between experiential praxis and biblical interpretation (an exploratory model).[107] That is why this and the following chapter are a continuation of the previous hermeneutical chapters and could just as easily precede as proceed them. The final chapters are not the application of a hermeneutic; they are the other half of the ongoing dialectic between a biblically inspired eschatological imagination and community participation in those eschatological realities, which aids the interpretive process. A linear hermeneutical model, common in many hermeneutics textbooks (even in Pentecostal schools), starts with arriving at the proper interpretation of a text and then moves toward applying it in practice as the final step.[108] In this scenario, a study of the biblical text alone *is* enough to arrive at the meaning of the text; the resultant praxis does not factor into the interpretative process and in fact the hermeneutical task can be

---

107. See discussion in 5.2 and Avery, *Models*, 16.

108. A popular example would be J. Scott Duvall and J. Daniel Hays, *Grasping God's Word: A Hands-On Approach to Reading, Interpreting, and Applying the Bible*, 2nd ed. (Grand Rapids: Zondervan, 2005) and the abridged version *Journey into God's Word: Your Guide to Understanding the Bible* (Grand Rapids: Zondervan, 2008). I am aware of these books being used as core textbooks in Hermeneutics courses at least two Pentecostal schools. See Cartledge, "Practical Theology," who argues that the evangelical "applied theology" of applying biblical texts in a linear manner is not conducive to the pneumatologically orientated way Pentecostals read texts (164–5).

considered complete without the actual experience of practicing the text.[109] This linear approach can be simplified as a "the-Bible-says-so" type of praxis where the goal is a re-enactment of what the readers interpret from the Bible.

Pentecostals historically and in contemporary scholarship place much more emphasis on the dialectical feature of praxis in biblical interpretation. Study of the biblical text alone *is not* enough. This is particularly true, argues Johns, when discussing the gender problem. As a Pentecostal woman reading the Scriptures, she laments: "I need more than 'the right interpretation' to save me from despair. . . . hermeneutics alone cannot save us."[110] Johns then creatively exhorts that we must move "beyond 'what the text meant' or 'what the text means' into the realm of 'what new world is being created by the text' and 'how are women to be found in this new world'?"[111] Interpretation of Scripture is influenced and validated by experience through praxis and vice versa in a dialectical encounter.[112]

Pentecostal scholars argue that devoid of practicing the biblical text, we will not understand the meaning of the text, for the same Spirit who inspires the biblical message also inspires practices in line with the s/Spirit of that message.[113] In his five elements of Pentecostal hermeneutics, Roger Stronstad uses experience as a sort of inclusio in the interpretive process, where the study of the text is preceded by experiential presuppositions and ends with experiential verification.[114] Applied to eschatological praxis, the more the readers participate experientially—and experimentally—in the unfolding eschatological drama within the text, the more they can imagine and understand the full promises contained within the text. In this way, an eschatological Pentecostal praxis can be considered more experimental or even playful as it sheds light on the possible meaning of the text.[115]

A helpful way to understand the experimental feature of pre-enactment praxis is to consider its pre-critical proclivities. As Archer and others argue, Pentecostals

---

109. See Duvall and Hays's four steps of "The Interpretive Journey" in *Grasping God's Word*, 19–27.

110. Johns, "Grieving, Brooding, Transformation," 144.

111. Johns, "Grieving, Brooding, Transformation," 145.

112. See Archer, *Pentecostal Hermeneutic*, 256–7, 134–5; Yong, *Spirit-Word-Community*, 13.

113. See Robby Waddell, *The Spirit of the Book of Revelation* (Blandford Forum, UK: Deo, 2006), 101, 111, 118.

114. Stronstad, "Pentecostal Experience and Hermeneutics," 14–30. He elsewhere states that "the Pentecostal experience is a valid hermeneutical presupposition." See Roger Stronstad, "The Biblical Precedent for Historical Precedent," *Paraclete* 27, no. 3 (1993): 1.

115. For play in conversation with the biblical text, see Vondey, *Beyond Pentecostalism*, 66–77. For the "playfulness" of Pentecostal theology, see Vondey, *Pentecostal Theology*, esp. 12–14, 132–3. See also Wolfgang Vondey, "Religion as Play: Pentecostalism as a Theological Type," *Religions* 9, no. 3 (2018): 80, https://doi.org/10.3390/rel9030080.

have an appreciation for and similarities to the pre-critical interpretive methods of premodern patristic and mystic interpreters who strongly prioritize the role of praxis in interpretation.[116] A useful example of this pre-critical praxis approach and its similarities with my proposed pre-enactment praxis is Douglas Burton-Christie's monographic study of fourth-century desert monastics' approach to reading and interpreting the Bible.[117] Burton-Christie argues that the desert monastics considered experience a primary way to interpret biblical texts and to enter more deeply into the world of the text.[118] Far from a linear re-enactment of the text where one's actions follow the prescribed behavior of an already-decided interpretation, the monastics emphasized the unknowability of what a text might mean until it was put into practice. Because texts are meant to be encountered and practiced, the meaning of a sacred text could not be determined until experimented with in praxis. As Burton-Christie concludes, the desert monastics "were convinced that only through *doing* what the text enjoined could one hope to gain any understanding of its meaning."[119] This praxis-centered approach created a dialectic, or what Burton-Christie describes as a hermeneutical circle, of praxis and interpretation where the meaning of the text can only be understood as it is acted out and brought to life.[120]

Of particular interest for this chapter's proposal of a pre-enactment praxis model is the role of the eschatological imagination for these pre-critical interpreters and its dialectical relationship with eschatological participation. The sacred texts did not describe the world only as it is but projected a new world that is yet to come. Therefore, the challenge of the interpreter-practitioner was to pre-enact experimentally that new world as much as possible in order to better imagine and understand the world of possibilities projected by the text.[121] In this way, posits Burton-Christie, "the horizon of one's life could become fused with the horizon of the text" as the transforming power of the text is unleashed in praxis.[122] The scope of the text—and its power to transform

---

116. Archer, *Pentecostal Hermeneutic*, 125. See Timothy B. Cargal, "Beyond the Fundamentalist-Modernist Controversy: Pentecostals and Hermeneutics in a Postmodern Age," *Pneuma* 15, no. 2 (Fall 1993): 163–87; Waddell, *Revelation*, 113. See also discussion in Oliverio, *Theological Hermeneutics*, 190–202. Stephenson sees this pre-critical interpretation of biblical texts by early Pentecostals as "detrimental" (*Types*, 3–4). For a non-Pentecostal endorsement of pre-critical methods, see Steinmetz, "The Superiority of Pre-Critical Exegesis."

117. Douglas Burton-Christie, *The Word in the Desert: Scripture and the Quest for Holiness in Early Christian Monasticism* (Oxford: Oxford University Press, 1993).

118. Burton-Christie, *Word in the Desert*, 23. Burton-Christie says they enter "a personal drama" (299).

119. Burton-Christie, *Word in the Desert*, 135; italics in the original.

120. See Burton-Christie, *Word in the Desert*, 23.

121. Burton-Christie, *Word in the Desert*, 19–20, 153.

122. Burton-Christie, *Word in the Desert*, 153, 165.

individuals and communities—becomes limited without the courage to enter into the future world of possibilities that are "stretching ahead of the sacred texts."[123] And the way to enter into that world is through the experimental acting out (pre-enactment) of the text's eschatological trajectory. Instead of following a prescribed re-enactment of a past world, these pre-critical interpreters saw themselves as potentially pre-enacting future worlds of possibility offered by the texts.[124] Therefore, there was no way to understand the text apart from praxis, for the full meaning was not contained in the words nor could interpretive study alone determine the meaning.

What pre-critical interpreters such as the desert monastics show us is that a pre-enactment praxis model provides the freedom to move beyond the restrictive re-enactment of biblical prescriptions or descriptions. An eschatologically based praxis features texts that project forward and provide room for experiential and experimental actions in dialectical relationship with the promises of the text. A re-enactment praxis model will never work for egalitarian praxis because egalitarian practices are not fully contained within the text, only hints and threads of future promises meant to be (pre)enacted by the reader-interpreter through experimental praxis. As Land argues, "New experiences would often be the occasion for finding new insights into Scripture."[125] Kevin Vanhoozer similarly asserts that the meaning of some biblical texts is not fully "realized" until they are put into practice.[126] Returning to Dulles on the importance of models, he argues that exploratory theological models contain the "capacity to lead to new theological insights."[127] "Thanks to the ongoing experience of the Christian community," he says, we "can discover aspects of the gospel of which Christians were not previously conscious."[128] Thus, without an exploratory pre-enactment praxis model that makes room for a dialectic between experimental participation and imaginative interpretation, lingering uncertainty about the role of women will allow the Pentecostal gender paradox to persist, even if re-enacting the most egalitarian of biblical texts. But Pentecostals can be confident that an eschatological praxis model that leads to newfound freedoms for women is, as the next section shows, still firmly placed in the authority of the biblical story and in line with the historical heart of movement.

---

123. Burton-Christie, *Word in the Desert*, 20, 23. He is citing here the work of Tracy, *Analogical Imagination* (see my Section 3.4.3 for more). The goal of transformation is key to Burton-Christie's understanding of the monastics (see Burton-Christie, 299–300).

124. See Burton-Christie, *Word in the Desert*, 185, 299–300.

125. Land, *Pentecostal Spirituality*, 67.

126. Vanhoozer, "Scripture and Hermeneutics," 47–8. This is part of Vanhoozer's "Theodrama" as a model for biblical interpretation (see also his *Drama of Doctrine*).

127. Dulles, *Models*, 17.

128. Dulles, *Models*, 18.

## 5.4.2 Pre-Enactment and Biblical Authority: The (Ongoing) Eschatological Drama

An important disclaimer for and defense of an eschatological praxis model is that, although experimental and not a strict re-enactment of biblical texts, it does not diminish the authority of the text nor reduce its importance for praxis. On the contrary, it heightens the need to engage with the text. N. T. Wright provides an astute and imaginative way of understanding the authority of the text in a way that supports my praxis model of emphasizing pre-enactment of the future over re-enactment of the past.[129] The Bible, he suggests, is like having the first four acts (Creation, Fall, Israel, Jesus) of a five-act play in which the actors must perform the fifth act in a way that continues, but is still consistent with, the trajectory of the first four acts.[130] In order to make sure the fifth act is a natural progression of the first four acts, the actors must immerse themselves in the first four acts, which are the undoubted "authority" for the final act; any behavior inconsistent with the first four acts would be called into question. However, states Wright, "This 'authority' of the first four acts would not consist—could not consist!—in an implicit command that the actors should repeat the earlier parts of the play over and over again," what I call a re-enactment praxis.[131] Therefore, an eschatological praxis is scriptural, yet unscripted, because the final script does not exist.[132]

Because the first four acts anticipate the fifth act, there is freedom to act with experimental innovation to discover the rightness and fittingness of the last act as it functions dialectically with the text of the preceding acts. Within the known four acts there are "hints of how the play is supposed to end. . . . without making clear the intervening steps," therefore requiring "an improvisatory performance of the final act as it leads up to and anticipates the intended conclusion."[133] Wright concludes that the task of those involved in the final act "is to reflect on, draw out, and implement the *significance* of the first four acts."[134] Wright's helpful model of authority for praxis sheds light on the vital importance of the previous chapter in establishing a unified eschatological–egalitarian narrative thread throughout the "acts" of the Bible. This biblical thread, while still being "in a state of needing

---

129. Including Wright here is not to say that all of his writings or approaches are conducive to Pentecostal theology or hermeneutics. For more on Wright's worldview-model in conversation with Pentecostalism, see Chapter 2 of Mikael Stenhammar, *The Worldview of the Word of Faith Movement: Eden Redeemed* (London: Bloomsbury T&T Clark, 2021). See also Janet Meyer Everts and Jeffrey S. Lamp, eds., *Pentecostal Theology and the Theological Vision of N.T. Wright: A Conversation* (Cleveland, TN: CPT, 2015).

130. See the full discussion of "The Five Acts" in Wright, *New Testament*, 140–3.

131. Wright, *New Testament*, 140.

132. See Castelo, "Improvisational Quality of Ecclesial Holiness," 103–4. This approach avoids the extremes of strict biblicism (the Bible says so) and solely intuition (the Spirit says so). See Stackhouse's Appendix "How Not to Decide on Gender," in *Finally Feminist*.

133. Wright, *New Testament*, 141–2. For more on "performing" the Scriptures see Vanhoozer, "Scripture and Hermeneutics," 48.

134. Wright, *New Testament*, 143; italics in the original.

completion,"¹³⁵ provides the authority for a liberating eschatological–egalitarian praxis that is in line with the biblical eschatological drama and its egalitarian trajectory, something early Pentecostals seemed to innately understand.

Early Pentecostals provide an interesting prototype for the viability of an eschatologically inspired pre-enactment praxis. Pentecostal pioneers desired to take the Bible seriously and rejected actions they deemed outside the scope of the biblical text.¹³⁶ But their understanding of the unfolding eschatological drama, and their place in it, allowed them to move beyond prescriptive re-enactments of the text toward a more experimental and experiential pre-enactment of promises within the text. A strong dialectical relationship existed between the belief that they were participating in eschatological realities and their understanding of the eschatological promises of Scripture. McQueen's study of early Pentecostals found there was no "preconceived eschatological script"; rather, there was an experimental, yet discerning, element to their praxis.¹³⁷ Land's work, which was one of the first to argue for a distinctive eschatological praxis among early Pentecostals,¹³⁸ has led to a growing list of scholars concluding, based on historical study, that early Pentecostal praxis was fueled primarily by eschatological concerns, including gender praxis.¹³⁹

In their work on early Pentecostal attitudes towards women, Barfoot and Sheppard argue that one of the main factors responsible for furthering equality between the sexes in Pentecostal ministry was "the community's eschatological belief that they were experiencing the 'latter rain' (Joel 2:23) in which 'your sons *and your daughters will prophesy*' (Joel 2:28)."¹⁴⁰ Eschatological participation in equality was more important than any official statements or doctrines. The egalitarian message and actions of many early Pentecostals found traction because they were placed in the context of eschatological hope; that is, women's increasing participation was a way of preparing the church for Christ's coming by pre-enacting what they believed the coming world would look like.¹⁴¹ Early Pentecostals believed they were participating in and advancing the unfolding eschatological drama through their Spirit-inspired egalitarian practices that

---

135. Wright, *New Testament*, 141.

136. Of course, see my Chapters 2 and 3 for fuller discussion of the brief argument here.

137. McQueen, *Pentecostal Eschatology*, 215. See also 296.

138. See discussion in my previous chapters, including the Introduction, but see also Land, *Pentecostal Spirituality*, 91–3, 114–15. This discovery led to Land's call for a contemporary eschatological activism among Pentecostals (see 73, 114, 224).

139. These works have already been discussed, especially in Chapter 2, but the literature is convincing on this point. See specifically Tackett, "Callings," 74; Althouse's study in *Moltmann*, 61–107; McQueen, *Pentecostal Eschatology*, 121; Ware, "Spiritual Egalitarianism," 231; Faupel, *Everlasting Gospel*, 20–3; Kenyon, "Ethical Issues," 402, 419–21; Archer, *Pentecostal Hermeneutic*, 171.

140. Barfoot and Sheppard, "Prophetic vs. Priestly," 4; italics in the original.

141. See Althouse, *Moltmann*, 28.

were pre-enactments of and preparation for the promised coming kingdom.[142] As the latter rain motif suggests, they were not pursuing re-enactments of past or prescribed biblical events but fresh experiences that gave new insight into the eschatological promises within the text.[143] Liberating practices for women emerged when Pentecostals sought to conform not to the present but to the world that was to come, and these practices continually fueled their eschatological imagination. This eschatologically inspired, experimental-dialectical praxis was the foundation for early Pentecostals' theological beliefs and articulations, including on the role of women.

Ecclesial restrictions upon women are eradicated when an eschatological praxis is adopted. Inequality between the genders, fueled by re-enactment praxis models, is out of step with the eschatological trajectory and drama of the biblical text, which teaches that the future gift of gender equality is a promise meant to be pre-enacted in the present.[144] As Pentecostals pre-enact eschatological–egalitarian promises rather than re-enact cultural complementarian prescriptions, they are free to become the present embodiment of the eschatological equality of God's kingdom, a hermeneutical act providing "tangible evidence of eschatological inevitability."[145] But just how far does this freedom extend? If the fullest extent of the promise is still in the future, are there justified limitations for praxis on this side of the *eschaton*? The last section addresses these potential concerns regarding the pre-enactment of eschatological–egalitarian promises.

### 5.4.3 Potential Concerns

Before applying the proposed praxis model in the next chapter, clarifications on three potential concerns regarding an eschatological praxis may be helpful. First, some may argue suggesting practices based on pre-enacting eschatological promises presents an over-realized eschatology, that is, expecting now what is only reserved for the future.[146] I am not proposing that an eschatological praxis model should be applied to *every* situation of Pentecostal life. An over-realized eschatology could be problematic for some theological issues such as divine healing, sanctification, or our eschatological union with God. However, when it comes to issues of equality and justice, concerns over an over-realized eschatology do not apply. The eschatological–egalitarian promises of Genesis 1–2, Galatians

---

142. See Faupel, *Everlasting Gospel*, 116; Green, *Lord's Supper*, 76; Tackett, "Callings," 86.
143. See Mittelstadt, "Reimagining Luke-Acts," 32; Land, *Pentecostal Spirituality*, 67. See 3.1.2 for more on the latter rain motif.
144. McQueen, *Joel*, 54; Cf. Gal. 5:25.
145. Augustine, *Pentecost*, 140. See also her *Spirit and the Common Good*, 60.
146. A common complementarian argument or concession is that yes, there will be no distinction in roles between men and women in the *eschaton*, but God has ordained temporary gender roles or hierarchy for the time being for the sake of order and structure in this world.

3:28, and Acts 2 are good news now, not just for the future.[147] Rather than conforming to the present form of this world that "is passing away," believers are to conform to the age that is to come to the fullest extent possible.[148] Gender equality may not be fully perfected on this side of the *eschaton*. The gender praxis problem may always exist to some extent as we attempt to practice the ideal of the *eschaton* in the midst of the real, the sinful structures and human brokenness that are not yet fully redeemed.[149] Even so, we must still do everything possible to reflect and anticipate the equality that is to come and "to actualize the new age in the midst of the old,"[150] pre-enacting God's egalitarian kingdom even in the midst of patriarchal and sexist systems. Although our actions alone cannot bring about the fullness of future equality, we are still called to act in eschatological fidelity to what we know is promised and in the process participate in the unfolding eschatological drama that is transforming all creation.[151] In this way, egalitarian practices become signposts and anticipations of the final equality of God's kingdom.[152]

A second concern is the potential "risk" involved in adopting a model that is a pre-enactment of something that is promised rather than a re-enactment of something prescribed. Whereas the latter instills confidence in those desiring a dogmatic approach to praxis and leads to definitive actions, the former involves imaginative and dialectical experimentation and improvisation that requires a malleable approach to praxis. Therefore, the next chapter, while proposing an eschatological-egalitarian praxis, is only a starting point for exploring the trajectory of egalitarian possibilities based on eschatological promises, rather than a strict or immutable ecclesiastical model. Rather than a linear and potentially hierarchical approach where decisions concerning gender are made on paper from an ivory tower, an eschatological approach must allow for experimentation on the ground and involve people—always a risk!—in the hermeneutical process. Still, sustaining an eschatological praxis is not possible without actual theoretical articulation, which is part of the reason for this chapter, and which also leads to the third concern about the role of the intellect in an imaginative, praxis-oriented model.

An eschatological approach to gender recruits the imagination more than the intellect so that transformative praxis is given priority over the formation of opinions. However, one must recognize the (ironic) truth that only the intellect

---

147. See Sallie McFague, *Models of God: Theology for an Ecological, Nuclear Age* (Philadelphia: Fortress, 1987), 44.

148. 1 Cor. 7:29-31; Cf. Matt. 6:10; Rom. 12:2; Eph. 1:10-11. The advice on marriage in 1 Cor. 7 is a good example.

149. See Yong, *Renewing*, 184.

150. Snodgrass, "Galatians 3:28," 179; See Wright, *Surprised by Hope*, 221.

151. See Althouse, "Pentecostal Eschatology," 214; Bauckham and Hart, *Hope Against Hope*, 182-3; Hart, "Eschatology," 267.

152. See Land, *Pentecostal Spirituality*, 45.

can establish its own inferiority to the imagination.¹⁵³ So "while the goal is practical, the way there is theoretical."¹⁵⁴ Although Pentecostals must *show* more than *tell* the world God's plan for gender equality,¹⁵⁵ the articulation or telling of an eschatological–egalitarian ethic still plays a crucial role in establishing a liberating praxis for women in the church. Although this chapter presents an intellectual basis for an eschatological–egalitarian praxis, the goal is the transformation of women and men through actual practices that recruit the eschatological imagination.

Proposing a model or theory—important as it is—is not the same as attaining or practicing it.¹⁵⁶ As Dulles contends, we assess models "by living out the consequences to which they point."¹⁵⁷ Therefore, an important disclaimer for this chapter and this project as a whole is what Burton-Christie discovered as foundational to the pre-critical approach of the desert monastics: "more words about the meaning of a particular text would not contribute as much toward clarifying its meaning as a humble attempt to practice it."¹⁵⁸ Therefore, the next chapter precedes the current chapter in importance, even if following it in order. The Pentecostal gender praxis problem exists largely because theory or models have been given more attention than actual practices and rarely do the two complement each other or receive equal attention in a single work. Smith argues that transformation is often lacking because we have used "flawed models . . . that have focused on convincing the intellect rather than recruiting the imagination."¹⁵⁹ Smith expects that when our imaginations are persuaded (more than our intellect), we will begin "*acting* in ways that embody" the coming kingdom.¹⁶⁰ Taking it a (dialectical) step forward, I argue that our participatory actions also help inspire (and grow) our imagination. The practical urgency of eschatological participation fuels the theological authority of the eschatological imagination and vice versa.

Adopting an eschatological praxis model presents some challenges, but mostly opportunities to participate in a hope-filled praxis that leads to a more just and egalitarian church and society.¹⁶¹ Concerns over an over-realized eschatology are invalid for a problem that is within our power to change, even if we eagerly await the fullness of its promise. No praxis model is perfect, but humility should not hinder the church from bold, even risky, experimentation based on eschatological promises. A pre-enactment model must prioritize the imagination

---

153. Smith, *Imagining*, xiii, 16. Smith is following Proust here (see 40–1, 73).
154. Smith, *Imagining*, 40.
155. To *show* more than *tell* is a part of Smith's argument (*Imagining*, 163).
156. See Burton-Christie, *Word in the Desert*, 161.
157. Dulles, *Models*, 19.
158. Burton-Christie, *Word in the Desert*, 155.
159. Smith, *Imagining*, 39.
160. Smith, *Imagining*, 157; italics in the original.
161. See Carbine, "Re-visioning the Public Church in a Feminist Perspective," 190. Carbine is concerned with political praxis and participation in her chapter, not the inner ecclesial praxis of the church (173).

over the dogmatic prescriptions and intellectual propositions of a re-enactment praxis, even if theoretical articulation helps bring us to that conclusion. Some risk is inherent in an eschatological praxis,[162] but also new possibilities to solve the gender praxis problem, aligning a strong hermeneutic with a liberating praxis. There must be room for experimental praxis as a part of the hermeneutical task; the dialectic does not work without it. It is this part of the eschatological dialectic or hermeneutical circle that this chapter has sought to explain and the next chapter practically applies. Proposing eschatology as the methodological starting point for approaching the gender question has the potential not only to close the gap between theory and practice but also to render the praxis gap nonexistent because of the interdependent relationship between eschatology and praxis.

## 5.5 Conclusion

This chapter connects several arguments that move this book closer to resolving the Pentecostal gender paradox while also making some original and important contributions to the general fields of theological praxis and eschatology. Previous Pentecostal works on gender have failed to connect an authorizing hermeneutical model for the ministry of women with a convincing and liberating egalitarian praxis model, creating a decades-long gender praxis problem in Pentecostalism. Thus, the purpose of this chapter was to create an eschatologically oriented praxis model consistent with the hermeneutical arguments of the previous chapters and their proposed dialectic. Rather than moving directly into practical suggestions that are potentially detached from the previous biblical-theological arguments, I have first constructed a praxis model that firmly connects theory with praxis and that informs and inspires the proposals in the closing chapter. I have suggested the viability of using pre-enactment theory as a form of eschatological praxis over against re-enactment praxis models that are unable to solve the gender problem for Pentecostals. To my knowledge, this is the first attempt to apply pre-enactment specifically to Christian practice.

This chapter (and especially the next) creates an example of how to solve what I have termed simply as the "Pentecostal gender praxis problem" and "eschatological praxis problem." To date, both theological works on women's equality in the church and eschatological works in general have suffered from a praxis deficit. An eschatological–egalitarian praxis has the potential to solve both problems and make a significant contribution to both fields. The eschatological pre-enactment praxis model proposed in this chapter and applied in the next offers an authoritative solution to the gender praxis problem because it is not an afterthought, a disconnected appendix to a theological argument that has already concluded. Rather, it is an essential part, perhaps even the starting point, of my proposed eschatological method and hermeneutic. Because Pentecostal theology

---

162. See Shields, *Eschatological Imagination*, 176.

is a "living praxis,"[163] moving toward an eschatological–egalitarian praxis is an essential and connected part of developing an eschatological–egalitarian theology.

Strict re-enactment praxis of past biblical events or prescriptions regarding gender is not a model compliant with current Pentecostal scholarship or the eschatological heart of the Pentecostal movement. This model, even when applied to more liberating texts, still upholds the gender paradox which limits the possibilities for women to freely act out their God-given callings. I have instead argued for an eschatological pre-enactment praxis model for gender roles that is dialectical, experiential, and experimental. This model displays fidelity to the egalitarian trajectory of the biblical text, contemporary developments in Pentecostal thought, current trends in eschatology, and the historical eschatological heart of the movement. Pentecostal gender praxis should not be confined to re-enacting past biblical events or prescriptions, but rather pre-enacting biblical eschatological–egalitarian promises that lead to complete freedom for women to act out their ecclesiastical vocations. Because Pentecostalism is a praxis-centered, eschatologically oriented movement, it is primely situated to embrace a fully liberating eschatological praxis for women and men in the church. The next chapter seeks to apply this liberating praxis model in the areas of Pentecostal leadership, education, and worship.

---

163. Vondey, *Pentecostal Theology*, 16–17, 28.

## Chapter 6

### PARTICIPATING IN THE *ESCHATON*

### TOWARD A PENTECOSTAL ESCHATOLOGICAL-EGALITARIAN PRAXIS

The goal of this chapter is to critically apply the eschatological hermeneutic and pre-enactment praxis model proposed in the previous chapters to ecclesial situations that are typically male-dominated in order to eschatologically reimagine Pentecostal gender praxis. Patriarchal gender practices within the three areas of Pentecostal organizational leadership, theological education, and corporate worship are critically examined under an eschatological lens for the purpose of modifying them—or in some cases constructing new practices—to correspond to the eschatological-egalitarian biblical trajectory proposed in the previous chapters. With the history, hermeneutics, and theory of an eschatological solution to the gender problem firmly articulated, the task remaining is to suggest how Pentecostals might confidently and practically pre-enact God's eschatological-egalitarian kingdom. Therefore, this chapter answers the all-important question of what an eschatological approach to gender looks like on the ground, while providing an important contribution to both the gender and eschatological praxis problem laid out in the previous chapter. The argument of this chapter is that an eschatologically based gender praxis is able both to *correct* practices that are male-dominated or favor the male experience as well as to *construct* practices that are congruent with the eschatological-egalitarian hermeneutic of imagination and participation proposed in this work. Pentecostal gender praxis based on present participation in eschatological-egalitarian realities has the power and potential to provide full freedom for women to live out their callings and use their voices in the church without restriction.

This chapter is likely the most challenging of this work. The purpose of the proposed eschatological hermeneutic is to create change in practices, to cut through the indecision, ambiguity, and inconsistency of the Pentecostal gender paradox. However, the eschatological emphasis of Pentecostalism has not been widely applied to Pentecostal ecclesiology or concrete practices;[1] few examples exist that flesh out the practical implications of one's eschatological existence,

---

1. Vondey, *Pentecostal Theology*, 249. For more on Pentecostal ecclesiology, see Vondey, *Pentecostal Theology*, 225–53. See discussion in the previous chapter, esp. 5.3.4.

despite many calls to do so.² The greatest challenge is not so much to create an eschatological argument for gender equality or to know what is eschatologically true. The challenge lies in implementing practices congruent with one's eschatological convictions, acting on the eschatological possibilities of the biblical text.³ Discovering eschatology as an early Pentecostal authorizing hermeneutic for the ministry of women (Chapter 2), establishing a unified eschatological–egalitarian biblical narrative thread (Chapter 4), and creating a preferred model for an eschatologically based praxis (Chapter 5) matters only to the extent that these arguments are brought to life in Pentecostal congregations and institutions. If all of history is moving toward an end where women are free to lead without restriction, how can the church as eschatological community participate in and represent those realities fully in the present?⁴

This chapter seeks to correct and construct gender practices eschatologically in the three areas of Pentecostal leadership, education, and worship. One chapter is not able to develop fully the gender practices for *all* aspects of these three areas. Therefore, each section focuses on select ways leaders can reimagine practices to be congruent with the eschatological–egalitarian ideal. Even so, the scope of this chapter is quite broad and requires justifications. First, eschatological pre-enactment praxis is dialectical, experiential, and experimental (Chapter 5). Rather than stating a static set of prescriptions on how Pentecostals might re-enact past biblical events, the proposed praxis encourages a dynamic interaction with the biblical text, believing experience can provide a hermeneutical lens for understanding Scripture.⁵ Churches can experiment with practices that seek to participate in the eschatological ideal of gender equality and the current unfolding eschatological drama that moves in that direction. Therefore, the idea is to give enough suggestions and space to "play" with a praxis model that is ongoing in its movement toward eschatological egalitarianism and its constant dialectic of imagination and participation.⁶ It is not the style of feminist or liberationist works

---

2. For example, see McQueen, *Joel*, 54–7. Pentecostal ecclesiology in general is fairly un(der)developed. See John Christopher Thomas, "1998 Presidential Address: Pentecostal Theology in the Twenty-First Century," *Pneuma* 20, no. 1 (Spring 1998): 17. See also Warrrington, *Pentecostal Theology*, 131–79 for further discussion. However, see Simon Chan, "Mother Church: Toward a Pentecostal Ecclesiology," *Pneuma* 22, no. 2 (Fall 2010): 177–208, as well as his Chapter 4 "Pentecostal Ecclesiology" in Chan, *Pentecostal Theology*.

3. See Alexander and Gause, *Women*, 109; Shields, *Eschatological Imagination*, 170.

4. For the church as eschatological community or people of God, see Yong, *Renewing*, 93; Vondey, *Pentecostal Theology*, 249–53; Avery Dulles, "The Church as Eschatological Community," in *The Eschaton: A Community of Love*, ed. Joseph Papin (Villanova, PA: Villanova University Press, 1971), 69–103.

5. See Studebaker, *From Pentecost to the Triune God*, 30.

6. Althouse discusses ritual or liturgical play as an important part of Pentecostal worship and for worshipping eschatologically, as play helps people envision alternative futures and break chains of oppression (Peter Althouse, "Betwixt and Between the Cross

to end a book with "the answers," for there are not always easy answers in the mess of injustice and real situations.[7] Furthermore, for Pentecostals, room must be left for "surprises of the Spirit" that may "rightly reorder the world in anticipation of the coming rule of God."[8]

Second, although the chapter does contain important theological contributions in several areas, the purpose of this chapter is not to develop a theology of Pentecostal leadership, education, or worship. That task has been taken up by Pentecostal scholars elsewhere. Rather, the goal is to give diverse examples of how gender practices can be eschatologically reimagined in various Pentecostal contexts. My work does not want to make the same mistake of many other biblical-theological works on gender as well as eschatological works in general, namely, offering very few suggestions on how ideas are actualized on the ground.[9]

My conviction throughout this work is that the biblically inspired eschatological imagination leads to participation in those eschatological realities in the present (and vice versa). This chapter aims to expand the repertoire of eschatological–egalitarian participation into the three areas of Pentecostal leadership, education, and worship. Each section for the three areas will critique male-dominated gender practices and images, many based on the inconsistency of re-enactment praxis, and then construct gender practices based on the authority, consistency, and hermeneutical priority of eschatological texts on gender and suggest how the church might pre-enact those eschatological promises. The specific practices addressed were chosen due to their tendency to be male-dominated and their debated status when it comes to equal female participation or representation. These are areas where women are sometimes strictly prohibited from leading or, more commonly, significantly underrepresented in their numbers, underheard in their voices, or overlooked in their experiences due to patriarchal systems. An effective feminist contribution to ecclesial practices must be able to both correct patriarchal practices that marginalize, omit, silence, or limit women, as well as (re)construct new praxis paradigms for how the church can fully support and give opportunity for the callings, gifts, and voices of women.[10]

The order of the sections intentionally moves from the macro-level of organizational structures and institutional practices to the micro-level of the localized context of church worship services where change can happen more

---

and the Eschaton: Pentecostal Worship in the Context of Ritual Play," in Martin, *Theology of Worship*, 276, 278–89). See Jean-Jacques Suurmond, *Word and Spirit at Play: Towards a Charismatic Theology*, trans. John Bowden (Grand Rapids: Eerdmans, 1995).

7. See Russell, *Household*, 87–8.
8. Yong, *Renewing*, 78.
9. See the "praxis problems" of the previous chapter.
10. For this "twofold approach" in feminist theology, see Susan Frank Parsons, "Preface," xiv. See also Procter-Smith's "marks" of a feminist liturgy ("Feminist Ritual Strategies," 501) as well as Ruether's comments on how a feminist approach changes practices in the church (*Sexism*, 193).

readily. An eschatological–egalitarian praxis can make faster inroads in localized worship settings where practices can change with less difficulty, which is why that section is the longest, contains the most suggestions, and acts as the culmination to my work. However, women will never be truly "free" to lead on the local level while institutional structures and educational practices continue to exclude them and their voices, whether intentionally or unintentionally. Therefore, the chapter seeks to first address these more difficult—and sometimes subtle—areas of exclusion. Change in practices may be implemented more slowly in these contexts, but my contention is that an eschatological praxis has the best chance to create change and to cut through the hesitancy concerning women's leadership in these areas. The praxis suggestions of each section are primarily geared toward Pentecostal leaders and pastors, those who have the influence to correct practices and construct new ways of leading, educating, and worshipping in conformity to eschatological–egalitarian promises.[11]

## 6.1 Organizational Leadership: Reifying Eschatological Equality

Reification has become a popular term in literature on communities of practice and participation.[12] In principle, reification refers to taking an abstract concept—here eschatological equality—and giving it physical representation. If a community of people or organization wants to achieve a certain way of doing things, it must discern how their vision will be made real in the life of the community to ensure participation in the vision. Explaining concepts to a congregation or community is not enough; ideas must be intentionally reified through concrete actions. For Pentecostals, simply explaining the eschatological–egalitarian trajectory of Pentecost or having policy or possibilities on paper will not achieve the desired outcomes. Pentecostal institutions and churches must find ways to intentionally reify the eschatological–egalitarian structure of God's reign through actual participation in its realities and by dismantling hierarchical gender structures, which typically favor men and the male experience. This section gives practical suggestions on how to do so in both denominational structures and the local church.

### 6.1.1 In Denominational Structures

In order for Pentecostals to construct practices that are congruent with the egalitarian structure of the coming kingdom, they must configure organizational

---

11. See also the "Impact" section of my Conclusion for some pastoral-type advice to Pentecostal leaders.

12. For a helpful overview, see Etienne Wenger, *Communities of Practice: Learning, Meaning, and Identity* (Cambridge: Cambridge University Press, 1998), 55–9.

leadership in a way that reifies the church's eschatological destiny.[13] As Russell argues, appealing to the "authority of the future" helps the church find the energy and vision for implementing structures that reflect the eschatological new community.[14] Non-egalitarian structures—namely, a lack of women in visible and prominent leadership roles—must be corrected, as they provide a distorted vision of God's eschatological intent, and they rob the church of the opportunity to provide a visible witness of God's future reign.[15] As an eschatological movement of the Spirit, Pentecostalism must find ways to intentionally reify eschatological expectations in present denominational and ecclesiastical structures in order to manifest the message it claims to bear.[16]

Women often feel isolated, objectified, marginalized, and even feared at the highest levels of leadership due to spoken and unspoken "rules" that hinder women from institutional decision-making.[17] The research on women in Pentecostal institutional leadership by both Catford and Alexander reveals a system of male patronage and a masculine culture that reflects the leadership style of men and leaves little room for the leadership qualities of women.[18] Women have lamented the difficulty in finding female examples and mentors on the denominational level as there are often no "prominent" or high profile women in visible Pentecostal denominational leadership.[19] A lack of an egalitarian leadership model and vision not only hurts women but also robs men in various ways, including the opportunity to learn from the "other half" of the church.[20] Eschatological–egalitarian realities

13. See Grenz and Kjesbo, *Women in the Church*, 178; McQueen, *Joel*, 55.

14. Russell, *Household*, 68; see also Grenz and Kjesbo, *Women in the Church,* 192.

15. Leeuwen, *Gender and Grace*, 46; Dempster, "Eschatology," 167, 186. See also Stephenson, *Dismantling*, 135.

16. See Moltmann, "Foreword," vii; Gutiérrez, *Theology of Liberation*, 147.

17. See Alexander and Bowers, *What Women Want*, 124–8. An example would be the so-called "Billy Graham rule" (see Tish Harrison Warren, "An Open Letter to Men Who Broke the Billy Graham Rule," *InterVarsity: Women in the Academy and Professions Blog*, April 4, 2017, http://thewell.intervarsity.org/blog /open-letter-men-who-broke-bil ly-graham-rule). See the experience of Jo Anne Lyon in her position of denominational leadership, "Men and Women Working Together," *Wesleyan Life*, accessed on April 25, 2022, at: https://wesleyan.life/men-and-women-working-together. See also Chopp, "Eve's Knowing," esp. 117–22; Roberta C. Bondi, *Memories of God: Theological Reflections on a Life* (Nashville: Abingdon, 1995), 60–4. According to Ruether, institutional structure is one of two specific areas where the church alienates women (the other being worship, addressed in 6.3). See Ruether, *Sexism*, 193.

18. See Catford, "Women's Experiences," 39–41; Alexander (in her summary of four early Pentecostal women leaders), *Limited Liberty*, 156.

19. Alexander and Bowers, *What Women Want*, 91–4.

20. See Ruether, *Sexism*, 179, 189–94. For more on how macho-masculinity harms men, even leading to health problems, see Russell, *Future*, 91. One example is that non-egalitarian positions or "separate spheres" ideology may overlook men's contributions in

cannot be experienced in Pentecostal circles if, as Yong observes, "more than half of its constituency is subordinated to the rest and/or marginalized from the centers of power and authority."[21] Overall, women report feeling trapped in a system of "vocational oppression" that promotes dependency upon male leaders rather than equal partnership between the sexes.[22]

What Alexander specifically found in her historical research of early female Pentecostal denominational leaders was that no articulated praxis framework existed that allowed future women to sustain the legacy of women's leadership,[23] opening the door for the gender paradox of the past century. There remains a "stained-glass ceiling" for women in leadership at the executive level of Pentecostal denominations.[24] For decades, men have been making decisions *for* women without women having a voice at the Pentecostal "men-only table of decision-making."[25] This male hierarchy trickles down into the local church, which is why this section (and chapter) begins with denominational structures and then moves to the local level. The more Pentecostal institutions intentionally reify eschatological equality, the more women at the local church level will be encouraged and empowered to lead.

The exclusion of women at the institutional level is at times subtle. Therefore, the development and promotion of an eschatological sensitivity and consciousness within denominations can help Pentecostals expose and correct non-egalitarian practices that reify male dominance. The interviews and research conducted by Alexander and Bowers report that Pentecostal women find an inhospitable environment within denominational structures and events.[26] They are often excluded from texts or photographs in denominational materials such as magazines and conference promotions. Minister retreats, support groups, and national and regional denominational meetings are dominated by men and male speakers and assume the participants are men (such as the still common use of the term "pastors' wives").[27] They do not address the lives, needs, and ministries of women ministers. Fewer than a quarter of women ministers felt

---

the home and in parenting (see Leeuwen, *Gender and Grace*, 10–11, and her chapter "The Case for Co-Parenting," 145–63; Stackhouse, *Partners*, 136, 151–7; Williams, "Evangelicals and Gender," 280–1). For the "stages" of the male conversion journey, see Ruether, *Sexism*, 189–91. Cf. Johns, "Conscientization," 153.

21. Yong, *Spirit Poured Out*, 191. See also here Ambrose, "Shaming the Men," 79–81.
22. Alexander and Bowers, *What Women Want*, 127, 124.
23. Alexander, *Limited Liberty*, 156.
24. See Stanley, "Shattering the Stained-Glass Ceiling," 83–6.
25. Alexander and Bowers, *What Women Want*, 123, 125.
26. The proceeding sentences follow the findings of Alexander and Bowers, *What Women Want*, esp. 82–3, 89, 91–3, 112–14, 124–8.
27. Anecdotally, while attending my wife's ordination retreat for the PAOC *as her spouse*, it was repeatedly assumed by leaders and participants without asking that *I* was the one seeking ordination.

denominational meetings and conferences encouraged their full participation and about half report "no support from denominational leaders" in their calling.[28] This situation can, and should, be corrected by the Pentecostal eschatological imagination. Pre-enacting eschatological ideals will ensure women hold positions of denominational leadership and provide intentional supports for female pastors and leaders. Denomination materials and conference promotions should clearly reify the expectation that women leaders and ministers will be participating. Furthermore, conference committees can require women's voices at the planning table, and participants can ask how a conference or event meets the needs of women ministers or encourages their participation.

Organizational structures within Pentecostal denominations and institutions must be intentionally corrected to accommodate and reify eschatological truths. In the words of Qualls, Pentecostal denominations must "put their rhetoric into action."[29] And as a "rhetoric of hope," eschatology "demands action."[30] One good example reported by Qualls is the Assemblies of God Women in Ministry Taskforce of the late 1990s.[31] This denominational taskforce was established not to create new policy or debate the gender issue, but rather to partner with local churches in order to reconcile existing egalitarian policy with actual practices.[32] Denominations can intentionally, through legislative action if necessary, promote and elect women to executive leadership positions and national governing bodies (and not just positions specifically intended to represent women!) as ways of reifying eschatological equality.[33] This increase in women leaders at the national and district levels will result in the voices of women pastors and leaders being equally heard at denominational events and conferences, a must for the gathered eschatological church. These practices must be reified not only in broader ecclesial structures and institutions of Pentecostal denominations but also in the local church. Equal access to and representation in local church senior leadership and in the pulpit is a necessary and crucial step in reifying eschatological equality in Pentecostal churches, which in turn will also prepare women leaders for potential inclusion on the denominational level.

### 6.1.2 In the Local Church

Patricia Dorsey's study of Southwest Assembly of God in Houston, TX reveals a common pattern: "Although women can hold any position at Southwest Assembly of God, there has never been a female Communion Elder, Trustee, Deacon, or

---

28. Alexander and Bowers, *What Women Want*, 112, 61. Crabtree and Qualls had similar findings in their survey of AG women ("Women," 314–16).
29. Qualls, *Forgive Us*, 185.
30. Shields, *Eschatological Imagination*, 173.
31. See Qualls, *Forgive Us*, 185–7.
32. Qualls, *Forgive Us*, 184.
33. See the example of the AG in 2017 reported by Qualls, *Forgive Us*, 199.

Senior Pastor. . . . Women have not served in any major decision-making capacity at the church."[34] While nothing on paper or in policy would hinder women from leading in these ways "the church body seems to prefer male leadership" and "congregants seemed content with the gender status quo."[35] Dorsey's study suggests that a monopoly of male leadership exists in Pentecostal churches so that only "half the church" is often represented in leadership.[36] Recent studies indicate that although the percentage of credentialed women ministers is growing, the number of women in lead or senior pastor positions has remained very low, less than 1 percent in some of the largest Pentecostal denominations.[37] Larger and more influential churches are even less likely to have women in a lead role or significant leadership roles.[38] As Hollingsworth and Browning explain, Pentecostal church leadership tends to be male-dominated and contains "deep-seated structural hindrances that prevent women from occupying top ministerial positions."[39] But as "the interim eschatological community," which provides a blueprint for and pre-enactments of God's egalitarian kingdom, Pentecostal churches must find ways to reify their eschatological–egalitarian beliefs or else risk reflecting a broken, backward-looking reality of the church instead of the flourishing and forward-looking community they are called to be.[40]

Co-equal representation in church leadership is the eschatological–egalitarian trajectory presented in passages such as Genesis 1–2 and Acts 2.[41] Many feminist works on the church, including Pentecostal ones, call for the elimination of all clericalism and hierarchical systems to correct and completely re-construct the failed patriarchal structure of the church. These helpful and thought-provoking works claim liberation for women is impossible within the existing incompatible structures that disempower women and perpetuate patriarchal tendencies.[42] They

---

34. Patricia Dorsey, "Southwest Assembly of God: Whomsoever Will," in *Religion and the New Immigrants: Continuities and Adaptations in Immigrant Congregations*, ed. Helen Rose Ebaugh and Janet Saltzman Chafetz (Walnut Creek, CA: AltaMira, 2000), 251.

35. Dorsey, "Southwest Assembly of God," 251, 253.

36. See Carolyn Custis James, *Half the Church: Recapturing God's Global Vision for Women* (Grand Rapids: Zondervan, 2011).

37. Such as the AG USA (see "Female Lead Pastors: A Discussion Worth Having," 1). Others place the number of churches led by women somewhere between 4 and 11 percent. See studies by Alexander and Bowers, *What Women Want*, 107; Crabtree and Qualls, "Women," 296. Cf. Ruether, *Sexism*, 178.

38. Alexander and Bowers, *What Women Want*, 119–20.

39. Hollingsworth and Browning, "Daughters," 169.

40. J. Christian Beker, *Paul the Apostle: The Triumph of God in Life and Thought* (Philadelphia: Fortress, 1980), 326; Stephenson, *Dismantling*, 189.

41. See previous discussion and Ruether, *Sexism*, 102; Nordling, "Gender," 502.

42. See, for example, Ruether, *Sexism*, 200–1, 206–7; Nicola Slee's chapter, "In Search of a Round Table: Ecclesiology in Feminist Perspective," in her *Faith and Feminism: An Introduction to Christian Feminist Theology* (London: Darton, Longman and Todd, 2003),

therefore call for a radical egalitarianism that removes all titles, official positions, and structures from the church. I have and will draw from these works for practical suggestions that help move toward the eschatological–egalitarian ideal. However, although I agree that "flatter structures" in churches will help women,[43] that ministry cannot be confined to clergy,[44] and that the activity of the Spirit often "subverts the status quo of the powerful,"[45] my approach is slightly less radical.

The proposal here recognizes that some form of structure—and the ubiquity of a "lead" or "senior" pastor—is likely to continue to exist in most Pentecostal churches,[46] although the hope is churches might reconsider some of those practices. But I am not arguing, as other works do, for the elimination of positions, ordination, or authority or power of any kind. Rather, I propose the eschatological redefining of power and authority as partnership instead of domination, a heightened emphasis on mutuality, and the inclusion of women at all levels of leadership in ways that reflect the eschatological–egalitarian trajectory of the Scriptures.[47] Therefore, the focus here is pragmatic, namely, how to correct the exclusion of women in positions of ecclesiastical power and move toward constructing a more equal and shared leadership between women and men as a way of participating in and reifying eschatological equality.

This reification of eschatological–egalitarian beliefs can be done in both grand and minor ways as all the activities and decisions of a church communicate or reify *something* about their beliefs. In churches where a woman is not the "lead" pastor but in a "support" role, churches may consider titles that reify less hierarchy and represent the shared leadership structure and co-equal responsibility to care for the church. This mutuality of responsibility can also be reified by listing the pastors in various orders on the church website or bulletin, rather than the usually male "senior" pastor always being listed first.[48] Other important eschatological

---

83–94, esp. 85; Stephenson, *Dismantling*, 3–4, 148, 167, and esp. 182–7. This, of course, is a key part of Stephenson's thesis that the current system of hierarchy must be dismantled, a Pentecostal "Exodus Community from Patriarchy" (see 175–80). Procter-Smith makes the important point that women can exercise dominion over men or other women, which is equality problematic for egalitarian leadership ("Feminist Ritual Strategies," 503).

43. See Crabtree and Qualls, "Women," 310, 313.
44. Macchia, "Baptized in the Spirit," 19.
45. Smith, *Tongues*, 45.
46. See Crumbley, "Sanctified Saints," 134.
47. For a similar approach, see here Russell, *Household*, 21–5, who calls for an alternative paradigm for exercising authority in new ways that reflect God's new household (using Jesus as example) and produce empowerment rather than dependence, ushering in the new kingdom of God (see also 66, 92). But Russell also does elsewhere suggest the possibility of creating communities that transcend the clergy-laity barrier (*Future*, 135).
48. See similar suggestions by Stephenson, *Dismantling*, 187.

reifications for Pentecostal churches include adopting co-gender ministry models,[49] requiring equal representation on church boards, fully accepting clergy couples without stereotyping one as the "pastor's wife" or insisting one (usually the male) must be more "in charge" than the other,[50] legitimizing the roles women hold with official titles such as pastor,[51] showing a "preferential option for women" in hiring,[52] and compensating women pastors equally to men (which is currently not the case in Pentecostal churches).[53] Steps like these move beyond "tolerating" women in ministry and toward constructing practices congruent with eschatological-egalitarian thinking.[54] Church leadership and decision-making must include the equal voice of women and men if it is to be an eschatological community. So-called "token representation" of women is not the goal,[55] but full and equal participation in church leadership. These small, but important, reifications within the church need to be supported with larger steps in key and visible areas of influence such as preaching.

In addition to using eschatological inclusivity in story and language from the pulpit—the *what* and *how* of preaching argued for in the worship section below—the very act of female preaching and leadership (the *who*) is a primary way for women to exercise their eschatological authority to lead and to recruit the eschatological imagination of the congregation.[56] Although many Pentecostal churches may "allow" women preachers or claim equal opportunity or access to the proclamation of the Word, very few reify their beliefs in the pulpit.[57] The absence of women in the pulpit slows or even reverses the eschatological

---

49. Stephanie L. Nance and Ava Kate Oleson, "Living a Theology of Co-Gender Ministry," in English de Alminana and Olena, *Women*, 349–67.

50. See Russell, *Future*, 130; Donna Day-Laver, "Clergy Couples: Are They Working?" *Daughters of Sarah* 3, no. 2 (March 1977): 1–3. For an opposing view, see Gordon T. Smith, "Spouses as Co-Pastors?" *Institutionally Sound: Leading Organizations to Mission Effectiveness Blog*, March 12, 2018, http://www.institutionalintelligence.ca/archive/spouses-as-co-pastors/.

51. Alexander and Gause, *Women*, 112.

52. Alexander and Gause, *Women*, 112. See the previously cited resource from AG leaders, "Female Lead Pastors: A Discussion Worth Having."

53. See the research by Alexander and Bowers on the "gender pay gap" in Pentecostal ministry (*What Women Want*, 101–5).

54. See Stephenson, *Dismantling*, 165.

55. See Ruether, *Sexism*, 178, 200–1.

56. For the importance of pulpit rhetoric in defeating patriarchal theology, see Joy E. A. Qualls, "Toward a Rhetoric of the Spirit: Assault, Abuse, and a Theology of Women's Empowerment," in Alexander et al., *Sisters, Mothers, Daughters*, 238.

57. See my ethnographic study of an influential Assemblies of God megachurch in Springfield, MO. Over several years of research and observation, only a few women ever spoke from the pulpit, and those that did were always guest speakers and not in-house women pastors, of which there were none. Joseph Lee Dutko, "This-Worldly Explanations

trajectory of Pentecost, whereas women preachers "portray an authentic picture of Pentecost's outcomes" and fuel the congregations' eschatological imagination.[58] In addition, women preachers will bring insights and perspectives to the Scriptures and Christian life previously overlooked or unspoken by male preachers.[59]

The importance of experience for theological reflection and convictions, touted in both Pentecostal and feminist theology, suggests the need for more opportunities for Pentecostal women preachers.[60] Because experience functions as a source of theological authority for Pentecostals,[61] experiencing the preaching of women is one of the primary ways to solidify their eschatological authority to lead. Rather than being "under the authority" of men, women function under the authority of God's eschatological–egalitarian plan. Experience provides a hermeneutical lens for understanding Scripture;[62] therefore, the more women can exercise their eschatological authority from the pulpit, the more the hermeneutical priority of eschatological texts on gender will become the adopted paradigm over patriarchal patterns in Scripture. In this way, women acting out their calling may precede, inform, or come alongside any debate or theologizing about the appropriateness of those actions.[63] As Stackhouse reflects on his own journey in this area of women leaders in the church, "the anomalies in my experience were accumulating at a rate too great to be accommodated by my paradigm."[64] This kind of experiential approach is what led to early leadership opportunities for women in Pentecostalism,[65] and still has the potential to turn the pulpit from a limiting symbol for women into a liberating one.[66]

A new paradigm and approach for the full inclusion and affirmation of women in Pentecostal organizational leadership is needed, one that aligns with the eschatological freedom articulated in the Scriptures and found in early

---

for Otherworldly Growth: Vitality in an Ozarks Megachurch" (MA thesis, Missouri State University, 2008), 13, 82, https://bearworks.missouristate.edu/theses/2455/.

58. Crabtree and Qualls, "Women," 306.

59. See 6.3.2 on story in preaching. See also Mary Catherine Hilkert, *Naming Grace: Preaching and the Sacramental Imagination* (New York: Continuum, 1997).

60. See Copeland, "Journeying," 32.

61. This is one of the primary arguments of Peter D. Neumann, *Pentecostal Experience: An Ecumenical Encounter* (Eugene, OR: Pickwick, 2012).

62. Studebaker, *From Pentecost to the Triune God*, 30.

63. See Sherilyn Benvenuti's provocative article, which argues that it is time to leave the debates and for women to simply be who God has called them to be: "Anointed, Gifted, and Called: Pentecostal Women in Ministry," *Pneuma* 17 (1995): 229–35.

64. Stackhouse, *Finally Feminist*, 22. He's using Thomas Kuhn's terminology here.

65. See my Chapter 2. For example, A. H. Argue encouraged the ministry and ordination of his daughters primarily because of his experience of Aimee Semple McPherson's ministry (Ambrose, "Zelma," 106–7).

66. See Payne, *Gender*, 135, who documents how early Pentecostal women used practices that formerly restrained them to instead resist norms.

Pentecostalism. The welcoming eschatological Spirit of Pentecost who invites a variety of voices, differences, and mutuality, is not fully reified by primarily male-only leadership.[67] In order to implement and pre-enact these eschatological promises, men must be willing to listen to women's voices, including the research on women's feelings cited above.[68] Pentecostal men need to hear the tongues of women "talking back," interpreting their words as a righteous and appropriate eschatological anger and as a sign of hope that they have not yet given up on the Pentecostal community.[69] The next part of this chapter turns to the significant role Pentecostal theological education can play in this task of eschatologically forming men and women. Incorporating women's voices in places of learning can both correct previously male-centered educational practices and begin to construct new ways of learning that reflect the eschatological–egalitarian ethic. An eschatological approach to Pentecostal education that incorporates the voices of women will prepare future Pentecostal pastors and leaders to expect and reify egalitarian leadership in Pentecostal organizations as well as recruit their imagination for eschatological–egalitarian participation in corporate worship settings.

## 6.2 *Theological Education: Forming an Eschatological Consciousness*

For Pentecostal leaders to overcome the gender paradox, an eschatological–egalitarian consciousness must inform both teaching and learning in Pentecostal schools and higher education, as well as any other place where there is formal or informal Pentecostal theological instruction.[70] Teachers need to develop intentional strategies to recruit the eschatological imagination, which leads to and works dialectically with egalitarian participation. This section provides

---

67. See Amos Yong's "welcoming" and "inviting" Spirit in *Hospitality and the Other: Pentecost, Christian Practices, and the Neighbor* (Maryknoll, NY: Orbis Books, 2008); Amos Yong, "The Inviting Spirit: Pentecostal Beliefs and Practices Regarding the Religions Today," in *Defining Issues in Pentecostalism: Classical and Emergent*, ed. Steven M. Studebaker (Eugene, OR: Pickwick, 2008), 29–45. For more on the differences and mutuality represented at Pentecost and how it transforms the participant, see Amos Yong, "The *Missio Spiritus* in a Pluralistic World: A Pentecost Approach to Dialogue, Hospitality, and Sanctuary," *Pittsburgh Theological Journal* 9 (Autumn 2018): 11–48, esp. Part I, 11–25. See also here Augustine, *Spirit and the Common Good*, 10, and Augustine, *Pentecost*.

68. On men listening to women, see Stackhouse, *Partners*, 173–7.

69. Stephenson, *Dismantling*, 180. For more on anger as an appropriate response in this situation, see Jean Baker Miller and Janet L. Surrey, "Revisioning Women's Anger: The Personal and the Global," in *Women's Growth in Diversity: More Writings from the Stone Center*, ed. Judith V. Jordan (New York: Guilford Press, 1997), 200.

70. For more on Pentecostal theological education see Amos Yong, *Renewing the Church by the Spirit: Theological Education after Pentecost* (Grand Rapids: Eerdmans, 2020).

pedagogical suggestions for how Pentecostals can incorporate more female voices and perspectives, including from feminist theologians, into the classroom. Examples are given of how an eschatological–egalitarian orientation to Pentecostal theological education might correct and construct teaching and theological formation in the three theological disciplines of eschatology, anthropology, and trinitarian theology.

Although it unpacks some of the logical theological implications of the proposed eschatological hermeneutic of my work, this section is not meant to be speculative. Rather, its focus is on how to create an egalitarian educational experience congruent with an eschatology of gender so that future Pentecostal leaders are prepared to construct worship that participates in eschatological–egalitarian realities and lead in a way that reifies their eschatological convictions. Eschatology, anthropology, and trinitarian theology are inextricably linked and together contribute to the way we think about organizational structures and gender inclusiveness in leadership (the previous section, 6.1), and the language used, stories told, and embodiment portrayed in worship (the next section, 6.3).

### 6.2.1 Eschatological Pedagogy: Incorporating Women's Voices

An eschatological–egalitarian approach to Pentecostal education will equally incorporate female voices, interpretations, and stories into theological instruction and the building (and critiquing) of theory and practice.[71] In other words, Pentecostal theological formation in general should be "feminist" in its most basic definition of considering women's experiences for theological reflection.[72] Keeping women and their thoughts, writings, and contributions at the margins of theological instruction is not consistent with the eschatological–egalitarian heart of Scripture or the Pentecostal movement. An Acts 2 understanding of the "last days" is that hearing all voices—particularly of both men and women—is integral to knowing and understanding God (Acts 2:17-18). Although feminist thinking has yet to find a home in orthodox theology,[73] books and resources written by Pentecostals from a feminist perspective and that draw from feminist sources are becoming more common.[74]

Despite its congruence with Pentecost-inspired thinking, embracing a feminist approach to Pentecostal theological pedagogy likely represents a major paradigm shift. But by ignoring feminist theology, Stephenson argues Pentecostals will

---

71. See the previously cited work of the Stone Center, *Women's Growth in Diversity*, as well as its other volume *Women's Growth in Connection*. See also Jeanne Stevenson-Moessner, ed., *Through the Eyes of Women: Insights for Pastoral Care* (Minneapolis: Fortress, 1996).

72. Ruether, *Sexism*, 13.

73. Stackhouse, *Partners in Christ*, 147. See Stackhouse on hearing the voice of women in scholarship particularly (*Finally Feminist*, 124-9).

74. See my introductory comments in Chapter 1.

continue to fuse "an ideology of Spirit empowerment with a hierarchical anthropology"; in other words, the gender paradox will continue to thrive.[75] Feminist theology helps to expose the patriarchal tendencies of theology and ecclesiastical structures that silence women. For example, systematic theology and its traditional order have been challenged by many feminist scholars as a male-centered epistemology.[76] A change several feminist theologians have suggested or implemented is putting methodology and theological rationale at the end of a work, challenging its unquestioned status by overly systematic male theologians.[77]

In her theological memoir, theologian Roberta Bondi (the first woman to attain tenured faculty status at Candler School of Theology, Emory University) reflects on her learning experience and how "theology was abstract, logical, propositional, and systematic, and so was its God."[78] She describes how she had to deconstruct her theological education, unlearning and relearning what Christian doctrines mean and do not mean to women in her time.[79] Bondi shares her experience in theological education not because her story is fascinating, but because "in many different versions it is the personal history of so many people."[80] Many theological students like Bondi (whether male or female) have had a similar experience as the one Ruether describes:

> Writings by women themselves or writings expressing alternative views to the dominant tradition have often been dropped out of the official tradition, and their remains have to be dug up through careful detective work. But the dominant male tradition about women is not hidden at all. It lies right on the surface of all the standard texts of Plato, Aristotle, Augustine, Aquinas, and the like and its message has been absorbed and taken-for-granted over the generations. It takes a new consciousness to go back and isolate this whole body of material as a problem rather than as normative tradition. . . . No professor ever taught me to recognize it as an "issue."[81]

---

75. Stephenson, *Dismantling*, 86.

76. See Ruether, *Sexism*, xvi. In her tenth-anniversary edition, she mentions that she used the traditional order in her groundbreaking volume because nothing else existed at the time of her writing.

77. Ruether, *Sexism*, xvii. For an example of putting methodology and rationale at the end of a work, see Russell, *Future*.

78. Bondi, *Memories*, 9.

79. Bondi, *Memories*, 17.

80. Bondi, *Memories*, 27.

81. Rosemary Radford Ruether, "Becoming a Feminist," in *Invitation to Christian Spirituality: An Ecumenical Anthology*, ed. John R. Tyson (Oxford: Oxford University Press, 1999), 457. Reprinted from Ruether's *Disputed Questions on Being a Christian* (Nashville, TN: Abingdon, 1982), 109–26.

For Pentecostals, I propose this "new consciousness" is an eschatological one, where the eschatological understanding of God's plan for equality informs Pentecostal theological inquiry.

There are several ways Pentecostal teachers can develop and teach this consciousness. For starters, they can introduce themselves and their students to feminist authors and thought. Ruether laments that "most male students and faculty still do not read [feminist] literature as a necessary part of their education and scholarship."[82] The theological world is just starting to come to grips with a history dominated by male readings and interpretations. Pentecostal educators should carefully choose textbooks and reading assignments, being aware of how women's voices might be left out. A few specific examples may be helpful in opening the conversation and imagination for how an eschatological education will incorporate the eschatological equal voices of "male and female" (Gen. 1:27; Gal. 3:28), "both men and women" (Acts 2:18).

Christopher Stephenson uses portions of *God, Sexuality, and the Self* for his undergraduate theological students at Lee University. Stephenson chose this trinitarian-focused text by Sarah Coakley because she models "a theologian who is a woman, a minister of the church, a sympathizer with charismatic phenomena, and a proponent of rigorous systematic theology."[83] For teaching a basic Introduction to Theology course at a Pentecostal university, I chose a textbook that was within Christian orthodoxy but that also incorporated feminist ideas, criticisms, and language into almost every topical chapter.[84] Hermeneutics or book study courses might suggest commentaries written by women for all classes and incorporate their insights into the classroom. Foundational courses for all incoming students (usually on the Bible or the essentials of Christianity) could require *The Women's Bible Commentary* as a textbook or for inclusion in their personal pastoral/theological libraries, as it represents "the first comprehensive attempt to gather some of the fruits of feminist biblical scholarship on each book of the Bible in order to share it with the larger community of women who read the Bible."[85] Including feminist thought and theology in the classroom will hopefully solve another problem, one antithetical to an eschatological praxis, the silence of women in higher education due to patriarchal pedagogy.

---

82. Ruether, "Letty Russell," 20.

83. Christopher A. Stephenson, "Sarah Coakley's *Théologie Totale*: Starting with the Holy Spirit and/or Starting with Pneumatology?" *JPT* 26, no. 1 (2017): 9.

84. Hanson, *Introduction to Theology*, vi (for rationale), 37–8 for an example.

85. Carol A. Newsom and Sharon H. Ringe, "Introduction to the First Edition," in *The Women's Bible Commentary*, rev., 3rd (expanded), and 20th anniversary ed., ed. Carol A. Newsom, Sharon H. Ringe, and Jacqueline E. Lapsley (Louisville, KY: Westminster John Knox, 2012), xxix. Other resources would be Schroeder and Taylor, *Voices Long Silenced*; Marion Ann Taylor, *Handbook of Women Biblical Interpreters: A Historical and Biographical Guide* (Grand Rapids: Baker Academic, 2012).

Despite the advances and increased number of women on campuses, Bible colleges, and Christian universities, studies have revealed many gender discrepancies in theology classrooms.[86] Women in these classes are more silent and passive than males, and research by Allyson Jule and Bettina Tate Pedersen determined that professors talk more to their male students and treat males differently.[87] Therefore, there needs to be open and honest discussions about these realities in Pentecostal educational circles, perhaps in the form of formal workshops or even full courses on gender or women's experiences in theological education.[88] One of the original impetuses for this current project was a course in graduate school entitled "Women's Voices: Issues in Women's Faith and Development."[89] The class, taught by a woman and consisting of eleven female and two male students (including myself), was filled with heartbreaking stories from women of what it is like to be a woman in the Christian world of theology and the church. Thus, reading the right theological textbooks is only half the battle. Women bring their own perspectives, experiences, insights, and questions—sometimes quite different than men's—to theological and biblical discussion in the classroom and other academic contexts. An eschatological consciousness that values the biblical hope for equality will correct the gender-based power imbalance in theological texts as well as in the classroom, while also seeking to construct new egalitarian ways of writing, teaching, and learning theology.[90]

In addition to adopting an eschatological pedagogy that incorporates the voices of women, Pentecostal teachers can also reassess how eschatology itself is taught as a theological discipline. Feminist theologians have often been antagonistic or at least dismissive toward traditional eschatology due to its male-centered, individualistic,

---

86. For the challenges historically faced by women in theological higher education, see the stories in Schroeder and Taylor, *Voices Long Silenced*, 192–6, 209–11, 249–53. See also the resource by Nancy Wang Yuen and Deshonna Collier-Goubil, eds., *Power Women: Stories of Motherhood, Faith, and the Academy* (Downers Grove, IL: IVP Academic, 2021). Of course, these observations are often true of non-theological educational settings as well. See the older, but still insightful, book by Nadya Aisenberg and Mona Harrington (based on interviews with academics), *Women of Academe: Outsiders in the Sacred Grove* (Amherst, MA: University of Massachusetts Press, 1988).

87. Pedersen, "Christian Feminist," 13. See also Allyson Jule, "Silence as Femininity? A Look at Performances of Gender in Theology College Classrooms," in Pedersen and Jule, *Being Feminist*, 35–58.

88. See Stephen J. Bergman and Janet L. Surrey, "The Woman-Man Relationship: Impasses and Possibilities," in Jordan, *Women's Growth*, 260–88, where they report experiences and results from gender workshops that help create a "shift to mutuality" in male-female relationships.

89. A course at Carey Theological College (Vancouver, BC) through Regent College (Vancouver, BC) taught by Barbara Mutch in Fall 2013.

90. See Hollingsworth and Browning, "Daughters," 170.

and otherworldly focus.[91] However, a more praxis-oriented Pentecostal eschatology aligns well with feminist thinking, and it can also learn from it. Land defines "good" Pentecostal eschatology as one that mobilizes into action and actual practices. "Bad" eschatology, on the other hand, "thrilled but did not mobilize."[92] In other words, eschatological practices that anticipate or pre-enact future promises are to be preferred over speculative eschatological timetables.[93] And most feminist theologians would agree. Citing others, Ruether explains that women may think of immortality different than men. Whereas men tend to fixate on death and have a more individualized concern for self-perpetuation, women focus more on the female birth experience and show concern for how to collectively nurture ongoing life on earth.[94] Eschatological hope that incorporates the voices and perspectives of women is less likely to focus on the self and more likely show concern for the condition of all humanity.[95] A female-oriented eschatology might focus more on how to make the world more livable for the children and generations to come,[96] moving pedagogical approaches away from abstract and systematic ideas and toward how theology can improve the lives of the marginalized, including women.

De-centering the future from oneself, or humans in general for that matter, as the main concern of eschatology is a common feminist redefining or rereading of eschatology. Therefore, like recent trends in Pentecostal eschatology, feminist theologians propose a more practical eschatology. For example, in a chapter on eschatology, McFague redefines eschatology to mean "living from a vision for a different present based upon a new future."[97] She presents suggestions for creating a more just and ethical present world, a this-worldly "ecoeschatology," over against concerning oneself with one's individual eschatological existence.[98] Many other feminist theologians or "eco-feminists" emphasize caring for creation as an important eschatological practice, partly because "feminists tend to see the degradation of nature as an extension of the degradation of women."[99] Teaching

---

91. See 1.1.1–1.1.2.

92. Land, *Pentecostal Spirituality*, 62–3, 73.

93. See Warrington, *Pentecostal Theology*, 323.

94. Ruether, *Sexism*, 235–6.

95. This anthropological connection to eschatology is a/the trend in eschatology in general. See Rausch, *Eschatology*, 91–7; Dermot A. Lane, *Keeping Hope Alive: Stirrings in Christian Theology* (1996; repr., Eugene, OR: Wipf & Stock, 2005), 26–8, 157–9; Tinder, *Hope*, 201; Brian D. Robinette, *Grammars of Resurrection: A Christian Theology of Presence and Absence* (New York: Crossroad, 2009), 165, 177.

96. See Phan's seven contributions of feminist eschatology ("Feminist Eschatology," 219–20).

97. McFague, *Body of God*, 198.

98. McFague, *Body of God*, 198.

99. Carmody, *Feminist Theology*, 231; see 91, 230–4. See also Celia Deane-Drummond, who writes her chapter on creation from an ecofeminist framework ("Creation," in Parsons, *Feminist Theology*, 190–205).

eschatology with the inclusion of female voices brings more perspectives to the table than the classic definitions of eschatology used in most Pentecostal institutions, definitions historically dominated by male-influenced worldviews. Furthermore, presenting alternative eschatologies can lead to more women sharing their experiences of how they think about eschatology, the afterlife, and how it impacts their Christian living.

This section on eschatological pedagogy contains examples of how an eschatological consciousness in Pentecostal education has the potential to correct and construct pedagogical approaches in order to incorporate the equal voices of "both men and women" (Acts 2:17) in Pentecostal places of learning. Before moving on to the implications of an eschatological–egalitarian praxis for Pentecostal worship, some necessary theological foundation from an eschatological perspective will help inform the argument for correcting and constructing the language used, stories told, and embodiment portrayed in worship, as well as continue this section's emphasis on forming an eschatological consciousness in theological education.

### 6.2.2 Eschatological Anthropology: Ontological Outcomes

Scholars contend that eschatology *is* anthropology in the future sense.[100] Chapter 4 argued hermeneutically that the prelapsarian *imago Dei* is filled with eschatological significance. According to Genesis 1:26–28, the question, "what does it mean to be made in the image of God?" is an eschatological one. Making humankind in the "image" and "likeness" of God includes both male and female as the representation of that image. Therefore, the hermeneutical insights gained in Chapter 4 may give some clues for investigating an eschatological anthropology and trinitarian theology, with an aim toward the practical implications of those eschatological doctrines for how we worship and image God in the present. The hermeneutical priority of eschatological texts on gender for interpreting Scripture leads to the ontological priority of our eschatological existence for determining praxis.[101]

Because humans are made in the image of God and share a common destiny of eschatological fellowship with God, a Pentecostal eschatological anthropology is helpful for determining the language we might use about God and for governing our human relations, worship practices, and overall eschatological formation in the present.[102] Edmund Rybarczyk argues that unlike other traditions, Pentecostals tend to make their anthropological formations based on humans as they were after the Fall and pay little attention to their prelapsarian state.[103] This

---

100. Robinette, *Grammars of Resurrection*, 165, 177.
101. See Rendtorff, *Ethics*, 1:81.
102. See Pannenberg, *Systematic Theology*, 2:224.
103. Edmund J. Rybarczyk, *Beyond Salvation: Eastern Orthodoxy and Classical Pentecostalism on Becoming Like Christ* (Carlisle, England: Paternoster, 2004), 216–17, 227.

postlapsarian emphasis has a profound effect on gender relations, as it overlooks the eschatological-egalitarian trajectory of the *imago Dei* of Genesis 1 and the restoration of its human embodiment at Pentecost.[104] Stephenson similarly argues that Pentecostals have understood anthropology primarily in terms of function rather than being, creating a dualistic anthropology that maintains restrictive practices for women and maintains gender hierarchy by focusing on women's empowerment (function) rather than personhood (ontology).[105] She concludes that what is needed is a theological argument that addresses the personhood of women.[106] I propose that an eschatological anthropology provides the best way forward for Pentecostals and gender praxis, as it addresses the ontological and not just the functional status of women.[107]

An eschatological anthropology has historically been problematic for women's equality. Discriminatory practices toward women in the present were often rooted in an eschatological anthropology that considered women inferior. Some church fathers equated maleness with the spiritual nature and femaleness with the carnal nature, and they therefore questioned whether women will exist in the resurrection or considered if the female body would be transformed in some way, perhaps even into male.[108] More common and accepted was the argument that the eschatological body will be sexless, an argument still put forward,[109] although it has mostly fallen out of favor as its theological and hermeneutical problems

---

See also here much of Augustine's chapter "From the Common Image to the Common Good" in her *Spirit and the Common Good*, 13–60. For more on Pentecostal theological anthropology, see Vondey, *Pentecostal Theology*, 175–97.

104. See Vondey, *Pentecostal Theology*, 187; cf. Rybarczyk, *Beyond Salvation*, 227.

105. See Stephenson, *Dismantling*, 78, 85, 89. See also Lisa P. Stephenson, "A Feminist Pentecostal Theological Anthropology: North America and Beyond," *Pneuma* 35, no. 1 (2013): 35–47. Johns makes a similar argument in "Spirited Vestments," grounded in the trinitarian *imago Dei*.

106. Stephenson, *Dismantling*, 89. Her contribution or solution is a pneumatological anthropology (see 134–5).

107. For indeed, part of the redemption of the "ontological brokenness" of the postlapsarian world is the "ontological renewal" of humanity (Augustine, *Spirit and the Common Good*, 17).

108. See Gospel of Thomas in 1.1.1. See discussion of this history in Ruether, *Sexism*, 247–9, including the views of Gregory of Nyssa, Augustine, Jerome, and Thomas Aquinas. Irenaeus and Tertullian argue that bodies will be raised with genitals. Like Augustine, Jerome argues the same but also subscribes to gender inequality and social hierarchy in heaven. For more, see Elizabeth Clark's review of Peter Brown's *Body and Society*, in *Journal of Religion* 70 (1990): 432–6.

109. Gregory of Nyssa most famously argued for a sexless resurrection body, as did Origen. See discussion in 4.3.3 on Gal. 3:28 for more. This thinking is particularly prominent in Eastern Christianity, which emphasizes a spiritual body free from sexual differentiation. For this perspective, see Karras, "Eschatology," who cites Gregory of Nyssa,

have been exposed.[110] The hermeneutical work done in Chapter 4 moves toward an eschatological egalitarian anthropology that affirms the goodness of men and women and frees women to lead in the present based on their eschatological status. Therefore, the goal is not to overcome our maleness and femaleness in anticipation of the eschatological eradication of gender, for that gender trajectory moves opposite to the eschatological trajectory of the biblical narrative. The goal is to become more fully male and female, embracing our eschatological identity initiated in Genesis 1, redeemed through Christ (Gal. 3:28), and restored and embodied by the Spirit (Acts 2:17-18). An eschatological anthropology leads to an eschatological consciousness that "we are and ever will be male and female followers of Jesus Christ,"[111] which has profound implications for ecclesial praxis.

Amos Yong's argument regarding eschatology and disability is helpful for moving toward a Pentecostal eschatological–egalitarian anthropology. Gender, of course, is not a disability, but like disability it is a strong identity marker of being human. Yong argues that "if there are no disabilities in the life to come, then that implicitly suggests our present task is to rid the world of such unfortunate and unwanted realities," a conclusion opposite his thesis.[112] Some traits, states Yong, "are so identity-constitutive that their removal would involve the obliteration of the person as well."[113] He seeks to correct the image of a disability-free paradise and expose the "normate biases" of most eschatological interpretations, for they dramatically affect how we think, behave, and what we deem as good in the

---

his sister Macrina, John Chrysostom, and Maximos the Confessor as those who argue that gender is not an ontological part of one's eschatological existence (253-4).

110. See Alan J. Torrance, "God, Personhood and Particularity: On Whether There is, or Should Be, a Distinctive Male Theological Perspective," in Campbell, *Gospel and Gender*, esp. 134-54. For more on the eschatological body and gender in the afterlife, including historical overviews, see Candida R. Moss, *Divine Bodies: Resurrecting Perfection in the New Testament and Early Christianity* (New Haven, CT: Yale University Press, 2019), 66-88, esp. 70-3; Coakley, *Powers and Submissions*, 153-67; Christopher West, *Theology of the Body for Beginners* (West Chester, PA: Ascension, 2009), esp. 53-9; Brian Edgar, "Biblical Anthropology and the Intermediate State," *Evangelical Quarterly* 74 (2002): 27-45 (Part I), 109-21 (Part II); John W. Cooper, *Body, Soul, and Everlasting Life: Biblical Anthropology and the Monism-Dualism Debate* (Grand Rapids: Eerdmans, 2000); William Hasker, *The Emergent Self* (Ithaca, NY: Cornell University Press, 1999); Caroline Walker Bynum, *The Resurrection of the Body in Western Christianity, 200-1336* (New York: Columbia University Press, 1995), 35-103 (Rausch, *Eschatology*, 83-5 follows her summary fairly closely); Graff, *Feminist Approaches to Theological Anthropology*.

111. Nordling, "Gender," 497.

112. Amos Yong, *The Bible, Disability, and the Church: A New Vision of the People of God* (Grand Rapids: Eerdmans, 2011), 118. See also his longer work, *Theology and Down Syndrome: Reimagining Disability in Late Modernity* (Waco, TX: Baylor University Press, 2007). See also here the important work of Moss, *Divine Bodies*, 53-65.

113. Yong, *The Bible, Disability*, 121.

present life.[114] Our eschatological anthropology matters greatly, argues Yong, for eschatological expectations generate present practices and "eschatological images . . . translate into churches—harbingers of the coming reign of God."[115] Yong suggests how an inclusive eschatological vision creates a different world in the present as our eschatological images, even if unconsciously, structure our attitudes toward people in the present.[116] Similarly, if gender is eradicated altogether in the *eschaton*—or a gender hierarchy is maintained—it would devalue the experience of gendered beings or imaging God in equal-gendered ways for both would become temporal constructs.

Like others, Yong argues for a biblically based embodied eschatological anthropology based on Jesus's resurrected body, which is transformed yet still maintains ontological continuity with the marks and traits of his earthly body and person, including gender.[117] The eschatological-egalitarian biblical narrative and Jesus's resurrected body reveal that humankind will be embodied and gendered beings forever.[118] Therefore, an eschatological anthropology has implications for understanding God's eschatological trinitarian being (and vice versa) because one of the primary markers of human beings' eschatological reflection of the likeness and image of God is gender (Gen. 1:26-27). These insights have implications for the gendered language we use about God. It is that practical problem the last subsection tackles before turning to how an eschatological orientation to these theological doctrines influences how we worship.

### 6.2.3 Eschatological Trinitarianism: Gender Implications

Eschatology is impossible to separate from trinitarian theology.[119] Historically, trinitarian theology has suffered from an androcentric bias, but both eschatological and feminist approaches to the Trinity have revealed new insights that can correct and reconstruct this core doctrine.[120] Despite the gender-balanced image-language of Genesis 1 and its reaffirmation in Galatians 3:28 and Acts 2, God has historically been described in male terminology, particularly the first and second members of the Trinity. Some theologians have attempted to "balance" the masculine imagery

---

114. Yong, *The Bible, Disability*, 118–20.
115. Yong, *The Bible, Disability*, 121.
116. Yong, *The Bible, Disability*, 135, 142.
117. See Yong, *The Bible, Disability*, 123–30; Yong, *Renewing*, 53; Nordling, "Gender," 498, 507. Yong's continuity and discontinuity argument is similar to Wright, *Surprised by Hope*.
118. See Nordling, "Gender," 497–8.
119. Karras, "Eschatology," 245; Yong, *Renewing*, 17.
120. Janet Martin Soskice, "Trinity and Feminism," in Parsons, *Feminist Theology*, 147. In *Pentecost to the Triune God*, Studebaker calls for Pentecostals to bring trinitarian theology to bear on important issues in contemporary Christian thought and life, which would/should include gender.

of the Father and Son by feminizing the Spirit.[121] As Carmody and others argue, this approach is both praiseworthy in some of the insights it provides, but also problematic in its line of thinking.[122]

Pneumatology provides a helpful and natural inroad for discussing the feminine characteristics of the triune God because the person of the Spirit is not historically tied to male imagery, is often referred to in female terms, and is frequently linked to women's equality, empowerment, liberation, and an overall inclusive vision.[123] Increased focus on the Spirit is certainly beneficial in drawing attention to the feminine characteristics of God and what is means to be in God's image.[124] In particular, Pentecostal pneumatology presents a helpful contribution and counterbalance to traditional (that is rational, functional, male-dominated) trinitarian theology and its Christocentrism and privileging of male identity.[125] The Spirit refuses easy categorization,[126] defies control (John 3:8), and challenges traditional power structures. However, simply feminizing the Spirit or moving from a Christocentric to pneumacentric theology is problematic.[127] Most feminist theologians are critical of this approach because it divides the masculine and feminine characteristics of God between the persons of the Trinity.[128] Furthermore, pneumatology has often been ignored, repressed, or subordinated in Christian

---

121. The most prominent example is Yves Congar, who speaks of the Spirit as *the* feminine person in the Trinity in *I Believe in the Holy Spirit*, vol. 3 (New York: Seabury, 1983). See also Donald Gelpi, *The Divine Mother: A Trinitarian Theology of the Holy Spirit* (Lanham, MD: University Press of America, 1984). Elisabeth Moltmann-Wendel and Jürgen Moltmann see potential in this approach in *God—His and Hers* (London: SCM, 1991), 36.

122. See Carmody, *Feminist Theology*, 202. For a summary of the options of gender language and the Trinity, see Miroslav Volf, "The Trinity and Gender Identity," in Campbell, *Gospel and Gender*, 157.

123. See Hollingsworth, "Spirit and Voice," 191 for a brief summary. For a full treatment, see Rebecca Button Prichard, *Sensing the Spirit: The Holy Spirit in Feminist Perspective* (St. Louis, MO: Chalice, 1999). See Slee, *Faith and Feminism*, 72, 80. For female imagery of the Holy Spirit in early Christian texts and throughout Christian history, see Ruether, *Sexism*, 59–60.

124. Carmody, *Feminist Theology*, 202–3. The central biblical metaphors for the Spirit are female or gender non-specific (see Slee, *Faith and Feminism*, 72).

125. See Studebaker, *From Pentecost to the Triune God*, esp. 96–7, 136, 146, 166.

126. Nicola Slee, "The Holy Spirit and Spirituality," in Parsons, *Feminist Theology*, 185.

127. Replacing an overemphasis on the Father or Son with an overemphasis on the Spirit is something Studebaker, for example, is aware of and defends himself against repeatedly in *From Pentecost to the Triune God* (see 136, 146, 166).

128. Most notable is the oft-cited article by Sarah Coakley, "'Femininity' and the Holy Spirit?" in *Mirror to the Church: Reflections on Sexism*, ed. Monica Furlong (London: SPCK, 1988), 124–35. See a similar critique by Slee, "The Holy Spirit as the Feminine in God? Pneumatology in Feminist Perspective," in her *Faith and Feminism*, 72–82. See also Soskice, "Trinity and Feminism," 135–50, esp. 143; Elizabeth A. Johnson, *She Who*

theology, potentially mirroring the marginalization of the female experience in Christianity.[129] Particularly problematic is that the Spirit is often incorrectly—and sometimes subconsciously—considered subordinate to the Father and Son and "pushed out" of theological discussion, heightening male hierarchy and reinforcing gender paradigms and stereotypes.[130]

A better approach to considering the gendered aspects of God in a trinitarian context, and one corresponding to eschatological thinking, is to affirm the equal feminine and masculine attributes contained within each member and the fullness of the Godhead.[131] Feminist theologians tend to approach the doctrine of the Trinity as both a source of and liberator from patriarchy, the former being historically true but the latter becoming more prominent.[132] Scholars have consistently argued that trinitarian doctrines impact gender constructions and that gender constructions influence perceptions of the Trinity.[133] Although some theologians advise to tread cautiously in drawing implications for gender from the Trinity,[134] most feminists have embraced the shift in trinitarian doctrines from symbol of hierarchical power, subordination, and role distinction to egalitarian

---

*Is: The Mystery of God in Feminist Theological Discourse*, 25th anniversary ed. (New York: Crossroad, 2007), 152.

129. Slee, *Faith and Feminism*, 73-4. See also Slee, "The Holy Spirit and Spirituality," 172; Anne Claar Thomasson-Rosingh, *Searching for the Holy Spirit: Feminist Theology and Traditional Doctrine* (London: Routledge, 2015).

130. Slee, *Faith and Feminism*, 74; Coakley, "Femininity"; Hollingsworth, "Spirit and Voice," 195; Rosemary Radford Ruether, "The Emergence of Christian Feminist Theology," in Parsons, *Feminist Theology*, 3; Studebaker, *From Pentecost to the Triune God*, 166. See also Lisa P. Stephenson, "Where the Wind Blows: Pneumatology in Feminist Perspective," in *T&T Clark Handbook of Pneumatology*, ed. Daniel Castelo and Kenneth M. Loyer (London: Bloomsbury T&T Clark, 2020), 327-35.

131. Carmody, *Feminist Theology*, 202-3; Johns, "Spirited Vestments," 182-3. For a good discussion on the feminine Divine and on God as both a Mother/Father figure, see Eleanor Rae and Bernice Marie-Daly, *Created in Her Image: Models of the Feminine Divine* (New York: Crossroad, 1990).

132. See Rees, "Sarah Coakley," 309; Catherine Mowry LaCugna, "God in Communion with Us: The Trinity," in LaCugna, *Freeing Theology*, 83-114.

133. Most notably, see Campbell, ed., *Gospel and Gender: A Trinitarian Engagement with Being Male and Female in Christ*. See specifically Volf's chapter, "The Trinity and Gender Identity," 155-78. See also here Alvin F. Kimel Jr., ed., *This Is My Name Forever: The Trinity and Gender Language for God* (Downers Grove, IL: InterVarsity, 2001). See especially the chapter by Stanley Grenz, "Is God Sexual? Human Embodiment and the Christian Conception of God," 190-212.

134. See Simon Chan's discussion in *Spiritual Theology: A Systematic Study of the Christian Life* (Downers Grove, IL: InterVarsity, 1998), 50-1; Stackhouse, *Finally Feminist*, 76-7.

centerpiece.¹³⁵ These theologians, including many Pentecostals, primarily place their argument in the social or relational dynamic of the Trinity as a vision of non-hierarchical equality and mutuality.¹³⁶ The triune God is not more male than female, and "it is the doctrine of the Trinity which saves the Christian doctrine of God from stifling androcentrism."¹³⁷ Rather than assigning male-only qualities to God or splitting the divine image into male or female or ignoring divine gender attributes altogether, an eschatological approach affirms the egalitarian nature of God's entire being and mines the implications for gender constructs in the present.

The above assessment of the gender implications of these core components of theological education is purposely brief, but it creates the necessary eschatological consciousness and framing for correcting and constructing practices in Pentecostal worship. Ignoring the practical implications of an eschatological understanding of humanity or God is where other works fall short. When it comes to how humans live as gendered beings, we must consider our eschatological identity in order to be "eschatologically reoriented" in our praxis.¹³⁸ Organizational structures, educational materials, and worship practices are consciously and unconsciously influenced by one's theological-ontological beliefs concerning anthropology and the Trinity. But it is not enough only to establish an eschatological theological anthropology or trinitarian theology that is egalitarian. As Stephenson argues, "In order to attend to the [gender] issue in a systemic fashion, the ecclesiological aspect of the problem must also be addressed. . . . In order to effect a real and lasting transformation, a new vision of the church must be envisioned and embraced."¹³⁹ Because "God is the last thing," one's focus should be on "the eschatological trinitarian presence," followed by what that means for present practice.¹⁴⁰ The present church is to reflect the eschatological-egalitarian ideal of community that is found in the eschatological Trinity.¹⁴¹

The church's worship is where the inclusion of women in organizational leadership and incorporation of women's voices and perspectives in education can come together. As Ruether states, the language and activity of worship is one of the primary areas where the church alienates women, which is why it is given ample

---

135. Hierarchical distinctions in the Trinity are the classic arguments of complementarians such as Wayne Grudem and John Piper. See discussion in Johns, "Spirited Vestments," 174–5. See Grey, *Three's a Crowd*, 2. See also here Giles, *The Trinity and Subordinationism*.

136. See Augustine, *Spirit and the Common Good*, 43, 58–60, 127; Johns, "Spirited Vestments," 180–3; Johnson, *She Who Is*, 227–35; Catherine Mowry LaCugna, *God for Us: The Trinity and Christian Life*, esp. the chapter "Persons in Communion" (New York: HarperSanFrancisco, 1973), 275, 279–82.

137. Soskice, "Trinity and Feminism," 139; cf. 147.

138. Nordling, "Gender," 506.

139. Stephenson, *Dismantling*, 167.

140. Land, *Pentecostal Spirituality*, 196.

141. Grenz, *Moral Quest*, 296.

attention in this chapter and provides the proper culmination to my work.[142] Reifying eschatological equality on the institutional level and listening to and incorporating women's voices in theological educational formation matter only to the extent that Pentecostals regularly participate in eschatological-egalitarian realities in their worship. Simply the inclusion of women is not enough, for it is in worship, and the entire liturgy and practices that make it up, that people are primarily formed and shaped.[143] The following section on worship begins with proposing Pentecostal worship primarily as eschatological formation before applying an eschatological-egalitarian praxis to the specific areas of imagination, story, and embodiment in worship, three areas influenced by an overall eschatological consciousness as well as an eschatological anthropology and trinitarian theology.

### 6.3 Corporate Worship: Participating in Eschatological–Egalitarian Realities

The primary context for Pentecostal formation and doctrinal reflection is worship,[144] and positioning worship as eschatological formation is the starting point for reimagining gender praxis in the church.[145] The day of Pentecost in Acts 2 provides the template for eschatological pre-enactment praxis in worship.[146] Awakening the eschatological imagination—that we are in the "last days" (v. 17)— leads to a call to eschatological participation in practices that mark the last days, which includes equal voice and participation for "both men and women" (v. 18). Therefore, where the Spirit is being "poured out" (vv. 17, 18) in the context of the gathered worshipping church (v. 1), people are being eschatologically formed and transformed into the embodiment of the future new humanity.[147] Discovering this future in the present is a communal activity in which the freedom is given to experience and then declare that "this is that" (v. 16) toward which the church is moving. In this way, the acts and activities of the church, and specifically egalitarian acts, become "prophetic signs" and "pointers" to the coming kingdom of God.[148]

These prophetic actions often contradict the past as well as the present in favor of anticipatory practices that are a "reminder of God's future" as the church

---

142. Ruether, *Sexism*, 193.
143. Susan A. Ross, "Church and Sacrament—Community and Worship," in Parsons, *Feminist Theology*, 232–3.
144. See Johns, *Pentecostal Formation*, 121–8; Alvarado, "Pentecostal Worship," 221–33; Vondey, *Pentecostal Theology*, 31; Smith, *Imagining*, 3.
145. Cf. Hebrews 12:22-24, where the present church shares in the eschatological worship that is already taking place.
146. For Pentecost as eschatological event and category, see 4.4.3 and Vondey, *Pentecostal Theology*, 276–7.
147. See Augustine, *Pentecost*, 19.
148. Augustine, *Pentecost*, 146. See also Johns, "Conscientization," 155.

becomes an eschatological symbol of the new creation.[149] The seduction of returning to the "old age" for those who have entered into the new eschatological life of the Spirit is a common New Testament theme and one relevant to discerning worship practices.[150] Instead of thinking from the perspective of a previous time and attempting to re-enact those practices, Pentecostal worship fueled by the eschatological imagination thinks from the perspective of the end of time for practices in the present time.[151] As Warrington observes, there has not been enough awareness in Pentecostalism of how the Spirit may desire to transform our world by bringing eschatological issues to reality *prior* to the *eschaton*.[152] It is in worship that Pentecostal churches receive the foretaste of what is to come and imaginatively participate in the realities of the New Jerusalem, including the equality of the sexes.[153] Worship is where believers are formed; it "rehumanizes us" and becomes an apprenticeship for the final day and a space where "the boundary between the present and future is breached."[154]

For early Pentecostals, each worship service was a "rehearsal and anticipation" of the kingdom to come.[155] As Castelo argues, seeing themselves as the eschatological people of God has carried both potential and peril for Pentecostals.[156] Early Pentecostals saw themselves as starting "anew" as the church and looked for evidence of this newness in the eschatological markers of the lame walking, the blind seeing, and daughters prophesying.[157] However, seeing themselves as a (forward) "movement" rather than a "church" caused them to not reflect ecclesiologically on their practices.[158] As Pentecostal praxis became slowly detached

---

149. Schwarz, *Eschatology*, 370–1. See Russell, *Future*, 103.

150. See Rom. 7:14-23; 1 Cor. 7:31; Gal. 5:17; Rev. 21:1, 5. See similar commentary by Fee, *God's Empowering Presence*, 821; Nordling, "Gender," 497, 507; Moltmann, "Liberating," 199–200.

151. This is similar to or drawing from Russell's eschatological metaphor of the "household of God" for praxis, which involves "working from the other end" (see her *Household*, 40, 76; *Future*, 15–16).

152. Warrington, *Pentecostal Theology*, 237–8.

153. Melissa Archer, "Worship in the Book of Revelation," in Martin, *Theology of Worship*, 121–2, 125. She uses the term "proleptic participation" (121). For more on worship as proleptic and eschatological, see Kimberly Ervin Alexander's "'Singing Heavenly Music': R. Hollis Gause's Theology of Worship and Pentecostal Experience," in Martin, *Theology of Worship*, 205–6. For more on eschatological worship, see Daniela C. Augustine, "Liturgy, Theosis, and the Renewal of the World," in Martin, *Theology of Worship*, 165–85, esp. 167. For worship and the eschatological imagination, see Althouse, "Betwixt and Between," 267, 269, 278.

154. Augustine, *Spirit and the Common Good*, 137; Archer, "Worship," 125–6.

155. Land, *Pentecostal Spirituality*, 62.

156. See Castelo, "Improvisational Quality of Ecclesial Holiness," 90–2.

157. Castelo, "Improvisational Quality of Ecclesial Holiness," 91–2.

158. Castelo, "Improvisational Quality of Ecclesial Holiness," 90.

from the eschatological imagination and its egalitarian impulses, patriarchal forms of worship and liturgy began to dominate and still do.[159] Vondey calls this the "doxological divide," where "although women are allowed to speak, shout, testify, sing, preach, pray, and prophesy, their voices are not always heard" as men still hold all the positions of power and influence (reflected by the word "allowed"), which shapes the way worship is conducted.[160]

The way most churches use liturgical language, tell stories, and perform sacramental acts in worship is "heavily colored by the male experience."[161] These practices within the worship service must be corrected and eschatologically reimagined in order to find congruence with the eschatological–egalitarian vision of the biblical text.[162] Smith argues that worship shapes us primarily through the "intertwining of embodiment, imagination, and story."[163] We are transformed, he suggests, through narrative, imagination, and ritual, which form the foundation for our liturgical practices.[164] Any account of worship formation must attend to these three areas, and in particular to the imagination.[165] Therefore, the following sections suggest how eschatological convictions may correct and construct gender praxis in these three areas in the way we eschatologically imagine God through the language of worship, tell God's story in a way that is gender-inclusive, and eschatologically embody God's presence through sacramental activities.

*6.3.1 Imagination: Eschatological Language*

This section proposes that a way to correct the male bias of language and to construct new images is through the eschatological consciousness proposed in the previous section. Thinking and living eschatologically frees us to consider alternatives for naming and imaging God in our worship and prayers and to use inclusive language in worship activities. Using the eschatological imagination and eschatological language may be the solution for the decades-long search for a "usable language" in worship that incorporates both genders and the experiences

---

159. This is part of the lament of Land, *Pentecostal Spirituality*, 208–9.

160. Vondey, *Perplexed*, 129–31.

161. Judith V. Jordan, "Clarity in Connection: Empathic Knowing, Desire, and Sexuality," in Jordan, *Women's Growth*, 65. For the need for new rituals and practices based on women's experiences, see Ross, "Church and Sacrament," 225.

162. Other areas, of course, could be addressed, such as singing and what eschatological messages are communicated through song (see Middleton's section "Singing Lies in the Church," 27–30 in his *New Heaven*).

163. Smith, *Imagining*, 15.

164. Smith, *Imagining*, 33. Smith uses the word "liturgical" as philosophical shorthand for embodied or material (19n44).

165. Smith, *Imagining*, 19, 162.

of women.[166] The power and importance of language in ordering gender relations is an issue commonly flagged in Pentecostal and other Christian feminist literature.[167] In her work on (re)affirming women in Pentecostalism, Blumhofer lists five practical tasks facing churches to create more inclusive, egalitarian worship. One of those tasks is to grapple with issues related to language, including (but not limited to) gender-inclusive language for God and the masculine language and imagery that governs most sermons, prayers, and songs in the church.[168] Qualls argues that the discrepancies and tensions about women in Pentecostal leadership "are profoundly rhetorical. They are primarily rooted in the way people use words, language, and symbols."[169] Male bias in the language of worship must be corrected and supplanted with new eschatological–egalitarian images.

The use of gender-inclusive language in early Pentecostal preaching, publications, and writings is surprising and ahead of its time. "Such language," argues McQueen, "was not forced but rather expressive of the way the community was actually living," that is, eschatologically.[170] However, as the eschatological imagination faded so too did inclusive egalitarian language, replaced instead with patriarchal imagery that marginalizes women. For example, in one speech at the 1927 General Council of the Assemblies of God, a man proudly depicted the movement as having begun as an "orphan girl" who had now grown "to be a mighty man."[171] In order to overcome patriarchal language like this, which hurts and alienates women, Pentecostal churches must find new language for imagining and imaging God in worship in ways that help women to flourish and that persuade both men and women of God's eschatological–egalitarian desire.[172]

Naming and imaging God solely through one gender has a tremendous impact on the equality of women in worship and everyday life.[173] Ruether argues that when we are incapable of imagining an alternative way to think or talk about God and gender, then sexism and biasing of language and symbols will continue to pollute the worship of the church.[174] Gender is a central way to experience and

---

166. A search articulated by Letty Russell in 1974 in *Human Liberation in a Feminist Perspective—A Theology* (Philadelphia: Westminster, 1974), 73.

167. See Stephenson, *Dismantling*, 169–72; Chopp, *Power to Speak*; Ruether, *Sexism*, 173–5.

168. Blumhofer, *Women and Church*, 5–7. Blumhofer has evangelicals in mind as well. The other tasks deal with learning from the past, writing inclusive histories, dealing with biblical and theological issues, and women's representation in leadership roles, all of which have been addressed in this work already.

169. Qualls, *Forgive Us*, 3.

170. McQueen, *Joel*, 83. See my Chapter 2.

171. Barfoot and Sheppard, "Prophetic vs. Priestly," 14.

172. See Chopp, *Power to Speak*, 2, 9; Qualls, *Forgive Us*, 28.

173. Hollingsworth, "Spirit and Voice," 195. She is summarizing the work of Sarah Coakley. See also Ruether, *Sexism*, 53; Volf, "Trinity and Gender," 157.

174. Ruether, *Sexism*, 178.

understand God in worship.[175] Therefore, eschatologically (re)imagining God and humans made in God's image challenges and ultimately corrects the way we name and image God. As humans wandered east of Eden (Gen. 3:24), the Edenic eschatological understanding of God and gender went with them, replaced with a male-dominant imaging of God. The eschatological worshipping community formed in the image of God gives equal weight to the male and female experience *and* the male and female attributes of God. One gender does not provide a better or superior image of God for worship; rather, God's eschatological being represents the fullness of both genders, and worship that is eschatologically nuanced will move in that direction in the language it uses to image and worship God.

The church's present worship must find ways to reflect and express the masculine and feminine attributes within the eschatological Trinity.[176] Language about God is always inadequate in describing the greatness of God's mystery, for we cannot yet fully see God as God is (1 John 3:2). Affirmative, kataphatic language about what or who God is like should always be balanced to a degree with apophatic disclaimers about what or who God is not like. God reveals God's self in gendered language and imagery, both male and female. However, God is also beyond human categories of gender or sexual distinction (John 4:24);[177] God is no more literally mother than God is literally father.[178] However, our language about God is necessarily gendered due to language limitations and so to worship the divine properly in spirit and in truth (John 4:24), the eschatological church must not privilege one gender above another in its language and descriptions of God.[179] Knowing we are gendered in the *eschaton*, and that our gendered existence is one of equality that reflects and images the egalitarian triune God, our present experience in worship should lead to language and imaging of God that reflects these eschatological-egalitarian truths.

The biblical text contains both male and female imagery for God and for describing divine activity.[180] In the Hebrew Scriptures,[181] God "gives birth" to Israel (Deut. 32:18) and describes herself as a woman in labor (Isa. 42:14)[182] and a nursing

---

175. See Sarah Coakley, "Is there a Future for Gender and Theology? On Gender, Contemplation, and the Systematic Task," *Criterion* 47 (2009): 2–11.

176. See Grenz, *Moral Quest*, 277.

177. See Sharon H. Ringe, "When Women Interpret the Bible," in *Women's Bible Commentary*, 6.

178. See Hanson, *Introduction to Christian Theology*, 21–3; Russell, *Household*, 52.

179. See Volf, "Trinity and Gender," 158.

180. Ruether, *Sexism*, 68.

181. For the formation of the male God image in the Ancient Near East, see Ruether, *Sexism*, Chapter 2, "Sexism and God-Language: Male and Female Images of the Divine."

182. See discussion of Isaiah 42 by Beth M. Stovell, "The Birthing Spirit, the Childbearing God: Metaphors of Motherhood and Their Place in Christian Discipleship," in *Making Sense of Motherhood: Biblical and Theological Perspectives,* ed. Beth M. Stovell (Eugene, OR: Wipf & Stock, 2016), 27–41, esp. 30–4.

mother (Isa. 49:15; cf. Isa. 66:13; Num. 11:12; Ps. 131:2). In the New Testament, Jesus self-describes himself as a searching woman (Luke 15:8-10), mother hen (Luke 13:34), and in a manner befitting a Middle-Eastern mother (Luke 15:20).[183] New Testament authors describe believers as newborn babies at Jesus' breast tasting his goodness (1 Pet. 2:2-3; cf. Heb. 5:12-14).[184] The God of Scripture performs domestic activities that would have culturally been considered "women's work" such as preparing food, raising children, and giving birth.[185] These are just a few of many examples of female metaphors for or feminine characteristics of God in the Scriptures or Christian history.[186] Patriarchal Christianity has made these images for God inappropriate or even heretical at times, but an eschatological approach corrects male-only images for God and frees the worshipping community to imagine God through feminine imagery and apart from patriarchal biases.[187] God can be described in worship as an understanding mother, loyal sister, or winsome

---

183. See here the insights of Kenneth Bailey on the Prodigal Son parable (Luke 15) in his *Jacob and the Prodigal: How Jesus Retold Israel's Story* (Downers Grove, IL: InterVarsity, 2003), 146. Cf. a parallel scene in Tobit 11:9 when Tobias returns and his *mother*, Anna, "ran up to her son and threw her arms around him . . . And she wept." Luke 15 and its absent mother, maternal-behaving father, and domestic-behaving woman have been interpreted both positively and negatively by feminist critics. For a negative assessment see Jane D. Schaberg and Sharon H. Ringe, "Gospel of Luke," in *Women's Bible Commentary*, 493–511; Susan Durber, "The Female Reader of the Parables of the Lost," *Journal for the Study of the New Testament* 45 (1992): 59–78; Bruce Malina and Jerome Neyrey, "Honor and Shame in Luke-Acts: Pivotal Values of the Mediterranean World," in *The Social World of Luke-Acts: Models for Interpretation,* ed. J. H. Neyrey (Peabody, MA: Hendrickson, 1991), 62. For a positive assessment, see Carol LaHurd, "Re-viewing Luke 15 with Arab Christian Women," in *A Feminist Companion to Luke*, ed. Amy-Jill Levine (New York: Sheffield, 2002), 252–3; Kenneth Bailey, *Finding the Lost: Cultural Keys to Luke 15* (Saint Louis: Concordia, 1992), 106, 203.

184. The word "good" in 1 Peter 2:3 is χρηστός evoking Jesus (Χριστὸς, Christ) as the source of spiritual milk for believers (v. 2). For more on the imagery of this passage, including its feminine (and masculine) associations, see Alicia D. Myers, "*Pater Nutrix*: Milk Metaphors and Character Formation in Hebrews and 1 Peter," in Stovell, *Motherhood*, 81–99, esp. 97.

185. See Jen Pollock Michel, *Keeping Place: Reflections on the Meaning of Home* (Downers Grove, IL: InterVarsity, 2017). However, one must be careful not to speak of any of the feminine characteristics of God in ways that make them subordinate to the "primary" male characteristics, which would only perpetuate gender hierarchy and gender stereotyping (see Ruether, *Sexism*, 61).

186. Perhaps the most extensive or well-known work here is Johnson's *She Who Is*, which contains hundreds of pages of examples and suggestions for images of God and speaking about God and God's persons.

187. Carmody, *Feminist Theology*, 37–8.

lover.[188] These images can be particularly appealing to Pentecostals who cherish a relational sense of the divine and experiencing God as a tender lover or intimate friend.[189] To worship the trinitarian God only as Father or depict God *always* as male is not only unbiblical but also potentially idolatrous.[190]

Consistent use and privileging of male imagery betrays the biblical and eschatological vision of the Godhead. Instead, using eschatologically based language directs worshippers toward the fuller eschatological mystery of the divine when we will know God for who God fully is. Does this mean that eschatological language for God in worship, including names and pronouns, should be gender-inclusive?[191] Historically, and especially in spiritual writings, using feminine language and names for God is not uncommon, such as Julian of Norwich's well-known descriptions of "Christ our Mother" in her *Revelation of Love*.[192] However, it is perhaps unlikely that Pentecostal leaders will start regularly using female or gender-inclusive pronouns for God interchangeably with male ones, although some Pentecostal scholars have.[193] A more likely first step toward representing the eschatological Trinity is to choose alternatives such as referring to God as "friend" or "Holy One" more than "father,"[194] "the divine" instead of "him," or to avoid

---

188. Carmody, *Feminist Theology*, 38; McFague, *Models of God*, 95–155. See the various articles in the chapter "God as She" in *Wisdom of Daughters*, 37–66.

189. Griffith and Roebuck, "Women," 1207.

190. Stackhouse, *Partners in Christ*, 148; Ruether, *Sexism*, 66. See also Sallie McFague, *Metaphorical Theology: Models of God in Religious Language* (Philadelphia: Fortress, 1982), 145-7, 177-83, 193-4.

191. For an evangelical response to inclusive feminist God-language that mostly concludes the church should stick with traditional language, see Alvin F. Kimel, ed., *Speaking the Christian God: The Holy Trinity and the Challenge of Feminism* (Grand Rapids: Eerdmans, 1992). For a heated exchange on the book see the review of Catherine LaCugna and response by the book's editor in Catherine Mowry LaCugna, "Review of *Speaking the Christian God: The Holy Trinity and the Challenge of Feminism*," *Pro Ecclesia* 3 (1994): 114-16; Alvin F. Kimel, "It Could Have Been . . . .," *Pro Ecclesia* 3, no. 4 (1994): 389-94. See discussion of this exchange in Kathryn Greene-McCreight, *Feminist Reconstructions of Christian Doctrine: Narrative Analysis and Appraisal* (Oxford: Oxford University Press, 2000), 4-5.

192. I count at least ten references to the motherhood of God or Jesus from 128-34 and 138-42 in Julian of Norwich, *Revelation of Love*, ed. and trans. John Skinner (New York: Image/Doubleday, 1996). See also Brant Pelphrey, *Christ Our Mother: Julian of Norwich* (London: Darton, Longman, & Todd, 1989). See also the writings of Mechthild of Magdeburg in Tyson, *Invitation to Christian Spirituality*, 168-71 (esp. 169).

193. For example, Ware uses S/He for God in "Spiritual Egalitarianism," 231n31. See also Chan, *Spiritual Theology*, 54.

194. The suggestion of McFague, *Metaphorical Theology*, 177-92. See also Ruether, *Sexism*, who uses God/ess frequently in her book, but does not recommend it for worship.

pronouns all together and simply repeat the word "God."[195] But the eschatological imagination should at least remind Pentecostal leaders that referring to God as "she" or "her" is no less accurate than "he" or "him."

Worshippers are often formed more by images than concepts.[196] Therefore, an inroad to imaginative eschatological–egalitarian language for God is through imaging God in prayer and worship in creative ways that are fully in line with biblical descriptions, such as God as a mother. Locating the self in relation to God through prayer involves offering people gender-inclusive images for God. These images do not cater only to the male experience, but rather use the whole canon of names for God so that worshippers can think about, pray to, and worship God in creative and healing ways.[197] For example, in her work on female survivors of childhood sexual abuse, Barbara Mutch found that survivors in therapy had a longing and desire to pray, but could not due to the negative "power-over" imagery for God in prayer.[198] But when survivors discovered new images for God, they were able to once again pray and ask for things they needed. In her memoir, Bondi expresses that "it is not enough for me to know that I am made a generic human being, in the image of God who is my Father. I am a woman and I must know that the image of God in which I am made is also the image of god who is my mother." She continues later: "to know myself as a woman in the image of God, to know God as Mother, and to know my own mother as a window into God: these three are inseparable."[199] "Pastors," she argues, "especially have a responsibility to make sure that the language of worship does not hurt people or make God distant."[200] A gender-inclusive vision of worship also means praying for life moments that reflect women's experiences, such as praying for labors, births, or women's work in the marketplace, as well as healing prayers for abortion, miscarriage, rape or domestic violence.[201]

Nonpatriarchal, inclusive language and imagery for God in worship is essential for the eschatological–egalitarian church and reducing the alienation women feel in worship.[202] Using all male language and metaphors for God conveys the idea that women are somehow less like God than males, something

---

195. The suggestion of Ringe, "When Women Interpret the Bible," 6.
196. See Smith, *Imagining*, 17–18.
197. See Grenz and Kjesbo, *Women in the Church*, 74; Ruether, *Sexism*, 173–4.
198. Barbara Mutch, "Images of God and Their Relationship to Prayer in the Experience of Female Survivors of Childhood Sexual Abuse" (DMin diss., Princeton Theological Seminary, 1995). See also James Newton Poling, *The Abuse of Power: A Theological Problem* (Nashville: Abingdon, 1991). For some of the dangers of clergy using the language of fatherly caring, which evokes feelings of dependence and fuel power as domination over others, see Russell, *Household*, 90–1.
199. Bondi, *Memories*, 83, 108.
200. Bondi, *Memories*, 47.
201. See Slee, *Faith and Feminism*, 90.
202. See Copeland, "Journeying," 36; Carmody, *Feminist Theology*, 38.

the eschatological–egalitarian narrative refutes.[203] Furthermore, male-dominant imagery for God endorses, even if unintentionally, patriarchal authority.[204] Instead, names and images for the divine should point toward an eschatological understanding for God that transcends the patriarchal (and sinful) limitations of this world and includes the experiences of women as well as men.[205] Before applying how this eschatological understanding influences the stories we tell in worship, a closing word on gender-inclusive language in the church in general is appropriate.

In addition to language that names and images God in worship, the eschatological imagination can have tremendous impact on gender language in the church as churches seek to verbalize a new world that is void of patriarchal language and images. The eschatological passages on gender are consistent in their inclusivity of "male *and* female" (Gal. 3:28; Gen. 1:27), "men *and* women" (Acts 2:18). Therefore, a simple, practical implication of the hermeneutical priority of these passages and being an eschatological community is to use balanced, egalitarian language in worship. Unbalanced or male-biased language is to move backward, not forward in God's plan for men and women. Simple practices that can be adopted by Pentecostal churches are using Bible translations that are gender-inclusive,[206] making sure official church documents such as constitutions or policy manuals do not refer to pastors or lead pastors as "he" or "him," and avoiding (or changing if public domain) congregational songs that use non-inclusive language such as "man," "sons," "sonship," or male-only pronouns.[207] For example, the lines "nor man's empty praise" or "let men their songs employ" from the hymns "Be Thou My Vision" and "Joy to the World" (both public domain) can be changed to

---

203. Volf, "Trinity and Gender," 158. For the "Power of Naming," see Chapter 3 of Russell, *Household*, 43–57. For a technical work about forming an image of God, see Ana-María Rizzuto, *The Birth of the Living God: A Psychoanalytic Study* (Chicago: University of Chicago Press, 1979).

204. Russell, *Household*, 52.

205. Ruether, *Sexism*, 46.

206. For example, translations that use "person" or "humankind" rather than "man" or "mankind." Two of the most widely accepted or available would be the NRSVue/NRSV (which the *Women's Bible Commentary* is principally based) or TNIV, both of which at least translate terms that refer to both genders or all people in inclusive ways (such as translating *adelphoi* as "brothers and sisters"). The 2011 NIV sought to find a balance between the non-inclusive 1984 NIV and the all-inclusive TNIV, but in my opinion falls short of being deemed an inclusive translation. For more on translations, see Ringe, "When Women Interpret the Bible," 1–9, esp. 6.

207. A few popular examples of congregational worship songs from recent history would be "Majesty (Here I Am)" by Delirious with the lyrics "Here I am / Knowing I'm a sinful man" (Martin Smith and Stuart Garrard, *World Service*, 2003), or the modern hymn "How Deep the Father's Love for Us" with lyrics "As wounds which mar the Chosen One / Bring many sons to glory" (Stuart Townend, *Say the Word*, 1990).

"nor vain empty praise" and "let all their songs employ," respectively. These polices would extend to using inclusive language during public speaking and avoiding anti-eschatological language that assumes pastors or leaders are male such as "pastors' wives" or "elders' wives."

Leaders may think these kinds of changes are insignificant or that male language does not bother worshippers, but as Ruether argues the layers of sexism are "vast . . . ranging from the most subtle to the most brutal."[208] The eschatological–egalitarian trajectory must start somewhere, and for some churches it will be in small changes as they initially embrace the eschatological–egalitarian biblical narrative. Eschatological language has the power to liberate rather than oppress and subordinate women, bringing (trans)formation through eschatological images of God and human flourishing in Pentecostal worship.[209] But the imagination, inspired by the biblical eschatological–egalitarian narrative trajectory, does not just correct and construct *how* Pentecostals talk in worship, but also *what* they talk about and the stories they tell. Changes in language are only a small or first step toward building an eschatological–egalitarian praxis. Participating in the *eschaton* requires a radical restructuring of worship to include the experiences, thoughts, and insights of women so that more than "half the story" of the human experience is communicated.[210]

### 6.3.2 Story: Eschatological Inclusivity

The stories we tell in worship, whether through the biblical story, Christian and denominational history, or present testimonies, shape our emotions and feelings and ultimately influence our actions.[211] The worshipping community's understanding of the world and what God is doing in it is grasped more through imagination and story than cognitive-based propositions, and these stories are "carried" in and through our practices.[212] Because of male dominance in Pentecostal worship services, the stories, experiences, and insights of women have been ignored or overshadowed. However, an eschatological approach to ecclesial storytelling places the stories of women from the past and present in the context of the egalitarian future. The eschatological outpouring of the Spirit at Pentecost emphasizes the need for multiple voices and languages over a single voice or language (Acts 2:5-11), a "heteroglossia" that pays attention to the language, stories, and participation of both men and women (Acts 2:17-18).[213] The eschatological–egalitarian church

---

208. Ruther, *Sexism*, 175.
209. See Chopp, *Power to Speak*, 68.
210. See Ann Loades, "Introduction," in *Feminist Theology: A Reader*, ed. Ann Loades (Louisville, KY: Westminster John Knox, 1990), 2–3.
211. Smith, *Imagining*, 38.
212. See Smith, *Imagining*, 30, 162. Smith is heavily influenced here by Charles Taylor and his "social imaginary" in *Modern Social Imaginaries* (Durham, NC: Duke University Press, 2000), 23–6.
213. Procter-Smith, "Feminist Ritual Strategies," 512. See also Holmes, "Acts 29," 198.

equally considers the stories of women in the three areas of preaching the biblical story, sharing personal story through testimony, and telling the story of the Christian and Pentecostal tradition. Because women's stories will be heard equally in the future, the eschatological church must make room to hear them now.

Preaching inspired by the eschatological imagination and its egalitarian narrative thread will elevate, celebrate, and grieve with the voices and stories of women in the Scriptures. Preachers fueled by the text's inclusive eschatological vision will seek to rescue biblical stories from their male-dominated interpretations and reimagine them through the eyes and experiences of women.[214] For Pentecostals, this might mean positioning Elizabeth, the first person in the New Testament said to be "filled with the Holy Spirit" (Luke 1:41), and her sister Mary as featured biblical prototypes of the Spirit-filled life.[215] Reimagining Mary as the "first Pentecostal" and "model charismatic," or the first to receive the baptism in the Spirit, places a woman as the original model of Pentecostal praxis.[216] Moving beyond pneumatological concerns, Mary can be featured for her model obedience (Luke 8:19-21) and celebrated at Christmas for how a woman's body is central to the incarnation. Continuing with Mary and the Gospels, preachers can regularly highlight the faithfulness of women who "were first at the Cradle and last at the Cross."[217]

A key figure like Mary is an easy first step in reimagining the place of women in the biblical story. However, few other women from the biblical text receive regular attention in homiletic proclamation; women of the Bible have been ignored despite the wealth of their words and stories in the biblical narrative.[218]

---

214. Ruether, *Sexism*, 1. For examples, see Mickelson's humorous way of reading Genesis 1-3 from a women's perspective in Hull, *Equal to Serve*, 245-50, and Ruether's "Feminist Midrash of the Gospel in Three Acts" (*Sexism*, 1-11).

215. Yong, *Renewing*, 57.

216. Josephine Massyngbaerde Ford, "Mary and the Holy Spirit," in *NIDPCM*, 863-4. The baptism in the Spirit is in reference to the coming of the Spirit upon Mary at Jesus' conception (864). For more on Mary and Pentecostals, see Lisa P. Stephenson, "Truly Our Sister?: Pentecostal Readings of Mary," in Isgrigg, Mittelstadt, and Wadholm, *Reception History*, 112-24, esp. 122-4; Yong, *Spirit Poured Out*, 194-5n60. For more on Marian piety, see Carmody, *Feminist Theology*, 246-7.

217. The famous quote of Dorothy L. Sayers from her 1938 essay, "Are Women Human?" later printed in 1947 and currently in book form in Dorothy L. Sayers, *Are Women Human? Penetrating, Sensible, and Witty Essays on the Role of Women in Society* (1971; repr., Grand Rapids: Eerdmans, 2005), 47.

218. Several great resources exist for uncovering the stories and words of women in the Bible. Lindsay Hardin Freeman identifies and discusses *every* woman in the Bible who speaks in *Bible Women: All Their Words and Why They Matter*, 3rd ed. (n.p.: Forward Movement, 2016). See also Dorothy A. Lee, *The Ministry of Women in the New Testament: Reclaiming the Biblical Vision for Church Leadership* (Grand Rapids: Baker Academic, 2021); Richard Bauckham, *Studies of the Named Women in the Gospels* (Grand Rapids: Eerdmans, 2002);

Eschatological inclusivity draws attention to overlooked and even unnamed women in the Scripture (Judg. 11:34, 40; Acts 21:8-9) and senses the urgency to bring their stories into worship. For example, when preaching on the Exodus, rather than solely focusing on Moses and Aaron, eschatological inclusivity will also feature the midwives—who defied Pharaoh's edict to put to death baby boys—as initial liberators and the beginnings of the freedom of Israel from Egyptian bondage.[219] The names and stories of Zipporah, Miriam, Jael, Ruth, Dorcas, Lydia, Junia, Phoebe, Priscilla, and many more will be said and told in the eschatological-egalitarian church. This egalitarian storytelling is not limited to the pulpit, but can and should be incorporated into small groups, youth ministries, and children's church curriculums. Stephenson recommends incorporating egalitarian material into Christian education programs for kids in Pentecostal churches, building an "appreciation for the full humanity of women at all ages."[220]

Inclusive preaching fueled by the eschatological–egalitarian imagination will not only name women and highlight their contributions to the biblical story, but also communicate the pain of women in the text and of women today reading the Scriptures. To include, recognize, and incorporate fully the experiences of women in the church, Pentecostal worship must engage the "texts of terror" such as the rape of Tamar (Gen. 38), the Levite's concubine (Judg. 19), and other difficult texts.[221] Casey Cole proposes an "orthopathic reading" of these texts, which has similarities with my work's proposed eschatological reading. She argues that a hermeneutic limited to orthodoxy or orthopraxy "may leave us trapped in the texts of terror."[222] Instead of asking, "what should we believe?" or "what should we do?" some texts invite us to ask, "what do we feel?" or "what do we long for?" Cole eventually hints at an eschatological reading of these texts when she suggests that these difficult

---

Finger and Sandhaas, *Wisdom of Daughters*, esp. Chapter 1, "Women in Scripture," which contains fifteen different essays on fifteen different women in Scripture. For proclamation of the Word in feminist perspective and what it might look like and entail, see Chopp, *Power to Speak*. For more on women and preaching, see Amy Oden, *In Her Words: Women's Writings in the History of Christian Thought* (Nashville: Abingdon, 1994), 280-1.

219. J. Cheryl Exum, "'You Shall Let Every Daughter Live': A Study of Exodus 1:8–2:10," *Semeia* 28 (1983): 63-82.

220. Stephenson, *Dismantling*, 193.

221. See Trible, *Texts of Terror*. Other examples include Gen. 16, 21:1-21; Judg. 11; 2 Sam. 13; as well as some of the Pauline texts on women. See here the compilation of essays in Johns and Stephenson, *Grieving, Brooding, and Transforming*; Frances Taylor Gench, *Encountering God in Tyrannical Texts: Reflections on Paul, Women, and the Authority of Scripture* (Louisville, KY: Westminster John Knox, 2015); Jonathan Kirsch, *The Harlot by the Side of the Road: Forbidden Tales of the Bible* (New York: Ballantine Books, 1997).

222. Casey S. Cole, "Taking Hermeneutics to Heart: Proposing an Orthopathic Reading for Texts of Terror via the Rape of Tamar Narrative," *Pneuma* 39 (2017): 266. See also Casey S. Cole, "The Binding of Jephthah: Learning Orthopathy from the Daughter of Judges 11," *JPT* 29, no. 2 (2020): 145-57.

texts cause us to anticipate and long for the future creation.[223] But that does not mean these texts can be easily dismissed if we are to create spaces where the voices and experiences of women are heard. These stories are about abandonment, triangulation, sexual violence, treating women as property and possession, and the loss of women's identity within the collective culture.[224] These are injustices that need to be named and exposed as they still reflect the contemporary experiences of many women and the damaged souls within church congregations. By not ignoring the texts of terror, the eschatological–egalitarian church will make room for the inclusion of the often-painful experiences of women and the Scriptures that may be a stumbling block to wounded souls.[225]

Eschatological inclusion also impacts the stories we tell about sin, servanthood, and suffering.[226] Freeing preaching and teaching in the church from male domination and ideas will challenge popular theological constructions in these areas as women sometimes construct, experience, or understand sin differently than men. Ruether argues that a huge barrier for Christian women in conservative traditions "is the identification of sin with anger and pride, and virtue with humility and self-abnegation."[227] Male teaching on sin and servanthood, she states, is "an ideology that reinforces female subjugation and lack of self-esteem," for to be "Christ-like" is to put others first and have no self of their own.[228] Equally including women means reevaluating common teachings on pride, humility, sin, servanthood, self-sacrifice, and self-denial.[229] Telling stories of sin from women's perspectives often recognizes sin more in structural systems and webs of relationship and not just in individual acts.[230] Furthermore, an inclusive view of sin—and preaching on women's experiences in the Bible—will address topics such

---

223. Cole, "Orthopathic Reading," 274.

224. For more, see Bob Ekblad, *Reading the Bible with the Damned* (Louisville, KY: Westminster John Knox, 2005).

225. See Elizabeth Liebert, "Coming Home to Themselves: Women's Spiritual Care," in Stevenson-Moessner, *Through the Eyes of Women*, 262–3.

226. On servanthood language and problems see Jacquelyn Grant, "The Sin of Servanthood," in *A Troubling in My Soul: Womanist Perspectives on Evil and Suffering*, ed. Emilie M. Townes (Maryknoll, NY: Orbis Books, 1993), 199–218. For a positive treatment of service from feminist perspective see Russell's chapter "God's Self-Presentation" in *Future of Partnership*, 61–77. For the problem of suffering as a Christian virtue, see Stephenson, "Toxic Spirituality," 35–8.

227. Ruether, *Sexism*, 186.

228. Ruether, *Sexism*, 186. See also a similar insight in Liebert, "Coming Home," 262–3.

229. See the insightful article by Brita L. Gill-Austern on how we (mis)understand Christian love ("Love Understood as Self-Sacrifice and Self-Denial: What Does It Do to Women?" in Stevenson-Moessner, *Through the Eyes of Women*, 304–21).

230. Ruether, *Sexism*, 215.

as the control of women's bodies by men and acts that dehumanize women (and men) such as rape, sexual violence, abuse, harassment, and pornography.[231]

Potentially most important for promoting an eschatologically inclusive vision in worship is incorporating the experiences, lives, and stories of women in testimony, applications, illustrations, and other practices of storytelling. One of the "marks" of an egalitarian liturgy is an emphasis on women's lives and relationships.[232] The eschatological trajectory of Jesus' ministry resulted in his using examples of women and women's experiences regularly in his teachings and parables, with some arguing he used more imagery and examples from women's lives than men's.[233] Jesus included women in theological discussion and used metaphors that made sense to their lives, keeping them from feeling alienated in his teaching.[234] Practices inspired by the eschatological–egalitarian imagination will reflect what women think, feel, desire, and know bodily.[235] For example, churches may spend time talking and praying about stillbirths, birth experiences, women's health issues, women's friendships, or the difficulty women face in the workplace.[236] Although the church and culture at large does "not readily tolerate and legitimize women's painful feelings in response to life events" there are many ways to affirm the experiences of women and "their attempts to bring theological meaning to their lives and relationships."[237] A church moving toward eschatological equality will allow space for women to share their testimonies, even if involving the painful stories of patriarchy.[238]

In addition to including biblical stories about women and the contemporary experiences of women, the church must practice celebrating the lives and stories of women throughout its history. Stories from past and present about women's achievements in the church can serve as a way to legitimize their callings and break down restrictions.[239] Women mothers, mystics, madams, monastics, martyrs,

---

231. See Ruether, *Sexism*, 217, 228, and various articles in the chapter "Women and Abuse" in *Wisdom of Daughters*, 129–52.

232. Procter-Smith, "Feminist Ritual Strategies," 501.

233. Grenz and Kjesbo, *Women in the Church*, 74. A few examples: Matt. 13:33; Luke 15:8-10; John 16:21.

234. See Carmody, *Feminist Theology*, 38. For theological discussion with women, see John 4:1-26.

235. See Bonnie J. Miller-McLemore, *Also a Mother: Work and Family as Theological Dilemma* (Nashville: Abingdon, 1994).

236. See Irene P. Stiver and Jean Baker Miller, "From Depression to Sadness in Women's Psychotherapy," in Jordan, *Women's Growth*, 223.

237. Stiver and Miller, "Depression to Sadness," 232; Joretta L. Marshall, "Sexual Identity and Pastoral Concerns: Caring with Women Who Are Developing Lesbian Identities," in Stevenson-Moessner, *Through the Eyes of Women*, 151.

238. See the Foreword by Rachel Held Evans in Bessey, *Jesus Feminist*, xiii.

239. For the importance of story for women's callings, see Linda Ambrose, "Aimee Semple McPherson: Gender Theory, Worship, and the Arts," *Pneuma* 39 (2017): 113–21.

maids, and ministers from across economic, educational, and ethnic spectrums have made contributions to Christian thought and practice over the centuries, and their stories need to be told. These women's stories, such as Thecla (first century), the first female Christian martyr, or Paula (fourth century), who knew the Scriptures by heart and chanted the Psalms in Hebrew, have been mostly ignored or hidden due to male bias. These women are just a few in an expansive list of women prophets, disciples, evangelists, preachers, reformers, and church planters.[240] Unveiling these women hidden in church history and telling their stories reminds the church that in every time and every place God has had his hand on women and men and revealed himself to and through both without gender preference. These stories of the impact of women's lives on the church show that the eschatological–egalitarian trajectory of the Spirit has always been at work in the church, even if some archeological digging is needed. Churches can, and should, take time to tell these stories from the pulpit and elsewhere in the church as well as find creative ways to feature them regularly, such as on International Women's Day or even Pentecost.

Within the Pentecostal tradition, telling the stories of women leaders is a primary way to inspire the eschatological–egalitarian imagination and to encourage present participation in egalitarian realities. Eschatologically inspired storytelling is a way to progress the egalitarian narrative thread of the Scriptures and its pre-enactment practices rather than regress into re-enactment practices. However, despite Pentecostals' treasuring of their spiritual experiences and telling stories through oral history, the stories of the "foremothers" of the Pentecostal faith have failed to regularly find their way into the mainstream story of Pentecostalism and its history, allowing the eschatological imagination and egalitarian renewal to wane.[241] In order to participate in eschatological–egalitarian realities in the worship of the church, the eschatological imagination must be recruited through story in order to see beyond structures and distinctions that limit women and provide the urgency to (pre)enact alternatives.[242] Pentecostal churches can tell the story of Agnes Ozman as the first North American to speak in tongues at Parham's Bible school, effectively launching the modern Pentecostal movement, or of Ellen Hebden's role in initiating the Canadian Pentecostal story.[243] Especially important are the well-developed call narratives of Pentecostal women that validated their ministry callings.[244] These narratives tell the stories of women who, often reluctant

---

240. See Nordling, "Gender," 501–2; Oden, *In Her Words*. See the resource by Michelle DeRusha, *50 Women Every Christian Should Know: Learning from Heroines of the Faith* (Grand Rapids: Baker Books, 2014), although Pentecostal women are conspicuously absent.

241. See Cavaness, "Leadership Attitudes," 112; Roebuck, "Hearing Women's Voices," 38–60; Leeuwen, *Gender and Grace*, 50–1; Poloma and Green, *Assemblies of God*, 98.

242. Procter-Smith, "Feminist Ritual Strategies," 513.

243. See 2.3.1. See also Edith L. Blumhofer, "Ozman, Agnes Nevada," in *NIDPCM*, 952.

244. On the call narratives, see Powers, "Pentecostal Hermeneutics," 319–29; Blumhofer, *Assemblies of God*, 1:357; Lawless, *Handmaidens of the Lord*, 76–84; Barfoot and Sheppard, "Prophetic vs. Priestly."

to accept the call, could not escape God's call to preach and lead.[245] These call narratives and testimonies of women superseded any Scriptural proof-texting or theologizing in early Pentecostalism with regard to the question of women's ability to lead.[246]

Churches need to consider—in light of the eschatological–egalitarian vision—whether their language, teachings, and stories in worship "repel or draw women in"[247] and if they perhaps "overlook those who are routinely overlooked, that is to say half the world's population."[248] But inspiring the eschatological–egalitarian imagination through the liturgical language used and inclusive stories told is still not enough. Pentecostals must also perform and enact in worship the imaginative language used and the stories told, so that liturgical actions become one of the primary ways the church tells the unfolding eschatological–egalitarian drama.[249] An egalitarian *vision* must lead to *visibility* as the imagination produces participation. Churches must embody and (pre)enact the story they tell by correcting historically male-dominated practices and creating new opportunities for women congruent with the eschatological–egalitarian ethic. One example is how the practice of the Lord's Supper can be eschatologically reimagined.

### 6.3.3 Embodiment: Eschatological Sacramentality

One of the sacramental practices historically most dominated by men or male clergy is presiding over the Lord's Supper;[250] therefore, it provides an important case study of how an eschatologically inspired praxis might correct the gendered assumptions of who leads Communion and construct new possibilities for shared leadership between genders.[251] The focus of this section is on how to embody eschatological–egalitarian realities in sacramental activities, primarily focusing

---

245. See some of the stories in my Chapter 2. See also Stephenson, *Dismantling*, 52 on McPherson's call.

246. English de Alminana, "Introduction," 5.

247. Crabtree and Qualls, "Women," 305.

248. A quote from the semi-autobiographical Canadian feminist novel *Unless* by Carol Shields (Toronto: Vintage Canada, 2002), 220.

249. Smith, *Imagining*, 109.

250. For the Lord's Supper as a sacrament and the role of sacramental activity within Pentecostal worship, see Joseph Lee Dutko, "Beyond Ordinance: Pentecostals and a Sacramental Understanding of the Lord's Supper," *JPT* 26 (2017): 252–71; Green, *Lord's Supper*, esp. 3, 81, 91, 128, 165, 177–8, and all of Chapter 3, "(Re)Discovering the Sacramentality of Early Pentecostalism"; Wolfgang Vondey and Chris W. Green, "Between This and That: Reality and Sacramentality in the Pentecostal Worldview," *JPT* 19 (2010): 243–64.

251. Other sacramental activities could be analyzed for how they might embody eschatological equality, such as baptism and foot washing, but I focus here on the Lord's Supper because it is perhaps the most male-dominated and the most regular and visible

on who (and who does not) preside over the Supper.²⁵² This section first exposes and critiques the biblical-theological reasons for the overrepresentation of males in presiding over the Lord's Table, then proposes how approaching the Eucharist eschatologically helps construct new ways of embodying egalitarian realities.

Women have historically been and felt excluded from representing Christ at the Lord's Table.²⁵³ One of the restrictions of 1931 placed upon all Assemblies of God women, even ordained, was to limit their ability to preside over the "ordinance" of the Lord's Supper.²⁵⁴ Wacker claims this early resolution, written by men, was out of concern for men being put in a "recipient role."²⁵⁵ The result is that many modern Pentecostal parishioners have never been led in Communion by a woman. Part of the problem is the underlying assumption that the person presiding over the Table must be *in persona Christi*—acting "in the person of Christ"—and therefore must be male.²⁵⁶ Even if the syllogism that "if Christ is God, then God is male, and therefore the male represents God" is deficient, it still "has emotional resonances that carry weight" and impact ecclesiastical practices.²⁵⁷ Influential theologians such as Thomas Aquinas have argued that because Christ was incarnated as male, only males can accurately re-present him at the Table.²⁵⁸ The patriarchalization of Christology has led to the tacit—and at times not-so-tacit—assumption that women cannot sacramentally represent Christ. Ruether believes this gender-exclusivity to sacramental representation is "the keystone of conservative reaction against women's ordination," for it presupposes that the "head" pastor or priest must be male to represent Christ as head of the church.²⁵⁹

Several differing Christologies and constructive counterarguments to this line of thinking have been offered. Grenz and Kjesbo argue that the representation of Christ is more vocal rather than actual in eucharistic celebrations. Because Christ

---

sacramental practice in most churches. But see Andrew Ray Williams, *Washed in the Spirit: Toward a Pentecostal Theology of Water Baptism* (Cleveland, TN: CPT, 2021).

252. The terms Lord's Supper, Supper, Communion, Eucharist, Lord's Table, and Table are used interchangeably.

253. For stories of women's experiences regarding Communion, see (no author, transcripts of group conversation), "Setting the Table: Meanings of Communion," in *Setting the Table: Women in Theological Conversation*, ed. Rita Nakashima Brock, Claudia Camp, and Serene Jones (St. Louis, MO: Chalice, 1995), 249–68.

254. See the 1931 AG General Council resolution mentioned in 3.2.

255. Wacker, *Heaven Below*, 171.

256. Susan A. Ross, "Sacraments: God's Embodiment and Women," in LaCugna, *Freeing Theology*, 202.

257. Elaine Storkey, "Who Is the Christ? Issues in Christology and Feminist Theology," in Campbell, *Gospel and Gender*, 107. Syllogism made famous by Daly in *Beyond God the Father*, 19. See also Johnson, "Christology: Redeeming the Name of Christ," esp. 119–20.

258. See Ruether, *Sexism*, 126 for discussion. Thomas Aquinas, *Summa Theologica*, pt.1, q.92, art.1–2; q.99, art.2; pt. 3, supp., q.39.1.

259. Ruether, *Sexism*, 126.

is the host and the presider primarily "serves as the mouthpiece for the risen Lord," the church's eucharistic doctrine is nothing but "enhanced by women representing Christ at the Lord's table."[260] Citing Galatians 3:28 as support, Grenz and Kjesbo state that including women in leading at the Table is the only way to represent fully the one who is (eschatologically) representative of all humanity.[261] Others argue for an alternative egalitarian Christology, often based on Galatians 3:28, that sees Christ as representative of the new humanity, both male and female.[262] Jesus coming in "human likeness" (Phil. 2:7) includes experiencing life from the vantage point of the oppressed and marginalized, which would include women. Even though Jesus was male, he penetrated the depths of the human experience of exclusion and marginality and thus learned how to empathize and realize his own male privilege.[263] Therefore, one possible reason for why the incarnate Christ was male is that only a male could have offered the radical critique of systems of power, including male/female hierarchy and relationships.[264] As such, male-only representation of Christ sends the opposite message intended by Jesus coming in the flesh. Arguments like this are helpful and thought-provoking, but not strong enough to overcome definitively the Pentecostal hesitancy surrounding sacramental embodiment. An eschatological approach to Pentecostal sacramentality that emphasizes the pneumatological and not just Christological dynamics of the Lord's Supper can open new possibilities for who leads Communion and how.

The Eucharist is as much a pneumatological and eschatological event as it is a Christological one.[265] Many early Pentecostals saw the Lord's Table as an anticipatory event, a preview or rehearsal of the kingdom that is to come.[266] And the primary link between the Eucharist and the final kingdom is the Holy Spirit,[267] signified by the *epiclesis* or calling of the Holy Spirit to come during the celebration of the Supper. Because of the eschatological disposition of the Spirit's

---

260. Grenz and Kjesbo, *Women in the Church*, 204.

261. Grenz and Kjesbo, *Women in the Church*, 204. See 202–5 for their full discussion on eucharistic representation.

262. See Ruether, *Sexism*, 127–31 for discussion of alternative and more egalitarian Christologies. See similar argument by Pannenberg, *Systematic Theology*, 3:391. See also the chapter by Carbine, "Re-visioning the Public Church in a Feminist Perspective," 173–92, esp. 179.

263. Following Yong's similar argument on disability here (*The Bible, Disability*, 128).

264. See Grenz and Kjesbo, *Women in the Church*, 209.

265. Dutko, "Beyond Ordinance," 261–7. See also Stephenson, *Types*, 127.

266. See Green's extensive research here in chapter 3 of *Lord's Supper*, esp. 102, 113–14, 141, 162. See also Gordon Smith's chapter on "Anticipation" in his *A Holy Meal: The Lord's Supper in the Life of the Church* (Grand Rapids: Baker Academic, 2005), 91–8.

267. See Geoffrey Wainwright, *Eucharist and Eschatology* (New York: Oxford University Press, 1981), 126–7.

work,²⁶⁸ turning one's attention to the Spirit in Communion is "almost of necessity a turn to eschatology."²⁶⁹ The eucharistic calling for the Holy Spirit to come—a practice Pentecostals would do well to adopt²⁷⁰—is primarily an eschatological and Pentecost-inspired longing.²⁷¹ Therefore, several Pentecostal theologians have argued for a primarily eschatological approach to the Lord's Supper in Pentecostal churches.²⁷²

The Lord's Supper is an "eschatological catalyst" that deepens and enlivens hope for the coming kingdom²⁷³ and a sign or foreshadow of the future reign of God.²⁷⁴ Therefore, it is no surprise that the Supper has often been compared to Pentecost and Acts 2, so much so that Orthodox theologian Alexander Schmemann suggests that "each Eucharist [is] a Pentecost."²⁷⁵ Like the coming of the Spirit at Pentecost, Communion is an event that begins to call a future world into existence,²⁷⁶ a promise of yet greater things to come.²⁷⁷ As Daniel Tomberlin argues, "the celebration of the Lord's Supper is a prophetic act of worship."²⁷⁸ Therefore, as an eschatological-pneumatological event similar to Acts 2, the practice of the Lord's

---

268. Bauckham and Hart, *Hope Against Hope*, 210. See previous discussion on the eschatological Spirit in 3.4.2.

269. Dayton, *Theological Roots*, 145.

270. See Macchia, *Baptized in the Spirit*, 252.

271. Jürgen Moltmann, "Pentecost and the Theology of Life," in *Pentecostal Movements as an Ecumenical Challenge*, ed. Jürgen Moltmann and Carl-Josef Kuschel (Maryknoll, NY: SCM, 1996), 124. For more on the *epiclesis* and the pneumatological center of the Supper, including its historical roots in the Eastern Christian tradition and its eschatological significance, see Dutko, "Beyond Ordinance," 261-7; Veli-Matti Kärkkäinen, *The Holy Spirit: A Guide to Christian Theology* (Louisville, KY: Westminster John Knox, 2012), 16, 33; Wainwright, *Eucharist and Eschatology*, 100-1; Alexander Schmemann, *For the Life of the World: Sacraments and Orthodoxy*, rev. ed. (Crestwood, NY: St. Vladimir's Seminary Press, 1973), 44.

272. This argument goes hand in hand with a sacramental understanding of the Supper over against the ordinance position (see Dutko, "Beyond Ordinance"; Vondey and Green, "Sacramentality," 258-60). The Eucharist may also contribute to a sounder eschatology, which is part of Wainwright's argument in *Eucharist and Eschatology*. See also Wolfgang Vondey, *People of Bread: Rediscovering Ecclesiology* (Mahwah, NJ: Paulist, 2008), 243-89.

273. Stephenson, *Types*, 123-4, 130. See also 127-8.

274. Yong, *Renewing*, 154, 184; Althouse, "Ascension," 245. For more, see Wainwright, *Eucharist and Eschatology*, 64-9.

275. Schmemann, *Life of the World*, 55.

276. J.-M.-R. Tillard, *Flesh of the Church, Flesh of Christ: At the Source of the Ecclesiology of Communion*, trans. Madeleine Beaumont (Collegeville, MN: Liturgical, 2001), 4. See Rausch's chapter "Eschatology and Liturgy" in his *Eschatology*, 123-40.

277. Wainwright, *Eucharist and Eschatology*, 91-2, 95.

278. Daniel Tomberlin, *Pentecostal Sacraments: Encountering God at the Altar* (Cleveland, TN: Center for Pentecostal Leadership and Care, 2010), 178.

Supper must embody the gender equality of the coming kingdom. As we "become partakers of the world to come" in the Lord's Supper, we must embody that world in the present.[279]

The Lord's Supper is an opportunity to participate imaginatively in eschatological–egalitarian realities. If eschatological hope finds some of its strongest expressions in the Eucharist,[280] then Pentecostals cannot separate the eschatological hope of gender equality from their practice of the Lord's Supper. As the Spirit is poured out on both male and female, both inherit the calling to be the continuing presence and ongoing revelation of the Risen Christ to the world.[281] One of the ways this is embodied is through both women and men presiding over the Table. Although many argue that the Eucharist is to be a sign and model of God's eschatological kingdom community,[282] repeatedly overlooked as an application is the participation and presiding of women at the Table in embodying that future kingdom.[283] Although women often exercise authority in or at other places in the church or worship service, the primary message of most Pentecostal churches is that the sacramental role of presiding over the Table belongs to men.[284] This is especially true in other traditions, which require a community to "import" a male pastor or priest to ensure the validity of the Eucharist in situations where only a female leader is available in the local congregation.[285]

The Lord's Supper is a liturgical opportunity to reinforce and embody the eschatological–egalitarian message of Pentecostal churches.[286] As Smith argues, we must experience something and feel it "in our bones" rather than process it only with our minds, what he calls "bodily intelligence."[287] Green makes a similar argument regarding the Lord's Supper. Using the Emmaus story as his example, he suggests it is in the Eucharist that our "eyes are opened" (Luke 24:31) to the correct meaning of Scripture and God's future plans.[288] He states elsewhere,

---

279. Schmemann, *Life of the World*, 42.

280. As argued by Rausch, *Eschatology*, 27. However Rausch, a Catholic theologian, does not suggest this means women could lead the Eucharist as evidenced by his exclusive male language in his section of suggestions for presiders over the Eucharist (133–5). See also Augustine, *Spirit and the Common Good*, 146, 148, 152, 154.

281. Ruether, *Sexism*, 130–1.

282. Althouse, "Ascension," 246.

283. For ways women can embody theological teachings, see Payne, *Gender*; Ambrose, "Aimee Semple McPherson," 113–15.

284. See Payne, *Gender*, 81–2. For group conversations from women about presiding at the Table, see "Setting the Table," 255–8.

285. Ross, "Sacraments: God's Embodiment and Women," 204.

286. See Stephenson, *Types*, 129.

287. Smith, *Imagining*, 53, 59.

288. See Chris E. W. Green, "'Then Their Eyes Were Opened': Pentecostal Reflections on the Church's Scripture and the Lord's Supper," *Pneuma* 35, no. 2 (2013): 220–34. Cf. Green, *Lord's Supper*, 324.

"As Christ comes to the church through the Spirit in the Eucharist-event, the celebrants' eyes are opened to see the one who has gone before us into the Eschaton, a vision that alters the very structure of their being, both communally and personally."[289] Because the imagination is eucharistically formed, what is done at the Table and who presides matter greatly in how Pentecostals think and feel about gender hierarchy as well as in how behaviors are formed.[290] Because of the eschatological significance of the Lord's Supper, asserts Green, "both *what* is done in the worship service and *how* it is done matter to the utmost."[291] The Lord's Table is an opportunity to embody and witness a glimpse of God's promised and preferred future, including egalitarian realities.[292]

Pentecostal churches can eschatologically embody equality in the Eucharist by ensuring that women frequently lead in presiding over the Table. As a prophetic pre-enactment, female leadership over the Supper reminds the congregation that in the kingdom to come, patriarchy will not have the final word. The Lord's Supper is a taste of the future where women and men will co-lead and rule together. Thus, an eschatological–egalitarian Communion praxis imagines a future kingdom of justice *and* places the present under judgment.[293] As Christ's victory over sin—including inequality and suppression of women's voices—is proclaimed in the Eucharist, that victory should be (pre)enacted and embodied through hearing and seeing women at the Table. Another way to eschatologically reorder our imagination at the Supper is to have a woman and man co-preside over the Table together. This equal representation provides a glimpse into the co-equal eschatological trajectory of the Scriptures. Whether women lead Communion alone or co-lead, congregations may have to look beyond ordained and credentialed minsters in situations where no female pastors serve in the church. As a place where distinctions and social standing are reordered,[294] it is fully appropriate for laity to lead in the celebration of the Supper.[295]

When considering the eschatological nature of the Lord's Supper,[296] it is not a stretch to say that participation in a non-egalitarian way may cause a group to be guilty of partaking "in an unworthy manner" (1 Cor. 11:27).[297] In Paul's words to the church in Corinth in Chapter 11, he is primarily angry because their meal was highlighting differences rather than unity and equality (vv. 18–19). When

---

289. Green, *Lord's Supper*, 324.

290. See Green, "Eyes Were Opened," 224–5. For the Eucharist's impact on behavior, see Tillard, *Flesh of the Church*, 72.

291. Green, *Lord's Supper*, 324n392; italics in the original.

292. See Green, *Lord's Supper*, 324–5.

293. See Rausch, *Eschatology*, 158–9, although his stance is not egalitarian.

294. See Don E. Saliers, *Worship as Theology: Foretaste as Glory Divine* (Nashville, TN: Abingdon, 1994), 60.

295. For an argument on laity leading communion, see Stephenson, *Types*, 124–5.

296. Matt. 26:29; Luke 22:16, 18; 1 Cor. 11:26.

297. See Gladd and Harmon, *Inaugurated Eschatology*, 122–3.

distinctions are reinforced through the Lord's Supper, Paul says it should not even be considered the Lord's Table at all (vv. 20–22). By not considering all persons present, including women, churches fail to discern the body and may be bringing eschatological judgment—rather than promises—upon themselves (v. 29). Instead, as perhaps the central act of the church's worship,[298] the eucharistic table should embody the coming egalitarian kingdom and serve as an opportunity to reimagine ecclesiastical gender roles.[299]

Communion in classical Pentecostal churches is a recurrent opportunity for the congregation to participate eschatologically in being transformed into the egalitarian new humanity.[300] The eschatological vision of the Eucharist represents what is and what is to come.[301] Because worship activities and spaces communicate beliefs about gender and authority,[302] female voices must be heard at the Table, and women need to be visibly seen as re-presenting Christ and the new humanity he represents. An eschatological–egalitarian approach to the Lord's Supper has the potential to capture the imagination of parishioners and lead to participation in egalitarian realities. It also may enrich and deepen the experience of Communion, given that some have argued the spiritual symbolism of feeding, comforting, and giving birth found in the practice are actually *better* represented by women or at least come more naturally.[303] Male overrepresentation in the Supper moves opposite the eschatological–egalitarian trajectory of the Scriptures and also deprives both genders of participating fully in the multidimensional mystery of the Eucharist that is best represented by both women and men standing on behalf of Christ at the Table.

As eschatological community, the worship of the church is meant to point to a greater and new reality. The church is called to stand "within the present as the embodiment of the world's future."[304] Luke Timothy Johnson argues that eschatological–egalitarian passages such as Galatians 3:28 suggest that the church is the sacramental sign and realization of the world's future possibilities.[305]

---

298. According to the World Council of Churches, *Baptism, Eucharist and Ministry*, Faith and Order Paper No. 111 (Geneva, Switzerland: World Council of Churches, 1982), 10.

299. The importance (and metaphor) of a broad and ethical eucharistic table has been used for decades in liberation theology. See Althaus-Reid, "Class, Sex and the Theologian," 25.

300. For this eschatological–egalitarian transformation in the Eucharist, see Ruether, *Sexism*, 209.

301. See Tillard, *Flesh of the Church*, 79 (cf. 68–9); *Baptism, Eucharist and Ministry*, 10–11.

302. See Payne, *Gender*, 81–94, on women and worship space.

303. Christine Gudorf, "The Power to Create: Sacraments and Men's Need to Birth," *Horizons* 14 (1987): 296–309.

304. Augustine, "Liturgy," 182.

305. See Johnson, *New Testament*, 416, 419.

Pentecostal worship in particular, with its performative nature,[306] must find ways to embody this "alternative reality," including the equal inclusion or participation of women and men in the church's language, story, and sacramental activity.[307] As a place of eschatological formation, Pentecostal worship can reimagine gender praxis in the church. *How* stories are told (language), *what* stories are told (inclusivity), and *who* tells the stories (embodiment) form and shape the people of God and their behaviors. The way the church talks, acts, and the stories it tells in worship matter greatly and prepare it for God's coming kingdom. Following the example of Paul's epistles, leaders do not use eschatological language for its own sake, but to encourage right-living congruent with the eschatological vision.[308] Unfortunately, Pentecostal churches and leaders rarely connect eschatology to worship praxis or egalitarian initiatives, but this also presents an opportunity for Pentecostals to reconsider their corporate worship and how it may (or may not) reflect God's eschatological–egalitarian kingdom.

## 6.4 Conclusion

The goal of this chapter was to eschatologically reimagine gender praxis in Pentecostalism by critically applying the hermeneutic and praxis models constructed in the previous chapters. An eschatological–egalitarian praxis corrects male-dominated practices and also constructs practices that reify eschatological equality in leadership, form an eschatological consciousness in education, and participate in eschatological realities in worship. Pentecostal ecclesial gender praxis through an eschatological lens rethinks *who* leads and makes decisions on the denominational and local level, reassesses *what* voices and materials are used in theological education, and reimagines *how* language, story, and embodiment are used in worship. Pre-enacting the promise of gender equality ensures women are given equal voice and opportunity in each of these Pentecostal areas of praxis.

Like other chapters in this work, there is a natural interconnectedness and dialectic between the sections. As the eschatological imagination influences the church's gender approach to language, storytelling, and sacramental activity, participation in egalitarian leadership has the potential to increase. As women participate more in leadership, the church's eschatological–egalitarian imagination will grow, which in turn will fuel further participation in egalitarian structures. No section by itself offers an adequately complete solution. Merely including more women in leadership is not enough if worship practices continue to reflect a patriarchal worldview. Incorporating and empowering women's voices in the

---

306. See Smith, *Tongues*, 31; Smith, *Imagining*, 15, 173.

307. Frank D. Macchia, "Signs of Grace: Towards a Charismatic Theology of Worship," in Martin, *Theology of Worship*, 154.

308. 1 and 2 Thess. is a good example (such as 1 Thess. 4:13–5:22). See Johnson, *New Testament*, 286–90 for more.

classroom will only make a difference to the extent that they can have a voice at the institutional and decision-making level of Pentecostal organizations. Empowering female pastors and preachers without also equally including women in the leadership and decision-making in the church will fall short of the church's calling to be a foretaste of God's eschatological community. Equally, theology and practices are intertwined in a dialectical relationship, each providing foundation and framework for the other.

Constructing an eschatological praxis, even if partial, supports the growing consensus that Pentecostal eschatology is not and should not be a detached subject or theological discipline that takes place in a vacuum. Eschatology cannot be contained to a single chapter in a systematic theology or attached as an appendix or theological afterthought to the more important matters that precede it. Incorporating eschatological insights into subjects such as theological anthropology and trinitarian theology shows that including—and beginning with—an eschatological framework in our theology impacts ecclesial gender praxis. Whether or not we think about human beings and God in eschatological terms has a profound impact on how we approach or create hierarchical structures in the present. The way we imagine our own eschatological existence and how we reflect God's eschatological being has practical implications for the worship, structures, and language of the church and whether we seek to correct or acquiesce to gendered privilege and hierarchy.

Previous hermeneutical and theological works that argue for gender equality lack a full-scale and integrated praxis, often settling for a few pages of methodologically disconnected or inconsistent suggestions at the end. Similarly, works on eschatology that advocate for its practical relevance often fail to offer specific examples, settling for generalizations instead of concrete applications. I termed this situation the "praxis problem" and sought in this chapter to offer a contribution to, as well as an example for, the fields of eschatology and theological gender studies by providing developed suggestions for how gender praxis is reimagined "on the ground" through an eschatological lens. By pre-enacting the promise of gender equality in leadership, education, and worship, Pentecostals are preparing the way for the eschatological–egalitarian kingdom. Rather than re-enacting and preserving the "old world" of patriarchy that is passing away, an eschatological–egalitarian praxis pre-enacts the new egalitarian world. Gender-based limitations move opposite the eschatological–egalitarian trajectory of the Scriptures, whereas equal voice and opportunity for women acts as a sign of the ultimate renewal of creation and move Pentecostals closer to the end to which they are called.

# CONCLUSION

A headline from the 1991 Canadian *Pentecostal Testimony* reads, "Next Generation of Women in Ministry, Please Stand Up!"[1] Unfortunately, for the last one hundred years no firm critical-theological ground has existed for Pentecostal women to stand confidently upon, denying them unhindered access to and participation in all levels of church ministry and leadership. My work has identified the reason for this "shaky ground" as the lack of a consistent theological authorizing hermeneutic for the ministry of women, which has caused perpetual indecision and inconsistency over women's leadership. This uncertainty has led to a century of paradoxical messages regarding the role of women within Pentecostalism, described as the competing impulses of affirmation and denial, exclusion and embrace, liberation and limitation. To date, no complete critical approach has been able to resolve this paradox in a way that incorporates the historical, biblical, theological, and ecclesiological questions surrounding the Pentecostal gender debate. Therefore, the question that launched this research project was if a methodological solution exists that can convincingly resolve the Pentecostal gender paradox. In other words, is there a firm and lasting ground for Pentecostal women to stand on, one built on a foundation consistent with Pentecostal history, hermeneutics, theology, and praxis?

### *Review of Major Contributions and Invitation to Further Research*

This project has argued that eschatology is not only a firm ground but the "final ground" on which present and future generations of Pentecostal women can confidently stand.[2] An eschatological resolving of the Pentecostal gender paradox presents a comprehensive and cohesive argument for gender equality that positions eschatology as the methodological starting point and authorizing hermeneutic for the ministry of Pentecostal women. My work represents the first full-scale attempt—Pentecostal or otherwise—to approach the gender question through

---

1. "Next Generation of Women in Ministry Please Stand Up!" *Pentecostal Testimony*, June 1991, 2.

2. For eschatology as a "final ground" for social issues, see Bauckham and Hart, *Hope against Hope*, 56.

an eschatological lens from beginning to end, concluding that because gender equality will be the way of God's kingdom in *the* end (*eschaton*), gender inequality must come to *an* end in the present. Other works have sought to address the Pentecostal gender problem solely through one or two types of argument, whether it be historical, biblical/hermeneutical, theological/ontological, or ecclesiological/practical. But to address fully the layers and complexity of the gender paradox, a unifying methodological thread needs to be consistently woven through each of these areas to make an integrated and convincing argument that frees Pentecostal women to act without reservation on their God-given vocational callings.

Eschatology is considered an unlikely source of liberation for women. Chapter 1 categorized three existing views within feminist theology on eschatology's relationship to gender and determined that eschatology is most often considered incompatible, irrelevant, or insufficient as a method for egalitarian arguments. However, a few Pentecostal scholars have hinted at the promise of an eschatological approach to gender issues and opened the door for further inquiry. This Pentecostal openness to eschatology as potential cantilever to freedoms for women is partly inspired by the early egalitarian and eschatological heart of the movement. Chapter 2 established through historical research that eschatology functioned as an authorizing hermeneutic for women leaders in early Pentecostalism, which led to newfound (though not complete) freedoms for women. Early writings and periodicals as well as three case studies of early Pentecostal women revealed a consistent pattern of how eschatology functioned as a cornerstone for the legitimization of the unrestricted ministry of women. Through historical research, eschatology emerged as not only a possible viable critical approach but also a potential valid and valuable solution to the Pentecostal gender paradox.

Due to related historical shifts in Pentecostal hermeneutics and eschatology, Chapter 3 investigated how the authorizing hermeneutic of eschatology was lost and eventually replaced with hermeneutical hesitancy and inconsistency that more strictly limited women. These hermeneutical and theological shifts removed eschatology from the center of Pentecostal praxis, a development concomitant with the decline of the prominent place of women in the Pentecostal movement. However, more recent developments in Pentecostal eschatology and hermeneutics have opened the door to (re)consider eschatology as egalitarian centerpiece. Chapter 3 thus began the construction and articulation of an eschatological–egalitarian hermeneutic of imagination and participation.

Chapters 4–6 (re)constructed the eschatological authorizing hermeneutic by first establishing the hermeneutical priority of eschatological texts on gender and weaving together the unified eschatological–egalitarian biblical narrative thread. Creation (Gen. 1–3), the ministry of Jesus (Gal. 3:28) and Pentecost (Acts 2:17-18) are three eschatologically significant narratives that establish an egalitarian trajectory that inspires the imagination and invites present participation. Part of the weakness in previous critical approaches to the gender problem is that they lack a thorough egalitarian praxis that is solidly built on and integrated into their methodological approach. Similarly, eschatological works in general tend to promise practical implications but often fail to deliver. Chapter 5 avoided these weaknesses by proposing a pre-enactment praxis model that is dialectical, experiential, and experimental over against a strict re-enactment model in order to solve both the gender praxis problem and eschatological praxis problem. The final chapter critically applied the hermeneutical and praxis models of the previous chapters to correct current patriarchal practices and construct suggestions for what an eschatological–egalitarian praxis might look like on the ground and particularly in Pentecostal leadership, education, and worship.

This work has proven the potential of eschatology as a critical, versatile methodological approach to an important social concern. Eschatology has historically suffered an estrangement from practical implications, but this study has shown a strong interdependence between eschatological beliefs and present practices, eschatological thinking and eschatological living. The successful outcome of this eschatological method opens the door for more topics and issues—both scriptural and cultural—to be examined through an eschatological lens. A benefit of this study is that an eschatological methodological model now exists for others to apply to other areas that do not initially appear to have direct eschatological connection. Full-scale eschatological approaches to racial, ecological, socio-economic, ecumenical, and global issues within Pentecostalism are some potential areas for further research. For example, what would an eschatological approach to other religions and interfaith dialogue look like? Although this study's focus is primarily the Pentecostal gender binary that limits women and advantages men in ecclesial life, the possibility exists to examine the implications of an eschatological methodology and hermeneutic for other gender and sexuality topics within Pentecostal life.[3] Domestic, educational, and vocational issues related to gender would also benefit from a comprehensive eschatological approach. Each chapter or set of chapters also makes the important contribution of introducing an eschatological lens to the specific areas of Pentecostal history, hermeneutics, and praxis. This eschatological method and its heuristic use merits consideration in each of these fields as an important Pentecostal way of thinking and being in the world.

Other traditions, faith communities, and geographic areas (outside of classical North American Pentecostalism) can also benefit from and test the conclusions of this study. Eschatology is often ethnically and geographically contextualized;[4] therefore, there is opportunity to examine the challenges and potential of an eschatological resolving of paradoxical gender practices in other parts of the world. Christian eschatological traditions outside of Pentecostalism can investigate how eschatology has affected women in their own tradition and how an eschatological

---

3. For a starting point, see Marius Nel, *LGBTIQ+ People and Pentecostals: An African Pentecostal Hermeneutical Perspective* (Zürich, CH: LIT Verlag, 2020).

4. For more on the different eschatologies in various places, see section 4 of Althouse and Waddell, *Eschatologies*, 315–400. For example, see Nel, *African Pentecostalism and Eschatological Expectations*.

method might contribute to solving their own questions or uncertainties concerning the ministry of women. Going even broader, the study of the relationship between eschatological beliefs and gender practices in other religions, including those with contrasting eschatological visions to Pentecostalism, might provide insight or inroads for tackling gender inequality in other religious contexts.[5] For example, how does belief in reincarnation influence gender practices in the present world? Different Christian traditions, geographical contexts, and even religions can benefit from an imaginative, eschatologically driven approach to the moral and ethical concerns of our time, and perhaps no issue is more important than gender inequality.

## Impact: Global and Ecclesiastical Implications

The introduction to this work analyzed how a solution to the gender problem in Pentecostalism would impact women globally. Indecision or ambiguity about women's equality is not just a Pentecostal theological problem; it is a global human problem. However, people's theology and religious beliefs do play a significant role in addressing gender (in)equality around the world. This is especially true in the two-thirds world where Pentecostalism continues to grow in number and influence. Some have featured Pentecostalism's positive impact on women's liberation and empowerment in these contexts, while others highlight Pentecostalism's alignment with theological belief systems that support patriarchal and misogynistic systems. Most conclude that the current situation is a mix of both, a confluence of competing trajectories, hermeneutical inconsistencies, and scriptural ambiguities about women, what this project initially introduced as the "gender paradox." Therefore, which direction Pentecostals take on the gender question and how they decide to sort through their uncertainty will have global implications for women. The hope for this work is that Pentecostals will confidently embrace eschatological equality as the final word in resolving any and all issues related to women's (in)equality.

Any authoritarian, misogynistic, or patriarchal tendencies within the Pentecostal movement, even in the developed world, feed into the overall oppression experienced by women around the globe. Theological justification of male dominance and women's inferior status is a matter of life or death for women in places of the world where they are frequently devalued, exploited, and commodified. Women's voices, experiences, rights, freedoms, and education have been suppressed in the church for centuries. Therefore, the sweet foretaste of God's eschatological–egalitarian kingdom also leaves a bitter taste as one presently considers the current global situation of inequality in churches and society, including in places where Pentecostalism is one of if not the dominant expression of faith. Eschatology is not an invitation to escape from this world and its injustices; rather, the experience of

---

5. See Yong, *Renewing*, 42–3. For the relationship between feminist theology and world religions, see Carmody, *Feminist Theology*, 61–5.

the eschatological Spirit is what enables people to understand better this world and engage its injustices more deeply. Belief in eschatological equality does not devalue the present work before us, but rather adds value and urgency to it as Pentecostal women and men pursue God's eschatological–egalitarian kingdom based on solid historical and hermeneutical grounds that inspire their praxis. I would like to close by offering three eschatologically driven action steps to Pentecostal ecclesiastical leaders (especially men) about pursuing this cause.

I have been asked many times over the course of my research why I have undertaken this project. After all, I am a man, and this is a "women's issue." My response is that this is not a women's issue, but a theological and gospel issue that reveals one's greater understanding of who God is, how God acts, and God's ultimate plan, including for men and women. The lack of public voice, visibility, and denominational influence for Pentecostal women is a problem for *all* who believe in God's unfolding eschatological plan. Both women *and* men are harmed by and need to seek liberation from patriarchy, male dominance, and any theology or praxis that is less than fully egalitarian. Eschatological egalitarianism is not a women's movement; it is a movement of the Spirit for all and involves the participation of all. As most positions of power and influence within Pentecostalism are still held by men, the movement toward an eschatological–egalitarian church specifically needs the support and participation of these leaders if it is to succeed. I suggest three action steps for Pentecostal leaders to be "in step" with the eschatological Spirit (Gal. 5:25): they must reflect critically, relate compassionately, and rally collectively.

Step one for Pentecostal leaders inspired by the eschatological–egalitarian vision is to reflect critically on the effects of sexism, male-dominated power structures, and all injustices past and present toward women in the church.[6] In religious terms, leaders need to repent and seek reconciliation between men and women. According to Scripture, the appropriate response to visions of the eschatological new age is repentance and change (Luke 3:7-18, responding to 3:4-6; Acts 2:37-38, responding to 2:16-21). As leaders encounter eschatological texts on gender, they can begin to align their practices with the egalitarian hope of the Scriptures, believing the egalitarian trajectory lost in Genesis 3 is being restored in the present through Christ (Gal. 3:28) by the Spirit (Acts 2:17-18). To embrace God's eschatological–egalitarian plan, Pentecostal leaders must continually work to liberate themselves from the sins of systemic sexism until the final day arrives. Hierarchy, domination, power, and control over women—whether subtle or overt, whether by men or women—dehumanize both sexes and distort their humanity and perception of each other, robbing them of mutual enrichment. Public and written confessions from church and denominational leaders, recognizing the hurt they have caused by their actions *and* their silence, is a first step toward eschatologically inspired healing between men and women. However, being

---

6. One of the calls of Alexander and Bowers, *What Women Want*, 127, and Ruether, *Sexism*, 178–82.

eschatologically formed into a new humanity also requires that leaders do the work to relate compassionately, to enter into the struggles of women in the church.

Step two is for Pentecostal leaders to listen and relate compassionately to the stories of women in order to understand better what it is like to be a woman in the church. When women are not given room or voice to express their frustrations and struggles, their alienation from the church grows deeper as the eschatological-egalitarian vision clashes with the reality of most churches. Women in Pentecostal environments report constant discrimination and lack of respect, and express fear of being labeled as "divisive" or "unscriptural" if they speak up, or being pejoratively labeled as a "feminist."[7] Many women convey intense difficulty in going to or being a part of a church where their voices and experiences are not represented, feeling that the message of the church is anything but "good news" for women. The inability of leaders to compassionately relate and listen is causing women, including many Pentecostals, to leave the church due to feeling marginalized and excluded from meaningful participation.

An approach more congruent with the eschatological vision is to create an inclusive and safe place where the voices, experiences, and frustrations of women can be heard.[8] Leaders can encourage women to speak up and can create listening groups for women to share their stories, perspectives, and pain of what it is like to worship and serve in male-dominated cultures and structures within the church. Leaders, and especially men, can become more aware of the incredible pressure put on women as mothers, wives, daughters, or in male-dominated professions. But church leaders must do more than just hear the stories of women. To truly show they relate, leaders must change their practices, inspired by the eschatological-egalitarian vision of the Scriptures.

In addition to adopting the eschatologically based worship and leadership practices of Chapter 6, leaders can relate by trying to see through the eyes of women in order to develop practices that show awareness of women's lives and experiences. Until women's experiences are a part of shaping Pentecostal worship and institutional decision-making, the eschatological vision is incomplete. Pastors and denominational leaders, especially men, who plan and prepare sermons, presentations, and conferences should ask, "What will this sound like to a woman? What will this be like for a mother? What will this feel like for someone who has experienced domestic, sexual, or physical abuse or some other abuse of power?" Asking these questions encourage men to be more careful and sensitive with the imagery and language they use so that they do not overlook half or more of their parishioners or constituents.

---

7. See Catford's survey research, "Women's Experiences," 39–40.

8. For example, our church on Vancouver Island, British Columbia, together went through the book *Jesus Feminist* by Sarah Bessey in a small group format that allowed women to share their experiences. For some suggestions, see Lauren J. Raley, "Toward a Pentecostal Ecclesiology: Making Room for Survivors of Gender-Based Violence," in Alexander et al., *Sisters, Mothers, Daughters*, 214–20.

One way in which leaders can learn to relate better is by regularly reading female authors and books or blogs about women's experiences. Topics such as childhood, motherhood, eating disorders, menstruation, reproduction, sexual violence and rape, domestic abuse, and simply everyday "normalized" instances of sexism experienced by women are commonly overlooked by churches and male leaders due to lack of exposure to female writers.[9] Relatedly, men should intentionally put themselves under the "authority" of female pastors, teachers, preachers, professors, and the like. These steps can also help male pastors offer pastoral care that is "female-friendly" and less gender-biased, helping bring theological meaning to the

---

9. Just a few reading suggestions (not previously cited) from various disciplines, which may enhance pastoral ministry to women: Kat Armas, *Abuelita Faith: What Women on the Margins Teach Us about Wisdom, Persistence, and Strength* (Grand Rapids: Brazos, 2021); Susannah Larry, *Sexualized Violence, the Bible, and Standing with Survivors* (Harrisonburg, VA: Herald, 2021); Beth Allison Barr, *The Making of Biblical Womanhood: How the Subjugation of Women Became Gospel Truth* (Grand Rapids: Brazos, 2021); Sheila Wray Gregoire, Rebecca Gregoire Lindenbach, and Joanna Sawatsky, *The Great Sex Rescue: The Lies You've Been Taught and How to Recover What God Intended* (Grand Rapids: Baker Books, 2021); Cheryl Bridges Johns, *Seven Transforming Gifts of Menopause: An Unexpected Spiritual Journey* (Grand Rapids: Brazos, 2020); Casselberry and Pritchard, *Spirit on the Move*; Stovell, *Making Sense of Motherhood*; Candida R. Moss and Joel S. Baden, *Reconceiving Infertility: Biblical Perspectives on Procreation and Childlessness* (Princeton, NJ: Princeton University Press, 2015); Elaine A. Heath, *We Were the Least of These: Reading the Bible with Survivors of Sexual Abuse* (Grand Rapids: Brazos, 2011); Joan D. Chittister, *The Story of Ruth: Twelve Moments in Every Woman's Life*, art by John August Swanson (Grand Rapids: Eerdmans, 2010); Kristina LaCelle-Peterson, *Liberating Tradition: Women's Identity and Vocation in Christian Perspective* (Grand Rapids: Baker Academic, 2008); Daphne C. Wiggins, *Righteous Content: Black Women's Perspectives of Church and Faith* (New York: New York University Press, 2005); Debra Rienstra, *Great with Child: Reflections on Faith, Fullness, and Becoming a Mother* (New York: Tarcher/Putnam, 2002); various authors in the chapter "Our Bodies, Ourselves" in *Wisdom of Daughters*, 109–28; Jeanne Stevenson-Moessner, ed., *In Her Own Time: Women and Developmental Issues in Pastoral Care* (Minneapolis: Fortress, 2000); Linda M. Blum, *At the Breast: Ideologies of Breastfeeding and Motherhood in the Contemporary United States* (Boston: Beacon, 1999); Ellyn Sanna, *Motherhood: A Spiritual Journey* (Mahwah, NJ: Paulist, 1997); Joan Borysenko, *A Woman's Book of Life: The Biology, Psychology, and Spirituality of the Feminine Life Cycle* (New York: Riverhead Books, 1996); Christie Cozad Neuger, ed., *The Arts of Ministry: Feminist-Womanist Approaches* (Louisville, KY: Westminster John Knox, 1996); Anne Lamott, *Operating Instructions: A Journal of My Son's First Year* (New York: Pantheon, 1993). For a catalogue of as many as 100,000 personal stories from over twenty-five countries (and counting), see Laura Bates's The Everyday Sexism Project (website), updated April 29, 2021, https://everydaysexism.com/. For resources for those in Canadian contexts, see the Canadian Women's Foundation (website), updated April 20, 2022, https://canadianwomen.org/.

journeys, lives, and relationships of women.[10] Compassionately relating to these experiences of women will inform further critical reflection and will also go a long way toward women feeling heard. However, only reflecting critically and relating compassionately is not enough. The last eschatological action step for ecclesiastical leaders is to rally collectively around the eschatological–egalitarian vision.

As Pentecostal male leaders still have more positional influence and authority than women, they must use their status to rally for the advocation, liberation, and empowerment of their female colleagues. The loudest voices for women's equality need not (and cannot) only be women! Men must fight the common notion, especially in North American churches, that women's equality is no longer a problem and that it is time to move on because women are now "equal" on paper in many Pentecostal churches. But as long as gender-based discrimination still exists in the church, Pentecostal leaders must continue imagining and participating in God's egalitarian kingdom. Leaders can teach and model the eschatological-egalitarian hope by proclaiming publicly the lack of women leaders and preachers as a sign of a worldly, lukewarm church unprepared for the kingdom to come.[11] Pentecostal men should speak out against any conservatism that tries to reign in the radical vision of God's eschatological plan of the co-equal leadership and participation of women and men.

Eschatologically driven leaders will not see sexism as a women's problem, but their problem, the church's problem, and a global problem. As people of the Spirit of Pentecost, Pentecostals should invite, affirm, and welcome the voices and leadership of women. Pentecostal leaders can recruit the eschatological-egalitarian imagination and invite participation by publicly affirming women leaders, providing opportunities for preaching and leadership, "sponsoring" them for promotions, and introducing them to persons of influence on the senior level.[12] Disaffiliating with the male-only, tight-knit network of promotions and decision-making may come at the risk of men losing their current status, privilege, and even jobs, but an eschatological consciousness will embolden men's advocacy for women.[13] This male advocacy and voice is especially important in countries and cultural contexts where women may face danger for speaking up or encounter more hurdles and resistance to the idea of women's equality. By reflecting critically, relating compassionately, and rallying collectively, Pentecostal leaders inspired

---

10. See Carolyn Stahl Bohler, "Female-Friendly Pastoral Care," in Stevenson-Moessner, *Through the Eyes of Women*, 27–49.

11. As Church of God in Christ minister Charles E. Brown did (see Hollingsworth and Browning, "Daughters," 161). For more on the importance of male leaders endorsing women and some examples (from the AG), see Qualls, *Forgive Us*, 181, 186–92.

12. These are some of the suggestions of Alexander and Bowers, *What Women Want* in chapter 4, "Are Women Flourishing as Ministers?" See also Deborah Menken Gill, "Called by God—What's a Women to Do and What Can We Do to Help Her," *Enrichment: A Journal for Pentecostal Ministry* 2, no. 2 (Spring 1997): 33–5.

13. Ruether, *Sexism*, 191–2.

by the eschatological-egalitarian imagination can take steps toward healing the gender divide in Pentecostalism.

## Concluding Word

It is time for Pentecostals to move past the questioning of women's leadership and stand boldly and firmly on eschatological-egalitarian convictions. Warrington warns Pentecostals that as people who use Pentecost and Acts as their model for unity they "need to be aware of the possibility that their questioning whether God may be working in other parts of the Church may be as inappropriate as the Jewish Christians in the early Church who were concerned about the possibility that God could be working among the Gentiles."[14] Pentecostal leaders need to develop an eschatological "hermeneutical courage" to articulate the right-now relevance of eschatological reflection the way Peter did at Pentecost.[15] The eschatological events that unfolded at Pentecost led to accusations of drunkenness (Acts 2:13), but Peter offered a counterinterpretation, one that was bold, surprising, and changed accepted ideas of how God works. Similarly, the promotion of women's equality may lead to accusations of espousing a liberal theology or feminist agenda, but Pentecostal women and men can be confident and declare with eschatological conviction that "this" points to "that," namely, God's eschatological plan for gender equality "in the last days" (Acts 2:16-17).

The action steps in these concluding chapters complete the first attempt or "sketch" of the hermeneutical circle or dialectic of eschatological imagination and egalitarian participation. However, the circle is meant to be traced over or started anew repeatedly, and the dialectic should continue to go back and forth. A conclusion is not meant to bring the process to an end: the curtain has not closed, and the eschatological drama is not complete. Rather, this work and its applications are the initial dress rehearsal in the ongoing attempt to present the best possible performance, with the realization that perfection will never come this side of the *eschaton*, and therefore the work will always be in process and never finished. Praxis suggestions and action steps are not the end of theological inquiry; rather, they are a (new) beginning for further reflection. It is perfectly acceptable to realize the penultimacy of all our actions and movements toward equality. We are not yet a community or world where men and women are equal, but I have argued that perhaps that world is not so far away and in fact is already among us, awaiting our eschatological participation.

---

14. Warrington, *Pentecostal Theology*, 179.
15. Smith, *Tongues*, 22, 34. For the role of courage for eschatological living, see Shields, *Eschatological Imagination*, 172-3.

# BIBLIOGRAPHY

Abraham, Joseph. "Feminist Hermeneutics and Pentecostal Spirituality: The Creation Narrative of Genesis as a Paradigm." *Asian Journal of Pentecostal Studies* 6, no. 1 (2003): 3–21.

Adewuya, J. Ayodeji. "Constructing an African Pentecostal Eschatology: Which Way?" In *Perspectives in Pentecostal Eschatologies: World Without End*, edited by Peter Althouse and Robby Waddell, 361–74. Eugene, OR: Pickwick, 2010.

Aisenberg, Nadya, and Mona Harrington. *Women of Academe: Outsiders in the Sacred Grove*. Amherst, MA: University of Massachusetts Press, 1988.

Alexander, Estrelda Y. "Introduction." In *Philip's Daughters: Women in Pentecostal-Charismatic Leadership*, edited by Estrelda Y. Alexander and Amos Yong, 1–15. Eugene, OR: Pickwick, 2009.

Alexander, Estrelda Y. *Limited Liberty: The Legacy of Four Pentecostal Women Pioneers*. Cleveland, OH: Pilgrim, 2008.

Alexander, Estrelda Y. "The Role of Women in the Azusa Street Revival." In *The Azusa Street Revival and Its Legacy*, edited by Harold Hunter and Cecil M. Robeck Jr., 61–77. Eugene, OR: Wipf & Stock, 2006.

Alexander, Estrelda Y. "When Liberation Becomes Survival." In *Women in Pentecostal and Charismatic Ministry: Informing a Dialogue on Gender, Church, and Ministry*, edited by Margaret English de Alminana and Lois E. Olena, 323–47. Leiden: Brill, 2017.

Alexander, Estrelda Y. *The Women of Azusa Street*. Cleveland, OH: Pilgrim, 2005.

Alexander, Estrelda Y., and Amos Yong, eds. *Philip's Daughters: Women in Pentecostal-Charismatic Leadership*. Eugene, OR: Pickwick, 2009.

Alexander, Kimberly Ervin. "'Singing Heavenly Music': R. Hollis Gause's Theology of Worship and Pentecostal Experience." In *Toward a Pentecostal Theology of Worship*, edited by Lee Roy Martin, 201–20. Cleveland, TN: CPT, 2016.

Alexander, Kimberly Ervin. "'With Blessings They Cover the Bitterness': Persisting and Worshipping Through Brokenness – Pentecostal Women and the Pentecostal Tradition(s)." In *Grieving, Brooding, and Transforming: The Spirit, The Bible, and Gender*, edited by Cheryl Bridges Johns and Lisa P. Stephenson, 135–58. Leiden: Brill, 2021.

Alexander, Kimberly Ervin, Melissa L. Archer, Mark J. Cartledge, and Michael D. Palmer, eds. *Sisters, Mothers, Daughters: Pentecostal Perspectives on Violence against Women*. Leiden: Brill, 2022.

Alexander, Kimberly Ervin, and James P. Bowers. *What Women Want: Pentecostal Women Ministers Speak for Themselves*. Lanham, MD: Seymour, 2013.

Alexander, Kimberly Ervin, and R. Hollis Gause. *Women in Leadership: A Pentecostal Perspective*. Cleveland, TN: Center for Pentecostal Leadership and Care, 2006.

Alexander, Paul. *Peace to War: Shifting Allegiances in the Assemblies of God*. Telford, PA: Cascadia, 2009.

Alfaro, Sammy. "'*Se fue con el Señor*': The Hispanic Pentecostal Funeral as Anticipatory Celebration." In *Perspectives in Pentecostal Eschatologies: World Without End*, edited by Peter Althouse and Robby Waddell, 340–60. Eugene, OR: Pickwick, 2010.

Althaus-Reid, Marcella. "Class, Sex and the Theologian: Reflections on the Liberationist Movement in Latin America." In *Another Possible World: Reclaiming Liberation Theology*, edited by Marcella Maria Althaus-Reid, Ivan Petrella, and Luiz Carlos Susin, 23–38. London: SCM, 2007.

Althouse, Peter. "Ascension—Pentecost—Eschaton: A Theological Framework for Pentecostal Ecclesiology." In *Toward a Pentecostal Ecclesiology: The Church and the Fivefold Gospel*, edited by John Christopher Thomas, 225–47. Cleveland, TN: CPT, 2010.

Althouse, Peter. "Betwixt and Between the Cross and the Eschaton: Pentecostal Worship in the Context of Ritual Play." In *Toward a Pentecostal Theology of Worship*, edited by Lee Roy Martin, 265–79. Cleveland, TN: CPT, 2016.

Althouse, Peter. "The Landscape of Pentecostal and Charismatic Eschatology: An Introduction." In *Perspectives in Pentecostal Eschatologies: World Without End*, edited by Peter Althouse and Robby Waddell, 1–21. Eugene, OR: Pickwick, 2010.

Althouse, Peter. "Pentecostal Eschatology in Context: The Eschatological Orientation of the Full Gospel." In *Perspectives in Pentecostal Eschatologies: World Without End*, edited by Peter Althouse and Robby Waddell, 205–31. Eugene, OR: Pickwick, 2010.

Althouse, Peter. *Spirit of the Last Days: Pentecostal Eschatology in Conversation with Jürgen Moltmann*. London: T&T Clark, 2003.

Althouse, Peter, and Robby Waddell. "The Pentecostals and Their Scriptures." *Pneuma* 38, no. 1–2 (2016): 115–21.

Althouse, Peter, and Robby Waddell, eds. *Perspectives in Pentecostal Eschatologies: World Without End*. Eugene, OR: Pickwick, 2010.

Alvarado, Johnathan E. "Pentecostal Worship and the Creation of Meaning." In *Toward a Pentecostal Theology of Worship*, edited by Lee Roy Martin, 221–33. Cleveland, TN: CPT, 2016.

Ambrose, Linda M. "Aimee Semple McPherson: Gender Theory, Worship, and the Arts." *Pneuma* 39 (2017): 113–21.

Ambrose, Linda M. "Shaming the Men into Keeping Up with the Ladies: Constructing Pentecostal Masculinities." In *Sisters, Mothers, Daughters: Pentecostal Perspectives on Violence against Women*, edited by Kimberly Ervin Alexander et al., 69–85. Leiden: Brill, 2022.

Ambrose, Linda M. "Thinking Through the Theological and Methodological Quandaries of Gender and Canadian Pentecostal History." *Canadian Journal of Pentecostal-Charismatic Christianity* 3 (2012): 70–88.

Ambrose, Linda. "Zelma and Beulah Argue: Sisters in the Canadian Pentecostal Movement." In *Winds From the North: Canadian Contributions to the Pentecostal Movement*, edited by Michael Wilkinson and Peter Althouse, 99–127. Leiden: Brill, 2010.

Anderson, Allan Heaton. *An Introduction to Pentecostalism: Global Charismatic Christianity*. 2nd ed. Cambridge: Cambridge University Press, 2014.

Anderson, Robert Mapes. *Vision of the Disinherited: The Making of American Pentecostalism*. Oxford: Oxford University Press, 1979.

Archer, Kenneth J. "Early Pentecostal Biblical Interpretation." *JPT* 9, no. 1 (2001): 32–70.

Archer, Kenneth J. *A Pentecostal Hermeneutic: Spirit, Scripture and Community*. Cleveland, TN: CPT, 2009.

Archer, Kenneth J. "A Pentecostal Way of Doing Theology: Method and Manner." *International Journal of Systematic Theology* 9, no. 3 (July 2007): 301–14.

Archer, Kenneth J. "Spirited Conversation About Hermeneutics: A Pentecostal Hermeneut's Response to Craig Keener's Spirit Hermeneutics." *Pneuma* 39 (2017): 179–97.

Archer, Melissa L. "Was the Spirit Poured Out on Women to Remain Silent in the Church? Reading 1 Corinthians 14.34–35 and 1 Timothy 2.11-15 in the Light of Pentecost." In *Grieving, Brooding, and Transforming: The Spirit, the Bible, and Gender*, edited by Cheryl Bridges Johns and Lisa P. Stephenson, 123–34. Leiden: Brill, 2021.

Archer, Melissa L. "Women in Ministry: A Pentecostal Reading of New Testament Texts." In *Women in Pentecostal and Charismatic Ministry: Informing a Dialogue on Gender, Church, and Ministry*, edited by Margaret English de Alminana and Lois E. Olena, 35–56. Leiden: Brill, 2017.

Archer, Melissa L. "Worship in the Book of Revelation." In *Toward a Pentecostal Theology of Worship*, edited by Lee Roy Martin, 113–38. Cleveland, TN: CPT, 2016.

Argue, Zelma. "Emergency Ministries: 'The Time Is Short.'" *The Pentecostal Evangel* 1 (December 2, 1939): 10–11.

Argue, Zelma. "Your Sons and Your Daughters." *Canadian Pentecostal Testimony* 1 (December 1920): 3.

Armas, Kat. *Abuelita Faith: What Women on the Margins Teach Us About Wisdom, Persistence, and Strength*. Grand Rapids, MI: Brazos, 2021.

Armstrong, Sally. *Ascent of Women*. Toronto, ON: Random House Canada, 2013.

Arrington, French L. "Dispensationalism." In *NIDPCM*, rev. ed, edited by Stanley M. Burgess and Eduard M. van der Maas, 584–6. Grand Rapids, MI: Zondervan, 2002.

Assemblies of God District/Network Superintendents. "Female Lead Pastors: A Discussion Worth Having." Curated by Gene Roncone (A Collaborative Resource). September 2021. https://penndel.org/wp-content/uploads/2021/09/Female-Lead-Pastors.pdf.

Augustine, Daniela C. "Liturgy, *Theosis*, and the Renewal of the World." In *Toward a Pentecostal Theology of Worship*, edited by Lee Roy Martin, 165–85. Cleveland, TN: CPT, 2016.

Augustine, Daniela C. *Pentecost, Hospitality, and Transfiguration: Toward a Spirit-inspired Vision of Social Transformation*. Cleveland, TN: CPT, 2012.

Augustine, Daniela C. *The Spirit and the Common Good: Shared Flourishing in the Image of God*. Grand Rapids, MI: Eerdmans, 2019.

Augustine, Daniela C., and Chris E. W. Green, eds. *The Politics of the Spirit: Pentecostal Reflections on Public Responsibility and the Common Good*. Lanham, MD: Seymour, 2022.

Augustine, Saint. *On Christian Teaching*. Translated by R. P. H. Green. Oxford: Oxford University Press, 2008.

Autry, Arden C. "Dimensions of Hermeneutics in Pentecostal Focus." *JPT* 3 (1993): 29–50.

"Back to Pentecost." *AF* 1, no. 2 (October 1906): 3.

Bailey, Kenneth. *Finding the Lost: Cultural Keys to Luke 15*. Saint Louis, MO: Concordia, 1992.

Bailey, Kenneth. *Jacob and the Prodigal: How Jesus Retold Israel's Story*. Downers Grove, IL: InterVarsity, 2003.

Barfoot, Charles H., and Gerald T. Sheppard. "Prophetic vs. Priestly Religion: The Changing Role of Women Clergy in Classical Pentecostal Churches." *Review of Religious Research* 22, no. 1 (September 1980): 2–17.

Barr, Beth Allison. *The Making of Biblical Womanhood: How the Subjugation of Women Became Gospel Truth*. Grand Rapids, MI: Brazos, 2021.

Barrett, C. K. *The Gospel According the St John*. London: SPCK, 1956.

Bartleman, Frank. *Azusa Street*. New Kensington, PA: Whitaker House, 1982.

Barton, Stephen C. *The Spirituality of the Gospels*. London: SPCK, 1992.

Bates, Laura. "The Everyday Sexism Project (website)." Updated April 29, 2021. https://everydaysexism.com/.

Bauckham, Richard. "Eschatology." In *The Oxford Companion to Christian Thought: Intellectual, Spiritual, and Moral Horizons of Christianity*, edited by Adrian Hastings, Alistair Mason, and Hugh Pyper, 206–9. Oxford: Oxford University Press, 2000.

Bauckham, Richard. *Gospel Women: Studies of the Named Women in the Gospels*. Grand Rapids, MI: Eerdmans, 2002.

Bauckham, Richard. *Studies of the Named Women in the Gospels*. Grand Rapids, MI: Eerdmans, 2002.

Bauckham, Richard, and Trevor Hart. *Hope Against Hope: Christian Eschatology at the Turn of the Millennium*. Grand Rapids, MI: Eerdmans, 1999.

Beale, G. K. "The End Starts at the Beginning." In *Making All Things New: Inaugurated Eschatology for the Life of the Church*, edited by Benjamin Gladd and Matthew S. Harmon, 3–14. Grand Rapids, MI: Baker Academic, 2016.

Beavis, Mary Ann, with Elaine Guillemin, and Barbara Pell, eds. *Feminist Theology with a Canadian Accent: Canadian Perspectives on Contextual Feminist Theology*. Ottawa, ON: Novalis, 2008.

Beker, J. Christian. *Paul the Apostle: The Triumph of God in Life and Thought*. Philadelphia, PA: Fortress, 1980.

Bell, E. N. "Some Complaints." *Word and Witness* 10, no. 1 (January 20, 1914): 2.

Bell, E. N. "Women Elders." *The Christian Evangel* 15 (August 1914): 2.

Benvenuti, Sherilyn. "Anointed, Gifted, and Called: Pentecostal Women in Ministry." *Pneuma* 17 (1995): 229–35.

Bergman, Stephen J., and Janet L. Surrey. "The Woman–Man Relationship: Impasses and Possibilities." In *Women's Growth in Diversity: More Writings from the Stone Center*, edited by Judith V. Jordan, 260–88. New York: Guilford, 1997.

Bertone, John A. "Seven Dispensations or Two-Age View of History: A Pauline Perspective." In *Perspectives in Pentecostal Eschatologies: World Without End*, edited by Peter Althouse and Robby Waddell, 61–94. Eugene, OR: Pickwick, 2010.

Bessey, Sarah. *Jesus Feminist: An Invitation to Revisit the Bible's View of Women*. New York: Howard Books, 2013.

Betz, Hans Dieter. *Galatians: A Commentary on Paul's Letter to the Churches in Galatia*. Philadelphia, PA: Fortress, 1979.

"Bible Pentecost." *AF* 1, no. 3 (November 1906): 1.

Billingsley, Scott. *It's a New Day: Race and Gender in the Modern Charismatic Movement*. Tuscaloosa, AL: University of Alabama Press, 2008.

Billson, Janet Mancini, and Carolyn Fluehr-Lobban, eds. *Female Well-Being: Toward a Global Theory of Social Change*. London and New York: Zed Books, 2005.

Blumhofer, Edith L. *Aimee Semple McPherson: Everybody's Sister*. Grand Rapids, MI: Eerdmans, 1993.

Blumhofer, Edith L. *The Assemblies of God: A Chapter in the Story of American Pentecostalism*. 2 vols. Springfield, MO: Gospel Publishing House, 1989.

Blumhofer, Edith L. "A Confused Legacy: Reflections of Evangelical Attitudes toward Ministering Women in the Past Century." *Fides et Historia* 22, no. 1 (Winter–Spring 1990): 49–61.
Blumhofer, Edith L. "Ozman, Agnes Nevada." In *NIDPCM*, rev. ed., edited by Stanley M. Burgess and Eduard M. van der Maas, 952. Grand Rapids, MI: Zondervan, 2002.
Blumhofer, Edith L. *Restoring the Faith: The Assemblies of God, Pentecostalism, and American Culture.* Urbana, IL: University of Illinois Press, 1993.
Blumhofer, Edith L. "Women in Evangelicalism and Pentecostalism." In *Women and Church: The Challenge of Ecumenical Solidarity in an Age of Alienation*, edited by Malanie A. May, 3–12. Grand Rapids, MI: Eerdmans, 1991.
Blumhofer, Edith L., and Chris R. Armstrong. "Assemblies of God." In *NIDPCM*, rev. ed., edited by Stanley M. Burgess and Eduard M. van der Maas, 333–40. Grand Rapids, MI: Zondervan, 2002.
Blum, Linda M. *At the Breast: Ideologies of Breastfeeding and Motherhood in the Contemporary United States.* Boston, MA: Beacon, 1999.
Bohler, Carolyn Stahl. "Female-Friendly Pastoral Care." In *Through the Eyes of Women: Insights for Pastoral Care*, edited by Jeanne Stevenson-Moessner, 27–49. Minneapolis, MN: Fortress, 1996.
Bondi, Roberta C. *Memories of God: Theological Reflections on a Life.* Nashville, TN: Abingdon, 1995.
Borysenko, Joan. *A Woman's Book of Life: The Biology, Psychology, and Spirituality of the Feminine Life Cycle.* New York: Riverhead Books, 1996.
Bowen, Pearl B. "Akron Visited with Pentecost." *AF* 1, no. 5 (January 1907): 1.
Bowers, James P. "Foreword." In *Women in Leadership: A Pentecostal Perspective*, edited by Kimberly Ervin Alexander and R. Hollis Gause, vii–ix. Cleveland, TN: Center for Pentecostal Leadership and Care, 2006.
Briggs, Sheila. "Galatians." In *Searching the Scriptures: A Feminist Commentary*, vol. 2, edited by Elizabeth Schüssler Fiorenza, 218–36. New York: Crossroad, 1994.
Brusco, Elizabeth E. *The Reformation of Machismo: Evangelical Conversion and Gender in Columbia.* Austin, TX: University of Texas Press, 1995.
Burton-Christie, Douglas. *The Word in the Desert: Scripture and the Quest for Holiness in Early Christian Monasticism.* Oxford: Oxford University Press, 1993.
Bynum, Caroline Walker. *The Resurrection of the Body in Western Christianity, 200–1336.* New York: Columbia University Press, 1995.
Byrd, Joseph. "Paul Ricoeur's Hermeneutical Theory and Pentecostal Proclamation." *Pneuma* 15, no. 2 (Fall 1993): 203–15.
Cahill, Lisa Sowle. *Sex, Gender, and Christian Ethics.* Cambridge: Cambridge University Press, 1996.
Campbell, Douglas A. "The Logic of Eschatology: The Implications of Paul's Gospel for Gender as Suggested by Galatians 3:28a in Context." In *Gospel and Gender: A Trinitarian Engagement with Being Male and Female in Christ*, edited by Douglas A. Campbell, 58–83. London: T&T Clark, 2003.
The Canadian Women's Foundation (website). Updated April 20, 2022. https://canadianwomen.org/.
Carbine, Rosemary P. "'Artisans of a New Humanity:' Re-Visioning the Public Church in a Feminist Perspective." In *Frontiers in Catholic Feminist Theology: Shoulder to Shoulder*, edited by Susan Abraham and Elena Procario-Foley, 173–92. Minneapolis, MN: Fortress, 2009.

Cargal, Timothy B. "Beyond the Fundamentalist–Modernist Controversy: Pentecostals and Hermeneutics in a Postmodern Age." *Pneuma* 15, no. 2 (Fall 1993): 163–87.
Carmody, Denise L. *Christian Feminist Theology: A Constructive Interpretation*. Cambridge: Blackwell, 1995.
Carr, Anne E. *Transforming Grace: Women's Experience and Christian Tradition*. San Francisco, CA: Harper & Row, 1988.
Cartledge, Mark J. *The Holy Spirit and Public Life: Empowering Ecclesial Praxis*. Lanham, MD: Lexington Books/Fortress Academic, 2022.
Cartledge, Mark J. "Practical Theology: Attending to Pneumatologically-driven Praxis." In *The Routledge Handbook of Pentecostal Theology*, edited by Wolfgang Vondey, 163–72. New York: Routledge, 2020.
Casselberry, Judith, and Elizabeth A. Pritchard, eds. *Spirit on the Move: Black Women and Pentecostalism in Africa and the Diaspora*. Durham, NC: Duke University Press, 2019.
Castelo, Daniel. "The Improvisational Quality of Ecclesial Holiness." In *Toward a Pentecostal Ecclesiology: The Church and the Fivefold Gospel*, edited by John Christopher Thomas, 87–104. Cleveland, TN: CPT, 2010.
Castelo, Daniel. "Patience as a Theological Virtue: A Challenge to Pentecostal Eschatology." In *Perspectives in Pentecostal Eschatologies: World Without End*, edited by Peter Althouse and Robby Waddell, 232–46. Eugene, OR: Pickwick, 2010.
Catford, Cheryl. "Explaining the Recent Increase in Numbers of CRC Women Pastors." PhD diss., Deakin University, 2008.
Catford, Cheryl. "Women's Experiences: Challenges for Female Leaders in Pentecostal Contexts." In *Raising Women Leaders: Perspectives on Liberating Women in Pentecostal and Charismatic Contexts*, edited by Shane Clifton and Jacqueline Grey, 26–50. Sydney: Australian Pentecostal Studies, 2009.
Cavaness, Barbara L. "Leadership Attitudes and the Ministry of Single Women in Assemblies of God Mission." In *Philip's Daughters: Women in Pentecostal-Charismatic Leadership*, edited by Estrelda Y. Alexander and Amos Yong, 112–30. Eugene, OR: Pickwick, 2009.
Cerillo, Augustus, Jr, and Grant Wacker. "Bibliography and Historiography of Pentecostalism in the United States." In *NIDPCM*, rev. ed., edited by Stanley M. Burgess and Eduard M. van der Maas, 382–405. Grand Rapids, MI: Zondervan, 2002.
Chan, Simon. "Mother Church: Toward a Pentecostal Ecclesiology." *Pneuma* 22, no. 2 (Fall 2010): 177–208.
Chan, Simon. *Pentecostal Theology and the Christian Spiritual Tradition*. Sheffield: Sheffield Academic, 2000.
Chan, Simon. *Spiritual Theology: A Systematic Study of the Christian Life*. Downers Grove, IL: InterVarsity, 1998.
Charette, Blaine. "Restoring the Kingdom to Israel: Kingdom and Spirit in Luke's Thought." In *Perspectives in Pentecostal Eschatologies: World Without End*, edited by Peter Althouse and Robby Waddell, 49–60. Eugene, OR: Pickwick, 2010.
Chopp, Rebecca S. "Eve's Knowing: Feminist Theology's Resistance to Malestream Epistemological Frameworks." In *Feminist Theology in Different Contexts*, edited by Elisabeth Schüssler Fiorenza and M. Shawn Copeland, 116–23. London: SCM, 1996.
Chopp, Rebecca S. *The Power to Speak: Feminism, Language, God*. New York: Crossroad, 1989.
Christ, Carol P. *Laughter of Aphrodite: Reflections on a Journey to the Goddess*. San Francisco, CA: Harper & Row, 1987.

*Church of God in Christ Official Manual*. Memphis, TN: Church of God in Christ Publishing, 1973.

"Church of God says Women Can't be Bishops." *The Christian Century*, August 27, 2010. Religious News Service. https://www.christiancentury.org/article/2010-08/church-god-says-women-can-t-be-bishops.

Clark, Elizabeth. "Review of *Body and Society*, by Peter Brown." *Journal of Religion* 70 (1990): 432–6.

Clark, Elizabeth. *Women in the Early Church*. Wilmington, DE: Glazier, 1983.

Clark, Matthew S. "An Investigation into the Nature of a Viable Pentecostal Hermeneutic." DTh diss., University of Pretoria, 1997.

Clifton, Shane. "Pentecostal Hermeneutics and First-Wave Feminism: Mina Ross Brawner, MD." *Journal of the Pentecostal Charismatic Bible Colleges* 2 (2006): Article 01. Accessed August 8, 2019. http://webjournals.ac.edu.au/ojs/index.php/PCBC/article/view/8854/8851.

Clifton, Shane. "Sexism and the Demonic in Church Life and Mission." In *Raising Women Leaders: Perspectives on Liberating Women in Pentecostal and Charismatic Contexts*, edited by Shane Clifton and Jacqueline Grey, 51–70. Sydney: Australian Pentecostal Studies, 2009.

Clifton, Shane, and Jacqueline Grey, eds. *Raising Women Leaders: Perspectives on Liberating Women in Pentecostal and Charismatic Contexts*. Sydney: Australian Pentecostal Studies, 2009.

Clouse, Bonnidell, and Robert G. Clouse, eds. *Women in Ministry: Four Views*. Downers Grove, IL: IVP Academic, 1989.

Coakley, Sarah. "The Eschatological Body: Gender, Transformation and God." In her book, *Powers and Submissions: Spirituality, Philosophy and Gender*, 153–67. Oxford: Blackwell, 2002.

Coakley, Sarah. "'Femininity' and the Holy Spirit?" In *Mirror to the Church: Reflections on Sexism*, edited by Monica Furlong, 124–35. London: SPCK, 1988.

Coakley, Sarah. *God, Sexuality, and the Self: An Essay "On the Trinity"*. Cambridge: Cambridge University Press, 2013.

Coakley, Sarah. "Is there a Future for Gender and Theology? On Gender, Contemplation, and the Systematic Task." *Criterion* 47 (2009): 2–11.

Cole, Casey S. "The Binding of Jephthah: Learning Orthopathy from the Daughter of Judges 11." *JPT* 29, no. 2 (2020): 145–57.

Cole, Casey S. "Taking Hermeneutics to Heart: Proposing an Orthopathic Reading for Texts of Terror via the Rape of Tamar Narrative." *Pneuma* 39 (2017): 264–74.

*Combined Minutes of the General Council of the Assemblies of God*. St. Louis, MO: Gospel Publishing House, 1914. In The Flower Pentecostal Heritage Center Archives. Accessed May 11, 2021. https://archives.ifphc.org/DigitalPublications/USA/Assemblies%20of%20God%20USA/Minutes%20General%20Council/Unregistered/1914/FPHC/1914_04_11.pdf.

Congar, Yves. *I Believe in the Holy Spirit*. Vol. 3. New York: Seabury, 1983.

Constitution and By-Laws of the General Council of the Assemblies of God. 1931. The Flower Pentecostal Heritage Center Archives. Accessed May 11, 2021. https://archives.ifphc.org/DigitalPublications/USA/Assemblies%20of%20God%20USA/Minutes%20General%20Council/Unregistered/1931/FPHC/1931.pdf.

Cooper, John W. *Body, Soul, and Everlasting Life: Biblical Anthropology and the Monism-Dualism Debate*. Grand Rapids, MI: Eerdmans, 2000.

Copeland, M. Shawn. "Journeying to the Household of God: The Eschatological Implications of Method in the Theology of Letty Mandeville Russell." In *Liberating*

Eschatology: Essays in Honor of Letty M. Russell, edited by Margaret A. Farley and Serene Jones, 26–44. Louisville, KY: Westminster John Knox, 1999.

Corley, Lisa Bernal, and Carol Blessing. "Speaking Out: Feminist Theology and Women's Proclamation in the Wesleyan Tradition." In *Being Feminist, Being Christian: Essays from Academia*, edited by Allyson Jule and Bettina Tate Pedersen, 127–56. New York: Palgrave Macmillan, 2006.

Cornwall, Robert. "Primitivism and the Redefinition of Dispensationalism in the Theology of Aimee Semple McPherson." *Pneuma* 14 (Spring 1992): 23–42.

"Correspondence." *The Promise* no. 2 (June 1907): 3–4.

Cotton, "Mother" Emma. "Inside Story of the Outpouring of the Holy Spirit, Azusa Street, 1906." *Message of the Apostolic Faith* 1, no. 1 (April 1939): 1–3.

Cox, Harvey. *Fire from Heaven: The Rise of Pentecostal Spirituality and the Reshaping of Religion in the Twenty-First Century*. Cambridge, MA: Da Capo, 1995.

Cox, Harvey. *The Seduction of the Spirit*. New York: Simon and Schuster, 1974.

Crabtree, Loralie Robinson, and Joy E. A. Qualls. "Women as Assemblies of God Church Planters: Cultural Analysis and Strategy Formation." In *Women in Pentecostal and Charismatic Ministry: Informing a Dialogue on Gender, Church, and Ministry*, edited by Margaret English de Alminana and Lois E. Olena, 295–319. Leiden: Brill, 2017.

Crumbley, Diedre Helen. "Dressed as becometh Holiness: Gender, Race and the Body in a Storefront Sanctified Church." In *Spirit on the Move: Black Women and Pentecostalism in Africa and the Diaspora*, edited by Judith Casselberry and Elizabeth A. Pritchard, 89–108. Durham, NC: Duke University Press, 2019.

Crumbley, Deidre Helen. "Sanctified Saints—Impure Prophetess: A Cross-Cultural Study of Gender and Power in Two Afro-Christian Spirit-Privileging Churches." In *The Spirit in the World: Emerging Pentecostal Theologies in Global Contexts*, edited by Veli-Matti Kärkkäinen, 115–34. Grand Rapids, MI: Eerdmans, 2009.

"Current News." *Canadian Pentecostal Testimony* 1 (December 1920): 1.

Czirak, Adam, Sophie Nikoleit, Friederike Oberkrome, Verena Straub, Robert Walter-Jochum, and Michael Wetzels, eds. *Performance zwischen den Zeiten: Reenactments und Preenactments in Kunst und Wissenschaft*. Bielefeld, DE: transcript Verlag, 2019.

Czirak, Adam, Sophie Nikoleit, Friederike Oberkrome, Verena Straub, Robert Walter-Jochum, and Michael Wetzels. "(P)reenactment." In *Affective Societies: Key Concepts*, edited by Jan Slaby and Christian von Scheve, 200–9. New York: Routledge, 2019.

Daly, Mary. *Beyond God the Father: Toward a Philosophy of Women's Liberation*. Boston, MA: Beacon, 1973.

Daly, Mary. *The Church and the Second Sex*. Boston, MA: Beacon, 1968.

Daniels, Joel. "Gender and Pentecostalism: Men Voting on Whether Women Should Get to Vote." Engaged Pentecostalism (website). October 26, 2017. http://engagedpentecostalism.com/gender-and-pentecostalism-men-voting-on-whether-women-should-get-to-vote/.

Day-Laver, Donna. "Clergy Couples: Are They Working?" *Daughters of Sarah* 3, no. 2 (March 1977): 1–3.

Dayton, Donald W. *Theological Roots*. Peabody, MA: Hendrickson, 1987.

Deane-Drummond, Celia. "Creation." In *The Cambridge Companion to Feminist Theology*, edited by Susan Frank Parsons, 190–205. Cambridge: Cambridge University Press, 2002.

Dempster, Murray W. "Christian Social Concern in Pentecostal Perspective: Reformulating Pentecostal Eschatology." *JPT* 1, no. 2 (1993): 51–64.

Dempster, Murray W. "Eschatology, Spirit Baptism, and Inclusiveness: An Exploration into the Hallmarks of a Pentecostal Social Ethic." In *Perspectives in Pentecostal*

*Eschatologies: World Without End*, edited by Peter Althouse and Robby Waddell, 155–88. Eugene, OR: Pickwick, 2010.

Dempster, Murray W. "Evangelism, Social Concern, and the Kingdom of God." In *Called and Empowered: Global Mission in Pentecostal Perspective*, edited by Murray W. Dempster, Byron D. Klaus, and Douglas Petersen, 22–43. Peabody, MA: Hendrickson, 1991.

DeRusha, Michelle. *50 Women Every Christian Should Know: Learning from Heroines of the Faith*. Grand Rapids, MI: Baker Books, 2014.

Dorsey, Patricia. "Southwest Assembly of God: Whomsoever Will." In *Religion and the New Immigrants: Continuities and Adaptations in Immigrant Congregations*, edited by Helen Rose Ebaugh and Janet Saltzman Chafetz, 234–57. Walnut Creek, CA: AltaMira, 2000.

Drogus, Carol Ann. "Private Power or Public Power: Pentecostalism, Base Communities, and Gender." In *Power, Politics, and Pentecostals in Latin America*, edited by Edward L. Cleary and Hannah W. Stewart-Gambino, 55–75. Oxford: Westview, 1998.

Dulles, Avery. "The Church as Eschatological Community." In *The Eschaton: A Community of Love*, edited by Joseph Papin, 69–103. Villanova, PA: Villanova University Press, 1971.

Dulles, Avery. *Models of the Church*. Expanded ed. New York: Image Books, 2002.

Durber, Susan. "The Female Reader of the Parables of the Lost." *Journal for the Study of the New Testament* 45 (1992): 59–78.

Dutko, Joseph Lee. "Beyond Ordinance: Pentecostals and a Sacramental Understanding of the Lord's Supper." *JPT* 26 (2017): 252–71.

Dutko, Joseph Lee. "This-Worldly Explanations for Otherworldly Growth: Vitality in an Ozarks Megachurch." MA thesis, Missouri State University, 2008. https://bearworks.missouristate.edu/theses/2455/.

Duvall, J. Scott, and J. Daniel Hays. *Grasping God's Word: A Hands-On Approach to Reading, Interpreting, and Applying the Bible*. 2nd ed. Grand Rapids, MI: Zondervan, 2005.

Dyrness, William A., and Oscar García-Johnson. *Theology Without Borders: An Introduction to Global Conversations*. Grand Rapids, MI: Baker Academic, 2015.

Edgar, Brian. "Biblical Anthropology and the Intermediate State." *Evangelical Quarterly* 74 (2002): 27–45 (Part I), 109–21 (Part II).

Ekblad, Bob. *Reading the Bible with the Damned*. Louisville, KY: Westminster John Knox, 2005.

English de Alminana, Margaret. "Introduction." In *Women in Pentecostal and Charismatic Ministry: Informing a Dialogue on Gender, Church, and Ministry*, edited by Margaret English de Alminana and Lois E. Olena, 1–29. Leiden: Brill, 2017.

English de Alminana, Margaret, and Lois E. Olena, eds. *Women in Pentecostal and Charismatic Ministry: Informing a Dialogue on Gender, Church, and Ministry*. Leiden: Brill, 2017.

Evans, Mary J. *Woman in the Bible: An Overview of All the Crucial Passages on Women's Roles*. Downers Grove, IL: InterVarsity, 1984.

Exum, J. Cheryl. "'You Shall Let Every Daughter Live': A Study of Exodus 1:8–2:10." *Semeia* 28 (1983): 63–82.

Farley, Margaret A., and Serene Jones. "Introduction." In *Liberating Eschatology: Essays in Honor of Letty M. Russell*, edited by Margaret A. Farley and Serene Jones, vii–xv. Louisville, KY: Westminster John Knox, 1999.

Faupel, D. William. *The Everlasting Gospel: The Significance of Eschatology in the Development of Pentecostal Thought*. 1996. Reprint, Blandford Forum: Deo, 2009.

Fee, Gordon D. *God's Empowering Presence: The Holy Spirit in the Letters of Paul.* Grand Rapids, MI: Baker Academic, 2009.

Fee, Gordon D. "Male and Female in the New Creation: Galatians 3:26–29." In *Discovering Biblical Equality: Complementarity Without Hierarchy*, edited by Ronald W. Pierce and Rebecca Merrill Groothuis, 172–85. Downers Grove, IL: InterVarsity, 2005.

Fee, Gordon D., and Douglas Stuart. *How to Read the Bible for All Its Worth.* 3rd ed. Grand Rapids, MI: Zondervan, 2003.

Finger, Reta Halteman, and Kari Sandhaas, eds. *The Wisdom of Daughters: Two Decades of the Voice of Christian Feminism.* Philadelphia, PA: Innisfree, 2001.

Ford, Josephine Massyngbaerde. "Mary and the Holy Spirit." In *NIDPCM*, rev. ed., edited by Stanley M. Burgess and Eduard M. van der Maas, 863–4. Grand Rapids, MI: Zondervan, 2002.

Frahm-Arp, Maria. *Professional Women in South African Pentecostal Charismatic Churches.* Leiden: Brill, 2010.

France, R. T. *Women In The Church's Ministry: A Test Case for Biblical Interpretation.* Grand Rapids, MI: Eerdmans, 1997.

Freeman, Lindsay Hardin. *Bible Women: All Their Words and Why They Matter.* 3rd ed. N.p.: Forward Movement, 2016.

Fulkerson, Mary McClintock. *Changing the Subject: Women's Discourses and Feminist Theology.* Minneapolis, MN: Fortress, 1994.

Gabriel, Andrew K. "Pneumatology: Eschatological Intensification of the Personal Presence of God." In *The Routledge Handbook of Pentecostal Theology*, edited by Wolfgang Vondey, 206–15. New York: Routledge, 2020.

Gause, R. Hollis. "Does the New Testament Prohibit Women Leaders?" In *Women in Leadership: A Pentecostal Perspective*, edited by Kimberly Ervin Alexander and R. Hollis Gause, 77–107. Cleveland, TN: Center for Pentecostal Leadership and Care, 2006.

Gaventa, Beverly. "Is Galatians Just a 'Guy-Thing'? A Theological Reflection." *Interpretation: A Journal of Bible and Theology* 54, no. 3 (July 2000): 267–78.

Gebara, Ivone. *Out of the Depths: Women's Experience of Evil and Salvation.* Translated by Ann Patrick Ware. Minneapolis, MN: Fortress, 2002.

Gelpi, Donald. *The Divine Mother: A Trinitarian Theology of the Holy Spirit.* Lanham, MD: University Press of America, 1984.

Gench, Frances Taylor. *Encountering God in Tyrannical Texts: Reflections on Paul, Women, and the Authority of Scripture.* Louisville, KY: Westminster John Knox, 2015.

"Gender Equality" (category archives). Pentecostals and Charismatics for Peace and Justice (PCPJ). Updated June 7, 2021. https://pcpj.org/category/gender-equality/.

Giles, Kevin. *The Trinity and Subordinationism: The Doctrine of God & the Contemporary Gender Debate.* Downers Grove, IL: InterVarsity, 2002.

Gill-Austern, Brita L. "Love Understood as Self-Sacrifice and Self-Denial: What Does It Do to Women?" In *Through the Eyes of Women: Insights for Pastoral Care*, edited by Jeanne Stevenson-Moessner, 304–21. Minneapolis, MN: Fortress, 1996.

Gill, Deborah M. "Called by God—What's a Women to Do and What Can We Do to Help Her." *Enrichment: A Journal for Pentecostal Ministry* 2, no. 2 (Spring 1997): 33–5.

Gill, Deborah M. "The Contemporary State of Women in Ministry in the Assemblies of God." *Pneuma* 17, no. 1 (Spring 1995): 33–6.

Gill, Deborah M., and Barbara Cavaness. *God's Women Then and Now.* Springfield, MO: Grace & Truth, 2004.

Gill, Lesley. "'Like a Veil to Cover Them': Women and the Pentecostal Movement in La Paz." *American Ethnologist* 17, no. 4 (1990): 708–21.
Gladd, Benjamin L., and Matthew S. Harmon. *Making All Things New: Inaugurated Eschatology for the Life of the Church*. Grand Rapids, MI: Baker Academic, 2016.
Glass, James J. "Eschatology: A Clear and Present Danger—A Sure and Certain Hope." In *Pentecostal Perspectives*, edited by Keith Warrington, 120–46. Carlisle: Paternoster, 1998.
"God Appointed Convention." *The Promise* no. 15 (March 1910): 1–2.
Goff, Ella M. "A Gentile's Pentecost in the 20th Century." *The Apostolic Messenger* 1, no. 1 (February/March 1908): 2.
Goldenberg, Naomi R. *Changing of the Gods: Feminism and the End of Traditional Religions*. Boston, MA: Beacon, 1979.
Gordon, Adoniram Judson (A. J.). "The Ministry of Women." *Missionary Review of the World* 7 (1894): 910–21. Reprint, *The Alliance Weekly*, May 1, 1948, 277–8, 286.
Gordon, T. David. "The Problem at Galatia." *Interpretation* 41 (1987): 32–43.
Gössmann, Elisabeth. "Zukunft" [Future]. In *Wörterbuch der Feministischen Theologie*, edited by Elisabeth Gössmann, et al., 440–1. Gütersloh: Gütersloher Verlagshaus, 1991.
Grainger, Joseph A. "Testimonies." *AF* 1, no. 12 (January 1908): 4.
Grant, Beth (A. Elizabeth). "Merchandised Women: Priceless, Called and Empowered." In *Women in Pentecostal and Charismatic Ministry: Informing a Dialogue on Gender, Church, and Ministry*, edited by Margaret English de Alminana and Lois E. Olena, 272–89. Leiden: Brill, 2017.
Grant, Jacquelyn. "The Sin of Servanthood." In *A Troubling in My Soul: Womanist Perspectives on Evil and Suffering*, edited by Emilie M. Townes, 199–218. Maryknoll, NY: Orbis Books: 1993.
Grant, Walter V. *Putting the Women in Their Place*. Dallas: Grant's Faith Clinic, n.d.
Graves, Michael. *How Scripture Interprets Scripture: What Biblical Writers Can Teach Us about Reading the Bible*. Grand Rapids, MI: Baker Academic, 2021.
Green, Chris E. W. "Does (Not) Nature Itself Teach You? Pentecostal Reflections on a Troubled and Troubling Text." *Pneuma* 38, no. 4 (2016): 456–75.
Green, Chris E. W. "'Then Their Eyes Were Opened': Pentecostal Reflections on the Church's Scripture and the Lord's Supper." *Pneuma* 35, no. 2 (2013): 220–34.
Green, Chris E. W. *Toward a Pentecostal Theology of the Lord's Supper: Foretasting the Kingdom*. Cleveland, TN: CPT, 2012.
Greene-McCreight, Kathryn. *Feminist Reconstructions of Christian Doctrine: Narrative Analysis and Appraisal*. Oxford: Oxford University Press, 2000.
Green, Garrett. *Imagining Theology: Encounters with God in Scripture, Interpretation, and Aesthetics*. Grand Rapids, MI: Baker Academic, 2020.
Gregoire, Sheila Wray, Rebecca Gregoire Lindenbach, and Joanna Sawatsky. *The Great Sex Rescue: The Lies You've Been Taught and How to Recover What God Intended*. Grand Rapids, MI: Baker Books, 2021.
Grenz, Stanley. *The Moral Quest: Foundations of Christian Ethics*. Downers Grove, IL: IVP Academic, 1997.
Grenz, Stanley. *Renewing the Center: Evangelical Theology in a Post-Theological Era*. 2nd ed. Grand Rapids, MI: Baker Academic, 2006.
Grenz, Stanley J., and Denise Muir Kjesbo. *Women in the Church: A Biblical Theology of Women in Ministry*. Downers Grove, IL: IVP Academic, 1995.
Grey, Jacqueline. "Biblical Hermeneutics: Reading Scripture with the Spirit in Community." In *The Routledge Handbook of Pentecostal Theology*, edited by Wolfgang Vondey, 129–39. New York: Routledge, 2020.

Grey, Jacqueline. *Three's a Crowd: Pentecostalism, Hermeneutics, and the Old Testament.* Eugene, OR: Pickwick, 2011.

Griffith, R. Marie. "Women's Aglow Fellowship International." In *NIDPCM*, rev. ed., edited by Stanley M. Burgess and Eduard M. van der Maas, 1209–11. Grand Rapids, MI: Zondervan, 2002.

Griffith, R. Marie, and David G. Roebuck. "Women, Role of." In *NIDPCM*, rev. ed., edited by Stanley M. Burgess and Eduard M. van der Maas, 1203–9. Grand Rapids, MI: Zondervan, 2002.

Gudorf, Christine. "The Power to Create: Sacraments and Men's Need to Birth." *Horizons* 14 (1987): 296–309.

Gundry-Volf, Judith M. "Beyond Difference? Paul's Vision of a New Humanity in Galatians 3.28." In *Gospel and Gender: A Trinitarian Engagement with Being Male and Female in Christ*, edited by Douglas A. Campbell, 8–36. London: T&T Clark, 2003.

Guroian, Vigen. "Fruits of Pentecost: The Christian Gardener." *The Christian Century* 113, no. 21 (July 3, 1996): 684–6.

Guroian, Vigen. "Liturgy and the Lost Eschatological Vision of Christian Ethics." *The Annual of the Society of Christian Ethics* 20 (2000): 227–38.

Gutiérrez, Gustavo. *A Theology of Liberation.* Rev. ed. Maryknoll, NY: Orbis Books, 1988.

Haddad, Mimi R. "Examples of Women's Leadership in the Old Testament and Church History." In *Women in Pentecostal and Charismatic Ministry: Informing a Dialogue on Gender, Church, and Ministry*, edited by Margaret English de Alminana and Lois E. Olena, 59–69. Leiden: Brill, 2017.

Hall, Anna. "Jesus is Coming." *AF* 1, no. 1 (September 1906): 4.

Hallum, Anne Motley. "Taking Stock and Building Bridges: Feminism, Women's Movements, and Pentecostalism in Latin America." *Latin American Research Review* 38, no. 1 (2003): 169–86.

Hampson, Daphne. *Theology and Feminism.* Oxford: Basis Blackwell, 1990.

Hanson, Bradley C. *Introduction to Christian Theology.* Minneapolis, MN: Fortress, 1997.

Harré, Rom. *Physical Being: A Theory for a Corporeal Psychology.* Oxford: Blackwell, 1991.

Harrison, Beverly Wildung. *Making Connections: Essays in Feminist Social Ethics.* Edited by Carol S. Robb. Boston, MA: Beacon, 1985.

Harrison, Verna. "Gender, Generation, and Virginity in Cappadocian Theology." *Journal of Theological Studies* 47 (1996): 38–68.

Harrison, Verna. "Male and Female in Cappadocian Theology." *Journal of Theological Studies* 41 (1990): 441–71.

Hart, Trevor. "Eschatology." In *The Oxford Handbook of Evangelical Theology*, edited by Gerald R. McDermott, 262–75. Oxford: Oxford University Press, 2010.

Hart, Trevor. "Imagination for the Kingdom of God? Hope, Promise, and the Transformative Power of an Imagined Future." In *God Will Be All in All: The Eschatology of Jürgen Moltmann*, edited by Richard Bauckham, 49–76. Edinburgh: T&T Clark, 1999.

Hasker, William. *The Emergent Self.* Ithaca, NY: Cornell University Press, 1999.

Hauke, Manfred. *God or Goddess? Feminist Theology: What Is It? Where Does It Lead?* Translated by David Kipp. San Francisco, CA: Ignatius, 1995.

Hayes, Zachary. *Visions of a Future: A Study of Christian Eschatology.* Collegeville, MN: Liturgical, 1989.

Heath, Elaine A. *We Were the Least of These: Reading the Bible with Survivors of Sexual Abuse.* Grand Rapids, MI: Brazos, 2011.

Hebden, Ellen. "How Pentecost Came to Toronto." *The Promise* no. 1 (May 1907): 2.

Hilkert, Mary Catherine. *Naming Grace: Preaching and the Sacramental Imagination.* New York: Continuum, 1997.
Hocken, Peter D. "Argue, Zelma." In *NIDPCM*, rev. ed., edited by Stanley M. Burgess and Eduard M. van der Maas, 331. Grand Rapids, MI: Zondervan, 2002.
Hollenweger, Walter. *The Pentecostals: The Charismatic Movement in the Churches.* Translated by R. A. Wilson. Minneapolis, MN: Augsburg, 1972.
Hollingsworth, Andrea. "Spirit and Voice: Toward a Feminist Pentecostal Pneumatology." *Pneuma* 29, no. 2 (2007): 189–213.
Hollingsworth, Andrea, and Melissa D. Browning. "Your Daughters Shall Prophesy (As Long as They Submit): Pentecostalism and Gender in Global Perspective." In *A Liberating Spirit: Pentecostals and Social Action in North America*, edited by Michael Wilkinson and Steven M. Studebaker, 161–84. Eugene, OR: Pickwick, 2010.
Holmes, Pamela M. S. "Acts 29 and Authority: Towards a Pentecostal Feminist Hermeneutic of Liberation." In *A Liberating Spirit: Pentecostals and Social Action in North America*, edited by Michael Wilkinson and Steven M. Studebaker, 185–209. Eugene, OR: Pickwick, 2010.
Holmes, Pamela M. S. "The 'Place' of Women in Pentecostal/Charismatic Ministry Since the Azusa Street Revival." In *The Azusa Street Revival and Its Legacy*, edited by Harold Hunter and Cecil M. Robeck Jr., 297–315. Eugene, OR: Wipf & Stock, 2006.
Holmes, Pamela M. S. "The Spirit, Nature, and Canadian Pentecostal Women: A Conversation with Critical Theory." In *Philip's Daughters: Women in Pentecostal-Charismatic Leadership*, edited by Estrelda Y. Alexander and Amos Yong, 185–202. Eugene, OR: Pickwick, 2009.
Holmes, Pamela M. S. "Zelma Argue's Theological Contribution to Early Pentecostalism." In *Winds From the North: Canadian Contributions to the Pentecostal Movement*, edited by Michael Wilkinson and Peter Althouse, 129–50. Leiden: Brill, 2010.
Holm, Randall. "Pentecost: Women's Emancipation Day?" *Eastern Journal of Practical Theology* 5, no. 2 (1991): 27–34.
Hove, Richard. *Equality in Christ? Galatians 3:28 and the Gender Dispute.* Wheaton, IL: Crossway, 1999.
Hull, Gretchen Gaebelein. *Equal to Serve: Women and Men in the Church and Home.* Old Tappan, NJ: Fleming H. Revell, 1987.
Hyatt, Susan C. "Spirit-Filled Women." In *The Century of the Holy Spirit: 100 Years of Pentecostal and Charismatic Renewal, 1901–2001*, edited by Vinson Synan, 233–63. Nashville, TN: Thomas Nelson, 2001.
"In the Last Days." *AF* 1, no. 9 (June to September 1907): 1.
Irizarry-Fernández, Aida. "A Communal Reading. See—Judge—Act: A Different Approach to Bible Study." In *Engaging the Bible: Critical Readings from Contemporary Women*, edited by Choi Hee An and Katheryn Pfisterer Darr, 47–80. Minneapolis, MN: Fortress, 2006.
Isgrigg, Daniel D. *Imagining the Future: The Origins, Development, and Future of Assemblies of God Eschatology.* Tulsa, OK: Oral Roberts University Press, 2021.
Isgrigg, Daniel D. "The Latter Rain Revisited: Exploring the Origins of the Central Metaphor in Pentecostalism." *Pneuma* 41, no. 3–4 (2019): 439–57.
Isherwood, Lisa. "Eschatology." In *An A to Z of Feminist Theology*, edited by Lisa Isherwood and Dorothea McEwan, 53–5. Sheffield: Sheffield Academic, 1996.
Jacobsen, Douglas. "Review Essay: Pentecostalism Today; A Review of Brill's Encyclopedia of Global Pentecostalism." *Pneuma* 44, no. 2 (2022): 251–60.
James, Carolyn Custis. *Half the Church: Recapturing God's Global Vision for Women.* Grand Rapids, MI: Zondervan, 2011.

Jeffries, A. G. "The Limit of Divine Revelation." *Weekly Evangel*, March 18, 1916, 6–8.
Jenkins, Philip. *The Next Christendom: The Coming of Global Christianity*. Rev. ed. Oxford: Oxford University Press, 2007.
Jewett, Paul K. *Man As Male and Female: A Study in Sexual Relationships from a Theological Point of View*. Grand Rapids, MI: Eerdmans, 1975.
Jobling, J'annine. *Feminist Biblical Interpretation in Theological Context: Restless Readings*. Hampshire: Ashgate, 2002.
Johns, Cheryl Bridges. "Grieving, Brooding, and Transformation: The Spirit, the Bible, and Gender." *JPT* 23, no. 2 (2014): 141–53.
Johns, Cheryl Bridges. *Pentecostal Formation: Pedagogy among the Oppressed*. Eugene, OR: Wipf & Stock, 1998.
Johns, Cheryl Bridges. "Pentecostal Spirituality and the Conscientization of Women." In *All Together in One Place: Theological Papers from the Brighton Conference on World Evangelization*, edited by Harold D. Hunter and Peter D. Hocken, 153–65. Sheffield: Sheffield Academic, 1993.
Johns, Cheryl Bridges. *Seven Transforming Gifts of Menopause: An Unexpected Spiritual Journey*. Grand Rapids, MI: Brazos, 2020.
Johns, Cheryl Bridges. "Spirited Vestments: Or, Why the Anointing Is Not Enough." In *Philip's Daughters: Women in Pentecostal-Charismatic Leadership*, edited by Estrelda Y. Alexander and Amos Yong, 170–84. Eugene, OR: Pickwick, 2009.
Johns, Cheryl Bridges, and Lisa P. Stephenson, eds. *Grieving, Brooding, and Transforming: The Spirit, the Bible, and Gender*. Leiden: Brill, 2021.
Johnson, Elizabeth A. "Christology: Redeeming the Name of Christ." In *Freeing Theology: The Essentials of Theology in Feminist Perspective*, edited by Catherine Mowry LaCugna, 115–37. New York: HarperOne, 1993.
Johnson, Elizabeth A. *She Who Is: The Mystery of God in Feminist Theological Discourse*. 25th anniversary ed. New York: Crossroad, 2007.
Johnson, Luke Timothy. *The Writings of the New Testament: An Interpretation*. Rev. ed. Minneapolis, MN: Fortress, 1999.
Jones, Ian, Janet Wootton, and Kirsty Thorpe. *Women and Ordination in the Christian Churches: International Perspectives*. New York: T&T Clark, 2008.
Jordan, Judith V. "Clarity in Connection: Empathic Knowing, Desire, and Sexuality." In *Women's Growth in Diversity: More Writings from the Stone Center*, edited by Judith V. Jordan, 50–73. New York: Guilford, 1997.
Jule, Allyson. "Silence as Femininity?: A Look at Performances of Gender in Theology College Classrooms." In *Being Feminist, Being Christian: Essays from Academia*, edited by Allyson Jule and Bettina Tate Pedersen, 35–58. New York: Palgrave Macmillan, 2006.
Jule, Allyson, and Bettina Tate Pedersen. "Introduction: Being Feminist, Being Christian." In *Being Feminist, Being Christian: Essays from Academia*, edited by Allyson Jule and Bettina Tate Pedersen, 1–8. New York: Palgrave Macmillan, 2006.
Julian of Norwich. *Revelation of Love*. Edited and translated by John Skinner. New York: Image/Doubleday, 1996.
Kahl, Brigitte. "Gender Trouble in Galatia? Paul and the Rethinking of Difference." In *Is There a Future for Feminist Theology?*, edited by Deborah F. Sawyer and Diane M. Collier, 57–73. Sheffield: Sheffield Academic, 1999.
Kärkkäinen, Veli-Matti. "Are Pentecostals Oblivious to Social Justice? Theological and Ecumenical Perspectives." *Missiology: An International Review* 29, no. 4 (2001): 417–31.

Kärkkäinen, Veli-Matti. *The Holy Spirit: A Guide to Christian Theology*. Louisville, KY: Westminster John Knox, 2012.

Karras, Valerie A. "Eschatology." In *The Cambridge Companion to Feminist Theology*, edited by Susan Frank Parsons, 243–60. Cambridge: Cambridge University Press, 2002.

Kay, William K., and Anne E. Dyer, eds. *Pentecostal and Charismatic Studies: A Reader*. London: SCM, 2004.

Keener, Craig. *Acts: An Exegetical Commentary*. Vol. 1. *Introduction and 1:1–2:47*. Grand Rapids, MI: Baker Academic, 2012.

Keener, Craig. *Galatians: A Commentary*. Grand Rapids, MI: Baker Academic, 2019.

Keener, Craig. "Luke's Perspective on Women and Gender." In *Acts: An Exegetical Commentary*, vol. 1, by Craig Keener, 597–638. Grand Rapids, MI: Baker Academic, 2012.

Keener, Craig. *Paul, Women, & Wives: Marriage and Women's Ministry in the Letters of Paul*. Peabody, MA: Hendrickson, 1992.

Keener, Craig. "Refining *Spirit Hermeneutics*." *Pneuma* 39, no. 1–2 (2017): 198–240.

Keener, Craig. *Spirit Hermeneutics: Reading Scripture in Light of Pentecost*. Grand Rapids, MI: Eerdmans, 2016.

Kenyon, Howard N. "An Analysis of Ethical Issues in the History of the Assemblies of God." PhD diss., Baylor University, 1988. Page references are to the dissertation.

Kenyon, Howard N. *Ethics in the Age of the Sprit: Race, Women, War, and the Assemblies of God*. Eugene, OR: Pickwick, 2019.

Kimel, Alvin F. "It Could Have Been . . . ." *Pro Ecclesia* 3, no. 4 (1994): 389–94.

Kimel, Alvin F., ed. *Speaking the Christian God: The Holy Trinity and the Challenge of Feminism*. Grand Rapids, MI: Eerdmans, 1992.

Kimel, Alvin F., ed. *This Is My Name Forever: The Trinity and Gender Language for God*. Downers Grove, IL: InterVarsity, 2001.

King, Ursula, ed. *Feminist Theology from the Third World: A Reader*. London: SPCK, 1994.

Kirk, Geoffrey. *Without Precedent: Scripture, Tradition, and the Ordination of Women*. Eugene, OR: Wipf & Stock, 2016.

Kirsch, Jonathan. *The Harlot by the Side of the Road: Forbidden Tales of the Bible*. New York: Ballantine Books, 1997.

Klause, Byron. "The Holy Spirit and Mission in Eschatological Perspective: A Pentecostal Viewpoint." *Pneuma* 27, no. 2 (2005): 322–42.

Koch, Margaret, and Mary Stewart Van Leeuwen. *After Eden: Facing the Challenge of Gender Reconciliation*. Grand Rapids, MI: Eerdmans, 1993.

Kristof, Nicholas D., and Sheryl WuDunn. *Half the Sky: Turning Oppression into Opportunity for Women Worldwide*. New York: Vintage Books, 2009.

Kroeger, Catherine Clark, and Mary J. Evans, eds. *The IVP Women's Bible Commentary*. Downers Grove, IL: InterVarsity, 2006.

LaCelle-Peterson, Kristina. *Liberating Tradition: Women's Identity and Vocation in Christian Perspective*. Grand Rapids, MI: Baker Academic, 2008.

LaCugna, Catherine Mowry, ed. *Freeing Theology: The Essentials of Theology in Feminist Perspective*. New York: HarperOne, 1993.

LaCugna, Catherine Mowry. *God For Us: The Trinity and Christian Life*. New York: HarperSanFrancisco, 1973.

LaCugna, Catherine Mowry. "God in Communion with Us: The Trinity." In *Freeing Theology: The Essentials of Theology in Feminist Perspective*, edited by Catherine Mowry LaCugna, 83–114. New York: HarperOne, 1993.

LaCugna, Catherine Mowry. "Introduction." In *Freeing Theology: The Essentials of Theology in Feminist Perspective*, edited by Catherine Mowry LaCugna, 1–4. New York: HarperOne, 1993.

LaCugna, Catherine Mowry. "Review of *Speaking the Christian God: The Holy Trinity and the Challenge of Feminism*." *Pro Ecclesia* 3 (1994): 114–16.

Ladd, George Eldon. *The Presence of the Future: The Eschatology of Biblical Realism*. Rev. ed. Grand Rapids, MI: Eerdmans, 1974.

LaHurd, Carol. "Re-viewing Luke 15 with Arab Christian Women." In *A Feminist Companion to Luke*, edited by Amy-Jill Levine, 248–68. New York: Sheffield, 2002.

Lambdin, Thomas O., trans. "The Gospel of Thomas." In *The Nag Hammadi Library in English*, 3rd ed., edited by James M. Robinson, 124–38. San Francisco, CA: HarperSanFrancisco, 1988.

Lamott, Anne. *Operating Instructions: A Journal of My Son's First Year*. New York: Pantheon, 1993.

Land, Steven Jack. *Pentecostal Spirituality: A Passion for the Kingdom*. 1993. Reprint, Cleveland, TN: CPT, 2010.

Lane, Dermot A. *Keeping Hope Alive: Stirrings in Christian Theology*. 1996. Reprint, Eugene, OR: Wipf & Stock, 2005.

Larry, Susannah. *Sexualized Violence, the Bible, and Standing with Survivors*. Harrisonburg, VA: Herald, 2021.

Lawless, Elaine. *Handmaidens of the Lord: Pentecostal Women Preachers and Traditional Religion*. Philadelphia, PA: University of Pennsylvania Press, 1988.

Lee-Barnewall, Michelle. *Neither Complementarian nor Egalitarian: A Kingdom Corrective to the Evangelical Gender Debate*. Grand Rapids, MI: Baker Academic, 2016.

Lee, Chang-Soung. "In the Beginning There was a Theology: The Precedence of Theology Over Experience in the Pentecostal Movement." Asia Center for Pentecostal Theology (website articles). Posted August 27, 2019. https://pentecost.asia/articles/in-the-beginning-there-was-a-theology-the-precedence-of-theology-over-experience-in-the-pentecostal-movement/.

Lee, Dorothy A. *The Ministry of Women in the New Testament: Reclaiming the Biblical Vision for Church Leadership*. Grand Rapids, MI: Baker Academic, 2021.

"Letters from Bro. Johnson." *AF* 1, no. 2 (October 1906): 3.

Lewis, Paul. "Indonesia." In *NIDPCM*, rev. ed., edited by Stanley M. Burgess and Eduard M. van der Maas, 126–31. Grand Rapids, MI: Zondervan, 2002.

Liebert, Elizabeth. "Coming Home to Themselves: Women's Spiritual Care." In *Through the Eyes of Women: Insights for Pastoral Care*, edited by Jeanne Stevenson-Moessner, 257–84. Minneapolis, MN: Fortress, 1996.

Lim, David. *Spiritual Gifts: A Fresh Look; Commentary and Exhortation from a Pentecostal Perspective*. Springfield, MO: Gospel Publishing House, 1991.

Loades, Ann. "Introduction." In *Feminist Theology: A Reader*, edited by Ann Loades, 1–11. Louisville, KY: Westminster John Knox, 1990.

Lohfink, Gerhard. *Jesus and Community*. Translated by J. P. Calvin. Philadelphia, PA: Fortress, 1984.

Lonergan, Bernard J. F. *Method in Theology*. Toronto, ON: University of Toronto Press, 1971.

Lord, Andrew M. "Mission Eschatology." *JPT* 11 (1997): 111–23.

Lord, Andrew M. "The Pentecostal-Moltmann Dialogue: Implications for Mission." *JPT* 11, no. 2 (2003): 271–87.

Luther, Martin. *On the Bondage of the Will*. Translated and edited by Philip S. Watson. In *Luther and Erasmus: Free Will and Salvation*, edited by E. Gordon Rupp and Philip S. Watson, 101–334. Philadelphia, PA: Westminster, 1969.

Lyon, Jo Anne. "Men and Women Working Together." *Wesleyan Life* (blog). Accessed April 25, 2022. https://wesleyan.life/men-and-women-working-together.

Ma, Julie C. "Changing Images: Women in Asian Pentecostalism." In *Philip's Daughters: Women in Pentecostal-Charismatic Leadership*, edited by Estrelda Y. Alexander and Amos Yong, 203–14. Eugene, OR: Pickwick, 2009.

Ma, Julie C., and Wonsuk Ma. *Mission in the Spirit: Towards a Pentecostal/Charismatic Missiology*. Eugene, OR: Wipf & Stock, 2010.

Macchia, Frank D. *Baptized in the Spirit: A Global Pentecostal Theology*. Grand Rapids, MI: Zondervan, 2006.

Macchia, Frank D. "Baptized in the Spirit: Towards a Global Theology of Spirit Baptism." In *The Spirit in the World: Emerging Pentecostal Theologies in Global Contexts*, edited by Veli-Matti Kärkkäinen, 3–20. Grand Rapids, MI: Eerdmans, 2009.

Macchia, Frank D. "Sighs Too Deep for Words: Toward a Theology of Glossolalia." *JPT* 1 (1992): 47–73.

Macchia, Frank D. "Signs of Grace: Towards a Charismatic Theology of Worship." In *Toward a Pentecostal Theology of Worship*, edited by Lee Roy Martin, 153–64. Cleveland, TN: CPT, 2016.

MacIntyre, Alasdair. *After Virtue: A Study in Moral Theory*. 2nd ed. Notre Dame, IN: University of Notre Dame Press, 1984.

MacRobert, Iain. *The Black Roots and White Racism of Early Pentecostalism in the USA*. New York: St. Martin's, 1988.

Malcomson, Keith. *Pentecostal Pioneers Remembered: British and Irish Pioneers of Pentecost*. N.p.: Xulon, 2008.

Malina, Bruce, and Jerome Neyrey. "Honor and Shame in Luke-Acts: Pivotal Values of the Mediterranean World." In *The Social World of Luke-Acts: Models for Interpretation*, edited by J. H. Neyrey, 59–78. Peabody, MA: Hendrickson, 1991.

Mariz, Cecília Loreto, and María Das Dores Campos Machado. "Pentecostalism and Women in Brazil." In *Power, Politics, and Pentecostals in Latin America*, edited by Edward L. Cleary and Hannah W. Stewart-Gambino, 41–54. Oxford: Westview, 1998.

Marshall, Joretta L. "Sexual Identity and Pastoral Concerns: Caring with Women Who Are Developing Lesbian Identities." In *Through the Eyes of Women: Insights for Pastoral Care*, edited by Jeanne Stevenson-Moessner, 143–66. Minneapolis, MN: Fortress, 1996.

Martin, Bernice. "The Pentecostal Gender Paradox: A Cautionary Tale for the Sociology of Religion." In *The Blackwell Companion to Sociology of Religion*, edited by Richard K. Fenn, 52–66. Oxford: Blackwell, 2001.

Martin, David. *Forbidden Revolutions: Pentecostalism in Latin America and Catholicism in Eastern Europe*. London: SPCK, 1996.

Martin, David. *Pentecostalism: The World Their Parish*. Oxford: Blackwell, 2002.

Martin, David. *Tongues of Fire: The Explosion of Protestantism in Latin America*. London: Basil Blackwell, 1990.

Martin, Lee Roy. *Pentecostal Hermeneutics: A Reader*. Leiden: Brill, 2013.

McFague, Sallie. *The Body of God: An Ecological Theology*. Minneapolis, MN: Augsburg, 1993.

McFague, Sallie. *Metaphorical Theology: Models of God in Religious Language*. Philadelphia, PA: Fortress, 1982.

McFague, Sallie. *Models of God: Theology for an Ecological, Nuclear Age*. Philadelphia, PA: Fortress, 1987.

McGee, Gary B. "Initial Evidence." In *NIDPCM*, rev. ed., edited by Stanley M. Burgess and Eduard M. van der Maas, 784–91. Grand Rapids, MI: Zondervan, 2002.

McPherson, Aimee Semple. "As a Bride Adorned: Glowing Sermon on the Glorious Second Coming of Christ." *The Bridal Call Foursquare* 9, no. 9 (1926): 3.

McPherson, Aimee Semple. *The Life Story of Aimee Semple McPherson*. Los Angeles, CA: Foursquare Publications, 1979.

McPherson, Aimee Semple. "The Servants and the Handmaidens: Baccalaureate Sermon." *The Bridal Call Foursquare* 8, no. 9 (February 1930): 5–6, 32.

McPherson, Aimee Semple. "Signs of the Times." *The Bridal Call Foursquare* 11, no. 2 (July 1927): 5–8, 28–9.

McPherson, Aimee Semple. *This Is That*. 1919. Reprint, New York: Garland, 1985.

McQueen, Larry R. "Early Pentecostal Eschatology in the Light of *The Apostolic Faith*, 1906–1908." In *Perspectives in Pentecostal Eschatologies: World Without End*, edited by Peter Althouse and Robby Waddell, 139–54. Eugene, OR: Pickwick, 2010.

McQueen, Larry R. *Joel and the Spirit: The Cry of a Prophetic Hermeneutic*. 1995. Reprint, Cleveland, TN: CPT, 2009.

McQueen, Larry R. *Toward a Pentecostal Eschatology: Discerning the Way Forward*. Blandford Forum: Deo, 2012.

Medina, Néstor. "Jürgen Moltmann and Pentecostalism(s): Toward a Cultural Theology of the Spirit." *Toronto Journal of Theology* 24, no. Supplement 1 (January 2008): 101–14.

Medina, Néstor. "The New Jerusalem versus Social Responsibility: The Challenges of Pentecostalism in Guatemala." In *Perspectives in Pentecostal Eschatologies: World Without End*, edited by Peter Althouse and Robby Waddell, 315–39. Eugene, OR: Pickwick, 2010.

Meeks, Wayne A. "The Image of the Androgyne: Some Uses of a Symbol in Earliest Christianity." *History of Religions* 13, no. 3 (February 1974): 165–208.

Merritt, Stephen. "Women." *Midnight Cry*, March 6, 1919.

Michel, Jen Pollock. *Keeping Place: Reflections on the Meaning of Home*. Downers Grove, IL: InterVarsity, 2017.

Middleton, J. Richard. *A New Heaven and a New Earth: Reclaiming Biblical Eschatology*. Grand Rapids, MI: Baker Academic, 2014.

Migliore, Daniel. *Faith Seeking Understanding: An Introduction to Christian Theology*. Grand Rapids, MI: Eerdmans, 1991.

Miller, Donald, and Tetsunao Yamamori. *Global Pentecostalism: The New Face of Christian Social Engagement*. Berkeley, CA: University of California Press, 2007.

Miller, Jean Baker, and Janet L. Surrey. "Revisioning Women's Anger: The Personal and the Global." In *Women's Growth in Diversity: More Writings from the Stone Center*, edited by Judith V. Jordan, 199–216. New York: Guilford, 1997.

Miller-McLemore, Bonnie J. *Also a Mother: Work and Family as Theological Dilemma*. Nashville, TN: Abingdon, 1994.

"Missionaries to Jerusalem." *AF* 1, no. 1 (September 1906): 4.

Mittelstadt, Martin W. "My Life as a Mennocostal: A Personal and Theological Narrative." *Theodidaktos: Journal for EMC Theology and Education* 3, no. 2 (September 2008): 10–17.

Mittelstadt, Martin W. *Reading Luke-Acts in the Pentecostal Tradition*. Cleveland, TN: CPT, 2010.

Mittelstadt, Martin W. "Reimagining Luke-Acts: Amos Yong and the Biblical Foundation of Pentecostal Theology." In *The Theology of Amos Yong and the New Face of Pentecostal*

*Scholarship: Passion for the Spirit*, edited by Wolfgang Vondey and Martin William Mittelstadt, 25–43. Leiden: Brill, 2013.

Moltmann, Jürgen. *The Coming of God: Christian Eschatology*. Translated by Margaret Kohl. Minneapolis, MN: Augsburg Fortress, 1996.

Moltmann, Jürgen. *God in Creation: A New Theology of Creation and the Spirit of God*. Translated by Margaret Kohl. Minneapolis, MN: Fortress, 1993.

Moltmann, Jürgen. "Liberating and Anticipating the Future." Translated by Margaret Kohl. In *Liberating Eschatology: Essays in Honor of Letty M. Russell*, edited by Margaret A. Farley and Serene Jones, 189–208. Louisville, KY: Westminster John Knox, 1999.

Moltmann, Jürgen. "Pentecost and the Theology of Life." In *Pentecostal Movements as an Ecumenical Challenge*, edited by Jürgen Moltmann and Carl-Josef Kuschel, 123–34. Maryknoll, NY: SCM, 1996.

Moltmann, Jürgen. *Theology of Hope: On the Ground and the Implications of a Christian Eschatology*. Translated by James W. Leitch. Minneapolis, MN: Augsburg Fortress, 1964.

Moltmann, Jürgen, and Frank D. Macchia. "A Pentecostal Theology of Life." *JPT* 4, no. 9 (1996): 3–15.

Moltmann-Wendel, Elisabeth, and Jürgen Moltmann. *God—His and Hers*. London: SCM, 1991.

Moore, Rickie D. "Canon and Charisma in the Book of Deuteronomy." *JPT* 1 (October 1992): 75–92.

Moss, Candida R. *Divine Bodies: Resurrecting Perfection in the New Testament and Early Christianity*. New Haven, CT: Yale University Press, 2019.

Moss, Candida R., and Joel S. Baden. *Reconceiving Infertility: Biblical Perspectives on Procreation and Childlessness*. Princeton, NJ: Princeton University Press, 2015.

Mühling, Markus. *T&T Clark Handbook of Christian Eschatology*. Translated by Jennifer Adams-Maßmann and David Andrew Gilland. London: Bloomsbury, T&T Clark, 2015.

Mutch, Barbara. "Images of God and Their Relationship to Prayer in the Experience of Female Survivors of Childhood Sexual Abuse." DMin diss., Princeton Theological Seminary, 1995.

Myers, Alicia D. "*Pater Nutrix*: Milk Metaphors and Character Formation in Hebrews and 1 Peter." In *Making Sense of Motherhood: Biblical and Theological Perspectives*, edited by Beth M. Stovell, 81–99. Eugene, OR: Wipf & Stock, 2016.

Nance, Stephanie L., and Ava Kate Oleson. "Living a Theology of Co-Gender Ministry." In *Women in Pentecostal and Charismatic Ministry: Informing a Dialogue on Gender, Church, and Ministry*, edited by Margaret English de Alminana and Lois E. Olena, 349–67. Leiden: Brill, 2017.

Nausner, Michael. "Toward Community Beyond Gender Binaries: Gregory of Nyssa's Transgendering as Part of his Transformative Eschatology." *Theology & Sexuality* 16 (2002): 55–65.

Nel, Marius. *An African Pentecostal Hermeneutics: A Distinctive Contribution to Hermeneutics*. Eugene, OR: Wipf & Stock, 2018.

Nel, Marius. *African Pentecostalism and Eschatological Expectations: He is Coming Back Again!* Newcastle upon Tyne: Cambridge Scholars, 2019.

Nel, Marius. *LGBTIQ+ People and Pentecostals: An African Pentecostal Hermeneutical Perspective*. Zürich, CH: LIT Verlag, 2020.

Nelson, Douglas J. "For Such a Time as This: The Story of Bishop William J. Seymour and the Azusa Street Revival." PhD diss., University of Birmingham, 1981.

Neuger, Christie Cozad, ed. *The Arts of Ministry: Feminist-Womanist Approaches.* Louisville, KY: Westminster John Knox, 1996.

Neumann, Peter D. "Experience: The Mediated Immediacy of Encounter with the Spirit." In *The Routledge Handbook of Pentecostal Theology*, edited by Wolfgang Vondey, 84–94. New York: Routledge, 2020.

Neumann, Peter D. *Pentecostal Experience: An Ecumenical Encounter.* Eugene, OR: Pickwick, 2012.

Newsom, Carol A., and Sharon H. Ringe. "Introduction to the First Edition." In *The Women's Bible Commentary*, rev., 3rd (expanded), and 20th anniversary ed., edited by Carol A. Newsom, Sharon H. Ringe, and Jacqueline E. Lapsley, xxvii–xxxi. Louisville, KY: Westminster John Knox, 2012.

Newton, Jon K. "The Full Gospel and the Apocalypse." *JPT* 26, no. 1 (2017): 86–109.

"Next Generation of Women in Ministry Please Stand Up!" *Pentecostal Testimony* (June 1991): 2.

Noble, Christopher. "Biblical Literalism and Gender Stability: A Christian Response to Gender Performance Theory." In *Being Feminist, Being Christian: Essays from Academia*, edited by Allyson Jule and Bettina Tate Pedersen, 181–203. New York: Palgrave Macmillan, 2006.

Nordling, Cherith. "Gender." In *The Oxford Handbook of Evangelical Theology*, edited by Gerald R. McDermott, 497–512. Oxford: Oxford University Press, 2010.

North, Maria E. "A Testimony." *The Apostolic Messenger* 1, no. 1 (February/March 1908): 3.

Oberkrome, Friederike, and Verena Straub. "Performing in Between Times." In *Performance zwischen den Zeiten: Reenactments und Preenactments in Kunst und Wissenschaft*, edited by Adam Czirak et al., 9–22. Bielefeld, DE: transcript Verlag, 2019.

O'Callaghan, Paul. *Christ Our Hope: Introduction to Eschatology.* Washington, DC: The Catholic University of America Press, 2011.

Oden, Amy. *In Her Words: Women's Writings in the History of Christian Thought.* Nashville, TN: Abingdon, 1994.

"The Old-Time Pentecost." *AF* 1, no. 1 (September 1906): 1.

Oliverio, L. William, Jr. "Reading Craig Keener: On Spirit Hermeneutics: Reading Scripture in Light of Pentecost." *Pneuma* 39 (2017): 126–45.

Oliverio, L. William, Jr. *Theological Hermeneutics in the Classical Pentecostal Tradition: A Typological Account.* Leiden: Brill, 2012.

Oliver, Simon. *Creation: A Guide for the Perplexed.* London: Bloomsbury, T&T Clark, 2017.

Olupona, Jacob K. "Africa, West." In *NIDPCM*, rev. ed., edited by Stanley M. Burgess and Eduard M. van der Maas, 11–21. Grand Rapids, MI: Zondervan, 2002.

O'Neill, Mary Aquin. "Anthropology: The Mystery of Being Human Together." In *Freeing Theology: The Essentials of Theology in Feminist Perspective*, edited by Catherine Mowry LaCugna, 139–60. New York: HarperOne, 1993.

Onishi, Bradley. "The Rise of #Exvangelical." *Religion and Politics*, April 9, 2019. John C. Danforth Center on Religion & Politics at Washington University (St. Louis). https://religionandpolitics.org/2019/04/09/the-rise-of-exvangelical/.

Osiek, Carolyn. "The Feminist and the Bible: Hermeneutical Alternatives." In *Feminist Perspectives on Biblical Scholarship*, edited by Adela Yarbro Collins, 97–105. Chico, CA: Scholars, 1985.

Ozman, Agnes N. *What God Hath Wrought: Life and Work of Mrs. Agnes N. O. LaBerge.* N.d. Reprint, New York: Garland, 1985.

Palmer, Phoebe. *The Promise of the Father; or, A Neglected Specialty of the Last Days*. Boston, MA: Henry V. Degan, 1859.
Pannenberg, Wolfhart. "Constructive and Critical Functions of Christian Eschatology." *The Harvard Theological Review* 77, no. 2 (April 1984): 119-39.
Pannenberg, Wolfhart. *Systematic Theology*. 3 vols. Translated by Geoffrey W. Bromiley. Edinburgh: T&T Clark, 2004.
Parham, Charles F. "Free Love." *Apostolic Faith* (Baxter Springs, AR) 1, no. 10 (December 1912): 4-5.
Parham, Sarah E. *The Life of Charles F. Parham, Founder of the Apostolic Faith Movement*. 1930. Reprint, New York: Garland, 1985.
Parsons, Susan Frank. "Preface." In *The Cambridge Companion to Feminist Theology*, edited by Susan Frank Parsons, xiii-xvii. Cambridge: Cambridge University Press, 2002.
Pauw, Amy Plantinga. "Some Last Words About Eschatology." In *Feminist and Womanist Essays in Reformed Dogmatics*, edited by Amy Plantinga Pauw and Serene Jones, 221-4. Louisville, KY: Westminster John Knox, 2006.
Payne, Leah. *Gender and Pentecostal Revivalism: Making a Female Ministry in the Early Twentieth Century*. New York: Palgrave Macmillan, 2015.
Payne, Philip B. *Man and Woman, One in Christ*. Grand Rapids, MI: Zondervan, 2009.
Pedersen, Bettina Tate. "Christian Feminist or Feminist Christian: What's Feminism Got to Do with Evangelical Christians." In *Being Feminist, Being Christian: Essays from Academia*, edited by Allyson Jule and Bettina Tate Pedersen, 9-34. New York: Palgrave Macmillan, 2006.
Pelphrey, Brant. *Christ our Mother: Julian of Norwich*. London: Darton, Longman, & Todd, 1989.
Penney, John Michael. *The Missionary Emphasis of Lukan Pneumatology*. Sheffield: Sheffield Academic, 1997.
"Pentecostal Faith Line." *AF* 1, no. 1 (September 1906): 3.
"Pentecostal Notes." *AF* 1, no. 10 (September 1907): 3.
"Pentecostal Work in Toronto." *The Promise* no. 12 (February 1909): 2-3.
"Pentecost in Woodland." *AF* 1, no. 4 (December 1906): 1.
Perkins, Charlotte. *His Religion and Hers: A Study of the Faith of Our Fathers and the Work of our Mothers*. Westport, CT: Hyperion, 1976.
Petersen, Douglas. "A Moral Imagination: Pentecostals and Social Concern in Latin America." In *The Spirit in the World: Emerging Pentecostal Theologies in Global Contexts*, edited by Veli-Matti Kärkkäinen, 53-66. Grand Rapids, MI: Eerdmans, 2009.
Peterson, Eugene. *Eat This Book: A Conversation in the Art of Spiritual Reading*. Grand Rapids, MI: Eerdmans, 2009.
Phan, Peter C. "Woman and the Last Things: A Feminist Eschatology." In *In the Embrace of God: Feminist Approaches to Theological Anthropology*, edited by Ann O'Hara Graff, 206-28. Maryknoll, NY: Orbis Books, 1995.
Pinnock, Clark H. "The Work of the Holy Spirit in Hermeneutics." *JPT* 2 (1993): 2-23.
Pinnock, Clark H., with Barry L. Callen. *The Scripture Principle: Reclaiming the Full Authority of the Bible*. 2nd ed. Grand Rapids, MI: Baker Academic, 2006.
Poling, James Newton. *The Abuse of Power: A Theological Problem*. Nashville, TN: Abingdon, 1991.
Poloma, Margaret. "Charisma, Institutionalization and Social Change." *Pneuma* 17 (Fall 1995): 245-53.

Poloma, Margaret, and John Green. *The Assemblies of God: Godly Love and the Revitalization of American Pentecostalism*. New York: New York University Press, 2010.

Pope-Levison, Priscilla. *Turn the Pulpit Loose: Two Centuries of American Women Evangelists*. New York: Palgrave Macmillan, 2004.

Powers, Janet Everts. "Pentecostalism 101: Your Daughters Shall Prophesy." In *Philip's Daughters: Women in Pentecostal-Charismatic Leadership*, edited by Estrelda Y. Alexander and Amos Yong, 133–51. Eugene, OR: Pickwick, 2009.

Powers, Janet Everts. "'Your Daughters Shall Prophesy': Pentecostal Hermeneutics and the Empowerment of Women." In *The Globalization of Pentecostalism: A Religion Made to Travel*, edited by Murray W. Dempster, Byron D. Klaus, and Douglas Petersen, 313–37. Oxford: Regnum Books, 1999.

"P/Re/Enact! Performing in Between Times." Conference at the Institute for Cultural Inquiry, Berlin, October 27–28, 2017. https://doi.org/10.25620/e171027.

Prichard, Rebecca Button. *Sensing the Spirit: The Holy Spirit in Feminist Perspective*. St. Louis, MO: Chalice, 1999.

Procter-Smith, Marjorie. "Feminist Ritual Strategies: The *Ekklēsia Gynaikōn* at Work." In *Toward a New Heaven and a New Earth: Essays in Honor of Elisabeth Schüssler Fiorenza*, edited by Fernando F. Segovia, 498–515. Maryknoll, NY: Orbis Books, 2003.

"The Promise of the Father and Speaking in Tongues in Chicago." *AF* 1, no. 9 (June to September 1907): 3.

Prosser, Peter. *Dispensationalist Eschatology and Its Influence on American and British Religious Movements*. Lewiston, NY: Edwin Mellen, 1999.

Qualls, Joy E. A. *God Forgive Us for Being Women: Rhetoric, Theology, and the Pentecostal Tradition*. Eugene, OR: Wipf & Stock, 2018.

Qualls, Joy E. A. "Toward a Rhetoric of the Spirit: Assault, Abuse, and a Theology of Women's Empowerment." In *Sisters, Mothers, Daughters: Pentecostal Perspectives on Violence against Women*, edited by Kimberly Ervin Alexander et al., 223–41. Leiden: Brill, 2022.

Rae, Eleanor, and Bernice Marie-Daly. *Created in Her Image: Models of the Feminine Divine*. New York: Crossroad, 1990.

Raley, Lauren J. "Toward a Pentecostal Ecclesiology: Making Room for Survivors of Gender-Based Violence." In *Sisters, Mothers, Daughters: Pentecostal Perspectives on Violence against Women*, edited by Kimberly Ervin Alexander et al., 207–22. Leiden: Brill, 2022.

Ratzinger, Joseph. *Eschatology: Death and Eternal Life*. 2nd ed. Translated by Michael Waldstein. Washington, DC: The Catholic University of America Press, 1988.

Rausch, Thomas P. *Eschatology, Liturgy, and Christology: Toward Recovering an Eschatological Imagination*. Collegeville, MN: Liturgical, 2012.

Rees, Janice. "Sarah Coakley: Systematic Theology and the Future of Feminism." *Pacifica: Australasian Theological Studies* 24, no. 3 (October 2011): 300–14.

Reid, Barbara. *Choosing the Better Part? Women in the Gospel of Luke*. Collegeville, MN: Liturgical, 1996.

Rendtorff, Trutz. *Ethics*. Vol. 1. Translated by Keith Crim. Philadelphia, PA: Fortress, 1986.

Rice, Monte Lee. "Practicing the Passion of Pentecost: Re-envisioning Pentecostal Eschatology through the Anatheistic Sacramentality of Richard Kearney." *Pneuma* 43, no. 1 (2021): 43–71.

Rienstra, Debra. *Great with Child: Reflections on Faith, Fullness, and Becoming a Mother*. New York: Tarcher/Putnam, 2002.

Ringe, Sharon H. "When Women Interpret the Bible." In *The Women's Bible Commentary*, rev., 3rd (expanded), and 20th anniversary ed., edited by Carol A. Newsom, Sharon H. Ringe, and Jacqueline E. Lapsley, 1–9. Louisville, KY: Westminster John Knox, 2012.

Rios, Elizabeth D. "'The Ladies are Warriors': Latina Pentecostalism and Faith-Based Activism in New York City." In *Azusa Street and Beyond: 100 Years of Commentary on the Global Pentecostal/Charismatic Movement*, edited by Grant McClung, 217–29. Gainesville, FL: Bridge-Logos, 2006.

Rizzuto, Ana-María. *The Birth of the Living God: A Psychoanalytic Study*. Chicago, IL: University of Chicago Press, 1979.

Robeck, Cecil M., Jr. *The Azusa Street Mission and Revival*. Nashville, TN: Thomas Nelson, 2006.

Robeck, Cecil M., Jr. "McPherson, Aimee Semple." In *NIDPCM*, rev. ed., edited by Stanley M. Burgess and Eduard M. van der Maas, 856–9. Grand Rapids, MI: Zondervan, 2002.

Robeck, Cecil M., Jr. "William J. Seymour: An Early Model of Pentecostal Leadership." *Enrichment: A Journal for Pentecostal Ministry* 11, no. 2 (Spring 2006): 50–1.

Robinette, Brian D. *Grammars of Resurrection: A Christian Theology of Presence and Absence*. New York: Crossroad, 2009.

Roebuck, David G. "'Cause He's My Chief Employer': Hearing Women's Voices in a Classical Pentecostal Denomination." In *Philip's Daughters: Women in Pentecostal-Charismatic Leadership*, edited by Estrelda Y. Alexander and Amos Yong, 38–60. Eugene, OR: Pickwick, 2009.

Roebuck, David G. "Limiting Liberty: The Church of God and Women Ministers, 1886–1996." PhD diss., Vanderbilt University, 1997.

Roebuck, David G. "Loose the Women." *Christian History* 17, no. 2, Issue 58 (1998): 38–9.

Roebuck, David G. "Pentecostal Women in Ministry: A Review of Selected Documents." *Perspectives in Religious Studies* 16, no. 1 (Spring 1989): 29–44.

Roebuck, David G., and Karen Carroll Mundy. "Women, Culture, and Post-World War Two Pentecostalism." In *The Spirit and the Mind: Essays in Informed Pentecostalism*, edited by Terry L. Cross and Emerson B. Powery, 191–204. Lanham, MD: University Press of America, 2000.

"The Role of Women as Described in Holy Scripture." In *Where We Stand: The Official Position Papers of the Assemblies of God*, 181–90. Springfield, MO: Gospel Publishing House, 2001.

"The Role of Women in Ministry." Assemblies of God Position Papers. Version from August 11, 2010. https://ag.org/Beliefs/Position-Papers/The-Role-of-Women-in-Ministry.

Ross, Susan A. "Church and Sacrament—Community and Worship." In *The Cambridge Companion to Feminist Theology*, edited by Susan Frank Parsons, 224–42. Cambridge: Cambridge University Press, 2002.

Ross, Susan A. "Sacraments: God's Embodiment and Women." In *Freeing Theology: The Essentials of Theology in Feminist Perspective*, edited by Catherine Mowry LaCugna, 185–209. New York: HarperOne, 1993.

Ruether, Rosemary Radford. "Becoming a Feminist." In *Invitation to Christian Spirituality: An Ecumenical Anthology*, edited by John R. Tyson, 454–7. Oxford: Oxford University Press, 1999. Reprinted from *Disputed Questions on Being a Christian*, edited by Rosemary Radford Ruether, 109–26. Nashville, TN: Abingdon, 1982.

Ruether, Rosemary Radford. "The Emergence of Christian Feminist Theology." In *The Cambridge Companion to Feminist Theology*, edited by Susan Frank Parsons, 3–22. Cambridge: Cambridge University Press, 2002.

Ruether, Rosemary Radford. "Eschatology and Feminism." In *Lift every Voice: Constructing Christian Theologies from the Underside*, rev. and expanded ed., edited by Susan Brooks Thistlethwaite and Mary Potter Engel, 129–42. Maryknoll, NY: Orbis Books, 1998.

Ruether, Rosemary Radford. "Eschatology in Christian Feminist Theologies." In *The Oxford Handbook of Eschatology*, edited by Jerry L. Walls, 328–42. Oxford: Oxford University Press, 2008.

Ruether, Rosemary Radford. *Sexism and God-Talk: Toward a Feminist Theology*. 10th anniversary ed. Boston, MA: Beacon, 1993.

Ruether, Rosemary Radford. "The Theological Vision of Letty Russell." In *Liberating Eschatology: Essays in Honor of Letty M. Russell*, edited by Margaret A. Farley and Serene Jones, 16–25. Louisville, KY: Westminster John Knox, 1999.

Russell, Letty M. "Authority and the Challenge of Feminist Interpretation." In *Feminist Interpretation of the Bible*, edited by Letty M. Russell, 137–46. Philadelphia, PA: Westminster, 1985.

Russell, Letty M. *Church in the Round*. Philadelphia, PA: Westminster John Knox, 1993.

Russell, Letty M. *Ferment of Freedom: A Guide to Help Women Relate the Christian Faith and Participation in Social Change*. New York: National Board of the Young Women's Christian Association of the USA, 1972.

Russell, Letty M. *The Future of Partnership*. Philadelphia, PA: Westminster, 1979.

Russell, Letty M. *Growth in Partnership*. Philadelphia, PA: Westminster John Knox, 1981.

Russell, Letty M. *Household of Freedom: Authority in Feminist Theology*. Philadelphia, PA: Westminster, 1987.

Russell, Letty M. *Human Liberation in a Feminist Perspective—A Theology*. Philadelphia, PA: Westminster, 1974.

Russell, Letty M. *The Liberating Word: A Guide to Nonsexist Interpretation of the Bible*. Philadelphia, PA: Westminster John Knox, 1977.

Rybarczyk, Edmund J. *Beyond Salvation: Eastern Orthodoxy and Classical Pentecostalism on Becoming Like Christ*. Carlisle: Paternoster, 2004.

Saliers, Don E. *Worship as Theology: Foretaste as Glory Divine*. Nashville, TN: Abingdon, 1994.

Sanna, Ellyn. *Motherhood: A Spiritual Journey*. Mahwah, NJ: Paulist, 1997.

Sawyer, Deborah F. *God, Gender and the Bible*. London: Routledge, 2002.

Sawyer, Deborah F., and Diane M. Collier, eds. *Is There a Future for Feminist Theology?* Sheffield: Sheffield Academic, 1999.

Sayers, Dorothy L. "Are Women Human?" 1938 essay. Reprinted in *Are Women Human? Penetrating, Sensible, and Witty Essays on the Role of Women in Society*, edited by Dorothy L. Sayers, 47. Grand Rapids, MI: Eerdmans, 1971. Reprinted again, 2005.

Schaberg, Jane D., and Sharon H. Ringe. "Gospel of Luke." In *The Women's Bible Commentary*, rev., 3rd (expanded), and 20th anniversary ed., edited by Carol A. Newsom, Sharon H. Ringe, and Jacqueline E. Lapsley, 493–511. Louisville, KY: Westminster John Knox, 2012.

Schmemann, Alexander. *For the Life of the World: Sacraments and Orthodoxy*. Rev. ed. Crestwood, NY: St. Vladimir's Seminary Press, 1973.

Schneiders, Sandra M. *Beyond Patching: Faith and Feminism in the Catholic Church*. New York: Paulist, 1991.

Scholer, David. "Galatians 3:28 and the Ministry of Women in the Church." In *Theology, News and Notes*, 19–22. Pasadena, CA: Fuller Theological Seminary, June 1998.

Schrage, Wolfgang. *The Ethics of the New Testament*. Translated by David E. Green. Philadelphia, PA: Fortress, 1988.

Schroeder, Joy A., and Marion Ann Taylor. *Voices Long Silenced: Women Biblical Interpreters through the Centuries*. Louisville, KY: Westminster John Knox, 2022.

Schüssler Fiorenza, Elisabeth. *Bread Not Stone: The Challenge of Biblical Interpretation*. 1984. Reprint, Boston, MA: Beacon, 1995.

Schüssler Fiorenza, Elisabeth. "A Critical Feminist Emancipative Reading. Invitation to 'Dance' in the Open House of Wisdom: Feminist Study of the Bible." In *Engaging the Bible: Critical Readings from Contemporary Women*, edited by Choi Hee An and Katheryn Pfisterer Darr, 81–104. Minneapolis, MN: Fortress, 2006.

Schüssler Fiorenza, Elisabeth. *In Memory of Her: A Feminist Theological Reconstruction of Christian Origins*. 10th anniversary ed. New York: Crossroad, 1994.

Schwarz, Hans. *Eschatology*. Grand Rapids, MI: Eerdmans, 2000.

Scorgie, Glen G. *The Journey Back to Eden*. Grand Rapids, MI: Zondervan, 2005.

Segovia, Fernando F., ed. *Toward a New Heaven and a New Earth: Essays in Honor of Elisabeth Schüssler Fiorenza*. Maryknoll, NY: Orbis Books, 2003.

"Setting the Table: Meanings of Communion" (transcripts of group conversations). In *Setting the Table: Women in Theological Conversation*, edited by Rita Nakashima Brock, Claudia Camp, and Serene Jones, 249–68. St. Louis, MO: Chalice, 1995.

Sheppard, Gerald T. "Pentecostals and the Hermeneutics of Dispensationalism: The Anatomy of an Uneasy Relationship." *Pneuma* 7 (Fall 1984): 5–33.

Sheriffs, Deryck. *The Friendship of the Lord: An Old Testament Spirituality*. Carlisle: Paternoster, 1996.

Shields, Carol. *Unless: A Novel*. Toronto, ON: Vintage Canada, 2002.

Shields, John M. *An Eschatological Imagination: A Revisionist Christian Eschatology in the Light of David Tracy's Theological Project*. New York: Peter Lang, 2008.

Sjorup, Lene. "Pentecostals: The Power of the Powerless." *Dialog: A Journal of Theology* 41, no. 1 (Spring 2002): 16–25.

Slee, Nicola. *Faith and Feminism: An Introduction to Christian Feminist Theology*. London: Darton, Longman and Todd, 2003.

Slee, Nicola. "The Holy Spirit and Spirituality." In *The Cambridge Companion to Feminist Theology*, edited by Susan Frank Parsons, 171–89. Cambridge: Cambridge University Press, 2002.

Smith, Christian A. "The Eschatological Drive of God's Mission." *Review and Expositor* 82 (Spring 1985): 209–16.

Smith, Gordon T. *A Holy Meal: The Lord's Supper in the Life of the Church*. Grand Rapids, MI: Baker Academic, 2005.

Smith, Gordon T. "Spouses as Co-Pastors?" *Institutionally Sound: Leading Organizations to Mission Effectiveness Blog*, March 12, 2018. http://www.institutionalintelligence.ca/archive/spouses-as-co-pastors/.

Smith, James K. A. *The Fall of Interpretation: Philosophical Foundations for a Creational Hermeneutic*. Downers Grove, IL: InterVarsity, 2000.

Smith, James K. A. *Imagining the Kingdom: How Worship Works*. Grand Rapids, MI: Baker Academic, 2013.

Smith, James K. A. *Thinking in Tongues: Pentecostal Contributions to Christian Philosophy*. Grand Rapids, MI: Eerdmans, 2010.

Snodgrass, Klyne. "Galatians 3:28—Conundrum or Solution?" In *Women, Authority, and the Bible*, edited by Alvera Mickelsen, 161–81. Downers Grove, IL: InterVarsity, 1996.

Soothill, Jane E. *Gender, Social Change and Spiritual Power: Charismatic Christianity in Ghana*. Leiden: Brill, 2007.

Soskice, Janet Martin. "Trinity and Feminism." In *The Cambridge Companion to Feminist Theology*, edited by Susan Frank Parsons, 135–50. Cambridge: Cambridge University Press, 2002.

Stackhouse, John G., Jr. *Evangelical Landscapes: Facing Critical Issues of the Day*. Grand Rapids, MI: Baker Academic, 2002.

Stackhouse, John G., Jr. *Finally Feminist: A Pragmatic Christian Understanding of Gender* Grand Rapids, MI: Baker Academic, 2005.

Stackhouse, John G., Jr. *Partners in Christ: A Conservative Case for Egalitarianism*. Downers Grove, IL: InterVarsity, 2015.

Stackhouse, Reginald. *The End of the World?: A New Look at an Old Belief*. New York: Paulist, 1997.

Stanley, Susie C. "'Laying a Straw in Her Way': Women in Pentecostalism." *Enrichment: A Journal for Pentecostal Ministry* 11, no. 2 (Spring 2006): 110–16.

Stanley, Susie C. "Shattering the Stained-Glass Ceiling." In *The Wisdom of Daughters: Two Decades of the Voice of Christian Feminism*, edited by Reta Halteman Finger and Kari Sandhaas, 83–6. Philadelphia, PA: Innisfree, 2001.

Stanley, Susie C. "Wesleyan/Holiness and Pentecostal Women Preachers: Pentecost as the Pattern for Primitivism." In *Philip's Daughters: Women in Pentecostal-Charismatic Leadership*, edited by Estrelda Y. Alexander and Amos Yong, 19–37. Eugene, OR: Pickwick, 2009.

Starling, David I. *Hermeneutics as Apprenticeship: How the Bible Shapes Our Interpretive Habits and Practices*. Grand Rapids, MI: Baker Academic, 2016.

Steigenga, Timothy J. *The Politics of the Spirit: The Political Implications of Pentecostalized Religion in Costa Rica and Guatemala*. Lanham, MD: Lexington, 2001.

Steinmetz, David. "The Superiority of Pre-Critical Exegesis." *Theology Today* 37, no. 1 (April 1980): 27–38.

Stephenson, Christopher A. "Sarah Coakley's *Théologie Totale*: Starting with the Holy Spirit and/or Starting with Pneumatology?" *JPT* 26, no. 1 (2017): 1–9.

Stephenson, Christopher A. *Types of Pentecostal Theology: Method, System, Spirit*. Oxford: Oxford University Press, 2013.

Stephenson, Lisa P. *Dismantling the Dualisms for American Pentecostal Women in Ministry: A Feminist-Pneumatological Approach*. Leiden: Brill, 2012.

Stephenson, Lisa P. "A Feminist Pentecostal Theological Anthropology: North America and Beyond." *Pneuma* 35, no. 1 (2013): 35–47.

Stephenson, Lisa P. "Toxic Spirituality: Reexamining the Ways in Which Spiritual Virtues can Reinforce Violence Against Women." In *Sisters, Mothers, Daughters: Pentecostal Perspectives on Violence against Women*, edited by Kimberly Ervin Alexander et al., 33–48. Leiden: Brill, 2022.

Stephenson, Lisa P. "Truly Our Sister?: Pentecostal Readings of Mary." In *Receiving Scripture in the Pentecostal Tradition: A Reception History*, edited by Daniel D. Isgrigg, Martin W. Mittelstadt, and Rick Wadholm Jr., 112–24. Cleveland, TN: CPT, 2021.

Stephenson, Lisa P. "Where the Wind Blows: Pneumatology in Feminist Perspective." In *T&T Clark Handbook of Pneumatology*, edited by Daniel Castelo and Kenneth M. Loyer, 327–35. London: Bloomsbury, T&T Clark, 2020.

Stevenson-Moessner, Jeanne, ed. *In Her Own Time: Women and Developmental Issues in Pastoral Care*. Minneapolis, MN: Fortress, 2000.

Stevenson-Moessner, Jeanne, ed. *Through the Eyes of Women: Insights for Pastoral Care*. Minneapolis, MN: Fortress, 1996.

Stiver, Irene P., and Jean Baker Miller. "From Depression to Sadness in Women's Psychotherapy." In *Women's Growth in Diversity: More Writings from the Stone Center*, edited by Judith V. Jordan, 217–38. New York: Guilford, 1997.

Storkey, Elaine. *Scars Across Humanity: Understanding and Overcoming Violence against Women*. Westmont, IL: IVP Academic, 2018.

Storkey, Elaine. "Who Is the Christ? Issues in Christology and Feminist Theology." In *Gospel and Gender: A Trinitarian Engagement with Being Male and Female in Christ*, edited by Douglas A. Campbell, 105–23. London: T&T Clark, 2003.

Stovell, Beth M. "The Birthing Spirit, the Childbearing God: Metaphors of Motherhood and Their Place in Christian Discipleship." In *Making Sense of Motherhood: Biblical and Theological Perspectives*, edited by Beth M. Stovell, 27–41. Eugene, OR: Wipf & Stock, 2016.

Stovell, Beth M., ed. *Making Sense of Motherhood: Biblical and Theological Perspectives*. Eugene, OR: Wipf & Stock, 2016.

Stronstad, Roger. "The Biblical Precedent for Historical Precedent." *Paraclete* 27, no. 3 (1993): 1–10.

Stronstad, Roger. *The Charismatic Theology of St. Luke*. Peabody, MA: Hendrickson, 1984.

Stronstad, Roger. "Pentecostal Experience and Hermeneutics." *Paraclete* 26, no. 1 (Winter 1992): 14–30.

Stronstad, Roger. *The Prophethood of All Believers: A Study in Luke's Charismatic Theology*. Sheffield: Sheffield Academic, 1999.

Studebaker, Steven M. *From Pentecost to the Triune God: A Pentecostal Trinitarian Theology*. Grand Rapids, MI: Eerdmans, 2012.

Studebaker, Steven M. "Toward a Pneumatological Trinitarian Theology: Amos Yong, the Spirit, and the Trinity." In *The Theology of Amos Yong and the New Face of Pentecostal Scholarship: Passion for the Spirit*, edited by Wolfgang Vondey and Martin William Mittelstadt, 83–101. Leiden: Brill, 2013.

Sutton, Matthew Avery. *Aimee Semple McPherson and the Resurrection of Christian America*. Cambridge, MA: Harvard University Press, 2007.

Suurmond, Jean-Jacques. *Word and Spirit at Play: Towards a Charismatic Theology*. Translated by John Bowden. Grand Rapids, MI: Eerdmans, 1995.

Swartley, William. *Slavery, Sabbath, War, and Women: Case Issues in Biblical Interpretation*. Scottdale, PA: Herald, 1983.

Swoboda, A. J. *Tongues and Trees: Towards a Pentecostal Ecological Theology*. Blandford Forum: Deo, 2013.

Synan, Vinson, ed. *The Century of the Holy Spirit: 100 Years of Pentecostal and Charismatic Renewal, 1901–2001*. Nashville, TN: Thomas Nelson, 2001.

Tackett, Zachary Michael. "Callings, Giftings, and Empowerment: Preaching Women and American Pentecostalism in Historical and Theological Perspective." In *Women in Pentecostal and Charismatic Ministry: Informing a Dialogue on Gender, Church, and Ministry*, edited by Margaret English de Alminana and Lois E. Olena, 73–98. Leiden: Brill, 2017.

Taylor, Charles. *Modern Social Imaginaries*. Durham, NC: Duke University Press, 2000.

Taylor, Marion Ann. *Handbook of Women Biblical Interpreters: A Historical and Biographical Guide*. Grand Rapids, MI: Baker Academic, 2012.

Terrien, Samuel. *Till the Heart Sings: A Biblical Theology of Manhood and Womanhood*. Grand Rapids, MI: Eerdmans, 1985.

Thomas, John Christopher. "1998 Presidential Address: Pentecostal Theology in the Twenty-First Century." *Pneuma* 20, no. 1 (Spring 1998): 3–19.

Thomas, John Christopher. "'Where the Spirit Leads': The Development of Pentecostal Hermeneutics." *Journal of Beliefs & Values: Studies in Religion & Education* 30, no. 3 (December 2009): 289–302.

Thomas, John Christopher. "Women, Pentecostals and the Bible: An Experiment in Pentecostal Hermeneutics." *JPT* 5 (1994): 41–56.

Thomasson-Rosingh, Anne Claar. *Searching for the Holy Spirit: Feminist Theology and Traditional Doctrine*. London: Routledge, 2015.

Thompson, Matthew K. "Eschatology as Soteriology: The Cosmic Full Gospel." In *Perspectives in Pentecostal Eschatologies: World Without End*, edited by Peter Althouse and Robby Waddell, 189–204. Eugene, OR: Pickwick, 2010.

Thompson, Matthew K. *Kingdom Come: Revisioning Pentecostal Eschatology*. Blandford Forum: Deo, 2010.

Tillard, J.-M.-R. *Flesh of the Church, Flesh of Christ: At the Source of the Ecclesiology of Communion*. Translated by Madeleine Beaumont. Collegeville, MN: Liturgical, 2001.

Tinder, Glenn. *The Fabric of Hope: An Essay*. Grand Rapids, MI: Eerdmans, 1999.

Tomberlin, Daniel. *Pentecostal Sacraments: Encountering God at the Altar*. Cleveland, TN: Center for Pentecostal Leadership and Care, 2010.

"Tongues as a Sign." *AF* 1, no. 1 (September 1906): 2.

Torrance, Alan J. "God, Personhood and Particularity: On Whether There Is, or Should Be, a Distinctive Male Theological Perspective." In *Gospel and Gender: A Trinitarian Engagement with Being Male and Female in Christ*, edited by Douglas A. Campbell, 134–54. London: T&T Clark, 2003.

Tracy, David. *The Analogical Imagination: Christian Theology and the Culture of Pluralism*. New York: Crossroad, 1981.

Trible, Phyllis. *God and the Rhetoric of Sexuality*. Philadelphia, PA: Fortress, 1978.

Trible, Phyllis. *Texts of Terror: Literary-Feminist Readings of Biblical Narratives*. Philadelphia, PA: Fortress, 1984.

Tucker, Ruth A. *Women in the Maze: Questions and Answers on Biblical Equality*. Downers Grover, IL: InterVarsity, 1992.

Tucker, Ruth A., and Walter Liefeld. *Daughters of the Church: Women and Ministry from New Testament Times to the Present*. Grand Rapids, MI: Zondervan, 1987.

"Untitled Testimonies." *The Apostolic Messenger* 1, no. 1 (February/March 1908): 2.

Vanhoozer, Kevin J. *The Drama of Doctrine: A Canonical-Linguistic Approach to Christian Theology*. Louisville, KY: Westminster John Knox, 2005.

Vanhoozer, Kevin J. "Scripture and Hermeneutics." In *The Oxford Handbook of Evangelical Theology*, edited by Gerald R. McDermott, 35–52. Oxford: Oxford University Press, 2010.

Van Leeuwen, Mary Stewart. *Gender and Grace*. Downers Grove, IL: InterVarsity, 1990.

Volf, Miroslav. "After Moltmann: Reflections on the Future of Eschatology." In *God Will Be All in All: The Eschatology of Jürgen Moltmann*, edited by Richard Bauckham, 233–57. Edinburgh: T&T Clark, 1999.

Volf, Miroslav. "On Loving with Hope: Eschatology and Social Responsibility." *Transformation* 7 (July/September 1990): 28–31.

Volf, Miroslav. "The Trinity and Gender Identity." In *Gospel and Gender: A Trinitarian Engagement with Being Male and Female in Christ*, edited by Douglas A. Campbell, 155–78. London: T&T Clark, 2003.

Vondey, Wolfgang. *Beyond Pentecostalism: The Crisis of Global Christianity and the Renewal of the Theological Agenda*. Grand Rapids, MI: Eerdmans, 2010.

Vondey, Wolfgang. *Pentecostal Theology: Living the Full Gospel*. London: Bloomsbury, T&T Clark, 2017.

Vondey, Wolfgang. *Pentecostalism: A Guide for the Perplexed*. London: Bloomsbury, 2013.

Vondey, Wolfgang. *People of Bread: Rediscovering Ecclesiology*. Mahwah, NJ: Paulist, 2008.

Vondey, Wolfgang. "Religion as Play: Pentecostalism as a Theological Type." *Religions* 9, no. 3 (2018): 80. https://doi.org/10.3390/rel9030080.

Vondey, Wolfgang, and Chris W. Green. "Between This and That: Reality and Sacramentality in the Pentecostal Worldview." *JPT* 19 (2010): 243–64.

Vondey, Wolfgang, and Martin W. Mittelstadt. "Introduction." In *The Theology of Amos Yong and the New Face of Pentecostal Scholarship: Passion for the Spirit*, edited by Wolfgang Vondey and Martin William Mittelstadt, 1–24. Leiden: Brill, 2013.

Vondey, Wolfgang, and Martin William Mittelstadt, eds. *The Theology of Amos Yong and the New Face of Pentecostal Scholarship: Passion for the Spirit*. Leiden: Brill, 2013.

Wacker, Grant. *Heaven Below: Early Pentecostalism and American Culture*. Cambridge, MA: Harvard University Press, 2001.

Waddell, Robby. "Apocalyptic Sustainability: The Future of Pentecostal Ecology." In *Perspectives in Pentecostal Eschatologies: World Without End*, edited by Peter Althouse and Robby Waddell, 95–110. Eugene, OR: Pickwick, 2010.

Waddell, Robby. *The Spirit of the Book of Revelation*. Blandford Forum: Deo, 2006.

Waddell, Robby, and Peter Althouse. "The Promises and Perils of the Azusa Street Myth." *Pneuma* 38, no. 4 (2016): 367–71.

Wadholm, Rick, Jr. "'Until I, Deborah, Arose' (Judges 4–5): A Pentecostal Reception History of Deborah Toward Women in Ministry." In *Receiving Scripture in the Pentecostal Tradition: A Reception History*, edited by Daniel D. Isgrigg, Martin W. Mittelstadt, and Rick Wadholm Jr., 93–111. Cleveland, TN: CPT, 2021.

Wainwright, Geoffrey. *Eucharist and Eschatology*. New York: Oxford University Press, 1981.

Ware, Frederick L. "Spiritual Egalitarianism, Ecclesial Pragmatism, and the Status of Women in Ordained Ministry." In *Philip's Daughters: Women in Pentecostal-Charismatic Leadership*, edited by Estrelda Y. Alexander and Amos Yong, 215–33. Eugene, OR: Pickwick, 2009.

Wariboko, Nimi. *The Pentecostal Principle: Ethical Methodology in New Spirit*. Grand Rapids, MI: Eerdmans, 2012.

Warren, Tish Harrison. "An Open Letter to Men Who Broke the Billy Graham Rule." *InterVarsity: Women in the Academy and Professions Blog*, April 4, 2017. http://thewell.intervarsity.org/blog/open-letter-men-who-broke-billy-graham-rule.

Warrington, Keith. *Pentecostal Theology: A Theology of Encounter*. London: T&T Clark, 2008.

Watson, Natalie K. *Feminist Theology*. Grand Rapids, MI: Eerdmans, 2003.

Webb, William. *Slaves, Women, and Homosexuals: Exploring the Hermeneutics of Cultural Analysis*. Downers Grove, IL: InterVarsity, 2001.

Wedenoja, William. "Jamaica (I)." In *NIDPCM*, rev. ed., edited by Stanley M. Burgess and Eduard M. van der Maas, 141–5. Grand Rapids, MI: Zondervan, 2002.

Wenger, Etienne. *Communities of Practice: Learning, Meaning, and Identity*. Cambridge: Cambridge University Press, 1998.

West, Christopher. *Theology of the Body for Beginners*. West Chester, PA: Ascension, 2009.

Westermann, Claus. *Creation*. Translated by John Scullion. Philadelphia, PA: Fortress, 1974.
White, Alma. *The New Testament Church*. Bound Brook, NJ: The Pentecostal Union, 1912.
"Who May Prophesy." *AF* 1, no. 12 (January 1908): 2.
Wiebe, Ben. *Messianic Ethics: Jesus' Proclamation of the Kingdom of God and the Church in Response*. Waterloo, ON: Herald, 1992.
Wiggins, Daphne C. *Righteous Content: Black Women's Perspectives of Church and Faith*. New York: New York University Press, 2005.
Wilkinson, Michael, and Linda M. Ambrose. *After the Revival: Pentecostalism and the Making of a Canadian Church*. Montreal, QC and Kingston, ON: McGill-Queen's University Press, 2020.
Wilkinson, Michael, and Peter Althouse. *Catch the Fire: Soaking Prayer and Charismatic Renewal*. Dekalb, IL: NIU Press, 2014.
Wilkinson, Michael, and Steven M. Studebaker. "Pentecostal Social Action: An Introduction." In *A Liberating Spirit: Pentecostals and Social Action in North America*, edited by Michael Wilkinson and Steven M. Studebaker, 1–19. Eugene, OR: Pickwick, 2010.
Williams, J. Rodman. "The Holy Spirit and Eschatology." *Pneuma* 3, no. 2 (Fall 1981): 54–8.
Williams, Sarah C. "Evangelicals and Gender." In *Global Evangelicalism: Theology, History and Culture in Regional Perspective*, edited by Donald M. Lewis and Richard V. Pierard, 270–95. Downers Grove, IL: IVP Academic, 2014.
Wilson, Dwight J. "Eschatology, Pentecostal Perspectives On." In *NIDPCM*, rev. ed., edited by Stanley M. Burgess and Eduard M. van der Maas, 601–5. Grand Rapids, MI: Zondervan, 2002.
Wilson, J. R. *Why Church Matters: Worship, Ministry, and Mission in Practice*. Grand Rapids, MI: Brazos, 2006.
Witherington, Ben, III. *Women and the Genesis of Christianity*. Cambridge: Cambridge University Press, 1990.
Witherington, Ben, III. *Women in the Earliest Churches*. Cambridge: Cambridge University Press, 1988.
Woodhead, Linda. "Feminism and the Sociology of Religion: From Gender-Blindness to Gendered Difference." In *The Blackwell Companion to Sociology of Religion*, edited by Richard K. Fenn, 67–84. Oxford: Blackwell, 2001.
Woodhead, Linda. "God, Gender and Identity." In *Gospel and Gender: A Trinitarian Engagement with Being Male and Female in Christ*, edited by Douglas A. Campbell, 84–104. London: T&T Clark, 2003.
Woodworth-Etter, Maria. *A Diary of Signs and Wonders: A Classic*. 1916. Reprint, Tulsa, OK: Harrison House, 1980.
Woodworth-Etter, Maria. *Marvels and Miracles: God Wrought in the Ministry of Mrs. M. B. Woodworth-Etter for Forty-Five Years*. Indianapolis, IN: n.p., 1922.
Woodworth-Etter, Maria. "Women's Rights in the Gospel." In *Signs and Wonders God Wrought in the Ministry for Forty Years*, edited by Maria Woodworth-Etter. Indianapolis, IN: n.p., 1916. Reprint in the chapter "Maria Beulah Woodworth-Etter" in *A Reader in Pentecostal Theology: Voices from the First Generation*, edited by Douglas Jacobsen, 24–30. Bloomington, IN: Indiana University Press, 2006.
"The Work in Virginia." *AF* 1, no. 2 (October 1906): 3.
World Council of Churches. *Baptism, Eucharist and Ministry*. Faith and Order Paper no. 111. Geneva: World Council of Churches, 1982.

Wright, N. T. *The New Testament and the People of God*. Minneapolis, MN: Fortress, 1992.
Wright, N. T. *Surprised by Hope: Rethinking Heaven, the Resurrection, and the Mission of the Church*. New York: HarperOne, 2008.
Wright, N. T. "Women's Service in the Church: The Biblical Basis." A Paper Presented at the Symposium "Men, Women and the Church," St John's College, Durham, September 4, 2004. Posted July 12, 2016. https://ntwrightpage.com/2016/07/12/womens-service-in-the-church-the-biblical-basis/.
Yong, Amos. *The Bible, Disability, and The Church: A New Vision of the People of God*. Grand Rapids, MI: Eerdmans, 2011.
Yong, Amos. *In the Days of Caesar: Pentecostalism and Political Theology*. Grand Rapids, MI: Eerdmans, 2010.
Yong, Amos. *Hospitality and the Other: Pentecost, Christian Practices, and the Neighbor*. Maryknoll, NY: Orbis Books, 2008.
Yong, Amos. "The Inviting Spirit: Pentecostal Beliefs and Practices Regarding the Religions Today." In *Defining Issues in Pentecostalism: Classical and Emergent*, edited by Steven M. Studebaker, 29–45. Eugene, OR: Pickwick, 2008.
Yong, Amos. "Jesus the Proto-Feminist." In his *Who Is the Holy Spirit? A Walk with the Apostles*, 146–8. Brewster, MA: Paraclete, 2011.
Yong, Amos. "The *Missio Spiritus* in a Pluralistic World: A Pentecost Approach to Dialogue, Hospitality, and Sanctuary." *Pittsburgh Theological Journal* 9 (Autumn 2018): 11–48.
Yong, Amos. *Renewing Christian Theology: Systematics for a Global Christianity*. Waco, TX: Baylor University Press, 2014.
Yong, Amos. *Renewing the Church by the Spirit: Theological Education After Pentecost*. Grand Rapids, MI: Eerdmans, 2020.
Yong, Amos. *The Spirit Poured Out on All Flesh: Pentecostalism and the Possibility of Global Theology*. Grand Rapids, MI: Baker Academic, 2005.
Yong, Amos. *Spirit-Word-Community: Theological Hermeneutics in Trinitarian Perspective*. Eugene, OR: Wipf & Stock, 2002.
Yong, Amos. *Theology and Down Syndrome: Reimagining Disability in Late Modernity*. Waco, TX: Baylor University Press, 2007.
Yuen, Nancy Wang, and Deshonna Collier-Goubil, eds. *Power Women: Stories of Motherhood, Faith, and the Academy*. Downers Grove, IL: IVP Academic, 2021.
Zickmund, Brown. "The Struggle for the Right to Preach." In *Women and Religion in America*, vol. 1, The Nineteenth Century, edited by Rosemary Radford Ruether and Rosemary Skinner Keller, 193–241. San Francisco, CA: Harper & Row, 1981.

# INDEX

abuse   25, 234, 240, 256–7
Acts. *See also* Joel 2/Acts 2; Luke-Acts; Pentecost
   1:1   164, 168
   1:4-8   116
   1:8   164
   2:1-4   163
   2:5-11   236
   2:12   168
   2:16 (*see* this-is-that, hermeneutic(s))
   2:16-17   259
   2:16-18   2, 161
   2:16-21   255
   2:17   1, 64, 66, 74, 104, 107, 115, 170, 220
   2:17-18   28, 55, 64, 70, 74, 131, 141, 161–5, 167, 170, 173, 181, 215, 222, 236, 252, 255 (*see also* Pentecost)
   2:18   217, 235
   2:20   166
   2:37-38   255
   2:41   167
   7:59-60   163
   15:1-32   117, 136
   20:27   140
   21:8-9   238
androgyny   36, 153–7
anthropology   36, 41, 215–16, 220–3, 226, 227, 250
Aquinas, Thomas   36, 216, 243
Argue, Zelma   56, 67, 70–1, 106
Assemblies of God   10, 57, 66, 79, 92, 93, 102–7, 109, 111, 161, 177, 209, 230, 243
Augustine of Hippo   35, 135, 216
authority
   eschatological   71, 75, 95, 134, 137, 205, 212, 213
   of the future   44–6, 127, 138, 207
   male/female   4, 8, 24, 44–5, 58, 76, 88, 94, 104–7, 109, 110, 144, 159, 162, 168, 208, 211, 213, 235, 248, 257, 258 (*see also* hierarchy)
   to preach   58, 64–5, 67–8, 70–1 (*see also* preaching)
   of Scripture   118–19, 127–9, 135–6, 147–8, 191, 195 (*see also* hermeneutical priority)
   theological   19, 132, 187, 199, 213
Azusa Street mission and revival   58, 61, 63, 66, 79–81, 92, 103, 112

Bell, E. N.   105, 107, 111
body. *See also* androgyny; anthropology; resurrection
   eschatological   36–8, 182, 221–3
   women's   26, 36, 221, 237, 240
   in worship   29, 179, 242, 243, 246

calling (of/on women)   6, 69, 70, 72–4, 86, 95, 103, 177, 209, 213, 240, 241. *See also* preaching
Canada   26, 57, 62, 63, 67, 72, 76, 81, 82, 88, 106, 109, 241. *See also* Pentecostal Assemblies of Canada
children   37, 71, 219, 232, 238
church. *See also* ecclesiology; women
   as eschatological community   127, 152–3, 165, 166, 168, 183, 186, 204, 210, 228, 238, 248, 250
   local   8, 177, 205, 206, 208, 209, 249
Church of God (Cleveland, TN)   8, 107, 108, 110
Church of God in Christ (COGIC)   103–5
complementarian   4, 106, 118, 149, 151, 153, 156, 197, 226
conscientization   49–50, 52
creation. *See* Genesis 1–3 (creation)

dialectic(s)   27, 29, 93, 121–4, 127, 128, 173, 180, 185, 190–3, 195, 199–200, 250, 259

dispensationalism 20, 92–3, 100–1, 103, 111, 113–16, 129
divorce 67, 147

ecclesiology 95, 176, 180, 186, 203, 226, 228, 251, 252. *See also* Church
ecology 16, 48, 189, 219, 253
egalitarian 19, 28–30, 34, 35, 39, 45, 51–3, 55–61, 64, 65, 71, 75–8, 81, 83, 85–9, 91–5, 98, 103, 106–8, 110, 112, 116, 118–21, 132, 137, 139, 142, 145, 147–52, 160, 161, 168–73, 175–8, 180, 181, 190, 191, 194, 196, 198–201, 203, 206–10, 214, 215, 225–7, 229, 230, 235–8, 240, 241, 243, 244, 248–50, 252, 255, 258, 259. *See also* complementarian; women
   in Pentecostalism 10, 25, 28, 55, 61, 81, 83, 107, 112
   Pentecostalism as 2, 5, 10, 25
   praxis 52, 57, 106, 119, 175–6, 181, 190, 194, 198, 200, 206, 227, 236, 252
Ephesians
   5:22-23 171, 133
epistemology 21, 78, 216
eschatology. *See also* dispensationalism; latter rain
   in Christian theology 13–14, 182–3, 188, 218
   and ethics 13, 16, 17, 19, 115, 116, 132, 182, 185, 188, 189, 219, 253
   in feminist theology 32–8, 40, 41, 43, 45, 46–8, 217 (*see also under* patriarchy)
   function of 55, 86–8
   and hermeneutics (*see under* hermeneutics)
   and method 5, 13, 18, 20–1, 29, 45, 51, 187, 253
   over-realized 197
   and Pentecost (*see under* Pentecost)
   in Pentecostalism 15–18, 38, 50, 52, 56, 61–2, 76, 83, 84, 87–8, 92, 93, 95, 98, 101, 112, 118, 121, 134, 166, 185
   in Pentecostal theology 15, 48, 113–16, 186, 188, 219–20, 250
   and pneumatology 124–6, 167, 244–5
   and praxis (*see* praxis)
   types 19, 37, 39, 87, 101, 186, 219
eucharist. *See* Lord's Supper

Fall 36, 111, 144–9, 153–5, 170, 195, 220
Farrow, Lucy 62, 63, 79
feminism 31–3, 35–6, 40–1, 56, 83, 84, 205, 217, 219
   fear of 12, 108, 256, 259
feminist theology 33–5, 37–43, 46–8, 50, 118, 132, 134, 141–3, 150, 162, 214, 216, 217, 219, 223, 224
   and Pentecostals 127, 137, 148, 163, 215–17, 219
1 Corinthians
   7:3-4 155
   7:18-19 155
   7:29-31 198
   7:31 228
   11:2-16 168, 171
   11:3 171, 133
   11:5 181
   11:9 147
   11:26 247
   11:27 247
   12:13 151
   14:34-35 94, 133, 171, 178, 181
   15:42-44 36
1 Timothy
   2:11-15 104, 133, 171
   3:2-7 103
Foursquare (ICFG) 72–3, 82, 107
fundamentalism 12, 20, 59, 94, 101, 103, 115

Galatians
   1:4 160
   1:6 150
   3:1 150
   3:1–5:1 152
   3:6-29 155
   3:26-28 151, 170
   3:27 151, 156, 157, 159–60, 170
   3:27-29 152, 157
   3:28 28, 64–6, 68, 103–7, 111–12, 117, 131, 139–40, 141–4, 148, 149–50, 151, 152, 153, 154, 155, 156, 157–62, 170, 171, 173, 217, 222, 223, 235, 244, 248, 252, 255

4:19   151
4:21-31   151
4:28-5:1   150
5:6   156
5:13   151
5:16   160
5:16-18   160
5:16-21   151
5:16-26   150
5:17   228
5:24-26   151
5:25   160, 255
6:2   151
6:14-16   150
6:15   152, 156, 157
gender. *See* gender paradox; women
  eradication of (*see* androgyny)
gender debate. *See* gender paradox
gender equality. *See* egalitarian; women
gender paradox   4–5, 9–13, 17, 18, 21–2, 24, 26–9, 31, 39, 49, 51, 56, 77, 83, 89, 91–3, 98, 108, 112, 116, 117, 120, 122, 131, 136, 137, 139, 171, 178, 181, 201, 208, 216, 254
  causes of   5, 9, 28, 91, 93, 98, 117, 208, 216
  definition   2, 7, 10, 24, 94, 254
  as hermeneutical issue   9, 28–9, 92, 108, 120, 131, 134, 136, 171, 172
  resolving of   4, 12, 18, 29, 77, 85, 87, 116, 129, 134, 178, 200, 251
Genesis
  1:1   142
  1:2   148, 152
  1:26   146
  1:26-27   170, 223
  1:26-28   144, 147, 220, 222, 223
  1:27   144, 148, 150, 152–4, 157, 159, 217, 235
  1:28-30   140
  1:31   145, 149, 155
  2:4-25   144
  2:7-21   143
  2:18   143, 145
  2:18-24   143
  2:21-22   154
  2:22   143
  2:22-23   35
  2:24   170
  3:1   142
  3:16   145, 147
  3:20   143
  3:21   170
  3:24   231
  5:2   153
  12:3   152
  16   238
  18:18   152
  21:1-21   238
  38   238
Genesis 1–3 (creation)   28, 131, 141–9, 170, 173, 237, 252. *See also* Fall; *imago Dei*
God. *See also* Holy Spirit; Jesus
  and gender   224, 230, 231–2, 235 (*see also under* language)
  language for (*see under* language)
  as mother   231–4
Gordon, A. J.   59, 172
Gregory of Nyssa   35, 36, 154, 221

Hebden, Ellen   81–3, 241
hermeneutic(s)
  authorizing   3, 5, 9–10, 28, 56, 65, 67, 86, 91, 93, 103, 108, 120, 129, 131, 173, 252
  eschatological   28–9, 60, 65, 67, 68, 71, 76, 84, 87, 89, 91–4, 96, 99, 101, 103–4, 108, 112, 123–4, 127, 129, 131, 134, 137, 138, 140, 168, 169, 171–3, 252, 259
  and experience   78, 92, 103, 118, 127–8, 192, 198, 204
  latter rain (*see* hermeneutic(s), eschatological)
  liberating   92, 109, 117
  literal (*see* hermeneutic(s), restorationist)
  Pentecostal   92, 94, 95, 99, 101, 103, 112, 113, 116, 119, 121, 124, 126, 127, 131, 137, 158, 168, 181, 192, 252
  restorationist   92–3, 95, 97–9, 103, 105, 116, 171, 173
  this-is-that   169, 227
  and women (*see* women)
hermeneutical circle   122, 124, 129, 173, 193, 200, 259

hermeneutical inconsistency  5, 9, 12, 28–9, 60, 86, 91, 104, 129, 131, 136, 172, 173, 181, 250, 252, 254. *See also* gender paradox
hermeneutical priority  28, 93, 118, 131–2, 134–42, 147–8, 158–9, 166–8, 170, 171, 173, 175, 205, 213, 220, 235, 252
hermeneutical problems. *See* gender paradox; *specific scripture references*
hierarchy  33, 39, 44, 66, 101, 111, 134, 139, 143–5, 147, 150–1, 153, 154, 157, 159–60, 162, 172, 178, 208, 210, 211, 221, 223, 225, 244, 255. *See also* patriarchy
Holy Spirit  11, 26, 49, 68, 70–1, 96, 98, 99, 110, 115, 117, 119–20, 124–8, 138, 148, 159–60, 163, 164, 168, 178, 190, 205, 211, 215–16, 227–8, 237, 244, 245, 258. *See also* Joel 2/Acts 2; outpouring; Spirit baptism
  eschatological  51–2, 65, 112, 115, 123, 127, 147, 170, 214, 255
  feminizing of  224
  in hermeneutics  116–18, 122, 124, 136, 138

imagination  19, 30, 49, 86, 119, 121, 123, 125–6, 170, 181, 186, 188, 190, 198–200, 214, 229, 236, 242, 247–8
  eschatological  4, 14, 19, 21, 28, 34, 57, 60, 61, 64, 68, 74, 75, 88–9, 92, 98–9, 114, 123–6, 128, 139–42, 148, 159, 160, 162, 168, 188, 193, 197, 199, 212, 214, 227–9, 234, 235, 237, 241
  Pentecostal  78, 115, 126
  pneumatological  116, 126
*imago Dei*  145, 146, 220, 221. *See also* anthropology; Genesis, 1:27; ontology
intellect, role of  11, 78, 91, 95, 127, 198–200
Isaiah
  2:2  165
  42  231
  42:14  231
  49:5-6  152
  49:15  232

  66:13  232
  eschatological Spirit in  51, 165–6

Jesus
  as gendered body  36, 223, 243–4
  hermeneutics of  135, 147–8, 162
  in Luke-Acts  163–5, 168
  ministry of  140, 159–62, 168, 170
  second coming of  20, 61–5, 68, 70, 71, 73–5, 84–5, 95, 101, 196
  and women  160–2, 164–5, 169, 232, 240
Joel 2/Acts 2  51, 64, 65, 70–1, 74–5, 84–5, 89, 94, 100, 103, 106, 108, 112, 117, 164
Joel 2 prophecy  2, 51, 59, 61, 69, 74, 93, 165, 169, 170, 196. *See also* Joel 2/Acts 2
John
  4  161
  11:21-27  161

language  236, 249–50, 256
  in the church  212, 226, 229–31, 234, 242
  eschatological  68, 75, 85, 99, 229, 233, 249
  gender-inclusive  224, 229, 230, 233, 235–6
  for God  45, 220, 223, 230–1
latter rain  17, 61, 63, 67, 70, 85, 87–8, 92, 93, 95, 98–103, 105, 110, 121, 129, 196, 197
leadership. *See* women
Lord's Supper  105, 109, 242–8
Luke
  1:40  169
  2:36-38  169
  4:18-19  160, 164
  7:22-23  164
  7:28-35  160
  8:1-4  169
  11:20  160
  11:27-28  169
  12:35-40  160
  15  232
  22:16  247
Luke-Acts  52, 122, 135, 163, 165, 169
  women in  169

McPherson, Aimee Semple  56, 67, 69, 72–6, 82, 89, 107
Mark
  1:15  160, 164
  2:18-22  160
  5:21-43  168
  14:1-9  161
Matthew
  7:12  135
  15:21-28  161
  19:1-12  147
  22:34-40  135
  28:1-10  161
misogyny. *See* sexism
motherhood  73, 241, 256
  of God (*see* God)
  imagery in the Bible  69, 151, 232
mutuality  144, 145, 148, 151, 155, 211, 214, 226

new creation  37, 43, 44, 48, 51, 132, 137, 145, 146, 148–50, 152, 154, 155, 157–8, 160, 162, 167, 170, 173, 228

ontology  29, 52, 220, 221, 223, 226
ordinances. *See* Lord's Supper; water baptism
ordination  6, 8–9, 72, 105–6, 211, 243
outpouring (of the Spirit), 51, 57, 64, 66, 85, 93, 94, 115, 140, 163–8, 170, 236. *See also* Joel 2/Acts 2; Pentecost
Ozman, Agnes  61, 80, 83, 241

Parham, Charles  61, 80, 241
patriarchy  25, 36, 40, 139, 145, 151, 161, 205, 216, 225, 232, 235, 240, 243, 247, 249–50, 255
  in the Bible  134, 137, 139–40, 147–8, 171, 213
  and eschatology  37, 39, 48
  in Pentecostalism  23–5, 203, 230, 254
pedagogy  29, 140, 215–19
Pentecost  62, 63, 99, 166, 184, 213–14, 241, 245, 259. *See also* Acts 2
  at Azusa  62–5, 81

  day of  1, 85, 115, 118, 164–6, 170, 184, 221, 227, 236, 259
  as eschatological event  51, 60, 65, 100, 163, 165–9
  as hermeneutic  11, 59, 135, 140, 163, 166, 167
  narrative of  2, 28, 131, 140, 141, 163, 169, 170, 173, 186, 252
Pentecostal Assemblies of Canada  57, 106–7, 177
Pentecostalism. *See also under* eschatology; women
  definition  1
  global  22–6, 115–16, 254
  history  5, 15, 55–9, 61, 77–8, 83
Pentecostal scholarship  11–12, 14–16, 21, 49, 52
Pentecostal theology  11, 19, 78, 127, 135, 163, 183–5, 187, 201
pneumatology  11, 50–1, 114–16, 121–6, 148, 163, 167, 189, 224–5, 237, 244, 245
political activism  25, 114, 180, 189
praxis  41, 52, 172, 178, 181, 187, 191, 192, 194, 195, 198, 199, 205, 208, 259. *See also under* egalitarian
  eschatological  113, 175, 176, 180–3, 186–8, 190, 192, 194–8, 220, 226, 250
  liberating  50, 116, 162, 177, 178, 191, 199
  models  176–81, 191, 193–5, 198, 200, 204
  Pentecostal  11, 78, 91, 113, 176, 181, 183–7, 190, 192, 219, 229, 237
prayer  82, 110, 229–34, 240
preaching  64, 67, 73, 83, 209, 212–13, 230, 236–9, 241, 256, 258. *See also* authority
  women  57–8, 61–75, 81–2, 89, 103, 106, 107, 109, 117, 212–13, 242, 250, 257
prelapsarian  142–3, 146, 148, 153, 159, 220. *See also* Fall; Genesis 1–3 (creation)
primitivism  60, 98–100

resurrection  36–8, 48, 154, 157, 161, 221
rhetoric  9, 19, 209, 230

sacramentality. *See* Lord's Supper
Scripture
    interpretation of (*see* hermeneutics)
    prohibitive passages for women
        (*see under* women)
sexism   26, 40, 125, 145, 177, 198, 230,
    236, 254–5, 257, 258. *See also*
    patriarchy
Seymour, William   66, 79–80, 107
sin   144–5, 239–40, 247
Spirit baptism   61, 63, 65, 80–2, 84, 86,
    88, 94, 124, 126, 167, 168, 173, 178,
    184, 237
submission. *See* subordination
subordination   9, 25, 35, 81, 109–11,
    122, 143–5, 148, 178, 208, 224, 225,
    236
systematic theology   14, 15, 35, 40, 216,
    217, 250

testimony   62–5, 79, 81, 82, 236, 237,
    240, 242
texts of terror   133, 238
tongues, speaking in. *See* Spirit baptism
Trinity   215, 217, 223–6, 233
    eschatological   223, 226, 231,
        233

water baptism   105, 151, 159
Wesleyan-Holiness movement
    59–60, 158

women
    decline of in Pentecostalism   5–6, 9,
        12–13, 50, 51, 57, 86, 102–3, 106–8,
        112, 121, 177, 256
    discrimination against   4, 26, 207–8,
        212, 221
    exclusion of   13, 19, 22, 79, 83, 106,
        206–9, 211, 213, 229, 236, 243,
        250, 256
    injustice against   13, 22, 26–7, 79,
        146, 208, 220, 240, 254, 255
    as lead/Sr. pastors   10, 83, 177, 209–10
    liberation of   23, 26, 28, 53, 84, 197,
        210, 252, 254
    prohibitive Scriptures concerning   59,
        69, 109–10, 112, 133, 134, 139, 159,
        167
    restrictions on   4, 6, 10, 25, 88, 91, 92,
        104–5, 107, 109, 111, 117, 118, 129,
        159, 171, 177, 197, 205, 221, 243.
        *See also* ordination; subordination
    role of   4, 11, 33, 68, 73, 75, 79, 85–6,
        92, 94, 97–8, 101, 104, 106, 111,
        116–17, 133, 161–2, 178, 194, 212
    silence of   94, 98, 107, 117–18, 129,
        171, 178, 181, 216–18, 256
    violence against   25–6, 239–40, 254, 257
Woodworth-Etter, Maria   56, 67–70, 75
worship   78, 81, 203, 206, 215, 220–1,
    226–31, 234, 236, 238, 241–2,
    245–7, 256

www.ingramcontent.com/pod-product-compliance
Lightning Source LLC
Chambersburg PA
CBHW071234230426
43668CB00011B/1426